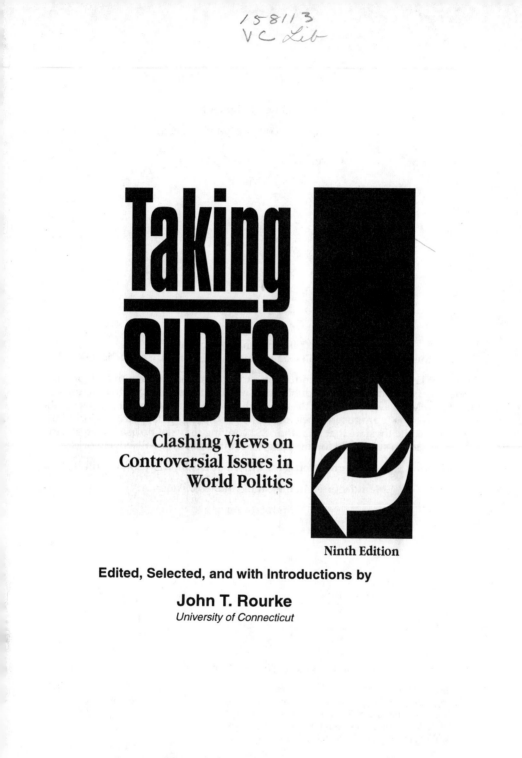

Taking SIDES

Clashing Views on Controversial Issues in World Politics

Ninth Edition

Edited, Selected, and with Introductions by

John T. Rourke
University of Connecticut

Dushkin/McGraw-Hill
A Division of The McGraw-Hill Companies

For my son and friend—John Michael

Photo Acknowledgments

Cover image: © 2000 by PhotoDisc, Inc.

Cover Art Acknowledgment

Charles Vitelli

Library of Congress Cataloging-in-Publication Data

Main entry under title:
    Taking sides: clashing views on controversial issues in world politics/edited, selected, and
with introductions by John T. Rourke.—9th ed.
    Includes bibliographical references and index.
    1. World Politics—1989–. I. Rourke, John T., *comp.*

909.82
ISSN: 1094-754X

0-697-39141-8

 Printed on Recycled Paper

PREFACE

In the first edition of *Taking Sides*, I wrote of my belief in informed argument:

> [A] book that debates vital issues is valuable and necessary.... [It is important] to recognize that world politics is usually not a subject of absolute rights and absolute wrongs and of easy policy choices. We all have a responsibility to study the issues thoughtfully, and we should be careful to understand all sides of the debates.

It is gratifying to discover, as indicated by the success of *Taking Sides* over eight editions, that so many of my colleagues share this belief in the value of a debate-format text.

The format of this edition follows a formula that has proved successful in acquainting students with the global issues that we face and generating discussion of those issues and the policy choices that address them. This book addresses 17 issues on a wide range of topics in international relations. Each issue has two readings: one pro and one con. Each is accompanied by an issue *introduction*, which sets the stage for the debate, provides some background information on each author, and generally puts the issue into its political context. Each issue concludes with a *postscript* that summarizes the debate, gives the reader paths for further investigation, and suggests additional readings that might be helpful. I have also provided relevant Internet site addresses (URLs) in each postscript and on the *On the Internet* page that accompanies each part opener.

I have continued to emphasize issues that are currently being debated in the policy sphere. The authors of the selections are a mix of practitioners, scholars, and noted political commentators.

Changes to this edition   The dynamic, constantly changing nature of the world political system and the many helpful comments from reviewers have brought about significant changes to this edition. There are 10 completely new issues: *Do Serious Threats to U.S. Security Exist?* (Issue 1); *Will Creating a Palestinian State Promote Peace in the Middle East?* (Issue 2); *Should We Be Guardedly Optimistic About Russia's Economic and Political Future?* (Issue 3); *Should Multinational Corporations Be Concerned With the Global Public Good?* (Issue 6); *Would the Use of Nuclear Weapons Necessarily Violate the International Law of War?* (Issue 10); *Should an International Criminal Court Be Established?* (Issue 11); *Do U.S. Efforts to Stem the Flow of Drugs from Abroad Encourage Human Rights Violations?* (Issue 13); *Would World Affairs Be More Peaceful If Women Dominated Politics?* (Issue 14); *Does Ritual Female Genital Surgery Violate Women's Human Rights?* (Issue 16); and *Should the Kyoto Treaty Be Supported?* (Issue 17).

i

Thus, approximately 60 percent of the issues and readings are new. Yet there is also a carryover of a goodly number of issues and readings that faculty who used the eighth edition indicated they wanted retained. Some of these issues are virtually timeless, such as Issue 12, *Should Foreign Policymakers Minimize Human Rights Concerns?* Other issues remain at the forefront of international debate, such as Issue 4, *Should China Be Admitted to the World Trade Organization?* It is also well to note that many of the issues have both a specific and a larger topic. For instance, Issue 9, *Should a Permanent UN Military Force Be Established?* is about the specific topic of strengthening the UN's peacekeeping (or peacemaking) ability, but it is also about more general topics. These include whether or not to give international organizations supranational powers; the issue about the propriety of interventionism using UN, NATO, or international forces; and the argument by some small countries that there is a growing neocolonialism in the world today.

A word to the instructor   An *Instructor's Manual With Test Questions* (both multiple-choice and essay) is available through the publisher for instructors using *Taking Sides* in the classroom. A general guidebook, *Using Taking Sides in the Classroom*, which discusses methods and techniques for integrating the pro-con approach into any classroom setting, is also available. An on-line version of *Using Taking Sides in the Classroom* and a correspondence service for *Taking Sides* adopters can be found at http://www.dushkin.com/usingts/. For students, we offer a field guide to analyzing argumentative essays, *Analyzing Controversy: An Introductory Guide*, with exercises and techniques to help them to decipher genuine controversies.

Taking Sides: Clashing Views on Controversial Issues in World Politics is only one title in the Taking Sides series. If you are interested in seeing the table of contents for any of the other titles, please visit the Taking Sides Web site at http://www.dushkin.com/takingsides/.

A note especially for the student reader   You will find that the debates in this book are not one-sided. Each author strongly believes in his or her position. And if you read the debates without prejudging them, you will see that each author makes cogent points. An author may not be "right," but the arguments made in an essay should not be dismissed out of hand, and you should work at remaining tolerant of those who hold beliefs that are different from your own.

There is an additional consideration to keep in mind as you pursue this debate approach to world politics. To consider objectively divergent views does not mean that you have to remain forever neutral. In fact, once you are informed, you ought to form convictions. More important, you should try to influence international policy to conform better with your beliefs. Write letters to policymakers; donate to causes you support; work for candidates who agree with your views; join an activist organization. *Do* something, whichever side of an issue you are on!

Acknowledgments   I received many helpful comments and suggestions from colleagues and readers across the United States and Canada. Their suggestions have markedly enhanced the quality of this edition of *Taking Sides*. If as you read this book you are reminded of a selection or an issue that could be included in a future edition, please write to me in care of Dushkin/McGraw-Hill with your recommendations.

My thanks go to those who responded with suggestions for the ninth edition:

Scott Bennett
Pennsylvania State
   University

Lewis Brownstein
SUNY College at New Paltz

Gary Donato
Three Rivers Community
   Technical College

June Teufel Dreye
University of Miami

Roger Durham
Aquinas College

Timothy L. Elliot
Brigham Young University

Kevin Ellsworth
Arizona State University

Donald Grieve
Northwood University

Dennis Hart
Kent State University

Ngozi C. Kamalu
Fayetteville State University

Wei-Chin Lee
Wake Forest University

Nelson Madore
Thomas College

Timothy Nordstrom
Pennsylvania State
   University

Arnold Oliver
Heidelberg College

Peter Sanchez
Loyola University

John Seitz
Wofford College

Zhe Sun
Ramapo College of
   New Jersey

Melvin M. Vuk
New Mexico State University

Jutta Weldes
Kent State University

I would also like to thank Ted Knight, list manager for the Taking Sides series, and David Brackley, senior developmental editor, for their help in refining this edition.

John T. Rourke
University of Connecticut

CONTENTS IN BRIEF

CONTENTS

R. James Woolsey, former director of the CIA, argues that the end of the cold war has given Americans a false sense of security and that the country needs to keep its military guard up. Carl Conetta and Charles Knight, codirectors of the Project on Defense Alternatives at the Commonwealth Institute in Cambridge, Massachusetts, contend that no military challenge comparable to that of the Soviet Union exists, except as a distant possibility.

Professor of social ethics Herbert C. Kelman contends that to move the Middle East peace process forward, Israel and the Palestinians have to commit themselves to a solution that includes the creation of a Palestinian state. Douglas J. Feith, who served as a Middle East specialist on the National Security Council during the Reagan administration, argues that a Palestinian state would endanger Israel's security.

Stephen Sestanovich, special adviser to the secretary of state for the New Independent States (former Soviet republics), argues that it is important to take advantage of the current opportunity to advance democracy and economic health in Russia. Professor of political science Peter Reddaway contends that Russia faces a future full of uncertainty.

Professor of political science Robert S. Ross contends that the World Trade Organization (WTO) should admit China in order to incorporate that country into the global economy. Greg Mastel, vice president for policy planning and administration at the Economic Strategy Institute in Washington, D.C., argues that the integrity of the WTO would be damaged if China were admitted without significant legal and economic reform.

Business professor Murray Weidenbaum argues that the integration of the American economy with the world is both inevitable and desirable. Professor of political science Gregory Albo maintains that globalization is neither irreversible nor, in its present form, desirable.

Dominic A. Tarantino, former chairman of Price Waterhouse World Firm, Ltd., contends that business leaders should take personal responsibility for the well-being of the entire globe. Professor Manuel Velasquez argues that since there is no way to enforce morality, companies that act ethically will be disadvantaged and therefore cannot be expected to do so.

United Nations executive James P. Grant contends that one way to jump-start solutions to many of the world's problems is to extend more assistance to impoverished countries. The editors of the *Economist*, a well-known British publication, suggest that the usual ways in which international aid is distributed and spent make it a waste of resources.

Tom Bethell, Washington correspondent for the *American Spectator*, contends that the drive toward denuclearization is likely to leave the United States exposed to its enemies. George Lee Butler, a retired U.S. Air Force general and former commander of the Strategic Air Command, advocates the elimination of all nuclear weapons.

Joseph E. Schwartzberg, a professor of geography, proposes a standing UN Peace Corps military force of international volunteers to better enable the UN to meet its peacekeeping mission. John F. Hillen III, a lieutenant in the U.S.

Army, criticizes the idea of a permanent UN army on several grounds and concludes that such a force is unworkable.

Abdul G. Koroma, a justice on the International Court of Justice, argues that the destructive power of nuclear weapons means that their use would necessarily violate the law of war. Stephen M. Schwebel, a justice on the International Court of Justice, maintains that in some circumstances the use of nuclear weapons can be justified under international law.

Beth K. Lamont, the American Humanist Association's alternative nongovernmental organization representative to the UN, affirms the need to advance the importance of international law as a mandatory standard of the conduct of countries and individuals. Lee A. Casey and David B. Rivkin, Jr., who both practice law in Washington, D.C., argue that the International Court of Justice will harm the very quest for justice that it purports to advance.

Alan Tonelson, a fellow of the Economic Strategy Institute in Washington, D.C., contends that the United States' human rights policy ought to be jettisoned. Michael Posner, executive director of the Lawyers Committee for Human Rights, maintains that the United States should continue to incorporate human rights concerns into its foreign policy decisions.

Eyal Press, a writer and a journalist, argues that in its effort to control drugs at one of their major sources, Latin America, the Clinton administration is threatening human rights in Latin America and constitutional rights in the United States. General Barry McCaffrey, director of the Office of National Drug Control Policy, contends that alleviating the threat that drugs pose requires cooperation between the United States and the countries of Latin America and that success promises to ameliorate the corrosive effect of drugs in both regions.

Francis Fukuyama, Hirst Professor of Public Policy at George Mason University, contends that a truly matriarchal world would be less prone to conflict and more conciliatory and cooperative than the largely male-dominated world that we live in now. Professor of political science Mary Caprioli contends that when women assume more political power and have a chance to act aggressively, they are as apt to do so as men are.

Daniel Pipes, editor of *Middle East Quarterly*, argues that just as those who considered the Soviet threat a myth were naive, so are those who dismiss the threat from Islamic fundamentalists naive. Zachary Karabell, a researcher in the Kennedy School of Government at Harvard University, holds that it is wrong to view Islam as a monolith whose adherents pose a threat to the stability of the international system.

Efua Dorkenoo, a consultant on issues of women's health to the World Health Organization, argues that the practice in some regions of the world of performing clitoridectomies on young women and girls violates their fundamental human rights. Scholar Eric Winkel maintains that if the practice of ritual clitoridectomy is to be changed or discarded, the change should come from within Islam and not through the imposition of external cultural values.

Bill Clinton, president of the United States, contends that we have a clear responsibility and a great opportunity to conquer global warming by supporting the Kyoto treaty. J. Kenneth Blackwell, treasurer of the state of Ohio, argues that the U.S. administration's support of the Kyoto treaty is based on inadequate climatological data.

INTRODUCTION

World Politics and the Voice of Justice

John T. Rourke

Some years ago, the Rolling Stones recorded "Sympathy With the Devil." If you have never heard it, go find a copy. It is worth listening to. The theme of the song is echoed in a wonderful essay by Marshall Berman, "Have Sympathy for the Devil" (*New American Review*, 1973). The common theme of the Stones' and Berman's works is based on Johann Goethe's *Faust*. In that classic drama, the protagonist, Dr. Faust, trades his soul to gain great power. He attempts to do good, but in the end he commits evil by, in contemporary paraphrase, "doing the wrong things for the right reasons." Does that make Faust evil, the personification of the devil Mephistopheles among us? Or is the good doctor merely misguided in his effort to make the world better as he saw it and imagined it might be? The point that the Stones and Berman make is that it is important to avoid falling prey to the trap of many zealots who are so convinced of the truth of their own views that they feel righteously at liberty to condemn those who disagree with them as stupid or even diabolical.

It is to the principle of rational discourse, of tolerant debate, that this reader is dedicated. There are many issues in this volume that appropriately excite passion—for example, Issue 15 on whether or not Islamic fundamentalism represents a threat to political stability and Issue 8 on whether or not the world needs to have nuclear weapons at all. Few would find fault with the goal of avoiding nuclear destruction—indeed, of achieving a peaceful world. How to reach that goal is another matter, however, and we should take care not to confuse disagreement on means with disagreement on ends. In other cases, the debates you will read do diverge on goals. Herbert Kelman, for example, argues in Issue 2 that creating an independent Palestinian state is the best road to peace in the Middle East. Douglas Feith disagrees, stressing what he sees as the disingenuousness of the Palestinians and predicting that a Palestinian state would make the Middle East even more dangerous for Israel than it already is.

As you will see, each of the authors in all the debates strongly believes in his or her position. If you read these debates objectively, you will find that each side makes cogent points. They may or may not be right, but they should not be dismissed out of hand. It is also important to repeat that the debate format does not imply that you should remain forever neutral. In fact, once you are informed, you *ought* to form convictions, and you should try to act on those convictions and try to influence international policy to conform better with your beliefs. Ponder the similarities in the views of two very different leaders, a very young president in a relatively young democracy and a very old emperor in a very old country: In 1963 President John F.

Kennedy, in recalling the words of the author of the epoch poem *The Divine Comedy* (1321), told a West German audience, "Dante once said that the hottest places in hell are reserved for those who in a period of moral crisis maintain their neutrality." That very same year, while speaking to the United Nations, Ethiopia's emperor Haile Selassie (1892–1975) said, "Throughout history it has been the inaction of those who could have acted, the indifference of those who should have known better, the silence of the voice of justice when it mattered most that made it possible for evil to triumph."

The point is: Become Informed. Then *do* something! Write letters to policymakers, donate money to causes you support, work for candidates with whom you agree, join an activist organization, or any of the many other things that you can do to make a difference. What you do is less important than that you do it.

APPROACHES TO STUDYING INTERNATIONAL POLITICS

As will become evident as you read this volume, there are many approaches to the study of international politics. Some political scientists and most practitioners specialize in *substantive topics*, and this reader is organized along topical lines. Part 1 (Issues 1 through 4) begins with a regional issue on the international system, which is currently an emphasis of many scholars. R. James Woolsey engages in debate with Carl Conetta and Charles Knight about whether or not serious threats remain to U.S. security in the post–cold war era. Issue 2, as noted, takes up the Middle East and the possible creation of an independent state for the Palestinians. The future of Russia and how that should affect Western, especially U.S., policy is the subject of Issue 3. The regional focus then changes to China in Issue 4. The basic question is whether or not that country should be admitted into the World Trade Organization (WTO). In many ways, though, the WTO issue is symbolic of whether or not China's human rights policy and other objectionable elements of its foreign and domestic policy should be overlooked in establishing normal commercial and diplomatic relations with Beijing.

Part 2 (Issues 5 through 7) focuses on international economic issues, including the desirability of the ever-increasing degree of economic interdependence; whether or not multinational corporations should try to operate in the public good; and whether or not foreign aid should be substantially increased or drastically reduced. Part 3 (Issues 8 and 9) deals with military security. The world has been threatened by atomic destruction for more than a half century. But some say that nuclear weapons have kept the peace. In Issue 8 Tom Bethell maintains that it would be a mistake for the United States to get rid of its nuclear weapons. George Lee Butler, a former commander of U.S. nuclear forces, takes the opposite point of view and says that it is time to create a world that is free of nuclear weapons. In Issue 9 the call to create a permanent UN peacekeeping force is debated.

Part 4 (Issues 10 and 11) examines controversies surrounding the application of international law in world politics. The first debate explores whether or not using nuclear weapons would necessarily violate the international law of war. In a larger sense, the debate is about the law of war in general, which has once again come to the fore in world politics, given the atrocities committed during recent years in Bosnia, Rwanda, Kosovo, and elsewhere. The issue on the law of war flows into the debate in Issue 11, which evaluates the wisdom of establishing a permanent international criminal court to punish those who violate the law of war. It is easy to advocate such a court as long as it is trying and sometimes punishing alleged war criminals from other countries. But one has to understand that one day someone from one's own country could be put on trial.

Part 5 (Issues 12 through 17) takes up global moral, social, and environmental issues. Issues 12 and 13 are related to the issues in Part 4 in that they involve human rights. In Issue 14 the debate turns to the potential impact of the growing role of women on the level of violence in the world. Certainly, equity demands that women have the same opportunity as men to achieve leadership positions. But will that equity also promote a decrease in world violence? Therein lies the debate. The focus switches to religion in Issue 15. Some analysts maintain that the lines of division and conflict in world politics will focus on broad cultural groups, with Muslims being one such group. This broader question is in the background of the debate over whether or not Islamic fundamentalism represents a danger to global tranquility. The intersection of human rights and religion within the context of cultural practices is at the center of the debate in Issue 16 over whether or not the largely North African practice of performing what is called female genital mutilation by critics and female circumcision by supporters should be banned. Finally, the environment is addressed in Issue 17, which focuses on the degree of danger posed by global warming and whether or not the strong measures stipulated in the Kyoto treaty should be adopted.

Political scientists also approach their subject from differing *methodological perspectives*. We will see, for example, that world politics can be studied from different *levels of analysis*. The question is: What is the basic source of the forces that shape the conduct of politics? Possible answers are world forces, the individual political processes of the specific countries, or the personal attributes of a country's leaders and decision makers. Various readings will illustrate all three levels.

Another way for students and practitioners of world politics to approach their subject is to focus on what is called the realist versus the idealist debate. Realists tend to assume that the world is permanently flawed and therefore advocate following policies in their country's narrow self-interests. Idealists take the approach that the world condition can be improved substantially by following policies that, at least in the short term, call for some risk or self-sacrifice. This divergence is an element of many of the debates in this book.

DYNAMICS OF WORLD POLITICS

The action on the global stage today is vastly different from what it was a few decades ago, or even a few years ago. *Technology* is one of the causes of this change. Technology has changed communications, manufacturing, health care, and many other aspects of the human condition. Technology has also led to the creation of nuclear weapons and other highly sophisticated and expensive conventional weapons. Issue 8 frames a debate over whether or not, having created and armed ourselves with nuclear weapons, we can and should reverse the process and eliminate them. Technology also has its negative byproducts, and one of them may be global warming caused by the vastly increased discharges of carbon dioxide and other "greenhouse" gases into the atmosphere that have resulted from industrialization, the advent of air conditioning, and many other technological advances. These effects are taken up in Issue 17.

Another dynamic aspect of world politics involves the *changing axes* of the world system. For about 40 years after World War II ended in 1945, a bipolar system existed, the primary axis of which was the *East-West* conflict, which pitted the United States and its allies against the Soviet Union and its allies. Now that the cold war is over, one broad debate is over whether or not there are potential enemies to the United States and, if so, who they are. The advocates on either side of Issue 1 disagree about whether or not there is any current threat. Issues 3 and 4 deal with Russia and China, two cold war antagonists of the United States. Some people believe that one or both of these countries, or even both of them in alliance, could pose a threat in the future. As such, the two debates, beyond the specific issues involved in them, also deal with how to interact with former and potential enemies.

Technological changes and the shifting axes of international politics also highlight the *increased role of economics* in world politics. Economics have always played a role, but traditionally the main focus has been on strategic-political questions—especially military power. This concern still strongly exists, but it now shares the international spotlight with economic issues. One important change in recent decades has been the rapid growth of regional and global markets and the promotion of free trade and other forms of international economic interchange. As Issue 5 on economic interdependence indicates, many people support these efforts and see them as the wave of the future. But there are others who believe that free economic interchange undermines sovereignty and the ability of governments to regulate multinational corporations. Whether or not these multinational corporations should self-regulate through conscious concern with the global public good is the point of controversy in Issue 6, and the degree to which the few relatively wealthy countries in the world should assist the many relatively poor countries in the world to develop economically is debated in Issue 7.

Another change in the world system has to do with the main *international* actors. At one time states (countries) were practically the only international actors on the world stage. Now, and increasingly so, there are other actors. Some actors are regional. Others, such as the United Nations, are global actors. Issue 9 examines the call for strengthening the peacekeeping and peacemaking capability of the United Nations by establishing a permanent UN military force. And Issue 11 focuses on whether or not a supranational criminal court should be established to take over the prosecution and punishment of war criminals from the domestic courts and ad hoc tribunals that have sometimes dealt with these cases in the past.

PERCEPTIONS VERSUS REALITY

In addition to addressing the general changes in the world system outlined above, the debates in this reader explore the controversies that exist over many of the fundamental issues that face the world.

One key to these debates is the differing *perceptions* that protagonists bring to them. There may be a reality in world politics, but very often that reality is obscured. Many observers, for example, are alarmed by the seeming rise in radical actions by Islamic fundamentalists. As Issue 15 illustrates, the image of Islamic radicalism is not a fact but a perception; perhaps correct, perhaps not. In cases such as this, though, it is often the perception, not the reality, that is more important because policy is formulated on what decision makers *think*, not necessarily on what *is*. Thus, perception becomes the operating guide, or *operational reality*, whether it is true or not. Perceptions result from many factors. One factor is the information that decision makers receive. For a variety of reasons, the facts and analyses that are given to leaders are often inaccurate or represent only part of the picture. The conflicting perceptions of Israelis and Palestinians make the achievement of peace in Israel very difficult. Many Israelis and Palestinians believe fervently that the conflict that has occurred in the region over the past 50 years is the responsibility of the other. Both sides also believe in the righteousness of their own policies. Even if both sides are well-meaning, the perceptions of hostility that each holds means that the operational reality often has to be violence. A related aspect of perception is the tendency to see oneself differently than some others do. Partly at issue in the debate over China's desire to join the World Trade Organization, as discussed in Issue 4, is whether the country should be able to join as a less developed country (as China sees itself) and take advantage of fewer restrictions, or whether China should be admitted as a major economic power (as the United States sees it) and have to abide by all the WTO's rules requiring lowering barriers to trade and investment.

Perceptions, then, are crucial to understanding international politics. It is important to understand objective reality, but it is also necessary to comprehend subjective reality in order to be able to predict and analyze another country's actions.

LEVELS OF ANALYSIS

Political scientists approach the study of international politics from different levels of analysis. The most macroscopic view is *system-level analysis*. This is a top-down approach that maintains that world factors virtually compel countries to follow certain foreign policies. Governing factors include the number of powerful actors, geographic relationships, economic needs, and technology. System analysts hold that a country's internal political system and its leaders do not have a major impact on policy. As such, political scientists who work from this perspective are interested in exploring the governing factors, how they cause policy, and how and why systems change.

After the end of World War II, the world was structured as a *bipolar* system, dominated by the United States and the Soviet Union. Furthermore, each superpower was supported by a tightly organized and dependent group of allies. For a variety of reasons, including changing economics and the nuclear standoff, the bipolar system has faded. Some political scientists argue that the bipolar system is being replaced by a *multipolar* system. In such a configuration, those who favor *balance-of-power* politics maintain that it is unwise to ignore power considerations. The debate in Issue 1 about current and future threats to U.S. security reflects the changes that have occurred in the system and the efforts of Americans to decide what, if anything, the United States needs to be militarily prepared to counter.

State-level analysis is the middle, and the most common, level of analysis. Social scientists who study world politics from this perspective focus on how countries, singly or comparatively, make foreign policy. In other words, this perspective is concerned with internal political dynamics, such as the roles of and interactions between the executive and legislative branches of government, the impact of bureaucracy, the role of interest groups, and the effect of public opinion. The Kyoto treaty, which is debated in Issue 17, represents a case where U.S. interest groups have and will clash with one another in an attempt to get the administration to withdraw its support of the treaty or, failing that, to try to block ratification of the treaty in the U.S. Senate. It will be, to a large degree, the environmentalists versus the business groups.

A third level of analysis, which is the most microscopic, is *human-level analysis*. This approach focuses, in part, on the role of individual decision makers. This technique is applied under the assumption that individuals make decisions and that the nature of those decisions is determined by the decision makers' perceptions, predilections, and strengths and weaknesses. Human-level analysis also focuses on the nature of humans. Issue 12 explores the degree to which decision makers should apply their own or their society's moral standards to foreign policy decisions.

REALISM VERSUS IDEALISM

Realism and idealism represent another division among political scientists and practitioners in their approaches to the study and conduct of international relations. *Realists* are usually skeptical about the nature of politics and, perhaps, the nature of humankind. They tend to believe that countries have opposing interests and that these differences can lead to conflict. They further contend that states (countries) are by definition obligated to do what is beneficial for their own citizens (national interest). The amount of power that a state has will determine how successful it is in attaining these goals. Therefore, politics is, and ought to be, a process of gaining, maintaining, and using power. Realists are apt to believe that the best way to avoid conflict is to remain powerful and to avoid pursuing goals that are beyond one's power to achieve. "Peace through strength" is a phrase that most realists would agree with.

Idealists disagree with realists about both the nature and conduct of international relations. They tend to be more optimistic that the global community is capable of finding ways to live in harmony and that it has a sense of collective, rather than national, interest. Idealists also maintain that the pursuit of a narrow national interest is shortsighted. They argue that, in the long run, countries must learn to cooperate or face the prospect of a variety of evils, including nuclear warfare, environmental disaster, or continuing economic hardship. Idealists argue, for example, that armaments cause world tensions, whereas realists maintain that conflict requires states to have weapons. Idealists are especially concerned with conducting current world politics on a more moral or ethical plane and with searching for alternatives to the present pursuit of nationalist interests through power politics.

Many of the issues in this volume address the realist-idealist split. Realists and idealists differ over whether or not states can and should surrender enough of their freedom of action and pursuit of self-interest to cooperate through and, to a degree, subordinate themselves to international organizations. This is one basis of disagreement in Issue 9, which contemplates a permanent UN military force. Realists and idealists also disagree on whether or not moral considerations should play a strong role in determining foreign policy. The proper role of morality is the focus of debate between realist Alan Tonelson and idealist Michael Posner in Issue 12. In a more applied sense, in Issue 13 the U.S. "drug czar" Barry McCaffrey answers the charge, represented by Eyal Press, that the weapons supplied to some Central and South American countries to fight drugs are often used to suppress domestic opposition in those countries. Just as in *Faust*, as mentioned at the beginning of this introduction, the urge to do good is fraught with peril.

THE POLITICAL AND ECOLOGICAL FUTURE

Future *world alternatives* are discussed in many of the issues in this volume. Issue 1, for example, debates whether or not the current world situation portends anarchy. The debate in Issue 7 on the North providing aid to the South is not just about humanitarian impulses; it is about whether or not the world can survive and be stable economically and politically if it is divided into a minority of wealthy nations and a majority of poor countries. Abraham Lincoln once said, "A house divided against itself cannot stand." One suspects that the 16th president might say something similar about the world today if he were with us. Another, more far-reaching alternative is an international organization taking over some (or all) of the sovereign responsibilities of national governments. Issue 9 on UN peacekeeping forces, Issue 11 on establishing an international criminal court, and Issue 4 on the World Trade Organization all focus on the authority of the international organizations to assume a degree of limited supranational (above countries) power.

The global future also involves the ability of the world to prosper economically while, at the same time, not denuding itself of its natural resources or destroying the environment. This is the focus of Issue 17 on global warming.

THE AXES OF WORLD DIVISION

It is a truism that the world is politically dynamic and that the nature of the political system is undergoing profound change. As noted, the once-primary axis of world politics, the East-West confrontation, has broken down. Yet a few vestiges of the conflict on that axis remain.

In contrast to the moribund East-West axis, the *North-South axis* has increased in importance and tension. The wealthy, industrialized countries (North) are on one end, and the poor, less developed countries (LDCs, South) are at the other extreme. Economic differences and disputes are the primary dimension of this axis, in contrast to the military nature of the East-West axis. Issue 7 explores these differences and debates whether or not the North should significantly increase economic aid to the South.

The North-South division is one of the outstanding issues in the debate over the Kyoto treaty in Issue 17. The poorer countries of the South have claimed and won an exemption from the requirement to cut down greenhouse gas emissions. Their argument is that they give off much less of such gases than the industrialized countries do. Moreover, say the countries of the South, they will not be able to achieve industrialization if they are required to curtail their economic activity. Some in the North, especially in the economic sector, argue that saddling the North with restrictions and not applying them to the South will not solve the problem (because increased emissions in the South will offset declining emissions in the North) and will also result in unacceptable economic burdens to the North.

Then there is the question of what, if anything, will develop to divide the countries of the North and replace the East-West axis. The possibility for tension is represented in several issues. Some believe that the remnants of the USSR, especially Russia, will one day again pose a threat to the rest of Europe. That concern is a backdrop to Issue 3. A provocative idea of political scientist Samuel Huntington is that cultures will be the basis of a new, multiaxial dimension of global antagonism. If that comes to pass, then it might be that most of what Huntington calls the Western countries will be one step in the formation of one part of the axis. One opposing group that might form around politically resurgent Muslims (as discussed in Issue 15) is what Huntington calls the Islamic civilization.

INCREASED ROLE OF ECONOMICS

As the growing importance of the North-South axis indicates, economics are playing an increased role in world politics. The economic reasons behind the decline of the East-West axis is further evidence. Economics have always played a part in international relations, but the traditional focus has been on strategic-political affairs, especially questions of military power.

Political scientists, however, are now increasingly focusing on the international political economy, or the economic dimensions of world politics. International trade, for instance, has increased dramatically, expanding from an annual world exports total of $20 billion in 1933 to $6.5 trillion in 1997. The impact has been profound. The domestic economic health of most countries is heavily affected by trade and other aspects of international economics. Since World War II, there has been an emphasis on expanding free trade by decreasing tariffs and other barriers to international commerce. In recent years, however, a downturn in the economies of many of the industrialized countries has increased calls for more protectionism. This is related to the debate in Issue 4 on China's application to join the WTO. Yet restrictions on trade and other economic activity can also be used as a diplomatic weapon. The intertwining of economies and the creation of organizations to regulate them, such as the WTO, is raising issues of sovereignty and other concerns. This is a central matter in the debate in Issue 5 between Murray Weidenbaum and Gregory Albo over whether or not the trend toward global economic integration is desirable.

The level and impact of international aid is another economic issue of considerable dispute. Issue 7 examines the question of whether massive foreign aid would help the less developed countries (and the developed countries as well) or actually hinder economic progress in the less developed countries.

CONCLUSION

Having discussed many of the various dimensions and approaches to the study of world politics, it is incumbent on this editor to advise against your becoming too structured by them. Issues of focus and methodology are important both to studying international relations and to understanding how others are analyzing global conduct. However, they are also partially pedagogical. In the final analysis, world politics is a highly interrelated, perhaps seamless, subject. No one level of analysis, for instance, can fully explain the events on the world stage. Instead, using each of the levels to analyze events and trends will bring the greatest understanding.

Similarly, the realist-idealist division is less precise in practice than it may appear. As some of the debates indicate, each side often stresses its own standards of morality. Which is more moral: defeating a dictatorship or sparing the sword and saving lives that would almost inevitably be lost in the dictator's overthrow? Furthermore, realists usually do not reject moral considerations. Rather, they contend that morality is but one of the factors that a country's decision makers must consider. Realists are also apt to argue that standards of morality differ when dealing with a country as opposed to an individual. By the same token, most idealists do not completely ignore the often dangerous nature of the world. Nor do they argue that a country must totally sacrifice its short-term interests to promote the betterment of the current and future world. Thus, realism and idealism can be seen most accurately as the ends of a continuum—with most political scientists and practitioners falling somewhere between, rather than at, the extremes. The best advice, then, is this: think broadly about international politics. The subject is very complex, and the more creative and expansive you are in selecting your foci and methodologies, the more insight you will gain. To end where we began, with Dr. Faust, I offer his last words in Goethe's drama, *"Mehr licht,"* ... More light! That is the goal of this book.

On the Internet . . .

U.S. Department of State Web Site Index
The information in this index of the U.S. Department of State is organized into categories, from foreign policy and the Middle East to regions and the United Nations.
http://www.state.gov/www/ind.html

WWW Virtual Library: International Affairs Resources
Hosted by Elizabethtown College in New Jersey, this site contains approximately 1,100 annotated links relating to a broad spectrum of international affairs. The sites listed are those that the Webmaster believes have long-term value and have further links to help in extended research.
http://www.etown.edu/home/selchewa/international_studies/firstpag.htm

Global Information Access Net
This site is hosted by the University of Pittsburgh as one of the National Resource Centers under Title VI of the U.S. Higher Education Act. The site has a good list of URLs that link to centers that study regional issues.
http://www.ucis.pitt.edu/dbinfo/

PART 1

Regional Issues

The issues in this section deal with countries that are major regional powers. In this era of interdependence among nations, it is important to understand the concerns that these issues address and the actors involved because they will shape the world and will affect the lives of all people.

■ Do Serious Threats to U.S. Security Exist?

■ Will Creating a Palestinian State Promote Peace in the Middle East?

■ Should We Be Guardedly Optimistic About Russia's Economic and Political Future?

■ Should China Be Admitted to the World Trade Organization?

ISSUE 1

Do Serious Threats to U.S. Security Exist?

YES: R. James Woolsey, from Statement Before the Committee on National Security, U.S. House of Representatives (February 12, 1998)

NO: Carl Conetta and Charles Knight, from "Inventing Threats," *The Bulletin of the Atomic Scientists* (March/April 1998)

ISSUE SUMMARY

YES: R. James Woolsey, former director of the Central Intelligence Agency, argues that the end of the cold war has given Americans a false sense of security and that the country needs to keep its military guard up against a range of threats.

NO: Carl Conetta and Charles Knight, codirectors of the Project on Defense Alternatives at the Commonwealth Institute in Cambridge, Massachusetts, contend that the United States continues to spend vast sums of money on its military despite the fact that the Soviet Union is gone and that no comparable military challenge exists, except as a distant possibility.

Prior to World War II, the United States participated in world politics only fitfully. In part, this stemmed from a feeling of security based on the fact that the country is guarded by three vast bodies of water and has only two, relatively weak, neighbors, Canada and Mexico.

A great deal of the sense of security was shattered by World War II and its aftermath. Looming ideological threats—first fascism, then communism—backed by military might seemed to loom just over the horizon. Military technology also perceptually narrowed the distance between the United States and potential danger. During World War II, aircraft carriers, submarines, long-range bombers, and other weapons systems were developed or improved to the point that the possibility of an enemy attacking the United States seemed increasingly real. Soon, however, the sense of danger from these weapons systems was far eclipsed by the extraordinary killing power of atomic weapons.

Even after the victories over Germany and Japan in World War II, in the minds of many the tide seemed to be turning against the United States in the post–World War II years of the late 1940s and the 1950s. The Soviet Union rapidly developed its own atomic, then hydrogen, bombs. Eastern Europe, North Korea, China, North Vietnam, and other places joined the seemingly unified Communist bloc. There was a "red scare" in the United States, and a demagogue named Senator Joseph McCarthy convinced many Americans that disloyal Communists had infiltrated government, the media, and elsewhere and were plotting to subvert the country. In the late 1950s the Soviets seemed to eclipse U.S. missile technology when they launched the first satellite, then put the first person in space.

After World War II the United States demobilized most of its military forces and slashed its military spending. The onset of the cold war reversed this trend, and the threats, real or imagined, epitomized by the nuclear weapon–armed, communist, officially atheist Soviet Union led to an immense buildup of American military power and the expenditure of a huge proportion of the U.S. budget for defense.

After that, the size of the U.S. military and the U.S. military budget ebbed and flowed. After some cutbacks the military establishment again increased during the Vietnam War era. After the Vietnam War ended, military spending and personnel both plunged, only to rise again during the years roughly equivalent to the presidency of Ronald Reagan. Then the waning of the cold war in the late 1980s again reversed the trend.

The final episode in the cold war roller-coaster ride of defense personnel and spending came on Christmas day 1991, when for the last time the Soviet hammer-and-sickle flag was lowered from atop the spires of the Kremlin in Moscow and the Russian flag was raised in its stead. The Soviet Union had collapsed and had been replaced by Russia and a number of other, smaller former Soviet republics. What had been a declining sense of threat seemingly dissipated even more rapidly.

By 1992, the last year of the presidency of George Bush, the world looked safer to Americans than it had seemed in many decades. Not only was the cold war over, but in early 1991 high-tech, American-led forces had routed Iraqi forces during the Persian Gulf War. In sum, the majority of the most fearsome enemies were gone or had moderated; less-potential opponents, such as Iraq, could, it seemed, be easily handled by U.S. military might.

However, the degree to which threats ended or only seemed to is debatable. The Russian nuclear arsenal remains massive, and the Chinese nuclear arsenal is growing. India and Pakistan joined the nuclear weapons club in 1998, and they and a number of other countries are developing missiles that can carry nuclear, chemical, biological, and other types of warheads over extended distances. Moreover, numerous countries are suspected of building or harboring ambitions to build weapons of mass destruction.

After a continuing decline in real dollar defense spending during most of the 1990s, the debate on the level of spending has once again come to the fore. In the first of the following selections, former CIA head R. James Woolsey contends that there are serious threats to U.S. national security and that U.S. forces must be well funded to meet the danger. Carl Conetta and Charles Knight contend that defense spending advocates like Woolsey are inventing or inflating threats.

YES
R. James Woolsey

THREATS TO UNITED STATES NATIONAL SECURITY

I am going to limit [my] remarks to what I would regard as the salient threats to American security, serious damage to the country, such as would be caused by an attack on us or a major war. There are a number of other interesting and important threats, in a sense, which we can discuss in questions, if the committee is interested.

One important preliminary matter. During the cold war, we became very accustomed to talking about threats and even validated threats and this was possible because the Soviet Union was, at least in its weapons development and the planning of its military operations, a relatively predictable place with respect to development, doctrine, military plans. We could focus our intelligence on key nodes, test ranges, on recruiting a Polish officer as a spy on the Warsaw Pact staff to steal their war plans and so on.

We got to be used to the idea that we should really only respond to reasonably clear extrapolations of what we, in fact, saw. That was not an irrational approach during the cold war, because of the nature of our enemy and because we had to economize and spend money on what was truly important.

But, this approach, in my judgment, needs to be substantially modified in the post-cold war era. People such as [Iraqi leader] Saddam Hussein and [North Korean leader] Kim Jong Il are far more unpredictable and irrational than the Soviet leaders ever were. It is dangerous, I believe, to assume that military developments and deployments in regimes such as these are going to follow some relatively predictable pattern.

I said on a number of occasions, and my staff, when I was DCI [director of central intelligence], used to wince when they heard it because they heard it so often, that we were in a situation similar to that of having struggled with a dragon for 45 years and killed him and now finding ourselves in a jungle full of a lot of poisonous snakes. That, in many ways, the snakes were much harder to keep track of than the dragon ever was.

I think that is the essence of the problem. Just as [Supreme Court Justice Oliver Wendell] Holmes used to say, in order to understand the law, you have to look at it as a bad man would, and in order to understand the post-cold

From U.S. House of Representatives. Committee on National Security. *Threats to United States National Security*. Hearing, February 12, 1998. Washington, D.C.: Government Printing Office, 1998. (S.Hrg 105-40.)

war era, we must all try, and it is a very difficult task, indeed, to look at the world through the eyes of a Saddam Hussein or a Kim Jong Il.

Now, starting with Russia and China, these are the only two countries that can destroy the United States today within the 30 minute flight time of an ICBM [intercontinental ballistic missile]. I believe that fundamentally, with Russia and China today, the United States need have no fundamental serious strategic differences with Russia at all, and with China, the one underlying one, where we are likely to have a serious strategic difference is the future of Taiwan or, at least, China's potential attempt to resolve the Taiwan issue by force.

But, nonetheless, neither of these two countries is in a stable situation yet. Both are in considerable political and economic flux and neither has established the rule of law. It is therefore, I think, quite important for us to look at the problems that might arise in the future with them and the problems that do exist today.

One of the most serious aspects of the current situation in Russia is that the degree of corruption and the fiscal problems of the Russian state have created a very poor state of morale, pay and behavior inside the Russian military forces. The conventional forces, most of them, are in worse shape, but even the strategic rocket forces are not immune to these problems.

There are some uncertainties that the general staff and the strategic rocket forces face with respect to nuclear weapons. First of all, because their conventional forces are in such poor shape, the Russians are moving toward a doctrine of potential first use of nuclear weapons and a much higher reliance on nuclear weapons than they had before.

Tongue in cheek, I might say they are adopting the views of the early [former Secretary of State Henry] Kissinger, circa late 1950's, early 1960's, with respect to reliance on nuclear weapons. They have lost some important warning systems that are outside Russia that were in the Soviet Union, but are not in Russia, and it is quite troubling to contemplate what might happen in some crisis if there were a misunderstanding, such as there might have been in part with respect to the famous recent incident of the Norwegian sounding rocket.

We, ourselves, in the United States, have had command post exercises in the Strategic Air Command once or twice over the years temporarily mistaken for the real thing. And, in one famous incident many years ago, when [Soviet leader Nikita] Khruschev was actually inside the United States, a brand new radar in the ballistic missile early warning system tracked the rising of the moon as a flight of incoming Soviet ICBM's. The Canadian general who was on duty at NORAD looked at his television screen, saw that Khruschev was in the cornfields or Disneyland or wherever and said, this just cannot be true.

But, the point is, that in times of tension it is plausible that something most unexpected could happen. I believe that the lessons for us from that circumstance with respect to Russian nuclear forces is the importance of discussions with the Russians to try to find ways to ameliorate this situation, but also, at least in my judgment, a vigorous approach toward ballistic missile defense for the United States, at least to the level that could deal with unauthorized and accidental launches.

A second problem with Russia is that many of those who managed the Soviet

Union's security establishment, whether in technology, intelligence or in military expertise, are now for hire on both the white and the black markets. This makes Russia a serious source of proliferation, for example, to Iran as the chairman mentioned. A recent series in [the Russian newspaper] *Izvestia* spoke in some detail about senior Russian military officers having provided assistance to [Japanese cult leader] Aum Shinrikyu, prior to Aum's chemical attack in the Tokyo subway.

One of the most difficult aspects of all of this is the inter-penetration of the security services, organized crime and some aspects of Russian business. If any of you are in Geneva, let us say, or Vienna sometime in the next few years and you should run into a very well dressed, prosperous looking Russian, let us say, a $2,000 suit and Gucci's and he says to you that he wants to talk to someone in the states about a joint venture for the export of oil or some other purpose, he may be what he says he is, a businessman. He may be a Russian intelligence officer under commercial cover. He may be a senior member of some organized crime group. But, what is really interesting is that there is at least some chance that he is all three, and indeed, that none of those three institutions has any particularly serious problem with that.

China presents the case of a dictatorship that has successfully begun a major economic modernization, but the disruption that will likely occur as the inefficient state owned enterprises are shifted in their organization and employment structure and the regional tensions that this sets up in China, along with other economic difficulties between the prosperous South and Coast and the less than prosperous North and Interior could lead Chinese leaders to take refuge, even more than they have in the past, in nationalism. The focus of nationalism for them is likely to be to regain Taiwan.

This is the one issue which I think might cause a major rupture between the United States and a nuclear power which today could threaten the United States. After we demonstrated, I believe, weakness and vacillation for several years, in my judgment, the Chinese were genuinely surprised two years ago when they launched ballistic missiles into the waters near Taiwan and the United States, in fact, responded by sending two aircraft carriers.

But, I think the lesson of that period is that it is dangerous to give China reason to doubt our resolve on this issue of the importance of a peaceful resolution of any differences in the Taiwan straits. A Chinese invasion of Taiwan is not really in the cards for many years. They lack the lift and the relevant types of military capability, but the seizure of one or more of the offshore islands, ballistic missile attacks using conventional warheads with excellent guidance, such as GPS, against targets in Taiwan, these are some of the types of things that could create a crisis and a confrontation with China.

I want to speak briefly to three rogue governments, North Korea, Iraq and Iran. Except during our periodic crises in the Mideast, the Korean Demilitarized Zone (DMZ) remains the most likely place in the world for the United States to get involved in a land war. There are several situations that create a serious risk that the North might expect some types of early successes and lead Kim Jong Il, even with the decrepit state of his nation, to try some wild throw of the dice.

The concentration of North Korean forces close to the DMZ, the concentration of South Korea's population in industry on the southern side of the DMZ, some imbalances in military capability, particularly South Korea's sparse investment in artillery and some North Korean capabilities, such as their special operations forces, their possession of ballistic missiles equipped with chemical and/or bacteriological weapons, the initiation of operational status for the Nodong [a medium-range ballistic missile], which could conceivably threaten our bases in Japan.

We have seen our military force structure erode since the gulf war,... and although there have been some important improvements in capabilities such as smart weapons, nonetheless, I think particularly from this committee's point of view, it is important that our capacity to fight two major regional wars simultaneously must be said to be in doubt.

If we are engaged in the Mideast at some point in hostilities, doubtless Kim Jong Il will notice. And, if we are engaged in Korea, doubtless Saddam will notice. If the [North Korean] Taepo Dong 2 missile has been developed and deployed by the time of any crisis or war on the Korean peninsula, the situation could be grave, indeed, because it would probably be able to reach at least some cities in Alaska, carrying possibly a bacteriological warhead. It is not unimaginable that the North Koreans would be able to produce one or two nuclear warheads from the fissionable material they were probably able to acquire from the earlier operation of their reactor. But, in many cases, bacteriological will do just as well as nuclear for a weapon of blackmail.

So, although in any war of duration, the decrepit nation of North Korea would not

be able to prevail against the combined forces of the United States and South Korea, the threat of a quick grab of the northern part of South Korea is a serious one, I believe, as long as this North Korean state and military pull together. If there were a simultaneous crisis in the Mideast or if the Taepo Dong 2 were developed and deployed, the situation could be extremely grave.

I would add, North Korea, of course, remains a very dangerous and serious proliferator, as well as creating these other direct threat problems.

The conclusion I draw from this is that theater and national ballistic missile defense for the United States and several important improvements for South Korea's defenses, especially artillery, are quite important.

Second, Iraq. Certainly, Saddam has proven his willingness to take risks. He has proven his ruthlessness and his lack of feeling for his own people and his stubbornness. The two fundamental problems are that Iraq sits on or near a huge share of the world's oil. In the late summer of 1990, Saddam was about 100 miles away from controlling over half of the world's proven reserves. Saddam doubtless holds at least stocks of chemical and bacteriological weapons and the means to deliver them against our friends and allies and against U.S. forces in the region, and the capacity to rebuild that capability, even if it is taken from him.

The problem is seriously complicated, in my judgment, by the fact that there are no easy fixes to this situation, by a short bombing campaign or by any other means. Even in the unlikely event that Saddam agreed to full and complete U.N. inspections and even if his supplies of chemical and bacteriological weapons, his capacity to produce them and his ballistic missiles were destroyed by inspectors or by air attack, if the inspections ceased, and they would have to be very, very vigorous inspections indeed, he would soon be capable of reaching some degree of devastation again.

For example, SCUDs [missiles] are available in many places in the world, especially to a country that has billions of dollars of oil revenue annually, and it is only a little harder to make anthrax than it is to run a small microbrewery, a parallel that was drawn by the Deputy Director of the Advanced Research Project Agency in the Pentagon in an excellent paper, unclassified paper, on bacteriological warfare, which I would urge that this committee seek and review.

Anthrax is relatively easy to make and the manufacturing equipment and the stocks for bacteriological and chemical weapons can be disbursed, can be hidden from inspectors, can be hidden from intelligence collection, perhaps in deep bunkers that even advanced and accurate conventional weapons cannot destroy.

I believe the problem with Saddam has been made worse by our flaccid responses in 1994 to the Iraqi Intelligence Service's attempt to assassinate former President Bush and in 1996 to Saddam's murderous assault against the north. He has doubtless concluded that almost no matter what he does, he will only have to endure air strikes for a limited period of time and that he can use those to rally support, especially in the Arab world.

Thus, in my judgment, it will do little good only to try to use air strikes to delay and disrupt the Iraqi capability to manufacture and use weapons of mass destruction for a limited period of time. Air attacks may show some success to that end, but Saddam will doubtless force innocent civilians to be placed at likely attack points or even kill them himself and claim that U.S. air strikes were responsible. In a few months, there would be a new crisis.

The fundamental problem is the Ba'athist Regime which Saddam heads and it seems to me that is the problem we must confront. As a shorthand, we often speak of Saddam as the problem and this focus on the individual can even lead to such proposals as I believe are extremely irresponsible when made by former senior Clinton administration advisor George Stephanopoulos in December that the United States provide "direct support" for a "inside job" to assassinate Saddam. In addition to being illegal under the current governing executive order, impractical and destructive of much of what we try to stand for in the world, such an effort, even if successful, would be quite likely to give us another Ba'ath Nationalist of Saddam's tribe.

Instead, I believe we need a solid program to break the power of Saddam's regime. Some elements of that program could include air strikes, but we should try to maintain our forces in the region for a sustained period of time in a condition to attack so that we can achieve some surprise at some point. An attack now against what are doubtless dispersed weapon stockpiles would be less likely to be effective. Republican Guard is also now probably dispersed to help make air attack against it less effective, and we would want to make sure that we attack in such a way as to cause maximum damage to the Republican Guard, since it is much of the source of the regime's power.

Yet, as I understand the current position of the Administration, it suggests that only attacks against weapon stockpiles are now being contemplated. The commanding general has more broadly spoken about attacks against the instruments of power in Saddam's regime, which I believe is a much better formulation. But, given the Administration's statements, in my view, limited strikes, especially if executed at a time that Saddam expects them, would succeed in doing very little that is useful. If air strikes occur within the next few weeks, this may be the most telegraphed punch in military history.

There are other important components to break the power of the Iraqi regime and I believe they should be undertaken promptly. They could include destroying the Iraqi air defense system by air strikes and then establishing and maintaining a no-fly zone over the entire country, a step which would make it much harder for the regime to move Republican Guard forces quickly by helicopter to counter rebellions by dissident regular forces in the future, such as have happened in the past.

It might also include recognizing a government in exile, providing vigorous air protection for the Kurds in the north, which we did not do 2 years ago, and the Shia [members of a Muslim sect] in the south, which we did not do in 1991 against the regime.

Now, it will be said by some that many members of our once effective gulf war coalition would not support such steps. But, it seems to me that the United States has more success in building coalitions when it takes firm, clear, sustainable positions than when it plays for short-term publicity or sending signals with military forces. It is aggravating in the extreme that the Saudis will apparently not permit us to conduct air strikes from Saudi territory, but we must understand that the Saudis or anyone else in the region

cannot reasonably be expected to support pinprick air attacks such as in 1994 and 1996 or even longer bombing campaigns that merely retard Saddam's program for weapons of mass destruction.

They must then continue to live next door to the angered viper, while we are free to withdraw thousands of miles away. A decisive and coherent long-term program to bring down the Ba'athist Regime in Iraq, of which air strikes from time to time may well be a very important part, seem to me to be the only course of action at this point that has any chance of success.

Briefly, on Iran, Mr. Chairman, unlike the case with the Iraqi regime, I believe that the threats that are potentially posed by Iran may plausibly be ameliorated by peaceful means. Now, this is far from certain, but it is much more likely now that the reigning clergy, centered around Ayatollah Khamenei has seen the dramatic rejection of their candidate for president and the overwhelming vote of the Iranian people for President Khatami in the last election. Now, President Khatami has very little formal power, especially over the military and the instruments of state power, such as the Iranian Intelligence Service that continues to provide substantial aid to Hezbollah and other terrorist groups.

But, nevertheless, in spite of the rule of those in the clergy who support terror at home and abroad, there are important forces in Iran who want better relations with the West, even with the United States. There is something there to work with. I believe it is a major error to blame Islam or Shia Islam for the state of affairs in Iran today. The limited number of clergy, I believe a minority of the Shia clergy, have designated themselves as rulers under the doctrine of the walayat al-faqih of Ayatollah Khamenei, but I believe there is ample evidence that they do not represent the majority opinion even of the Shia clergy in Iran.

Nonetheless, Iran is a terrorist state. It is a state that rules by force. It is a state that conducts terrorist operations abroad and that is seeking to acquire ballistic missiles and weapons of mass destruction, recently, with rather substantial Russian help.

In my judgment, one of the most important lessons of what is happening in Iran with respect to its weapons programs is that it will, before long, be a threat to our friends and allies in the region and that whatever we decide to do about the ABM [Anti-Ballistic Missile] Treaty, we should not even be discussing limitations on theater systems with the Russians.

Terrorism, finally. The risk that terrorists might use weapons of mass destruction in my view constitutes the number one threat to our national security. Much attention has been focused on fissionable material and small, stolen nuclear weapons, both in government planning and in the media and these are important, and ... steps that the Congress has adopted to approach and deal with this problem are of substantial contribution to national security.

But, the most troubling threat, I believe, is biological weapons. They may be quite small, they may be much more easily constructed, even than a crude nuclear weapon, and the raw material for some of the most fearsome ones such as anthrax is readily available. Indeed, it grows in a number of cow pastures in the world, unlike fissionable material, which requires a great deal of effort to produce.

Biological or chemical weapon terrorism could be undertaken by purely do-mestic sources, such as another [Oklahoma City bomb terrorist] Timothy McVeigh or a group with similar views. It could be undertaken by a group inside the United States that is inspired by individuals from abroad, such as the blind sheikh conspiracy in New York. It could be undertaken pursuant to covert encouragement by a foreign government through an intermediary organization, such as Iran working through Hezbollah. It could be undertaken directly by a foreign intelligence service, possibly as a false flag operation, in which Iranians masquerade as Iraqis or Iraqis masquerade as Iranians, and it could even be undertaken by special military forces of a foreign country, for example, with a diesel submarine covertly launching a land attack cruise missile with a biological warhead, or a freighter launching a SCUD.

Each of these types of terrorism, whether using biological weapons or some other, requires different responses. For example, for purely domestic and many foreign inspired domestic threats, the FBI's ability to penetrate such groups with informants is the main line of defense. For terrorist operations that are planned or launched from abroad, espionage managed by the CIA or acquired by intelligence sharing between the CIA and friendly intelligence services is really the only likely source of advance warning.

In the case of biological weapons, once an attack has been launched, the availability of sensors to detect it promptly and medication that can be administered quickly to large numbers of people could mean the difference someday between, say, hundreds of casualties in such an event and hundreds of thousands of casualties in such an event.

Today, unfortunately, there are a number of terrorist groups, both foreign and domestic who, for ideological or religious reasons, are not seeking a place at the table. They are seeking to blow up the table and to kill everyone sitting there. It is important for us to realize that the nature of some of these groups, Aum Shinrikyu is only one example, and the widespread information about terrorist techniques on the Internet and otherwise, creates a radically new terrorist situation compared to even the recent past. There is no silver bullet that will stop terrorism, but there is a major need for a thorough and coordinated U.S. Government response.

A final thought [is]... about oil. Although I disagree rarely and with trepidation with my old and good friend, Jim Schlesinger,... I would want to say this. Although there are several circumstances that might pose serious threats to the United States and I have mentioned some, confusion in the command and control system of Russia, a confrontation with China over Taiwan, a war on the Korean peninsula, a domestic terrorist threat, a number of the near and long-term threats to the United States seem to be centered in the Mideast and the importance of the Mideast is driven by two facts.

First, if you add the Caspian Basin to the Persian Gulf, it sits on approximately three-quarters of the world's known oil reserves. Second, the states that control almost all of this oil are either governed today by psychopathic predators or by vulnerable autocrats. Moreover, for historical reasons going back to the period after World War I and earlier, there is a great deal of resentment against the West, including now, particularly against us and Israel and the whole region is a potpourri of religious extremism, economic stagnation and large populations of unemployed youths. Some wealthy individuals such as Usima ben Laden are freelance sponsors of terrorism and work on weapons of mass destruction with millions and millions of dollars at their disposal.

Finally, Asia is quite likely, even with its current economic difficulties, as it grows and urbanizes, to increase substantially the world's demand for oil in the next century. A projection two years ago in *Fortune Magazine* calculated that once China and India reach what is today South Korea's level of energy consumption per capita, which would be several decades, because South Korea is still a very prosperous country, nonetheless, at that point, those two countries alone would require almost 120 million barrels of oil daily, given their current consumption patterns. The whole world today uses just over 70 million barrels a day.

These huge types of jumps in oil consumption probably are not going to occur because something will intervene by way of alternatives and the like, but the point is, the pressure will be there and we will at least see an increase and probably a substantial increase in the tens to hundreds of billions of dollars that now flow to the Mideast to hundreds of billions to trillions through the first half of the next century. These funds, because of the nature of that region, are going to support governmental and private activity that, in many cases, are not in the United States' interest, to put it mildly.

So, not as a matter of promoting autocracy in the United States... at all, but as a matter of world stability, I can think of no single, more important long term strategic issue than finding some way to reduce the world's dependence on Mideast oil.

NO

Carl Conetta and Charles Knight

INVENTING THREATS

It was a remarkable admission for a chairman of the Joint Chiefs: "I'm running out of demons. I'm down to [North Korea's leader] Kim Il Sung and [Cuba's leader Fidel] Castro."

The context for Gen. Colin Powell's 1991 remarks to Congress was the dissolution of the Warsaw Pact and America's recent victory in the Gulf War. When the Soviet Union collapsed soon after, an article in *Aerospace Daily*, a leading defense industry newsletter, recalled Powell's remarks and predicted: "Pentagon Budget Headed for $150 Billion—Half Current Level—By 1996."

But what a difference a few years can make. When he unveiled the "Quadrennial Defense Review" [in] May [1997], Defense Secretary William Cohen warned that "new threats and dangers, harder to define and more difficult to track, have gathered on the horizon." Contrary to *Aerospace Daily's* forecast, Secretary Cohen sees keeping the Pentagon budget at $250 billion or slightly more—about 77 percent of the 1991 level.

BREAKING WITH REALITY

The quadrennial review seeks to lead the United States into the next century with a defense budget only 23 percent lower than the average for the Cold War period of 1976–90. Despite Secretary Cohen's warning, however, there is no profusion of actual threats to justify this course. The preservation of high levels of spending instead reflects a novel way of thinking and talking about military requirements.

Beginning with efforts at the Rand Corporation during the late 1980s, the focus of defense planners has shifted from "the clear and present danger" of Soviet power to the intractable problem of "uncertainty." Along with this shift has come a new type of Pentagon partisan—the "uncertainty hawk."

From Carl Conetta and Charles Knight, "Inventing Threats," *The Bulletin of the Atomic Scientists* (March/April 1998). Copyright © 1998 by The Educational Foundation for Nuclear Science, 6042 South Kimbark, Chicago, Illinois 60637, USA. Reprinted by permission of *The Bulletin of the Atomic Scientists*. References omitted.

The uncertainty hawks forsake "threat-based" planning for new methods variously called "adaptive," "capability-based," or "scenario-based" planning. These methods seek to release planning from the "tyranny of scenario plausibility," as Rand analyst James Winnefeld puts it. Any hypothetical danger that seems remotely "possible" is deemed worthy of attention. In this approach, the concrete assessment of interests, adversaries, and trends matters less than does the unfettered exercise of "worst case" thinking.

A fixation on uncertainty colors all of the major post—Cold War policy blueprints—the quadrennial review, the 1993 "Bottom Up Review," and even the independent National Defense Panel report, "Transforming Defense," which was issued in December. Lost in these documents, however, is any real appreciation of America's profound post-Cold War security windfall.

PUZZLING EVIDENCE

No nation even approximates America's current combination of size, stability, economic vitality, military prowess, and geographic insulation. The strength of America's allies further reinforces its substantial security margin.

The [industrialized] countries of the Organization for Economic Cooperation and Development—the "West"—now account for three-quarters of the world's economic activity. And these states, along with other long-time American allies, account for 72 percent of world military spending. In contrast, current and potential adversary states—including Russia and China—account for 18 percent.

Another measure: Despite its absolute reduction in military spending, the U.S.

share of worldwide military spending increased from 27.5 to 32 percent between 1986 and 1995. In 1986, the United States spent only two-thirds as much on defense as did "potential threat states" (the Warsaw Pact states, China, Cuba, Iran, Iraq, North Korea, Libya, Syria, and Vietnam). In 1995, it spent 76 percent more than the group.

Western dominance is also reflected in the arms trade. The U.S. share of the arms export market grew from 22 to 49 percent from 1986 to 1995. Meanwhile, the aggregate share of all NATO countries grew from 44 to 78 percent. This change occurred in the context of a 55 percent contraction in the market. Thus, not only has the general diffusion of military power slowed dramatically, it has come substantially under the control of the United States and its allies.

But recent official Defense Department analyses miss both the forest and the trees. With the collapse of Soviet power and the return of U.S. defense spending to pre-Reagan levels, threat assessment has taken a great leap backward. The 1993 Bottom Up Review set the post-Cold War standard, promoting the image of regional "rogues" wielding huge arsenals of armored vehicles and combat aircraft.

But all tanks are not equal, as the Gulf War demonstrated. Quality makes a difference. Consider North Korea, which is invariably held up as a potential foe. A simple "bean count" of the North Korean arsenal adds up to almost 4,000 tanks and more than 700 combat aircraft.

However, a 1995 study by the Brookings Institution, which used a Pentagon methodology that takes quality into account, cut the challenge down to size. It showed the North Korean military as possessing the equivalent of less than 4.5 U.S. heavy divisions and 2.5 fighter wings

—about 1,500 tanks and 250 fighters. And even this calculation overlooked America's war-winning advantages in troop quality; logistics; and communications, intelligence, and information systems.

TWILIGHT OF THE ROGUES

Rather than redress the shortcomings of the Bottom Up Review, last year's quadrennial review compounds them. Notably, it fails to revise the estimated strengths of regional foes, despite their having suffered four years of decline.

In contrast, the National Defense University's "Strategic Assessment 1997," which is not an official document, observes that the Korean situation was "significantly different at the end of 1996 than it was in 1993." Surveying the poor state of the armed forces and economies of both North Korea and Iraq, the assessment concludes that the United States most likely will face "declining military challenges in both areas, especially in Korea."

Turning to Iran, the other *bête noire* of U.S. planners, the assessment similarly finds that Iran's conventional forces "on the whole are not improving" and their "ability to conquer ground is deteriorating." The Iranian military, the assessment suggests, has not recovered from the Iran-Iraq war, nor has the Iranian economy recovered from the 1979 revolution. Economic stagnation and sanctions together have held Iran's planned $10 billion military modernization program to less than 40 percent of its goals.

The concurrent decline of North Korean, Iraqi, and Iranian power is not merely fortuitous. Stripped of superpower patronage, these nations stand exposed to global trends that disfavor rigid and narrow economies. The military assessment—about 1,500 tanks and 250 fighters. And cent of these states, and others like them, was dependent on a circumstance that no longer exists—the East-West Cold War.

THE MASQUE OF UNCERTAINTY

Against the evidence—of a diminished and diminishing threat—uncertainty hawks describe the strategic environment as turbulent, allowing for few, if any, reliable forecasts.

"The real world defies prediction," says Rand's Winnefeld.

"The new strategic landscape is not rigid and linear, but highly fluid and unpredictable," says David Abshire, president of the Center of Strategic and International Studies.

These visions of uncertainty and instability lie at the core of both the quadrennial review and Transforming Defense. Similarly, "Joint Vision 2010" frames its force development program with the observation that "accelerating rates of change will make the future environment more unpredictable and less stable."

The agnosticism of the uncertainty hawks extends not only to the specifics of discrete future events, such as the presidential succession in Russia or the role of the mullahs in Iran, but also to the general character and magnitude of possible threats. Uncertainty envelops events and trends equally. Even with regard to its future national interests, goes the prevailing mantra, the United States is groping in twilight, if not in the dark.

"Uncertainty is a dominating characteristic of the landscape," wrote Paul Davis, editor of a 1994 compendium of Rand Corporation planning studies, "New Challenges for Defense Planning." "Most striking is the fact that we do not even know who or what will constitute the most serious future threat."

The new planning methods supposedly tame uncertainty by varying assumptions about America's future national interests, the identity and number of possible threats, the character and magnitude of these threats, how fast they could develop, and how quickly the United States could respond. The result is a vast array of hypothetical scenarios that serve to define requirements.

Winnefeld argues that in addition to breaking free from plausibility, planners must consider "discontinuous scenarios … in which there is no plausible audit trail or storyline from current events."

Among the "non-standard" scenarios that Rand analysts favor are defending the Ukraine or the Baltics against Russia, civil wars in Russia and Algeria, a variety of wars with China, contention with Germany, and wars aligning Iraq and Syria against Turkey, and Iraq and Iran against Saudi Arabia.

Along these lines, the quadrennial review uses unnamed "wild card" scenarios to help define requirements. Although it describes the scenarios as individually improbable, the review asserts that, given the whole set, there is a better than even chance that one or more will occur.

Of course, to prepare for "one or more" wild cards, the United States would have to hedge against the whole pack. One of the Pentagon's wild cards may be a scenario involving war in 2015 with China and North Korea—the Navy recently used that scenario to test the cost-effectiveness of its planned replacement for today's cruisers and destroyers.

PLAYING WITH WILD CARDS

Simulations—including nonstandard ones—can aid planning. But to what end? And to what effect? Exploring "wild cards" to identify warning signs or to define limits is one thing. Using them to establish force structure or modernization requirements is quite another.

Conflict scenarios, both wild and tame, can gain more credibility in the telling than they deserve. Cognitive researcher Massimo Piattelli-Palmarini calls this the "Othello Effect," referring to the trail of plausible but false suppositions that led Othello to murder his wife, Desdemona.

We have seen the Othello Effect writ large in the development of the two-war concept, the principal driver of U.S. defense policy since the end of the Cold War. The "need" to retain the ability to fight and quickly win two near-simultaneous major regional wars has kept defense spending high, and will continue to do so in the future.

Although both the 1993 and 1997 defense reviews link the two-war requirement to Korean and Persian Gulf scenarios, these were also described as merely illustrative. Officially, the two-war requirement is generic. As the quadrennial review puts it: "We can never know with certainty when or where the next major theater war will occur," or "who our next adversary will be."

The issue, however, is not the ability of the United States to predict events, but its willingness to clarify and weigh interests —at least when it comes to sending hundreds of thousands of Americans to war.

Outside Europe, only the Korean peninsula and the Persian Gulf qualify as areas in which perceived U.S. interests, vulnerable allies, and significant threats might converge to compel *very large-scale* U.S. intervention. Recognizing this helps to contain both uncertainty and military requirements. Similarly, stricter attention to risk factors would put into perspective the supposed need for a capability to fight two wars *simultaneously*.

Since 1945 the United States has fought three major regional conflicts—one every 15 or 20 years. Whether the future holds more major wars or fewer, two-war contingencies will occur much less often than single-war contingencies—even if war in one region boosts the chances of an attack elsewhere.

A "second war capability" might cost America two-thirds as much as the first —perhaps $50 billion a year. But it would serve its full purpose only a fraction as often. Is it worth spending $3 trillion dollars over 60 years to meet a double war contingency that might occur only once, if at all?

Of course it would be worth spending that kind of money—if delaying a full response to the second war would entail a catastrophic loss for the nation, But what possible regional war scenario could fit that description? Where are the adversaries and interests of sufficient magnitude to justify the expense?

The quadrennial review holds tenaciously to the two-war strategy as originally conceived, but cracks are appearing elsewhere. The December 1997 National Defense Panel report, for instance, calls the entire concept into question. Noting that "the current posture minimizes near-term risk at a time when danger is [already] moderate to low," the panel suggests that the two-war construct "may have become a force-protection mechanism—a means of justifying the current force structure."

However, the panel does not hold out any hope of budget reductions. Instead, it seeks to redirect more resources toward preparing for the putative security challenges of the post-2010 world. These are gathered under the headings of "Asymmetric Warfare," "Military-Technical Revolution," and a "Re-emergent Peer Competitor."

ASYMMETRIC WARFARE

Both 1997 defense reviews and joint Vision 2010 suggest that the West's foes may turn to unconventional methods and weapons to sap or circumvent Western strengths. The quadrennial review, for instance, speaks of "increasingly sophisticated asymmetric challenges involving the use of chemical, biological, and possibly nuclear weapons; attacks against the information systems of our forces and national infrastructure" as well as insurgency, terrorism, and environmental destruction. Joint Vision 2010 asserts that "our most vexing future adversary may be one who can use rapid improvements in its military capabilities that provide asymmetrical counters to U.S. strengths, including information technologies."

The Vietnam War amply illustrated the potential of asymmetric warfare—and its limits as well. Although masters of unconventional war, the North Vietnamese and their Viet Cong allies were dependent for success on the shield and support of a superpower—the Soviet Union—as well as neighboring China. Outside similar circumstances, the potential of asymmetric methods is limited.

In the post-Soviet era, few if any "non-peer" nations would plan or attempt a major military confrontation with the United States, although they might blunder into it, as Iraq did in 1990. Still, none can afford to set aside the funds needed to indulge dare-the-superpower fantasies, even by asymmetric means. Primarily, what will shape the armed forces of regional powers and developing nations in the coming decades will be local challenges such as old-fashioned cross-border threats and internal insurgencies.

The real core of the asymmetric warfare threat involves the spread of cheap ballistic missiles and weapons of mass destruction. This poses a real, but well-defined potential threat—mostly to U.S. regional operations. Compared to former Soviet capabilities, the threat is quite limited. And all of the recent defense reviews implicitly acknowledge this by recommending that only a small part of U.S. military forces and investment be devoted specifically to meeting this challenge.

To find a more sophisticated and comprehensive threat, scenario writers must work backwards from perceived Western vulnerabilities. "What would it take to defeat the United States?" is the question that animates their visions of asymmetric warfare. But the fact that we can spot theoretical "windows of vulnerability" does not mean that real-world foes could climb through them.

TECHNOLOGY DIFFUSION

When uncertainty hawks turn to assess the danger of technology diffusion, the actual capabilities and efforts of potential foes matter less than formal access to the military marketplace. The National Defense Panel, for instance, sees the future as providing "all nations with more or less equal access to defense-related technologies."

Similarly, Joint Vision 2010 leaves no doubt about where this leads: "Wider ac-cess to advanced technology along with modern weaponry ... and the requisite skills to maintain and employ it will increase the number of actors with sufficient military potential to upset existing regional balances of power."

What is lacking in these analyses is any general evidence of a rising curve of technological competence among our likely adversaries. Russell Travers, an analyst with the Defense Intelligence Agency, surveyed the modernization efforts of U.S. allies and adversaries alike in a Spring 1997 Washington Quarterly article, concluding that the idea that America is in danger of losing its technological superiority "does not hold up." Similarly, in a 1994 Foreign Affairs article, Ethan Kapstein of Harvard University's Olin Institute wrote that "by the early twenty-first century, the United States will be the sole producer of the world's most advanced weaponry." This is because "rising costs and declining defense budgets are putting pressure on the world's inefficient defense producers, and most of them are collapsing under the strain."

The plain fact is that all but a handful of nations lack the capacity to build, buy, integrate, support, and effectively use cutting-edge military systems in significant quantities. Nonetheless, the use of formal "market access" models to gauge the diffusion problem treats anyone's technology as though it were everyone's. Thus, every advance in American capabilities motivates the next. This suggests a continuous, solitary arms race in which the United States labors to outdistance its own shadow. In the end, technical feasibility alone defines requirements.

As with asymmetric warfare, the real core of the diffusion threat is the potential proliferation of medium-range missiles and weapons of mass destruction. The prospect of any more intensive technological competition than this hinges on the emergence of a major new rival to the United States.

THE THREAT WITH NO NAME

The quadrennial review sees the rise of a peer competitor as improbable before 2015. However, like the Bottom Up Review before it, it hedges against an earlier-than-expected arrival. To help decide near-term policy, it relies on simulations of war in 2014 with what might be called a "half-way peer"—a regional great power with armed forces significantly larger and more capable than those of Iraq, Iran, or North Korea.

The plausibility of this scenario depends on its details, which the review typically neglects to provide. Who is this threat? Why are we fighting it? What capabilities have planners given it? Even setting these questions aside, fighting simulated contests 17 years in advance begs the issue of how best to prepare for challenges that do not exist today and may not exist tomorrow.

The regional great powers and peer competitors that currently enthrall planners are only hypothetical constructs. Separating hypothesis from reality would be a process of emergence. Superpowers do not take shape easily or quickly. Their advent takes time and involves an extraordinary convergence of circumstances and trends—political, economic, geographical, and military. Tracking these provides a way to gauge the real danger of peer emergence.

Meeting the challenge of a peer rival, should one begin to gestate, would involve a race between its emergence and the ability of the United States to reconstitute sufficient additional military power. Given its incomparable military-industrial base, the United States would enjoy a unique advantage in any such competition. Today's huge gap between the United States and any potential rival defines America's strategic reaction time —its margin of safety.

But not for uncertainty hawks. They argue that the historical example of Nazi Germany's rapid ascent makes a reconstitution strategy untenable. But today's armed forces take much longer to develop than those of the 1930s. Combat vehicle and aircraft development, for instance, takes three to five times as long.

And even in the 1930s, for that matter, major threats did not spring up full grown. By 1928 Germany's manufacturing output was already 50 percent of the combined total of France, Great Britain, and Russia. Its per capita output was much higher. By 1935 Germany was leading the world in military spending.

The prime candidates for future peer rival status are Russia and China. A dozen years of dedicated investment might resuscitate a significant portion of the Russian armed forces. But the emphasis is on the "might." Russia's military is in ruins. And, Russia would have to rehabilitate its economy and governing structures before it could begin to rebuild its military strength.

The Chinese "threat" is even more iffy. If China's economy holds out, it might in 30 years be able to mount a Soviet-style challenge. Meanwhile, China is just beginning to inject 1980s technology into select portions of its armed forces. The National Defense University's "Strategic Assessment 1997" surmises that China's military in 1996 was "probably two decades away from challenging or holding its own against a modern military force." Paul Goodwin of the National War College puts "the window for China becoming one of the world's major military powers... at somewhere between 2020 and 2050."

Surveying the prospects worldwide, Russell Travers, the Defense Intelligence Agency analyst, concludes that "no military or technical peer competitor to the United States is on the horizon for at least a couple of decades."

CERTAIN FORCE

Uncertainty has breathed new life into declining and hypothetical threats. And current policy prescribes that the U.S. military do more than simply respond or prepare to respond to these threats. The quadrennial review proposes an expanded peacetime role for the Pentagon in shaping the strategic environment. "Environment shaping" is meant to encompass all the diffuse ways, apart from crisis response, that the U.S. military might protect and promote U.S. interests. Key to environment shaping are overseas presence, military assistance programs, and military-to-military contacts.

An important environment-shaping goal for the Pentagon is to discourage military competition with America and stem the emergence of hostile regional hegemons. As the quadrennial review sees it, the United States can stop difficult relationships from evolving into military contests by projecting a sense of overwhelming and unbeatable American power. And it can stem arms races by winning them in advance.

Of course, this assumes that countries will not view such preemptory moves as reason enough to gear up their own military efforts. Strategic Assessment 1997 warns that this type of toughest-kid-on-the-block dissuasion is a "two-edged sword" because it may "lead others to believe that their interests are at risk, in which case they may decide they have no choice other than the use of force."

Current U.S. defense policy embraces a uniquely high standard for defense sufficiency: the maintenance of U.S. military superiority over all current and potential rivals. As Defense Secretary Cohen states, with remarkable hyperbole: "Without such superiority, our ability to exert global leadership and to create international conditions conducive to the achievement of our national goals would be in doubt."

TUNNEL VISION

There is no escape from uncertainty, but there is relief from uncertainty hysteria. It begins with recognizing that instability has boundaries—just as turbulence in physical systems has discernible onset points and parameters. The turbulence of a river, for instance, corresponds to flow and to the contours of the river's bed and banks. It occurs in patches and not randomly.

Despite uncertainty, statements of probability matter. They indicate the weight of the evidence—or whether there is any evidence at all. Uncertainty hawks would flood our concern with a horde of dangers that pass their permissive test of "non-zero probability."

In so doing they establish an impossible standard of defense sufficiency: absolute and certain military security. Given finite resources and competing ends, something less will have to do. Strategic wisdom begins with the setting of priorities—and priorities demand strict attention to what appears likely and what does not.

The world may be less certain and less stable today than during the Cold War, but it also involves less risk for America. Risk is composed of equal parts probability and utility—chances and stakes.

With the end of global superpower contention, America's stake in most of the world's varied conflicts has diminished. So has the magnitude of the military threats to American interests. This permits a sharper distinction between interests and compelling interests; turbulence and relevant turbulence; uncertainties and critical uncertainties. And these distinctions will pay dividends whenever the country turns to consider large-scale military endeavors, commitments, and investments.

U.S. defense policy documents speak of military threats, however uncertain. But they fail to deal with the opportunity cost of continuing high defense expenditures. In a world in which economic issues have displaced military issues as the central focus of global competition, the failure to take a hard look at opportunity costs is critical.

A recent Rand Corporation paper argued against reduced defense spending on the basis that "the U.S. defense burden is now quite low by historical standards."

Defense Secretary Cohen likewise accentuates the post-Cold War decline in the proportion of gross national product that America devotes to defense.

But it is a peculiar parochialism that compares today's defense investment rate with that of the Reagan era while ignoring comparisons between the United States and its economic competitors. The United States continues to invest far more of its national product in defense than its allies, far more than the world average, and far more than its chief economic competitors. U.S. defense policy is oblivious to the strategic opportunity costs of high levels of military spending. And it is this lapse that gives license to the speculative methods and overweening goals of the uncertainty hawks.

In disregarding the requirements and consequences of increased global economic competition, present policy makes an unacknowledged bet about the future. The Soviet Union is gone and no comparable military challenge to the West exists, except as a distant possibility. Nonetheless, say the hawks, the American prospect depends as much as ever—if not more so—on the specifically military aspects of strength. Of this, the uncertainty hawks are certain.

POSTSCRIPT

Do Serious Threats to U.S. Security Exist?

Defense planning is one of the toughest of all policy-making areas because (to paraphrase President John Kennedy) if you make a mistake in domestic policy, it can hurt you; if you make an error in defense policy, it can kill you. For a general discussion of the relationship between military development and capability and world politics, see Barry Buzan and Eric Herring, *The Arms Dynamic in World Politics* (Lynne Rienner, 1998).

One task that makes defense planning difficult is determining a threat estimate—not only for now but for the future as well—and devising a strategy to counter them. Are there dangers? What are they? How many soldiers and how many weapons and what types are needed to provide for the common defense? Yes, the cold war is over. And, yes, Russia represents little threat for now. Yet it is also the case that a new, peaceful world order has not arrived. Perils persist and may proliferate in the future. The level and reality of these threats is what has been debated in the selections by Woolsey and by Conetta and Knight. To better understand U.S. defense policy, consult Wyn Bowen and David Dunn, eds., *American Security Policy in the 1990s* (Ashgate, 1996).

Some analysts contend that Americans should not let down their guard because doing so will necessitate crash spending when the next crisis breaks out. This view is found in Daniel Goure and Jeffrey Ranney, *Averting the Defense Train Wreck in the New Millennium* (CSIS Press, 1999). For the moment, the thinking in the White House has shifted in this direction, away from cutting defense spending further and toward limited increases. For FY 2000 President Bill Clinton had proposed an increase to $261 billion and another $13 billion in national security spending for programs outside the Department of Defense (DoD), such as nuclear warhead development, which is in the Department of Energy. Defense spending will be 15 percent of the federal budget. The administration projects that defense spending will rise to $200 billion plus another $14 billion non-DoD funding by 2004.

Many people will not agree with this policy. The facts are that the United States' defense budget constitutes about one-third of all the money spent on defense by all the countries of the world. Indeed, the 1997 U.S. defense budget was about equal to the combined defense budgets of the next six largest defense budgets (in descending amounts, Russia, Japan, France, Germany, Great Britain, and China). Critics will ask why this is the case, in an era where some planes (the B-2 bomber) cost $2 billion each and when U.S. military might far outstrips any single opponent.

ISSUE 2

Will Creating a Palestinian State Promote Peace in the Middle East?

YES: Herbert C. Kelman, from "Building a Sustainable Peace: The Limits of Pragmatism in the Israeli-Palestinian Negotiations," *Journal of Palestine Studies* (Autumn 1998)

NO: Douglas J. Feith, from "Wye and the Road to War," *Commentary* (January 1999)

ISSUE SUMMARY

YES: Herbert C. Kelman, director of the Program on International Conflict Analysis and Resolution at Harvard University, contends that to move the Middle East peace process forward, Israel and the Palestinians have to commit themselves to a solution that includes the creation of a Palestinian state.

NO: Douglas J. Feith, who served as deputy assistant secretary of defense and as a Middle East specialist on the National Security Council during the Reagan administration, argues that the Palestinian leadership remains hostile to Israel and that a Palestinian state would endanger Israel's security.

The history of Israel/Palestine dates to biblical times when there were both Hebrew and Arab (Canaanite) kingdoms in the area. In later centuries, the area was conquered by many others; from 640 to 1917 it was almost continually controlled by Muslim rulers. In 1917 the British captured the area, Palestine, from Turkey.

Concurrently, a Zionist movement for a Jewish homeland arose. In 1917 the (British foreign secretary Arthur) Balfour Declaration promised increased Jewish immigration to Palestine. The Jewish population in the region began to increase slowly, then it expanded dramatically because of refugees from the Holocaust. Soon after World War II, the Jewish population in Palestine stood at 650,000; the Arab population was 1,350,000. Zionists increasingly agitated for an independent Jewish state. Conflict increased, and London turned to the UN for a solution. The UN plan to divide the area into Jewish and Palestinian Arab homelands never went into effect. Instead, when the British withdrew in 1947, war immediately broke out between Jewish forces and the region's Arabs. The Jews won, establishing Israel in 1948 and doubling their territory. Most Palestinian Arabs fled (or were driven) from Israel to refugee camps in Gaza and the West Bank (of the Jordan River), two areas that had been part of Palestine but were captured in the war by Egypt and Jordan, respectively. As a result of the 1967 Six Day War between Israel and Egypt, Jordan, and Syria, the Israelis again expanded their territory by capturing several areas, including the Sinai Peninsula, Gaza, the Golan Heights, and the West Bank. Also in this period the Palestine Liberation Organization (PLO) became the major representative of Palestinian Arabs. True peace was not possible because the PLO and the Arab states would not recognize Israel's legitimacy and because Israel refused to give up some of the captured territory. Since then, however, continuing violence has persuaded many war-exhausted Arabs and Israelis that there has to be mutual compromise to achieve peace.

The 1990s were a decade of fitful progress toward, then seeming retreat from, the goal of peace. Israelis and Palestinians met in Spain and held public talks for the first time in 1991. Israeli elections brought Rabin's Labor Party to power in 1992, and it was willing to compromise with the Arabs to a greater extent than its more conservative predecessor had been. Bilateral secret peace talks between the Israelis and Palestinians in Norway led to an agreement in 1993. Among the Oslo agreement's terms are provisions to increase over time both the level of Palestinian autonomy in Gaza and the West Bank and the amount of territory under Palestinian control. Palestinians gained limited control over Gaza and parts of the West Bank and established a quasi government, the Palestinian Authority.

Soon thereafter, in 1996, the conservative Likud Party headed by Prime Minister Benjamin Netanyahu came to power. Netanyahu dismissed any possibility of an independent Palestine, said he would make tougher demands on the PLO, and pledged to expand Jewish settlements in the West Bank. He also argued that the Palestinians were not truly willing to accept the existence of Israel or to stem terrorist attacks on the country. This compounded the difficult issue of the fate of the some 200,000 Jews who were already in the West Bank and East Jerusalem, a potentially Palestinian-controlled area. Netanyahu further declared Jerusalem to be "the eternal capital of the Jewish people" and vowed never to return any part of the city to Arab control. This is also an explosive issue because of the emotional centrality of Jerusalem to all sides.

Pressure from a number of quarters, including the United States, has kept the Israelis and Palestinians talking. Meeting in 1997 at the Wye River Plantation in Maryland under the watchful eye of President Bill Clinton, Israel agreed to give the Palestinians control over about 40 percent of the West Bank. For their part, the Palestinians agreed to a security plan to protect Israel from Arab terrorist attacks and to remove language in the PLO charter that called for the destruction of the Jewish state. The immediate impact of the Wye River Agreement was negligible; each side accused the other of not living up to its end of the bargain. It is at that juncture that the following selections were written. In them, Herbert C. Kelman argues that a true Palestinian state (and true Palestinian acceptance of Israel) offers the path to peace. Douglas J. Feith holds that, given the attitudes of the Palestinian Authority, an independent Palestinian state will lead to war.

YES

Herbert C. Kelman

BUILDING A SUSTAINABLE PEACE

The prospects for Israeli-Palestinian peace are probably dimmer now than they have been at any time since the beginning of negotiations at the Madrid Conference in 1991. The Oslo agreement represented a major breakthrough in the conflict, which was made possible by the consummate pragmatism of the leaders on both sides; indeed, Oslo could stand as a virtual monument to pragmatism. Both Israeli prime minister Yitzhak Rabin and PLO [Palestine Liberation Organization] Chairman Yasir Arafat were persuaded of the political necessity of an early peace agreement and recognized that they needed each other to reach that agreement. They were not deterred by ideological dogma from making the necessary compromises as long as their fundamental interests—Israeli security and ultimate Palestinian statehood, respectively—were safeguarded. Out of these pragmatic commitments, Rabin and Arafat were able to develop a partnership that, in due course, probably would have achieved a mutually satisfactory agreement.

With the current Israeli government, that partnership has broken down. Prime Minister Benjamin Netanyahu and his coalition are not prepared to make the compromises required for achieving an agreement. Under the circumstances, it is highly unlikely that the strictly pragmatic, step-by-step process of exchanging concessions and confidence-building measures in the hope that this will eventually lead to some kind of agreement can succeed. Without the understanding that the two sides have to work together to shape a mutually acceptable agreement addressing the central concerns of both parties, the step-by-step approach will either collapse without an agreement or, if there is sufficient outside pressure, produce an agreement that is not workable and not conducive to a sustainable peace.

To save the peace process today, it is necessary to go beyond a pragmatic peace to a principled peace, opening the way to resolution of the conflict and to reconciliation. I am arguing, paradoxically, that at this low point in the peace process it is necessary to aim higher than the Oslo Accord—that, at this stage, there can be no peace without reconciliation. I am not speaking of reconciliation as a precondition for negotiation or as an instant outcome, but rather as a process. There is no way to sidestep the essential political give-and-take of negotiating an agreement, but the process and outcome of negotiations must be consistent with the requirements for ultimate reconciliation. Stated succinctly, this means that the negotiations must be anchored in the mutual acceptance of the other's nationhood and humanity.

THE OSLO ACCORD

To understand the significance of the Oslo Accord, it helps to note that there were in effect two processes going on at Oslo simultaneously and that the agreement reflects the effect of both: a process of distributive bargaining between two parties with unequal power and an initial, rudimentary stage of a process of reconciliation. At the risk of oversimplification, one might describe the Declaration of Principles (DOP) as primarily a product of distributive bargaining and the letters of mutual recognition exchanged between Arafat and Rabin as a product of a rudimentary process of reconciliation.

The DOP reflected—both in what it included and in what it omitted—the power differential between the parties. To be sure, some of the DOP's features created a clear opening for a Palestinian state, which indeed made it possible for the PLO to sign the agreement: It established a territorial base for the Palestinian Authority (PA) in Gaza and the West Bank and provided for the early empowerment of the PA. But it did not *guarantee* an independent Palestinian state; it did not explicitly prohibit the expansion of settlements (although it did rule out changes on the ground that would preempt the final status negotiations); it did not address the question of refugees except to defer

it to the final status negotiations. The items that did make it into the DOP —the terms of agreement—reflect the difference in power by favoring the stronger party. Moreover, the ambiguities that were purposely left in the DOP in order to make an agreement possible also work in favor of the stronger party, which is better positioned to resolve them in its own favor. It was this advantage, resulting from power-based, distributive bargaining, that led some Palestinian critics of Oslo to describe it as a Palestinian surrender and defeat. Interestingly, in characteristic mirror-image fashion, some Israeli and Jewish writers have criticized Oslo as a surrender by Israel. Thus, one writer described Oslo as "Zionist surrender that was driven by the palpable yearning of Israelis for normal life in a very dangerous neighborhood."

What these critics miss is that there was a second process going on alongside the distributive bargaining process, captured best by the letters of recognition. Although those letters also reflect the power differential in that Rabin's response to Arafat was much briefer and less specific in its commitment, the essence of this exchange of letters (and, by implication, of the DOP itself) is an act of mutual recognition. It is this exchange, more than the DOP, that states the underlying principle of the Oslo agreement. It provides the basis for a just solution—at least in the sense of pragmatic justice—that goes beyond the balance of power.

The breakthrough character of the Oslo agreement, from the Palestinian perspective, was Israel's recognition of the PLO as its negotiating partner. Because the PLO has, since the late 1960s, stood for the concept of an independent Palestinian state, recognition of the PLO clearly conferred legitimacy on that concept. It was tantamount to recognition of Palestinian peoplehood with the implication that, at the end of the day, a Palestinian state would be established. From the Israeli perspective, the breakthrough character of the Oslo agreement was Palestinian recognition of Israel's legitimacy, thus opening the door to recognition in the Arab world. Indeed, the Oslo Accord led, in short order, to an agreement between Israel and Jordan, to diplomatic relations between Israel and several Arab states, and to Israel's increasing economic integration in the region—gains that are now at risk because of the policies of the current government. In short, the mutual recognition of the Oslo agreement "represented a fundamental shift in the relationship between the two peoples. Acknowledging each other's legitimacy was a significant affirmation of the other's national existence, which the two sides had systematically denied to each other throughout the history of their conflict. . . . This conceptual breakthrough . . . is irreversible, even if the current peace process were to collapse."

The logic of the Oslo Accord was to move toward a final political outcome through a series of interim stages. There was no commitment on Israel's part that the final outcome would take the form of an independent Palestinian state, but the recognition of the PLO and some of the terms of the DOP clearly pointed in that direction. This was well understood by Palestinians, by Israelis, and by the rest of the world. In this sense, the Oslo agreement represented a move toward a principled solution of the conflict—toward a historic compromise, opening the way to reconciliation.

A POLITICAL PARTNERSHIP

In signing the Oslo agreement, with its far-reaching implications and limited commitments, both Rabin and Arafat took significant risks. Rabin took the risk that even if the experience of the interim period did not reassure Israel that a Palestinian state would be consistent with its own security requirements, the logic of the process might inexorably lead to a state anyway. He felt able to take that risk because the agreement contained no explicit commitment to a Palestinian state; thus the option of saying "no" in the end, though politically costly, remained available. Arafat took an even greater risk by signing an agreement that unambiguously recognized Israel—giving away what he used to call his last card—without an explicit promise of an independent state. He took the risk because his options were severely limited and because he had reason to believe that the process he was entering offered a high probability of a Palestinian state at the end of the day. Ultimately, the two leaders took these risks because their assessment of the political realities in relation to their interests led them to conclude that the time had come for a historic compromise based on mutual recognition.

Because both men also recognized that they needed each other to succeed in the peacemaking process, they entered into a political partnership despite serious reservations and initial distrust of each other. The evolving partnership between Rabin and Arafat, and the subsequent partnership between Peres and Arafat, were clearly limited. Each side tried to gain advantages for the interim negotiations and for the final status negotiations that lay ahead. Neither side observed the letter and the spirit of the Oslo agreement in all respects. The continuing settlement process during the Rabin and Peres era represented the most serious violation of the spirit of the agreement. Rabin, while often disdainful of the settlers, was clearly worried about the political costs of blocking settlement expansion; he missed an opportunity to dislodge the Hebron settlers after the Hebron massacre, when there was support for such a move in his cabinet. The PA, on its part, did not always adhere to the precise terms of the agreement with respect to such issues as establishment of PA offices in Jerusalem or the size of the security forces.

Despite its flaws, the partnership took hold in a way that partly transcended the balance of power. Each side was cognizant of the concerns and constraints of the other and refrained from creating situations that would be embarrassing or politically sensitive for the other side. They consciously tried to be responsive to each other and to avoid actions that might undermine their counterparts' political standing in their own community. They closed their eyes to occasional violations, with a degree of understanding of the political necessities that prompted them. Thus, the partnership developed during those years into a relationship characterized by significant elements of working trust and responsiveness at the leadership level.

One of the regrettable consequences of Rabin's and Arafat's consummate pragmatism is that they did not draw their publics into this evolving partnership. They preferred to see and present themselves as pragmatists yielding to necessity rather than as visionaries preparing for a process of long-term reconciliation. It seems that they did not trust their publics sufficiently to be able to share with them what I believe was their own readiness for a historic compromise. As a result, they did not educate their publics with respect to both the realities and the underlying principles that led them to Oslo and the subsequent partnership.

Rabin and Peres did not tell the Israeli public that the peace process was expected, ultimately, to lead to a Palestinian state. The evidence from public opinion data and informal observations suggests that the Israeli public would not have been surprised to hear that. It was generally understood, by both supporters and opponents of Oslo, that this was what the agreement meant. Instead of downplaying that fact, public education could have stressed that the successful unfolding of the process would probably lead to a Palestinian state and that such an outcome would be both just and in Israel's long-term interest. Such a message would have confirmed the Israeli public's expectations about the likely outcome and, at the same time, increased the perceived legitimacy of this outcome and the public's commitment to it as a goal that was necessary and right from the Israeli point of view.

Similarly, Arafat did not tell the Palestinian public that the Oslo agreement, although clearly pointing in the direction of a Palestinian state, did not guarantee this outcome. Nor did he explain to his public why he concluded that this was the best agreement he could achieve at this time, why he had strong reason to expect that it would ultimately lead to an independent state, and why the current process and its anticipated outcome were necessary and right, given the realities and the ultimate hopes of the Palestinian people. Just as Rabin underplayed the degree to which the Oslo agreement implied a Palestinian state, Arafat overplayed the degree to which a commitment to such a state had already been achieved. Neither leader told his public that there were risks, but that they were worth taking, or that there would inevitably be setbacks, but that they could be overcome.

Although the publics were not fully brought into the process, the partnership at the leadership level was sufficiently solid to allow Arafat and his Israeli counterparts to pursue the peace process in a pragmatic mode and wait until they had clear evidence of success before strengthening the public consensus in favor of a two-state solution as a fair and just historic compromise. Had Labor stayed in power, chances are good that the parties would eventually have achieved an agreement in the form of a two-state solution. But this pragmatic process could not survive the change in Israeli leadership that brought to power a coalition that was not committed to the political partnership that Arafat and the Labor party leaders had developed.

NETANYAHU'S APPROACH TO THE PEACE PROCESS

The approach to the peace process of the present Israeli government is qualitatively different from that of the previous government. Netanyahu has not made the strategic decision to end the conflict with a historic compromise based on mutual recognition. He has not accepted the Oslo agreement's implication that Israel will yield territory and control to an independent Palestinian state at the end of successful negotiations. He has shown no willingness to continue the political partnership with the PA that his predecessors established. He gives no consideration to what the Palestinians would need if a solution to the conflict is to be feasible from their point of view and politically acceptable to them. Indeed, he takes systematic steps that destroy the possibility of such solutions—for example, by unilaterally changing the status and demography of Jerusalem, expanding settlements, confiscating Palestinian lands, and blowing up Palestinian houses.

To be sure, Netanyahu has accepted certain political realities. A Palestinian self-governing authority is in place in Gaza and most of the West Bank cities, and it is universally recognized. Netanyahu does not intend to reoccupy these areas or to expel the Palestinians. He has thus found himself in a situation in which he has to deal with the PA as a territorially based political entity. His much-publicized handshake with Arafat visibly broke his long-standing taboo against negotiating with the PLO. In January 1997, he signed the Hebron agreement calling for partial redeployment of Israeli troops from Hebron and other West Bank areas. In June of that year, he presented a final status map to his inner cabinet, showing the areas of the West Bank (some 40 percent) that he might be prepared to turn over to the PA in a final agreement. By negotiating with the PA about redeployment and territory, Netanyahu demonstrated that he—along with a significant part of the Israeli Right—has recognized that the consequences of the Oslo agreement are not entirely reversible and is entertaining the concept of territorial compromise and some kind of partition of Greater Israel. Indeed, many settlers and right-wing ideologues; including members of his own party, are accusing him of selling out the cause by showing willingness to give up even a small part of the land.

Accusations from the more extreme elements of his coalition and constituency do constrain his ability to maneuver. But he has also given no indication that, in the absence of these constraints, he would vigorously pursue a peace process. While he accepts some of the new realities and responds to outside pressures when they become sufficiently persistent, it has become increasingly clear that he is not prepared to pay the price for peace. He remains committed to keeping as much of the land and as much control as possible. He has given no indication that he is prepared to allow the Palestinians to establish anything resembling a contiguous, viable, independent state on the pieces of land they may in the end be offered.

Netanyahu and much of the Zionist Right have now embraced the Oslo agreement and present themselves to the Israeli public and the American mediators as ready to pursue the peace process. However, as Ian Lustick points out in his detailed analysis, they use the Oslo agreement as a legal document rather than as the opening to a political partnership that it was intended to be. Netanyahu does not deal with the Palestinians as partners who are responsive to each other's concerns and constraints, but wields the terms of the agreement as a weapon against them, demanding that they honor certain specified terms before Israel will take the next step. These demands have been one-sided, have not considered the constraints of the Palestinian leadership, and have denied Israel's own failures to live up to its obligations under the accord.

Netanyahu has used the term "reciprocity" to frame his demands on the Palestinians. But reciprocity is a norm governing a relationship between equals, in which each party has both rights and obligations. In a relationship based on this norm, each party is expected to consider the needs, aspirations, and constraints of the other and to give the other what it asks for itself: reassurances regarding security, acknowledgment of identity, respect for dignity, understanding of sensitivities. A relationship can flourish only if both sides adhere to the norm of reciprocity. In Netanyahu's vocabulary, however, the word "reciprocity" is used as an ultimatum. For example, the Israeli government has refused to carry out the next (previously agreed-upon) stage of redeployment unless the PA takes certain "reciprocal" steps in curbing terrorism, such as arresting or extraditing a specified list of suspects. Yet security itself is best addressed in the context of a partnership, within a framework of reciprocal rights and duties, in which the parties jointly work out cooperative arrangements that are technically and politically feasible and consistent with the welfare and dignity of each. In this regard, the partnership between the Rabin/Peres government and the PA was actually quite successful in developing cooperative security arrangements that seemed to work, but that with the collapse of the partnership have been eroding.

Netanyahu's embrace of Oslo and demand for reciprocity seem designed to delay any further redeployment as long as possible and to set conditions that the Palestinians are likely to reject. The resultant breakdown of the negotiations could then be blamed on the Palestinians, setting the stage for Israel's unilateral imposition of a solution. It remains quite possible, however, that a combination of external and internal pressures may yet bring about a further Israeli redeployment and a return to the negotiating table. It is even possible that this government (though not without a great deal of internal opposition) will in the end agree to the establishment of some entity that could be called a Palestinian state. This possibility has been bruited by some of Netanyahu's associates. Their idea seems to be to turn over to the Palestinians whatever disconnected pieces of land they are prepared to offer and to tell the Palestinians that, if they wish, they can call it a state.

With or without negotiations, however, it is quite clear—from Netanyahu's map, his actions, and his pronouncements—that what he is prepared to offer the Palestinians, whether or not it is called a state, comes nowhere near to what Palestinians would minimally expect. It is, essentially, a limited autonomy in Gaza and several West Bank enclaves, excluded from Jerusalem, and heavily dependent on Israel. Even if this entity were to be called a state, it would lack the geographical contiguity, control over its population and resources, and all of the attributes of sovereignty, viability, and security that an independent state requires. Moreover, such a state would not solve the central problem of the Palestinian people, which is their lack of citizenship—a fundamental human right in the modern world. It would in effect be a set of Bantustans offering only the pretense of citizenship, without the capacity to protect the population or meet its needs. Even if the Palestinians accepted such an arrangement, it could not form the basis for a stable, sustainable peace.

The very fact that a Palestinian state is now being talked about by elements on the Israeli Right underlines the inevitability and growing legitimacy of a two-state solution based on territorial compromise.

It is a solution that is now almost universally viewed as a fair historic compromise, widely accepted by Palestinians, and increasingly by Israelis. But ironically, the Right's adoption of the concept of a Palestinian state poses a danger of distorting and trivializing that concept as a key element of a just solution to the conflict. If the Palestinian state envisaged in a two-state solution is to take the form that Netanyahu and his associates are prepared to accept, it will have lost its meaning as a way to terminate the conflict and establish a basis for long-term peace and cooperation.

It is no longer enough, therefore, to engage in a peace process that envisages a two-state solution without specifying what *kind* of two-state solution it is to be. One must be clear about the nature of the Palestinian state that will emerge from the final negotiations and its precise relationship to Israel.

THE NEED FOR A PRINCIPLED PEACE

To revive the peace process now, the parties need to recreate the working trust and reestablish the political partnership that have broken down. This can no longer be achieved by the step-by-step approach of distributive bargaining that seemed to be working when the Labor party was in power. The parties must now go beyond the pragmatism of the Oslo process and commit themselves to a *principled* outcome of the negotiations that not only serves the interests of both parties, as it must, but that is also fair and just. Thus, to restore Palestinian trust in the peace process, Israel must commit itself, on a principled basis, to a two-state solution as the end point of negotiations and negotiate the remaining issues on the premise of a Palestinian state. Such an Israeli commitment will allow the Palestinians, in return, to commit themselves to a principled two-state solution and thus help revive the political partnership....

ELEMENTS OF A PRINCIPLED PEACE

To move the peace process in the direction of a principled peace and ultimate reconciliation, there are four key ideas that need to be understood, promulgated, and acted upon in the coming negotiations....

Prior Commitment to a Two-State Solution

The Oslo agreement left the question of Palestinian statehood open until the end of the negotiations. With the total erosion of working trust, that option is no longer available. For the process to fulfill itself under the present circumstances, it must be clear at the outset that there will be a two-state solution and that only the modalities are the subject of negotiation. Such commitment can restore the trust necessary for productive negotiations to proceed.

Moreover, both sides' commitment to a two-state solution as the end point of the negotiations must be a *principled* commitment, comparable to the commitment of the South African parties to majority rule as the end point of their negotiations. The two-state solution must be adopted on the grounds that it is right—that it is perceived by the parties, and indeed by the rest of the world, as a just and fair historic compromise to the long and bitter conflict. Although this solution may not give each side all it wants and feels it deserves, it can at least address each side's basic

needs for identity, security, well-being, and self-determination, and it can serve both sides' long-term interests. Only a commitment to this kind of principled outcome can lead to a sustainable peace —to a stable, cooperative, and mutually enhancing relationship between the two states for the long term.

A Genuinely Independent Palestinian State

In a principled two-state solution, the Palestinian state, like Israel, must be sovereign, viable, and secure. If the state is to meet these criteria, it must have contiguous territory in the West Bank and a secure link between the West Bank and Gaza; it must be free of foreign troops and extraterritorial settlements; it must be able to exercise control over its land, resources, and population; and it must be able to secure the rights of its citizens.

In the debate about a two-state solution, it has to be made very clear that what Netanyahu and his government now envisage as the Palestinian entity is very different from a genuine Palestinian state, even if in the end they are willing to call it a state. What they seem prepared to offer would in effect continue the occupation, while allowing the Palestinians to establish a limited, nonsovereign autonomy, which could be called a state only in the sense that the South African Bantustans were called states. It is important to forestall the co-optation of the concept of a Palestinian state by the Israeli Right and its redefinition as another version of a Bantustan. In advocating and committing to a two-state solution, it is now essential to specify that what is being called for is a genuine Palestinian state possessing the essential attributes of an independent polity.

Meaningful Citizenship for the Palestinian People

The necessity of an independent Palestinian state at this historical juncture can perhaps be framed most persuasively in terms of the issue of citizenship. Citizenship is a central human right in the modern world, since it is a condition for assuring many other basic rights both at home and abroad. To lack citizenship is to lack protection, access to resources, and even personhood. One of the political and moral imperatives of an Israeli-Palestinian peace agreement is that it must provide meaningful citizenship to the Palestinian population of the West Bank and Gaza, as well as to the refugee population.

The only feasible and mutually acceptable vehicle for providing meaningful citizenship to the Palestinian people is a two-state solution that establishes a genuinely independent Palestinian state. The limited autonomy that the Netanyahu government envisages could offer the Palestinians under its jurisdiction passports and other trappings of citizenship. But even if it were called a state, it would be heavily controlled by Israel and would not have the capacity to offer the population most of the benefits and protection that citizenship normally entails. In effect, this arrangement would offer Palestinians the pretense of citizenship while denying them citizenship rights in the polity that controls their lives. . . .

Mutual Recognition of the Other's Nationhood and Humanity

Over the decades, the parties have engaged in systematic denial of each other's national identity, with the aim of delegitimizing the other's national movement and political aspirations. Clearly, if the parties are to conclude a principled agreement, conducive to sustainable peace and reconciliation, they will have not only to reverse this pattern, but also to take active steps to acknowledge the other's nationhood and humanity in word and deed. . . .

On the Israeli side, commitment to a genuinely independent Palestinian state, which would be able to offer full citizenship to its population, would represent the most concrete form of acknowledging Palestinian nationhood. . . . [In addition, there is need for official Israeli acknowledgment] that the Palestinians, as a nation, have rights in the land in which they have lived for generations; . . . an injustice has been done to them; and . . . an independent state providing Palestinian citizenship is designed to rectify the historical injustice by establishing their national rights.

[It is also necessary to reverse] the policies and practices of the Israeli government [that] seem designed to squeeze Palestinians out of large portions of the remaining land. In the densely populated and impoverished Gaza Strip, several thousand Israeli settlers occupy some 20 percent of the land and use a disproportionate amount of the water. In the West Bank, Israeli settlements are expanding, Palestinian land is being confiscated, Palestinians are denied building permits and houses built without permits are demolished, and water is in short supply for Palestinians—though not for their settler neighbors. In Jerusalem, there are deliberate attempts to reduce the number of Palestinian residents—for example, by denying building permits or by canceling the ID cards required for residency—while houses for Jewish occupants are being built or bought in the Palestinian parts of the city. The effect of these policies and practices is to leave the Palestinians very little space on which to establish a national presence in the country, to make it difficult for them to claim ownership of any part of Jerusalem, and to deprive them of the opportunity to lead normal lives.

... [O]nce Israel—perhaps the next Israeli government—takes the initiative in acknowledging Palestinian nationhood and humanity, it is essential that the Palestinian leadership be prepared to reciprocate. Notwithstanding Israel's power advantage, the Israeli public, if it is to support a principled peace and reconciliation, needs the reassurance that can only come from Palestinians' acknowledgment of Israelis' humanity and nationhood. At the human level, the core issue is Palestinian attitudes toward violence against Israelis. There must be no ambiguity about Palestinian renunciation of violence. Violence cannot be used as a bargaining chip or as a negotiating tactic that can be turned on and off as the situation requires. There can be no glorification of suicide bombers or rhetoric hinting that violence remains a political option. Violence must be renounced as a matter of principle, not only because it undermines the peace process, but because it kills and harms human beings. Palestinians will have to declare and demonstrate that they attach value to the lives and welfare of their Israeli neighbors. Clearly, Palestinians can offer this acknowledgment only in the context of genuine reciprocity.

As for acknowledging nationhood, Palestinians have come a long way in recognizing Israel's legitimacy—both in Arafat's letter to Rabin accompanying the Oslo agreement and in prior and subsequent actions of the Palestine National Council. Ultimately, however, they will need to take one further step required for a principled peace conducive to reconciliation: the acknowledgment that the Jewish people have authentic links to the land—that they are not just European colonial settlers engaged in an imperialist project, but a people that has returned to its ancestral homeland. Such an acknowledgment is extremely difficult and painful for Palestinians because it threatens the basic tenets of their national narrative. It can be made only in a context of genuine reciprocity. But a sustainable peace, conducive to reconciliation, ultimately requires each side to acknowledge that the other belongs in the land and has rights there. This acknowledgment of the other's nationhood began with the Oslo agreement but has been kept at a level of pragmatic accommodation. It now must be pushed to the level of principle.

CONCLUSION

Sustainable peace is not possible if the long-term relationship between the two peoples will be based on perpetuating Israeli power and Palestinian grievance: on Israel's continuing belief that it must maintain control over the lives of Palestinians, and on the Palestinians' continuing belief that Israel's existence is illegitimate. It is essential now to work toward a principled peace, based on the four components that I have described. It may seem utopian to advocate a more demanding process at a time when a less demanding, more pragmatic process is on the verge of collapse. But I believe that, with the right leadership, the two peoples are ready for such a principled approach. I would argue that it is the most realistic option under the present circumstances, with the capacity of setting a new dynamic into motion.

NO

Douglas J. Feith

WYE AND THE ROAD TO WAR

The Clinton administration has made a practice of quieting crises in faraway places by striking costly deals with international malefactors, buying the unsustainable from the unreliable. The dividend from these transactions—in Iraq, North Korea, the Balkans—has not been peace, security, or disarmament but, on occasion, signing ceremonies. Thus it was again this past October [1998], in the negotiations that President Clinton personally superintended at Maryland's Wye Plantation between Israeli Prime Minister Benjamin Netanyahu and Yasir Arafat, chairman of the Palestinian Authority (PA).

The Wye talks responded to a crisis in the Oslo "process"—the diplomacy based on the 1993 peace accords signed by Arafat and Israel's then-prime minister, the late Yitzhak Rabin. The process itself was suffering the death of a thousand Palestinian violations. Wye revived it with a new agreement that has been hailed not only for breaking a stalemate but for carrying the parties toward genuine peace and brightening prospects for an end to the entire Arab-Israeli conflict.

To say the least, such hopes are unrealistic. The Wye deal imparts the appearance of vitality to Oslo as one might paint the cheeks of an expiring patient. In line with the entire series of Palestinian-Israeli agreements of which it forms a part, it is likelier to produce war than peace and likelier to endanger than to promote U.S. interests in the region—in particular, the U.S. interest in a secure Israel.

* * *

The last such agreement between the parties was concluded in January 1997, when the recently-elected Netanyahu, intent on giving the Oslo experiment at least one more chance for success, consented to withdraw Israeli forces from the West Bank city of Hebron. He did so without first requiring the PA to cure any of its outstanding violations of promises made in earlier agreements.

The Hebron accord displeased many of Netanyahu's backers in the [right-of-center] Likud party. In Israel's 1996 election campaign, after all, Likud had charged incumbent Prime Minister Shimon Peres [of the left-of-center Labor party] with conducting a one-sided peace process in which Israel never

From Douglas J. Feith, "Wye and the Road to War," *Commentary* (January 1999). Copyright © 1999 by Douglas J. Feith. Reprinted by permission of *Commentary*. Notes omitted.

insisted successfully, or even sincerely, that the Palestinian side fulfill its obligations. After defeating Peres, Netanyahu had made "reciprocity" his government's byword. Now his core constituency threw back at him the very criticisms he had directed against Peres.

To distinguish his government's diplomacy from that of his predecessors, Netanyahu defended the Hebron deal by stressing, first, that *henceforth* "the fulfillment of the undertakings of one side would be dependent upon fulfillment by the other side," and, second, that Israel in its sole discretion would determine the extent of any further redeployments of forces. This, he reassured the Knesset, was "also the way in which the United States interprets the [Hebron] agreement." In a "Note for the Record," signed by the U.S. mediator Dennis Ross, there was a list of unfulfilled Palestinian pledges (to combat terrorism, confiscate illegal firearms, limit the number of Palestinian police, prevent hostile propaganda, and amend the PLO Charter), and there was an American promise that these "commitments will be dealt with immediately"; a letter from Secretary of State Warren Christopher likewise pledged an American effort to ensure "reciprocity." Vowing that there would be no new agreements until the PA complied with the old ones, Netanyahu won approval of the Hebron accords from the Israeli parliament.

Israel withdrew from Hebron. The PA, however, did not remedy—indeed, has not yet remedied—any of the violations listed in the Note for the Record. Nor did the Clinton administration fulfill its promise to press the PA on compliance. Nor was Israel allowed to determine on its own the scope of further redeployments. To the contrary, the Clinton administration developed its own proposal, endorsed by the PA, for a withdrawal from an additional 13 percent of the West Bank and the Gaza Strip. Then the PA and the U.S. pressured Israel over many months to accept the American proposal. Eventually, they succeeded in getting Netanyahu to do what he had vowed not to do.

On this slag heap of multilateral promise-breaking, the Wye talks convened in October.

* * *

The essence of the Wye River Memorandum, as the agreement is called, is a pledge from Israel to withdraw from more territory. In addition to laying out the terms for that withdrawal, a section entitled "Security" obliges the Palestinian side, "in conformity with prior agreements," to take steps to combat terror, collect illegal weapons, provide Israel with a list of its policemen, amend the PLO Charter, and so forth. The Memorandum refers many matters to committees—charged, among other things, with overseeing the PA's promises. On these committees the United States is to play a prominent role.

Netanyahu had agreed to the 13-percent withdrawal even before Wye began (on the condition that, in order to help contain the security risks for Israel, three of the thirteen percentage points would remain virgin territory as a "nature reserve"). So the main subject of negotiations was what the Palestinian side was offering. Consistent with his theme of reciprocity, Netanyahu wanted terms that would position him strongly to decline further moves in the Oslo process if the PA continued to fail to perform its duties. Arafat wanted the opposite—an agreement without clear commitments or enforcement mechanisms.

At Wye, administration officials continually told the press that they were in harmony with the Palestinians. What they focused on was protecting the Oslo process from present and future disputes over compliance. In practice, this meant not curing existing violations or preventing future ones but suppressing and precluding *complaints* about them. Although this may sound irrational, or just plain cynical, it follows logically from the belief that in the Oslo process lies the key to peace. For how better to preserve that process—i.e., sustain the negotiations, produce new agreements—than by making it difficult if not impossible for the Israeli side to prove the Palestinian side's violations? And how accomplish *that* except by crafting an agreement that may appear sound but meticulously omits the kinds of terms that competent people routinely include in commercial contracts: verification of compliance, surety mechanisms to enforce obligations, and provisions for termination in case of material breach?

Such are the Wye accords—documents replete with undefined terms, unaddressed contingencies, unauthorized interpretations, loopholes, and lacunae (grammatical errors, too). To get a sense of them, one must read at least a few provisions in full. Here, for example, are the paragraphs providing for a nature reserve. My comments are in italics:

> The Palestinian side has informed that it will allocate an area/areas amounting to 3 percent from the above Area (B) to be designated as Green Areas and/or Nature Reserves.

When must this allocation occur? What happens if it is later rescinded?

The Palestinian side has further informed that they will act according to the established scientific standards,

What standards? Who is authorized to alter them?

and that therefore there will be no changes in the status of these areas,

If the "scientific standards" are altered, can the PA claim the right to change the areas' status?

without prejudice to the rights of the existing inhabitants in these areas, including Bedouins;

If the PA wants to build a road, for whatever purpose, what is to prevent it from saying the road is needed in order to avoid prejudicing the rights of the existing inhabitants, thus nullifying the entire paragraph?

while these standards do not allow new construction in these areas, existing roads and buildings may be maintained.

Why not say simply that the Palestinian side shall, by a date certain, allocate the 3 percent permanently as a nature reserve and that, without advance approval of the two sides, no new construction shall take place there?

Now here in full is the section on illegal weapons, of which there are large quantities in the areas under PA control.

> (a) The Palestinian side will ensure an effective legal framework is in place to criminalize, in conformity with the prior agreements, any importation, manufacturing or unlicensed sale, acquisition or possession of firearms, ammunition or weapons in areas under Palestinian jurisdiction.

What are the standards for an "effective" legal framework? Who judges? What if the standards are lowered or ignored after Israel completes its 13-percent withdrawal?

(b) In addition, the Palestinian side will establish and vigorously and continuously implement a systematic program for the collection and appropriate handling of all such illegal items in accordance with the prior agreements. The U.S. has agreed to assist in carrying out this program.

What are the standards for assessing the adequacy of the PA's program? When does it begin? What does "implement" mean? Might Israel have to begin and perhaps complete its withdrawal before any direct action against terrorist groups is initiated? Even if direct action is taken early on, what are the consequences if it is halted or reversed a few months later? Will Israel then make a new agreement for additional withdrawals in return for PA reaffirmation of its Wye undertakings? Why not say, "The PA shall disarm within its area of control the terrorist organizations listed below . . ."?

(c) A U.S.-Palestinian-Israeli committee will be established to assist and enhance cooperation in preventing the smuggling or other unauthorized introduction of weapons or explosive materials into areas under Palestinian jurisdiction.

Why, again, is there no mention of particular action against any terrorist group? What about the importation by the PA itself of weapons impermissible under prior agreements, such as Katyushas and shoulder-fired rockets? What if the PA fulfills its duty to establish the committee, but reports it has not yet found an opportune time to disarm the terrorist cells? What if the PA informs the Americans that the Palestinian legislature refuses to approve action against illegal weapons? What commitment does Israel have from the United States in the event of unsatisfactory performance?

* * *

Similar criticisms apply to virtually every provision of the Wye Memorandum. Since the document, only nine pages long, was negotiated under the direct supervision of President Clinton, whose linguistic finesse has been well established in recent months, one cannot assume that its nonobligatory obligations and illusory promises are the result of inadvertence or of an inability to create nuance. No, the gaps and ambiguities were built in with care. They ensure that, down the road, Israel will not be able to establish easily or clearly that the Palestinians have violated their undertakings.

True, the Wye agreement includes a "time line," which breaks down each side's obligations into sequential steps, and Israeli officials have pointed to this feature as the agreement's key innovation. According to the Memorandum, indeed, the duties of the two parties "are to be carried out in a parallel phased approach" in accordance with the time line. But "parallel phased approach" is nowhere defined, and nowhere is it stated that any given step in the time line must precede any other. Nor is it specified that all steps in a given stage must occur before any obligations in a later stage become due.

Netanyahu has said that he will halt the Israeli redeployments, scheduled to occur in three stages over a 90-day period, if the PA does not fulfill its undertakings according to the time line. But the Memorandum does not actually say that Israel has the right to do so. In recent years, when Israel has suspended withdrawals due to the other side's violations, the PA has turned the tables by asserting that Israel's suspensions constitute violations of Oslo.

In any event, even if the "parallel phased approach" plays out according to Netanyahu's concept, Israel will have completed its redeployments within a brief period. From that point forward, the time line affords Israel no leverage with the PA. However tough-minded the idea may have been in its initial conception, it emerged from the negotiations as a dubious mechanism for ensuring reciprocity.

* * *

As if mushy drafting did not offer a sufficient impediment to enforcement of the PA's promises at Wye, the agreement assigns to the U.S.—in fact, to the Central Intelligence Agency—a pivotal role in assessing the parties' compliance. To believe that the CIA will actually help enforce Wye is to misunderstand both the agency and American policy.

Over the decades, the CIA has collected much information relating to arms control and peace agreements. But when violations of those agreements need to be assessed, it is powerfully resistant to functioning either as judge or prosecutor. During the cold war, for example, Defense Department officials found it an exercise in pulling teeth to get the CIA to provide clear reports of how the Soviet Union was violating the Anti-Ballistic Missile treaty, the Biological Weapons convention, and other international agreements.

As soon as something is made the subject of a peace or arms-control treaty, ordinary intelligence reports on the matter become politically and diplomatically sensitive. To avoid being drawn into a highly politicized dispute, the CIA, which does not see itself as in the business of treaty-enforcement, hedges its reports, taking pains to highlight gaps in the data, ambiguities in the available evidence, uncertainties in its estimates. Even the limited and grudging cooperation the Pentagon extracted during the cold war is likely to be denied to Israeli officials responsible for upholding the Oslo peace process.

Moreover, the Clinton administration has no desire to expose the PA's record. Since the Oslo process began in 1993, the State Department has issued a series of congressionally-mandated compliance reports; in them, PA violations have been either minimized or ignored. Wye reaffirmed the administration's determination to preserve the process despite PA violations, and the CIA can hardly be expected to cast doubt on something the government favors so intensely.

That is not all. The new U.S. role —neutral monitor of an agreement between Israel and the PA—is at odds with the existing relationship between the two democracies. American statutes commonly designate Israel a "major non-NATO ally." It is an ally's function to side with its fellow ally against those who would attack and destroy it. The United States can be neutral between Israel and the PA only if it assumes that the PA does not intend to destroy the Jewish state. But such an assumption would, in and of itself, disqualify the United States as a neutral party.

As a practical matter, the more deeply the U.S. enters into the role of monitor, the more it will resist favoring Israel on various matters *not* governed by the Wye or Oslo agreements: for example, relocating the U.S. embassy to Jerusalem. Anyone within the administration who might advocate a pro-Israel position on such an issue will encounter the objection that he is tainting the neutrality crucial to the role of monitor, which in turn is crucial to preserving the Oslo process.

Over time, the putative value of apparent neutrality will encourage neutrality in fact.

That the U.S.-Israeli "special relationship" has already frayed was manifested at Wye in the recklessness with which American officials toyed with the PA's threats to issue a unilateral declaration of independence. Arafat has said that, if Israel is not sufficiently forthcoming in negotiations, he will declare statehood on May 4, 1999 (the date on which "permanent status" of the PA-controlled areas was scheduled to take effect according to the 1993 Declaration of Principles and the 1994 Gaza-Jericho agreement). Such an act, far beyond violating Oslo, has catastrophic potential. It could provoke a war with Israel that might end up involving other states and endangering a multiplicity of American interests.

Washington had every opportunity at Wye to make known its unshakable rejection of such an act. American officials, for example, could have demanded that, as part of the Wye Memorandum, the PA formally renounce a unilateral declaration of independence. Washington could have said that if the Palestinians were intransigent on this point, they would bear the blame for the talks' failure. (On other issues, Israel was admonished at Wye in just these terms.) At the very least, the administration could have asserted that any such declaration by the PA would be deemed an unfriendly act toward the United States as well as a material breach of the Oslo agreements that would relieve Israel of any of its obligations thereunder. Washington could have made clear that it would not recognize a unilaterally declared Palestinian state, would work to ensure that other countries withhold recognition, and would terminate U.S. aid to the PA-controlled territories.

But, despite Israel's request for help on this issue, all that the Clinton administration was willing to provide was a letter from U.S. Ambassador Edward S. Walker, Jr. to Israel's cabinet secretary Dani Naveh:

> [A]s regards to the possibility of a unilateral declaration of statehood or other unilateral actions by either party outside the negotiating process that prejudge or predetermine the outcome of those negotiations, the U.S. opposes and will oppose any such unilateral actions.

This is far short of a vow not to recognize a state, and it puts the Palestinian threat—a virtual declaration of war—in the same category as disapproved "unilateral actions" by Israel, like building towns for Jews in the territories or apartments at Har Homa in Jerusalem.

* * *

This, then, was the breakthrough that administration officials congratulated themselves on having achieved at Wye. Since it was concluded, what has happened has been much like what happened before: Israel has withdrawn from additional territory, and has permitted the PA to operate its own airport. PA officials have written up security plans for committee consideration, but meanwhile have disclaimed any intention of fulfilling key promises they made in October. Thus, one top-level PA official announced early on that "there will be no vote" to amend the PLO Charter; another publicly contradicted the PA's promises regarding the arrest of terror suspects; and a third, the PA police chief, detailed how he means to circumvent the PA's commitment at Wye to reduce its police forces.

Since Wye, Palestinian terrorists have remained on the job. One post-Wye operation targeted Jewish children in a school bus near Gaza, another the Mahane Yehuda market in Jerusalem. And Palestinian newspaper articles and television broadcasts have continued repeatedly to condemn Israel—and Jews generally—in bigoted and incendiary language. On November 3, a religious program on the PA's official channel instructed viewers that "the Jews do not believe in God" and are "the seed of Satan and the devils." On November 7, the PA's official newspaper, *Al-Hayat Al-Jadeeda*, told its readers: "Corruption is part of the nature of the Jews.... If one studies their history, it becomes apparent that the Jews were subjected to losses and expulsions as a result of their wickedness and their despicable acts." Other examples abound.

* * *

Wye is said to have put Oslo back on track. So it has done—if by Oslo one means the whole history of one-sided Israeli concessions, of inflated Palestinian expectations, of Palestinian breaches of solemn undertakings, of Palestinian violence threatened and executed, and, crucially, of American rewards for Palestinian recalcitrance.

Oslo was meant to be an experiment. It was a test, in the aftermath of the cold war and the Gulf war, of whether peace might at last be available to Israel. It was a test, in other words, of PLO intentions. Whether or not Israel and the United States were prudent to embark on the experiment—to see whether land and authority provided by Israel would transform the PLO into a force for conciliation and against violence and war —the evidence, plentiful from the start, is now overwhelming that the experiment has failed. Building on the concessions Israel has already made, the PA has or will soon enjoy and undoubtedly exploit the capability to import weapons through its new air and sea facilities, to forge political alliances with the likes of Saddam Hussein, to protect terrorist organizations behind a wall of state sovereignty—in short, to continue its armed struggle to liberate all of Palestine.

Just as it has become increasingly clear that the dangers posed by Saddam Hussein in Iraq (as by Slobodan Milosevic in Serbia and Kim Jung Il in North Korea) cannot be effectively contained so long as the present regime there remains in power, it should be plain that there will be no peace between Israel and the Palestinians until the latter enjoy a different and better leadership than the corrupt, violent, and irresponsible police-state regime of the PA. The ability of the United States (or of Israel) to promote improvement in that leadership is limited. But the administration's current policy—increasing U.S. aid to the PA while winking at its violations of Oslo and its human-rights abuses—simply reinforces the regime's most dangerous traits. Down that road lie further misery for the Palestinians and, for Israel, war.

POSTSCRIPT

Will Creating a Palestinian State Promote Peace in the Middle East?

The Middle East's torment is one of the most intractable problems facing the world. In addition to the ancient territorial claims of Jews and Palestinian Arabs, complexities include long-standing rivalries among various religious and ethnic groups and countries in the region. To learn more about the Palestinians, consult Samih Farsoun, *Palestine and the Palestinians* (Westview Press, 1997). There are also great tensions within the two principal groups, the Palestinians and the Jews. Arab fundamentalist groups such as Hamas oppose the peace efforts, and moderate Arab leaders are sometimes in danger. Egypt's president Anwar Sadat was killed in 1981 after he signed a peace accord with Israel. There are also Jewish extremists, and it was one of them who gunned down Prime Minister Rabin in 1995.

Complicating matters for Israel is the fact that the country is divided between relatively secular Jews, who tend to be moderate in their attitudes toward the Palestinians, and orthodox Jews, who regard the areas in dispute as land given by God to the Jewish nation and who regard giving up the West Bank and, especially, any part of Jerusalem as sacrilege. Furthermore, there are at least 150,000 Israelis living in the West Bank, and removing them will be traumatic for Israel. The issue is also a matter of grave security concerns. The Jews have suffered mightily throughout history; repeated Arab terrorism represents the latest of their travails. It is arguable that the Jews can be secure only in their own country and that the West Bank (which cuts Israel almost in two) is crucial to Israeli security. If an independent Palestine centered in the West Bank is created, Israel would face a defense nightmare if new hostilities with the Palestinians were to occur.

Thus, for the Israelis the "land for peace" choice is a difficult one. Some Israelis are unwilling to cede any of what they consider the land of ancient Israel. Other Israelis would be willing to swap land for peace but are doubtful that the Palestinians will be assuaged. Still other Israelis think the risk is worth the potential prize: peace. Israeli attitudes are covered well in Asher Arian, *Security Threatened: Surveying Israeli Opinion on War and Peace* (Cambridge University Press, 1996).

Yasser Arafat and the Palestinian Authority also face great challenges. They must rein in those who advocate terrorism and who oppose the very existence of Israel. The Palestinians must also build viable governmental, social, economic, and other structures if they hope to achieve statehood. More on these tasks can be found in Glenn E. Robinson, *Building a Palestinian State: The Incomplete Revolution* (Indiana University Press, 1997).

ISSUE 3

Should We Be Guardedly Optimistic About Russia's Economic and Political Future?

YES: Stephen Sestanovich, from Statement Before the Committee on Foreign Relations, U.S. Senate (May 1998)

NO: Peter Reddaway, from Statement Before the Committee on Foreign Relations, U.S. Senate (May 1998)

ISSUE SUMMARY

YES: Stephen Sestanovich, ambassador-at-large and special adviser to the secretary of state for the New Independent States (former Soviet republics), argues that although it is impossible to guarantee that Russia will become an economically viable, stable democracy, it is vital to take advantage of the opportunity to advance democracy and economic health in Russia.

NO: Professor of political science Peter Reddaway charges that it is misguided to ignore or downplay the dangers inherent in many Russian trends and contends that Russia faces a future full of uncertainty.

Russia has experienced two momentous revolutions during the twentieth century. The first began in March 1917. After a brief moment of attempted democracy, that revolution descended into totalitarian government, with the takeover of the Bolshevik Communists in November and the establishment of the Union of Soviet Socialist Republics.

The second great revolution arguably began in 1985 with the elevation of reform-minded Mikhail S. Gorbachev to leadership in the USSR. Gorbachev's reforms, including *perestroika* (restructuring, mostly economic) and *glasnost* (openness, including limited democracy), unleashed strong forces within the USSR. The events of the next six years were complex, but suffice it to say that the result was the collapse of the Soviet Union. What had been the USSR fragmented into 15 newly independent countries. Of these former Soviet republics (FSRs), Russia is geographically the largest by far, it has the largest population, and it is, in reality and potential, the most powerful. Russia retained the bulk of the Soviet Union's nuclear weapons and their delivery systems. And although Russian military forces soon fell into disarray, the country's large population, its weapons manufacturing capacity, and the geostrategic importance gained from its huge landmass make it likely that the breakdown of Russia's conventional military capabilities will only be temporary. Moreover, with a well-educated populace, vast mineral and energy resources, and a large (if antiquated) industrial base, Russia has great economic potential.

Whatever its potential, Russia is experiencing vast problems, at least for the moment. The country's economy, for example, is in shambles. Russia's gross domestic product (GDP) from 1990 through 1997 declined by an annual average of 9 percent. Its per capita GDP in 1997, about $2,700, was less than one-tenth the U.S. per capita GDP. Inflation during this period averaged an annual 394 percent, and exports dropped 13 percent. This economic deterioration has devastated the Russian population. About one-third of all Russians live below the poverty line, and Russian longevity, the expected length of life, is actually declining. Russia's economic turmoil is also the primary cause of the decline of Russia's military. Hardest hit have been Russia's military personnel, who are ill-equipped, ill-trained, ill-housed, and ill-fed.

When Russia reemerged after the collapse of the USSR, President Boris Yeltsin offered the hope of strong, democratic leadership. Yeltsin was soon welcomed in Washington, and the Western countries, led by the United States, rushed to help the successor of their erstwhile enemy, the USSR. Most of the funds that have flowed to Russia have come from the International Monetary Fund (IMF), which is primarily funded by the United States and a handful of other industrialized countries. In mid-1998 outstanding IMF loans to Russia totaled almost $14 billion. One of the primary reasons for this change of heart toward Moscow was the belief by many that a democratic, economically stable Russia would be peaceful.

The years between the reestablishment of an independent Russia and the testimonies of Stephen Sestanovich and Peter Reddaway before the U.S. Senate, which are excerpted in the selections that follow, were full of turmoil. The economic situation improved somewhat, but that should be understood as an improvement from horrific to merely bad.

Democracy survived, but it was sometimes in peril. In 1992 the holdover (from the communist period) Russians and President Yeltsin had a confrontation over his demand for a new election and a new constitution. It ended only after a Yeltsin-ordered military attack on the legislative offices, in which many people were killed and wounded. Yeltsin was reelected president in 1996, but it was an ailing Yeltsin who was elected. Due to his age and alcohol he was frequently unable or nearly unable to carry out his duties. His popularity rating with the public sank to the single numbers. Russia remained stable, but it was clearly adrift.

It is against this background that Sestanovich and Reddaway gave testimony to Congress. In the following selections, Sestanovich argues that there are good prospects that democracy will survive in Russia and that the economy can recover. Reddaway contends that U.S. intervention is not only unlikely to make things better but could make things worse by alienating important elements of the Russian polity.

YES

Stephen Sestanovich

STATEMENT OF STEPHEN SESTANOVICH

In Moscow, President Yeltsin has put together a new government—one of youth, talent, and reformist conviction, and he has charged it with restoring momentum to his policies across the board. The direction that his new team takes and its ability to address the major challenges Russia faces will have important implications for Russian-American relations. It will have a major impact on questions that have been and will remain of particular concern both to this Administration and to members of Congress—whether it's Russia's ability to implement a tough and effective nonproliferation policy, the economic strategies necessary to attract foreign investment and encourage growth, the protection of religious liberty, or Russia's relations with its neighbors and the world.

How these questions are addressed will to a very large extent determine what kind of country Russia will be and what kind of role it will play in the world. On this, America's stand is clear: As President Clinton declared in his Berlin speech [in May 1998], "The secure, free and prosperous Atlantic community we envision must include a democratic Russia. For most of this century, fear, tyranny and isolation kept Russia from the European mainstream. Now Russians are building a democratic future. We have an enormous stake in their success. . . . We must support this Russian revolution."

Americans of both [political] parties have agreed that Russia's revolution deserves our support. They have seen that doing so serves American interests in the most palpable way. The Administration and Congress have worked together to give concrete support to this revolution. As Secretary Albright told the Senate Budget Committee: "Our highest priority is to ensure that NIS [New Independent States of the former Soviet Union] countries build peaceful ties with the West through free-market engagement and reliable democratic institutions."

To advance these interests in our relations with Russia, this Administration pursues a four-part agenda:

First, we seek to reduce the threat to the United States and to international peace posed by weapons of mass destruction. Russia itself no longer threatens America the way it did for so many decades. Ensuring that the remnants of

From U.S. Senate. Committee on Foreign Relations. Subcommittee on European Affairs. *Overview of Russian Foreign and Domestic Policy.* Hearing, May 20, 1998. Washington, D.C.: Government Printing Office, 1998.

the Soviet military-industrial complex do not threaten us or our allies remains a principal goal of U.S. policy.

Second, we support democracy and respect for human rights, including religious freedom. Just as Americans supported those who yearned to be free of communism throughout the Cold War, so now we must stand up for Russia's new generation of democrats as they build a civil society. A democratic Russia at peace with itself is more likely to be at peace with us and with the world.

Third, we strongly support Russia's continuing transition to a modern, market-based economy, coupled with Russia's integration into the world economy. A market economy is the essential complement to democracy and respect for fundamental human rights. It creates opportunities for those Russians who have put behind them the habits and outlook of the past. It provides opportunities for U.S. business to participate in Russia's revolution, as well.

Fourth, we seek a Russia cooperatively engaged with its neighbors and integrated into Euro-Atlantic and global communities. This is key to building a world based on equality among states rather than on confrontation and domination.

... [T]hese are extremely ambitious goals. Reaching them requires several things. One of them is bipartisan support. Since 1991, that support has by and large held firm. But I would be less than candid if I did not acknowledge that this bipartisan consensus is under very severe stress. In the face of these challenges there are plenty of people, possibly some members of this committee, who have begun to question whether these are in fact realistic aims for American foreign policy in 1998.

This Administration's answer to that question is, emphatically, yes. The key to restoring a measure of bipartisanship to our Russia policy is for us together to tackle the problems we face head on. The more thoroughly we talk through the difficulties that we encounter in our relations with Russia, the stronger, I believe, will be the case for the policy that we are pursuing.

Another prerequisite for achieving our goals is understanding what Russians are thinking. Russians are themselves divided about their policy goals.

There are, for example, those in Russia who understand that ratifying the START II treaty will enhance Russia's security and serve the urgent need of military reform; others prefer to block Russian-American agreements of any kind. There are those who see perfectly clearly that the flow of dangerous missile and nuclear technologies to Iran directly threatens Russia, but others believe they can make money from it and, to keep doing so, may try to subvert any strengthening of export controls. Many are committed to protecting the free exercise of religious faith in accordance with the Russian constitution and Russia's international obligations; others fear religious freedom and diversity. There are Russians who know that the long-term revival of their energy industry cannot succeed without foreign partnerships; others would rather let production slide than allow outsiders in. There are Russians who accept the independence of their neighbors and regard it as essential to Russia's security and democratic success; others want to reconstitute the Soviet Union no matter the price.

... [W]hat makes these differences serious isn't that we don't know where those who set Russian policy stand. We do. It was, after all, President Yeltsin who on Sunday emphasized to President Clinton his personal determination to use all the powers of his office to stop sensitive technology transfers to the Iranian missile program. It is the defense minister and foreign minister who are pushing START II ratification in the Duma [Russia's parliament]. And it was Sergey Kiriyenko who, as Energy Minister, committed himself to resolve problems faced by Russian-American joint ventures in the energy sector.

What makes the policy divisions I have described important—and what we must bear in mind as we deal with a Russia in transition—is their impact on the way policy is carried out. No matter the issue, the Russian system produces results —good, bad, or indifferent—only very slowly. The system itself is still undergoing profound change: The jurisdiction of government agencies is often poorly defined, their decisions are subject to constant challenge by the special interests affected, and bureaucrats who want to ignore a particular decree or law can sometimes take cover under another one with a diametrically opposite meaning.

I have dwelled on the difficulties that we face in pursuing our ambitious agenda toward Russia because some people conclude from these difficulties that we have had to give up and that we are now pursuing second-best results. We are not, and it would be unacceptable to do so.

The stakes are too high for us to accept second-best results. That was not this Administration's approach when it worked for the withdrawal of Russian troops from the Baltic states, when it concluded a trilateral U.S.-Russia-Ukraine agreement to remove nuclear weapons from Ukraine, when it completed the NATO-Russia Founding Act, when it stood behind the Russian reformers in their successful battle against inflation, or, frankly, when it stood with them against a communist resurgence.

It was said of every single one of these efforts that it could not succeed. And they definitely could not have succeeded without persistence, patience, and steady nerves. They could not have succeeded without continued bipartisan support for our Russia policy and for the resources that the Congress made available to advance our interests.

SECURITY/NONPROLIFERATION

Developing a post–Cold War security relationship with Russia that enhances mutual security through arms control treaties and engagement on nonproliferation remains one of America's top foreign policy priorities.

The Duma's delay in ratifying START II remains a source of frustration for us, and we hope that its action to postpone debate on ratification until September will be reconsidered. START II is manifestly in the interests of both the United States and Russia and should be approved.

Once START II is ratified, we are poised to begin talks on a follow-on accord that will cut both arsenals still further. We have already agreed that START III would cap strategic nuclear warheads at 2,000–2,500. We also have agreed to address transparency in nuclear warheads, fissile materials, and tactical nuclear weapons in the next treaty.

Destroying the world's stockpiles of chemical weapons is another challenge that we're tackling jointly with Russia, which acceded to the Chemical Weapons Convention in December. Under the Cooperative Threat Reduction (CTR) program, we are developing projects to eliminate Russia's chemical weapons production capacity and 14% of Russia's CW [chemical weapons] stockpile. Overall, the CTR program has provided approximately $1.3 billion to disarmament activities in Russia, including the destruction of over 360 strategic nuclear delivery vehicles, the safe dismantling of weapons of mass destruction infrastructure, and the secure storage of nuclear weapons and fissile materials.

In Birmingham last weekend, President Yeltsin joined in a G-8 [the major industrialized countries] condemnation of India's reckless nuclear weapons tests. The G-8 reaffirmed its shared commitment to prevent the proliferation of weapons of mass destruction and missile-related technology. This has been an area of great concern to Congress and to this Administration.

We have been engaged almost constantly with the Russian Government to find ways of stopping leaks of sensitive technology. We have discussed at length instances of involvement by Russian entities with Iran's ballistic program and pressed for immediate steps to halt it. The Russians have responded seriously, and our activities have intensified accordingly—between the President's envoy, Ambassador Gallucci, and Yuriy Koptev, the director of the Russian Space Agency (who recently held a sixth round in a series of consultations started with Ambassador Wisner last August); between Deputy Secretary of State Talbott and Deputy Foreign Minister Mamedov; between National Security Advisor Berger and his Russian counterpart, Andrei Kokoshin; between Secretary Albright and Foreign Minister Primakov; and between Presidents Clinton and Yeltsin.

Has there been progress? Yes.

First, Moscow has accepted the gravity of the problem and clearly stated its policy. President Yeltsin . . . [and] Prime Minister Kiriyenko [have both given] important reiterations of Russia's commitment to stop the spread of missile technology. To be frank, we had some concern that the message from the top had not been clear enough. This is no longer the case.

Second, Russia is putting in place a regulatory structure to control the flow of sensitive technology. Prime Minister Chernomyrdin signed an executive order strengthening Russia's export control system, giving the Russian Government broad powers (known as "catch-all" authority) to stop transfers of goods and services to foreign missile programs or programs for weapons of mass destruction. Last week, implementing regulations were issued. These guidelines:

- Establish supervisory bodies in all enterprises dealing with missile or nuclear technologies;
- Establish a range of measures for licensing military exports; and
- Specify a list of end-users for which exports are prohibited.

A separate order assigns the Russian Space Agency responsibility for oversight of the entire space rocket industry.

Third, we have set up a bilateral group where Russia's export control officials and experts work with ours to strengthen Moscow's export control system. We have sought for Russia to develop a system of export control legislation and regulation that is as tough and effective as the best in the world. We will work hand in glove with Russia to ensure this gets done.

Do we consider this major progress? Yes. Are we fully satisfied? Of course not.

Implementation is the crucial test. We will carefully monitor execution of this range of export control mechanisms, assist the Russians in every appropriate way, and continue to press Moscow to use this new authority to end all missile cooperation with Iran.

As you know, Secretary Albright [has] waived sanctions against Gazprom under the Iran and Libya Sanctions Act (ILSA). This waiver was based, in large part, on the progress I have outlined here toward accomplishing ILSA's primary objective of inhibiting Iran's ability to develop weapons of mass destruction and support terrorism. This Administration believes the waiver will encourage further progress in this direction and will be accompanied on our part by continued close monitoring.

Members of Congress have been active partners with the Administration in our dialogue with Russian officials about the problem of Russian cooperation with Iran.... Our goal is a Russian export control regime that is rigorous and meets Western standards. The actions the Russian Government has taken put it firmly on the right track.... [T]his Administration strongly opposes any form of nuclear cooperation between Russia and Iran. Given Tehran's demonstrated interest in acquiring a nuclear weapons capability, this is the only responsible position we can take. We have expressed this view repeatedly and at the highest levels within the Russian Government.

Moscow has given us assurances regarding Russia's nuclear cooperation with Iran, including President Yeltsin's assurance that Russia would not provide Iran with any militarily useful nuclear technologies, including a gas centrifuge facility and a heavy-water moderated reactor given the inherent proliferation risks of such reactors. We are, of course, aware that a senior Iranian official was recently in Moscow and, according to press accounts, Russian Atomic Energy Minister Adamov talked about expanded cooperation with Iran's nuclear program. We will continue to press Russia to ensure that cooperation does not go beyond the Bushehr reactor.

DEMOCRACY, HUMAN RIGHTS, AND RELIGIOUS FREEDOM

Religious freedom is a foundation stone of a free society and occupies an important place in the obligations that states assume as members in good standing of the international community. In October 1997, Russia enacted a restrictive and potentially discriminatory law on religion that includes troubling provisions establishing a hierarchy of religious communities and according preferential treatment to religions that have been present in Russia for an extended period of time. Some new religious organizations are required by the law to wait up to 15 years before acquiring basic legal rights.

This is a bad law. It was pushed through by those who do not share the principles of tolerance that are embodied in Russia's own constitution and its international commitments. Others in Russia, including millions of members of minority religious congregations, feel differently and value the freedoms that they have won during the past 10 years.

Enactment of the law and growing discrimination against minority religions and foreign missionaries in Russia's regions have been the subject of great concern. The President, Vice President, Secretary Albright, Ambassador Collins, and I have been active during the past year engaging with Russia to ensure that it upholds its commitments to protect religious freedom.

In seeking full Russian respect for its international obligations, we have been immeasurably helped by others who have articulated America's commitment to religion freedom. I want to thank you, Mr. Chairman, and Senator Hatch and Senator Bennett for traveling to Russia to discuss church-state relations with Russian authorities and to underscore U.S. concerns about the new law. Non-governmental organizations, such as Law and Liberty Trust, the Union of Councils, the National Conference on Soviet Jewry, the U.S. Catholic Conference, as well as church groups, have been actively and effectively engaged, as well.

Let me mention some of what has been accomplished.

- Russian government officials, including President Yeltsin and then-Prime Minister Chernomyrdin, pledged to the Vice President that the new law would not result in any erosion of religious freedom in Russia.
- In applying the law, the Russian Ministry of Justice has adopted a permissive approach to registering religious organizations with full legal rights, effectively bypassing elements of the 15-year rule. Last Thursday, the Ministry registered the Mormon Church with full legal rights.
- Presidential Administration officials have established two consultative mechanisms to engage with religious communities and to monitor application of the new law.
- The Presidential Administration and the Ministry of Justice have also promised to support efforts now underway by non-governmental organizations to challenge the constitutional-

ity of the law's retroactive provisions before the constitutional court.

The implementation of this law has provided encouraging evidence of the federal government's determination to respect its international obligations and to make sure that law enforcement conforms to constitutional standards. We are disappointed that the implementing regulations failed to clarify the law's ambiguities. Since enactment of the law, 25 cases of harassment by local officials have come to our attention. We and Ambassador Collins in Moscow have vigorously complained about these incidents. The federal government needs to be more active in reversing discriminatory actions taken at the local level and, when necessary, reprimanding the officials at fault. The State Department will continue to monitor this issue closely. . . .

Religious liberty is only one of the measures of the creation of a modern democratic order. The collapse of communism has permitted us to work with governments and with private groups across eastern Europe and Eurasia to foster the institutions essential for building a civil society.

In Russia, we have since 1991 initiated programs to support free and fair elections, the development of independent media, the promotion of accountable and responsive municipal government institutions, and the growth of a vibrant non-governmental sector. U.S.-sponsored programs have provided over 1,500 small grants that have nurtured environmental and human rights watchdog groups, women's organizations, public policy groups, and other non-governmental organizations. We have supported over 10,000 high-school exchange students. We are now exploring programs that will help foster religious tolerance. We have also worked to strengthen institutions that sustain the rule of law by training judges and reforming law school curricula to develop the next generation of legal professionals. Cooperation and training involving the FBI, Secret Service, DEA, Customs, and other U.S. agencies has helped us identify allies among Russian law-enforcement officers who can help tackle the scourges of corruption and international organized crime. These kinds of programs are a long-term investment in our security and an expression of Americans' deep-rooted sense of responsibility to support those who have survived tyranny and now want to build an open society.

THE U.S.-RUSSIA ECONOMIC RELATIONSHIP

Completing the transition from a centrally planned to a market economy is essential to Russia's prosperity, democracy, and long-term role as a constructive player in world affairs. The success of this transition is in our interest, and we will remain engaged in moving the process ahead.

Russia has made remarkable progress. The private sector produces 70% of Russia's GDP [gross domestic product], and tens of millions of Russians in start-up businesses are building the new Russian economy. After a decade of decline, Russia's economy may now be growing again. The Russian Government killed off the very high inflation that followed the collapse of the Soviet Union, dramatically reduced Russia's budget deficit, and built a strong ruble.

There are plenty of problems. Export revenues are being hit by falling world oil prices, the Asian flu has put the Russian and other emerging market economies under increased scrutiny and, in the past few days, Russian financial markets have been buffeted anew by developments in Asia and questions about the government's ability to manage economic policy. In particular, current market jitters underline the urgent need for tax reform and greater transparency in government decision-making.

U.S. and Russian leaders have placed a priority on investment and integration into the world economy as key building blocks of a dynamic, wealth-generating economy. At the 1997 Helsinki Summit, Presidents Clinton and Yeltsin called for improvements in Russia's investment climate and greater Russian participation in global institutions. Russia joined the Paris Club as a creditor member last year, has been invited to join APEC [Asia Pacific Economic Cooperation] meeting later this year, and has started serious efforts towards WTO [World Trade Organization] accession.

The "U.S.-Russia Binational Commission on Economic and Technological Cooperation"—formerly also known as the Gore-Chernomyrdin Commission—has been a key instrument of our policy. This Commission, which will continue with Prime Minister Kiriyenko, has successfully addressed diverse issues such as securing American participation in multi-billion dollar energy projects, simplifying customs procedures, and forging links between our industries and Russia's potentially vibrant high-technology sector.

Programs funded under the Freedom Support Act have been another instrument for helping Russia work through critical market reforms. We have funded a number of short- and long-term technical advisers to work with the Russian Government on creating new laws and institutions for a modern market economy. Our advisers have provided assistance to the government on monetary and fiscal policy, revamping the tax code, drafting commercial law, and preparing Russia's WTO accession commitments. These programs advance important U.S. interests, help improve conditions for U.S. traders and investors, and have been a sound investment in Russia and America's future. Congress has been wise to fund them.

Economic reform has had a certain ebb and flow over the past several years. There are those who favor open markets, those who favor oligopoly or insider capitalism, and still others who would defend a long-since defunct status quo. The last kind of thinking is the primary reason that progress has been so slow on reforming the tax code, normalizing land ownership, passing broader production-sharing legislation, and making progress on other investment climate priorities. Prime Minister Kiriyenko and his government appear determined to push ahead and address these issues. Together with the IMF [International Monetary Fund], the World Bank, and our friends and allies, the U.S. will continue to work closely with reform-minded Russian officials to promote an open entrepreneurial Russian economy, to the benefit of the Russian people and U.S. economic interests.

RUSSIA AND ITS NEIGHBORS

Our goal since the end of the Cold War has been a democratic, undivided Europe that includes Russia and all of the New Independent States. To achieve this, we have promoted the independence, sovereignty, and territorial integrity of these new states; encouraged their development as democratic, market-oriented countries adhering to the norms of responsible international behavior; and facilitated their integration into the Euro-Atlantic and global community of nations.

It is critical for Russia to be integrated into broader world structures. Let me elaborate this point by discussing two examples.

First is NATO [North Atlantic Treaty Organization]. It is no secret to say that the United States and Russia have disagreed profoundly over NATO enlargement. To make sure that the expansion of NATO occurred in a Europe that is whole and free, we worked to forge a cooperative NATO relationship with Russia codified in the NATO-Russia Founding Act signed one year ago in Paris. The NATO-Russia Permanent Joint Council is an essential element of integrating Russia. Its success will be important in completing the transition of European security from a kind of adversarial, zero-sum relationship we had with the Soviet Union to a cooperative one in which we work together.

Second is Russia's relations with its neighbors. We absolutely reject the idea of a Russia sphere of influence. But while some in the Russian political spectrum accuse us of trying to dominate the region—and some neighbors claim that Russia is out to dominate them—the reality is that the region will benefit from a cooperative, constructive Russia that trades with its neighbors and that helps to resolve differences with and among countries.

In this spirit we are working with Russia on problems that just a few years ago would have divided us. We are active co-chairs with France in the OSCE [Organisation for Security and Co-operation in Europe] Minsk Group process trying to resolve the conflict [between Armenia and Azerbaijan] in Nagorno-Karabakh. Russian and American soldiers are serving together under U.S. command to keep the peace in Bosnia. In energy, we regard the Caspian Pipeline Consortium route through Russia an essential element of a multiple pipeline strategy for moving Caspian Basin energy to international markets.

These efforts draw Russia into more cooperative relationships with its immediate neighbors and with the world as a whole. We believe inclusion is a sounder policy than isolation, but inclusion does not mean forgetting our interests or ignoring our differences. Secretary Albright put it well when she described the mandate for the NATO-Russia Permanent Joint Council. She said it was a forum where "we are not always going to agree.... We are not here to pretend or to paper over differences. We are here to work through them."

CONCLUSION

The common thread of our policy toward Russia is to address all four parts of the agenda I described together, comprehensively, and in a way that advances international peace and stability. We seek to demonstrate in practical ways the bene-

fits for Russia of being part of the international community and to ensure against the isolation that, for 70 years, produced such terrible consequences for Russia and the world.

The new government in Moscow understands the importance of integration. The top echelon of this new team represents something we have never seen before in any Russian Government. It is comprised exclusively of young governors and former regional administrators who made their mark in the country's most politically progressive provinces. They carry no Soviet-era baggage. They have, instead, first-hand knowledge of how markets function and an awareness that the average Russian cares more about his own government's ability to collect taxes fairly and provide services effectively than about NATO enlargement. They understand that in a democracy voters reward bottom-line results, not empty promises. This modern, progressive outlook should serve Russia well, and we look forward to working closely with this new team.

We cannot guarantee that democracy will triumph in Russia—that is for the Russian people to determine. But we owe it to ourselves to take full advantage of the opportunity to advance our broad agenda with Russia to secure a safer future for all Americans.

NO

Peter Reddaway

STATEMENT OF PETER REDDAWAY

Interpreting developments in Russia is difficult. Some analysts accuse others of holding Russia to an unreasonably high standard, given the ravages of 74 years of communism, and even of being "anti-Russian."

A typical response by the second group of analysts is that the first one ignores or downplays the dangers inherent in many Russian trends, wanting, for whatever motives, to be cheer-leaders, and thus ill-serves both Russia and the West.

I belong to the second group, but not out of any anti-Russianness. I believe that the US government and the West have, in general, pursued unwise policies towards Russia, and either do not realize this, or, for understandable if not laudable reasons, prefer not to acknowledge it by changing their policies.

Growing Anti-Americanism

One of the main consequences of this approach is already visible. When communism fell in 1991, pro-American feeling was widespread and strong in Russia. In recent years, however, resentment of the United States and bodies like the International Monetary Fund [IMF] has grown sharply, both among the Russian elite and among the population at large, because the economic "shock therapy" that we prescribed is working badly. The US is widely seen as bossing and trying to control Russia, as overwhelming it culturally through the invasion of US pop culture, McDonalds and Pizza Hut, and religious missionaries. Letters of instruction to the Kremlin from senior American officials are leaked to the Russian press and published. Thus when Russians have been asked in representative opinion polls to comment on such statements as "The US is utilizing Russia's weakness to reduce it to a second-rate power and a producer of raw materials," some 60–70% of them have "completely agreed" or "somewhat agreed" with the statement, while only about 20% have somewhat or completely disagreed.

In the perception of most Russians, both the US and President Yeltsin told them in 1991-92 that if their country followed the US's prescriptions, democracy and free markets could be built in a few years, without much pain, and before too long Russia would become stable and prosperous. Six

From U.S. Senate. Committee on Foreign Relations. Subcommittee on European Affairs. *Overview of Russian Foreign and Domestic Policy*. Hearing, May 20, 1998. Washington, D.C.: Government Printing Office, 1998.

years later, most Russians feel let down, and say that Yeltsin and the US did not deliver what they promised. As a result, the Russian government lacks legitimacy, and the US's motives are seen, however mistakenly, as self-interested and unfriendly to Russia. Among the elite, this perception has been strengthened by the eastward expansion of NATO [North Atlantic Treaty Organization] in the face of strong opposition from the entire spectrum of Russian elite opinion.

POPULAR FRUSTRATIONS

Here are some of the frustrations that typical Russians now feel: "Our political system," they say, "is not a tyranny, it's an attempt at democracy. Yet we don't have the rule of law. To a large extent we still have the rule of men. Our institutions are very fragile." Also, "We now have a lot of personal freedom, and plenty of enterprising people, but we don't have spare cash, and economic conditions are very difficult, so we can't make much use of our freedom." As an example, they might say: "Censorship is gone, but the media are owned by the government and the financial oligarchs, so we can't actually express ourselves very freely." On Russia's federalism, a typical view would be: "The regions are now more autonomous from central government than ever before in our history, but ordinary people don't benefit, because the local oligarchs are almost as corrupt and non-accountable to us as the Moscow ones are." To quote an actual poll, 84% of those asked to comment on the statement "Our public officials do not care much about what people like me think" either completely or somewhat agreed with it. The public approval ratings of leading politicians are remarkably low, and popular confidence in public institutions is typically in the 10–30% range, except for the army, which usually scores around 40%.

THE GOVERNMENT'S LACK OF LEGITIMACY

In other words, while the government is formally legitimate, because elections have so far been held, it lacks much real legitimacy. People see it—accurately in my view—as being much more concerned about the power and private interests of a small elite than about the public interest, or, in foreign policy, the national interest. Corrupt cliques control politics and economics, and care little about the population. They are not worried that social Darwinism is at work on the weak, the old, and the poor. As Boris Nemtsov, a deputy prime minister, said, "Russia, including its national leadership, must enter the 21st century only with young people." Or as Igor Chubais, brother of Anatoly Chubais, who ran the economy for Yeltsin until March, wrote in a book: "Russia . . . is of absolutely no interest to the present elite." The elite is concerned only with "power, money, and privileges." It sees the Russian people as "simply an annoying, tiresome nuisance, which, moreover, for some reason has to be paid wages."

The Scourge of Official Corruption

An important cause of the alienation of many Russians from the political system is the prevalence of official corruption. Especially worrying is the fact that, because corruption enables the whole political and economic system to work, it has seemingly become endemic. It substitutes for the rule of law. As Igor Chubais writes,

"All-pervasive corruption... strange as it may seem, carries out important social functions... In the absence of other social regulators, it has become one of the most important unifying forces in our country. Different sections of society and the state become inter-linked and acquire common interests. They... become capable of—at least in some fashion—functioning." All this explains why, although the Yeltsin administration has gone through the motions of six anti-corruption drives in six years, and hundreds of senior figures have been publicly accused of large-scale scams and machinations, and a few arrested, still not a single highly placed politician, businessman, or general has been both sentenced and jailed.

THE GOVERNMENT'S NON-ACCOUNTABILITY

Also, the government listens to the Russian people only when it is forced to. It wages a two-year war against Chechnya, one of Russia's constituent republics, without consulting the nation, and ends the war only when it finds it cannot win, and the death toll has mounted to some 80,000, most of the dead being civilians. It allows the payment of wages and pensions to be delayed for months, until, say, the miners become desperate and physically block the Trans-Siberian and Moscow-Vorkuta railroads. Then Prime Minister Kiriyenko offers to pay them a mere 14% of what he admits is a $600 million backlog.

The government's excuse for this chronic pattern of behavior is that despite six years of the IMF's loans, ministrations, and conditionalities, it does not have the cash to pay wages and pensions on time. At the same time, the top 5–10%

of the population lives a life of ease and conspicuous consumption. How serious, then, is the economic situation, and how long will it last?

THE STATE OF THE ECONOMY

Here is a snap-shot of the economy. According to the Organization for Economic Cooperation and Development (OECD), Russia's GDP [gross domestic product] has declined by a little over 40% since 1989 and has now bottomed out. The most recent estimates for its likely growth in 1998 vary from about zero to 2%. Inflation has been successfully brought down to an annualized rate of about 8% last month, however economists warn that "Russia's success in reducing inflation is undercut by the fact that the economy remains only partially monetarized, and the use of barter, dollars and money surrogates appears to be on the increase." Last year's budget deficit was 6.8% of GDP, and it is unclear whether this uncomfortably high figure will be reduced in 1998. Tax collection has become a chronic problem and is currently running at only 65% of projected levels. In 1996, as the OECD reports, "26 tax inspectors were reportedly killed, and many more injured or physically threatened, while 18 tax offices endured bomb blasts or shootings." Illegal capital flight is widely estimated to have been running at a rate of $10–15 billion a year for the last few years, easily outstripping Russia's total of aid loans and grants from abroad. The latter have nonetheless mounted fast, and, given the high level of domestic debt too, the OECD foresaw the possibility that "the total public debt could exceed 50% of annual GDP" by the end of 1997. Investment has fallen substantially throughout the 1990s, declining 5%

last year (less than usual), but continuing to decline in 1998. Thus the economy's capital stock has steadily aged. In particular, investment has been drastically squeezed by high interest rates. For most of this year the treasury bond rate has been 30%, and on May 18 the government defended the rouble by raising basic interest rates to 50%. For Russia's able but struggling entrepreneurs, these facts of life come on top of a business environment in which, first, racketeers routinely tax small and medium businesses, and second, contracts are hard to enforce, because criminals and corrupt officials can usually intimidate the courts. The media have reported the assassination of some 600 senior businessmen and a score or two of politicians over the last three years.

Since 1992 most prices have been freed, so goods are freely available. A few key prices are still controlled, such as those for apartment rents and household gas, the latter still being only 10–15% of the world market price. However, most prices are not much different from American levels, while average real incomes are only about one tenth of the US level. This gives some idea of the average Russian's standard of living. Moreover, 22% of the population now have incomes below the meager official level for subsistence, and real unemployment is about 10% and rising —in a country which is used to a virtual absence of joblessness. Russian agriculture has seen very little serious reform, and about half of the country's food supply is imported.

More generally, the Russian economy is dominated by crony capitalism, a phenomenon greatly facilitated by the above mentioned Anatoly Chubais. Last year Chubais switched his stance and began a campaign against crony capitalism. But it may have become so deeply embedded that it cannot be rooted out. Certainly, official efforts to combat the lack of transparency and the monopolistic tendencies in the economy have so far made only slow and intermittent progress, and have also suffered some reverses.

Finally, on the economy, the public sector has been neglected. Outside of Moscow, which is a different world from almost all the rest of Russia, the economic infrastructure and the environment have suffered badly. How deeply Russians are worried by environmental degradation can be seen from a new U.S.I.A. [United States Information Agency] survey.

This reports that some 68% of those polled hold that "protecting the environment should come first, even if it slows the growth of our country," while only 22% think that "economic growth should come first, even if the environment suffers as a result." In addition, the health, education, and research sectors have also deteriorated sharply. For example, because of the declining public health system and other negative factors, demographers expect the Russian population to decline from its present 147 million to about 135 million in 2020. Lastly, morale and discipline in the Russian military are at a worryingly low level, thanks in large part to a chronic lack of funding.

In short, six years of economic depression, continuing uncertainty about when, or whether, real growth will replace the current stagnation, and the fear that even if real growth develops it will take many years to improve the lot of ordinary people, have made the Russian people deeply skeptical about the IMF and its supposedly universal recipes for economic recovery. It is widely perceived as a tool of Western interests which will always put these interests and those of the Russian Establishment above the welfare of ordinary people. Most Russians did not like communism. Now they are wondering if they like capitalism—in the perverted form they see before them—any better.

FOREIGN POLICY

Against this background it is not surprising that Russian foreign policy has become increasingly critical of the U.S. and the West. Although the Yeltsin government is too dependent on the West to turn sharply against it, a continued cooling of relations, with more Russian acts of defiance over issues like Iran, Iraq, and Serbia, seems likely. More worrying is the danger that anti-Western feeling will continue to grow among ordinary Russians, thus creating the potential for future Russian governments to be more hostile towards the US and the West than the present one.

POLITICS AND THE FUTURE

President Yeltsin gives cause for many concerns, partly because his erratic physical (and even mental) health continues to deteriorate. Above all, though, his deep desire to hang on to power for as long as possible creates a situation fraught with danger. He fashioned the 1993 Constitution to give the presidency very broad powers, and has used these with great skill to rule largely by decree, and also to co-opt and outmaneuver most of the communist, nationalist, and democratic opposition, even though it has in general commanded much more popular support than he has. With strong US approval, he dispersed the first Russian parliament with tank fire in 1993, and he has often shown disdain or even contempt for its

constitutionally weak successor. By deploying cleverly his extensive powers of patronage, he has bought off most of his opponents, giving them small stakes in the status quo, and thus alienating them to a considerable extent from their political bases in the population.

In the business world, from 1991 onwards he quietly allied himself, first with the dynamic elements of the communist Establishment, who were appropriating many of the state's assets for themselves, and secondly with the emerging non-communist entrepreneurs. These groups, whose leaders are now known as the financial and business oligarchs, have been somewhat harder for him to control than the politicians, because the most skillful among them have developed a certain degree of autonomy from the government. In 1996 the oligarchs decided to get Yeltsin re-elected, even though his popular approval rating was around 5%, because their help would subsequently increase his dependence on them. However, the next presidential election, which, though not due until June 2000, has already obsessed the Russian Establishment for a year, is almost certain to be much more problematic than that of 1996.

At present Yeltsin shows every sign of intending to run, even though he will have already served two terms. His surrogates maintain that although the present Constitution allows only two terms, Yeltsin's first term was served mainly under the old Constitution, so a third term would be permissible. The bigger problem may well be, though, that this time the oligarchs do not seem to see him—given his all-round erraticness—as a candidate they want to back. On top of this, the oligarchs are currently divided among themselves, so the real possibility, or even probability, arises that the Establishment may be split two or even three ways in 2000. This means that the fragile Russian polity might easily be destabilized, if one or more of the contenders decides to try to win at all costs, and not to play by the rules. It also means that an only semi-Establishment figure like [former general and presidential candidate] Alexander Lebed could possibly have a chance of winning. Without doubt, too, serious competition between Establishment rivals, or between one or more of them and a non-Establishment figure, could carry promise as well as dangers: candidates would be more likely to address the real needs of the long-suffering Russian people.

In any case, Yeltsin is clearly on the move. His impulsive removal of Chernomyrdin as prime minister in March —when he at first appointed himself as Acting Prime Minister without realizing that this was forbidden by the Constitution—looks like a strong, possibly fatal blow to Chernomyrdin's already slim hopes. However, Mayor Yuri Luzhkov of Moscow is emerging as perhaps the strongest runner at this stage. Though closely linked by sections of the Russian press to criminal figures, he has skillfully managed to attract support from the three main sectors of public opinion, the nationalists, the communists, and the democrats, as well as from the Establishment. By contrast, the communist leader Gennady Zyuganov, who showed no will to win in his 1996 run-off with Yeltsin, is now faced with a slowly fracturing communist party, and in my view is not electable. And the leader of the democratic opposition, Grigory Yavlinsky, even though his Yabloko party is doing better than ever on the strength of its principled opposition to the government's economic policies and authoritarian tendencies, is probably too much of an intellectual to become President.

CONCLUSION

Thus Russia faces a future full of uncertainty. Big question marks hang over its political system, its economy, its military, its territorial integrity, and, at least under a post-Yeltsin government, its foreign policy. US and IMF policies towards Russia have, in my view, yielded little fruit. But they have contributed a lot to Russia's problems. The pro-American goodwill that we accumulated in Russia up to 1991 has, despite our good intentions, in many ways been squandered. We were much too sure we had the right recipes, and much too assertive in pushing them on the Russians. When we suspected they might not be right after all, we declined to stop and review them. We plowed on and hoped for the best. Now we are beginning to pay the price. If we stop now and review our stance, the price may be containable. Above all, we need to admit our mistakes, stop our continuous meddling in Kremlin politics and Russian economic policy, and have the Russian government take full responsibility for its decisions. If we don't do this, the price we pay for our mistakes will rise. We will increasingly alienate the Russian people—with consequences for our own interests and for Russian democracy and capitalism that could be very serious.

POSTSCRIPT

Should We Be Guardedly Optimistic About Russia's Economic and Political Future?

The debate over the future of Russia is not a matter of idle speculation. There are two very real policy considerations. The first involves the fact that the direction Russia takes in the future is likely to have important consequences for the world. Both the right and left wings of Russian politics favor a much more aggressive foreign policy. One likely right-wing candidate for the presidential campaign in 2000, former general Aleksandr Lebed, finished third in the first round of the 1996 election and has said, "He who shoots first laughs last." On the left, communist leader Gennadi Zyuganov, who finished second in 1996, has pledged to "restore the might of the Soviet state" and to follow "the foreign policies of pre-revolutionary [czarist] Russia."

The second real policy question is whether or not the United States should try to influence Russia's political and economic situation. The urge to do so is based on the theory that a democratic, prosperous Russia will be peaceful. There is considerable evidence that democracies are unlikely to engage in military conflicts with one another, but not all agree. For more on this debate, see Miriam F. Elman, ed., *Paths to Peace: Is Democracy the Answer?* (MIT Press, 1997). There are also doubts that democracy can survive in a country that is in such poor condition and that has no democratic tradition. On this matter, read Harry Eckstein et al., *Can Democracy Take Root in Post-Soviet Russia? Explorations in State-Society Relations* (Rowman & Littlefield, 1998)

Indicative of the uncertainty of Russia's political stability is the serious effort in the Duma (the Russian parliament) in May 1999 to impeach Yeltsin on a series of charges, including ruining the Russian military, causing deaths in the attack on parliament, and waging genocide on the Russian people by destroying the economy. The articles of impeachment all failed to gain the requisite votes to proceed, but some of the votes were close.

As a last note, there are numerous possible flash points between the United States and Russia. Although nuclear weapons have receded as a concern, at least for now, the Duma has yet to ratify the second Strategic Arms Reduction Treaty (START II). Also, Russia was highly critical of the opening of NATO membership in 1999 to the Czech Republic, Hungary, and Poland. A move to bring yet other Eastern European countries that lie close to Russia's borders into NATO is likely to spark a strong reaction. On this topic, see Hall Gardner, *Dangerous Crossroads: Europe, Russia, and the Future of NATO* (Greenwood, 1997).

ISSUE 4

Should China Be Admitted to the World Trade Organization?

YES: Robert S. Ross, from "Enter the Dragon," *Foreign Policy* (Fall 1996)

NO: Greg Mastel, from "Beijing at Bay," *Foreign Policy* (Fall 1996)

ISSUE SUMMARY

YES: Professor of political science Robert S. Ross contends that the World Trade Organization (WTO) should admit China in order to incorporate that country into the global economy.

NO: Greg Mastel, vice president for policy planning and administration at the Economic Strategy Institute in Washington, D.C., argues that the integrity of the WTO would be damaged if China were admitted without significant legal and economic reform.

China is a country in transition. It is moving, or trying to move, from a poor, largely agricultural economy to a wealthier, industrial economy. It retains its authoritarian, communist government, but it has adopted many of the trappings of a capitalist economy, including stock markets. Whereas China once rejected global trade and other international economic organizations, now it is trying to join them. Once called a "country without lawyers," China is now moving toward enacting commercial codes and other laws that regulate business and other activities.

China's unfulfilled desire to become a member of the World Trade Organization (WTO) is caught up in the issues of transition. It is possible, for example, to argue that China should be regarded as a less developed country (LDC) and admitted to the WTO as such. From a micro, per capita perspective, China is one of the world's poorest countries. The most telling statistic is that China's 1997 per capita gross national product (GNP) of $860 places it in the bottom 25 percent of all countries. Admission to the WTO as an LDC would give China a number of advantages not available to industrialized, economically developed countries (EDCs).

But it is also the case that from a macro perspective, China has one of the largest economies in the world. China's 1997 gross domestic product (GDP)—including Hong Kong, which is sometimes counted separately—was $1.2 trillion, making China's the sixth largest economy in the world. With $352 billion in goods exports in 1997 (again including Hong Kong),

China was the world's third largest exporter, surpassing Japan for the first time and trailing only the United States and Germany.

Whatever perspective one takes, there can be no disagreement that China is one of the world's fastest-growing economies. From 1990 through 1995, China's real GDP expanded an average of 11.6 percent annually. Moreover, China is rapidly industrializing. Its industrial sector has led the GDP growth, amassing an average 18.8 percent growth during the period. The country's exports have also increased rapidly, climbing 16.3 percent annually during 1990–1997. Again, manufactured goods lead the way, jumping from 48 percent of all exports to 85 percent.

One result of China's rising economic importance is that the United States and other EDCs are devoting increased attention to their economic relations with China. One key issue is its burgeoning trade surplus with the United States. During 1997 China (and Hong Kong) exported $76 billion in merchandise to the United States but took in only $28 billion in U.S. imports. The U.S. $48 billion trade gap trailed only the U.S. deficit with Japan and has evoked mounting criticism in the United States that Beijing is practicing one-way free trade.

One response by the United States, along with some other EDCs, has been to deny China's application for membership in the World Trade Organization. The WTO is the organizational structure that administers the General Agreement on Tariffs and Trade (GATT). This treaty was concluded in 1947 to promote free trade. For most of its existence, the name GATT caused confusion because it was both the name of a treaty and the name of the organization, which is headquartered in Geneva, Switzerland. That confusion ended in 1995 when the GATT organization was renamed the WTO.

By whatever name, the organization is at the center of global trade policy. GATT's initial membership was 23 countries; there are now 132 members of the WTO. These members account for more than 85 percent of all world trade. Membership in the WTO is important to China for a number of reasons. Among these is the fact that under WTO rules, the United States could not impose unilateral sanctions on trade with China because of concerns over human rights violations or other practices that are internal to China.

China contends that it should be admitted to the WTO with the status of an LDC, which would give it greater ability to protect its economy than is given to EDCs. Washington wants Beijing to forgo many of the protections because of its large economy. Washington also opposes Chinese membership based on Beijing's alleged unwillingness to enforce many commercial laws, such as other countries' patents and other intellectual property rights. Perhaps $2 billion in illegal ("pirated") copies of software, music CDs, and movie videos not only sell in China, but they also find their way into other countries.

In the following selections, Robert S. Ross and Greg Mastel take up the debate. Ross supports a WTO membership for China, while Mastel argues that China should be denied admittance until it institutes significant trade and market reforms.

YES

Robert S. Ross

ENTER THE DRAGON

The completion of the Uruguay Round of the General Agreement on Tariffs and Trade (GATT) and the establishment [in 1995] of the World Trade Organization (WTO) were truly major accomplishments. Together, they are helping to construct an international economic order characterized by liberal trade norms and dispute-settlement procedures that follow agreed-upon rules.

Challenges to the stability of this trade order could nonetheless arise from many sources. Economic factors such as unequal rates of growth and national recessions could elicit counterproductive foreign economic policies. Challenges could also come from powerful countries that refuse to play by the established rules of the WTO liberal trade regime and thus lead to destructive countervailing protectionist measures from their economic partners.

The post–World War II trade system faced such a challenge from Japan, whose effective export-promotion policies undermined the domestic industries of the advanced industrial economies, while its protectionist import restrictions prevented these industries from competing in the Japanese domestic market. Unfair Japanese trade practices brought about growing protectionism from Japan's major trading partners, including the United States and the European Union. Although Japan and its competitors have been able to contain the impact of their protectionist measures, Japanese protectionism has been a major factor contributing to the recent regionalization of the international economy and the emergence of trading zones characterized by special privileges for select WTO members.

THE CHALLENGE OF A RISING CHINA

Japan remains the country with the world's largest trade surplus, and its economic system remains mostly impenetrable. Nonetheless, the openness of the world economy may well be facing an even greater challenge from China's emergence as an economic power. If China's economy continues to grow at current annual rates of 8 to 10 per cent, and if it acquires advanced-technology capabilities, China's impact on the international economic system will dwarf that of Japan, even considering Japan's most influential period, during the

From Robert S. Ross, "Enter the Dragon," *Foreign Policy*, no. 104 (Fall 1996). Copyright © 1996 by The Carnegie Endowment for International Peace. Reprinted by permission.

1970s and 1980s. With favorable domestic economies of scale and a nearly unlimited supply of cheap labor, China could become a major export power capable of prevailing in the domestic markets of its economic competitors. If China simultaneously were to fail to offer opportunities for participation in its own domestic market, its policies could lead to destabilizing responses by all of the major economic powers.

Clearly, the challenge for the international community is to incorporate China into the global economy so that its behavior reinforces the contemporary trend toward trade liberalization. What is in dispute is the means by which this can be achieved. Chinese membership in the WTO is at the center of this debate. Correct management of China's application would have considerable implications for Chinese economic policy, for the role of the WTO in managing a liberal trade order, and for global economic stability. The dilemma is that there is no easy response to China's application.

Current Chinese trade practices are at wide variance with the WTO obligations assumed by the world's major trading powers. China's state-owned enterprises, which contributed approximately 31 per cent to China's total industrial output in 1995 and control strategic sectors of the economy, receive big subsidies and enjoy preferential access to government investment projects. Equally important, high tariffs and nontransparent government regulations protect China's private, collective, and state-owned manufacturers of consumer and industrial goods, further interfering with free trade. China's economic reforms and trade liberalization process have a long way to go before its economic policies meet WTO standards.

An equally important factor is the central government's failure to enforce a range of domestic policies meant to protect the rights of foreign businesses. China's ineffective protection of intellectual property rights is only the most obvious failure. Pervasive corruption throughout China and the absence of an effective central regulatory system weaken the government's ability to enforce international economic obligations on local governments and businesses. The absence of an effective legal system enforced by an independent judiciary compounds these problems, insofar as judicial recourse often is not an available remedy for injured parties. Corruption rather than law often determines the outcome of economic disputes in China.

China's growing economic power and its detrimental economic practices present the international community with a clear-cut policy objective: To persuade China to abandon its current practices for an economic system that complements the WTO's rule-based order. Moreover, if this process is delayed, China will develop sufficient economic power to resist pressures for reform. The United States faced this situation in its relations with Japan. By the time Washington actively sought change in Japan's trading system in the 1980s, Japan had developed the economic power to resist U.S. pressure. Washington failed to act when it had maximum leverage.

THE FAILURE OF CURRENT U.S. POLICY

The United States and its economic partners seek Chinese compliance with the WTO guidelines applicable to the major economic powers. Chinese membership in the WTO should be evaluated in terms of its contribution to this important agenda. Uncompromising adherence to rules and legal norms is a prerequisite to domestic order, but it is inappropriate for achieving interests in a world of states. Whether China today meets WTO standards is less important than adopting policies to promote the development of a Chinese economy compatible with the WTO. Practical pursuit of interest, rather than rigid adherence to principle, will best serve U.S. interests.

While it is in the interest of the United States and other industrial countries that China establish a liberal economic system as soon as possible, it is in China's interest to prolong its current policies. Although China has succeeded in expanding exports, the long-term expansion of its industrial base requires the use of the protectionist measures that Indonesia, Japan, South Korea, and Taiwan employed to assist their nascent industrial system prior to liberalization.

There is a conflict of interest between China and the global trading system that requires negotiation. Mere insistence that China abide by the rules before it is admitted to the WTO will not lead to a negotiated settlement. On the contrary, Chinese foreign trade officials argue that the U.S. price for Chinese admission into the WTO—rapid compliance with the trading rules applicable to the other major economic powers and a weakened industrial base—is too high. They have thus decided that China should remain outside of the WTO until the entry requirements are eased.

It is clear that WTO membership provides insufficient benefits to persuade China to liberalize its economy prematurely. Most-favored-nation (MFN) trade status assures China continued access to global markets. Although WTO textile regulations will eventually prove more advantageous than those of the Multi-Fibre Textile Agreement, the changing structure of Chinese trade is reducing the importance of textile exports to the Chinese economy. Equally important, improved access to international textile markets will not compensate China for a weakened industrial base. Given China's current ability to access markets, the benefit of WTO membership is primarily prestige. Beijing has determined that prestige is of little use in making China strong or in raising the standard of living of the Chinese people.

In this respect, contemporary China is different from the Japan of the 1960s. Whereas the United States had significant leverage over Japan in the early years of its post–World War II development, it lacks comparable leverage over China at a similar stage in China's development. The reason is that China has a far more open economy than Japan had at a similar stage of its development. Whereas Japan's trading partners could not sell to the Japanese market, China's trading partners have developed a significant interest in maintaining their access to the lucrative Chinese markets in consumer goods, aircraft, and infrastructure projects. This is not to say that the advanced industrial countries have no leverage over China, but that they have less leverage to compel China to open its markets fully. The result is a failed effort to use the prospect of Chinese membership in the WTO as an incentive for Beijing to liberalize its foreign economic policies.

The most profound implication of U.S. policy intransigence will be for China's future economic behavior. Not only has China *not* made the concessions demanded by Washington, but U.S. policy will merely encourage Beijing to persist in its current policies. Chinese isolation from the WTO and the resulting Chinese resentment of the major trading powers will likely enhance Beijing's proclivity to pursue mercantilist policies for national power rather than merely short-term protectionist policies for economic development.

Denial of Chinese membership in the WTO will not minimize the global impact of Chinese protectionism. China will affect the world trade system through its bilateral relationships: WTO member countries will seek bilateral accommodations with China in order to profit from its vast market, thus weakening the liberal trading order. This was the impact of U.S. and European bilateral arrangements with Japan. Denying China membership in the WTO may reflect principled adherence to the rules of trade and allow America to hold the moral high ground, but it will not realize American interests or the interests of America's major trading allies in maintaining a stable liberal economic order. Keeping China out of the WTO provides only the illusion of isolating the problem; it will not solve the problem.

A NEW DIRECTION

The United States has been negotiating Chinese admission into the GATT/WTO since 1988. The two sides remain far apart. It is time to reconsider the premises of U.S. policy.

Washington should support an accession agreement that acknowledges China's interest in protecting its industrial base. The agreement should also include a schedule for Chinese trade reform. The schedule might delay the reforms for longer than Washington would

like, but, once in the WTO, China will be required to follow through on the schedule. Indeed, one of the great missed opportunities of Washington's China policy was its failure to achieve Chinese membership in the GATT on terms negotiated by the Bush administration in 1989. If China had entered the GATT in 1989, it would be committed to a far more open trade system than is currently the case. Following the June 4, 1989, suppression of the Chinese democracy movement, Washington withdrew support for the agreement. Now China is under no obligation to conform to any GATT/WTO guidelines.

Moreover, the longer agreement is delayed, the longer the actual period of adjustment will be. The clock for Chinese adherence to WTO regulations does not start ticking until China joins the WTO. In addition, the longer China's entrance is postponed, the more powerful it will become, thus diminishing the organization's ultimate leverage. It is in the interest of the major economic powers to get the WTO clock ticking as soon as possible.

Chinese membership in the WTO will increase international leverage over China. Current efforts to coerce China to reform its economic system depend entirely on U.S. efforts. One of the reasons that U.S. negotiations with China for market access have failed is that the United States lacks support from its allies. By conducting negotiations within the multilateral setting of the WTO, the likelihood of maintaining a "united front" would be far greater, and the pressure on Beijing to compromise, more compelling. In addition, it would be politically easier for Chinese leaders to bow to WTO pressures than to unilateral U.S. insistence.

For any international regime to succeed, it must reflect the interests of its most important members. The United States acknowledged this fact throughout the Cold War when it allowed significant protectionism for its NATO allies and Japan in numerous economic sectors. It continued to do so during the Uruguay Round when it made concessions to Japan and France over agricultural products. While those compromises resulted in a less liberal trade agreement than the United States would have liked, they have enabled Europe and Japan to contribute to the integrity of the overall regime. As a result, the WTO may well be more stable and enduring. Accommodating Chinese interests may require concessions similar to those offered to Europe and Japan. But failure to include China in WTO negotiations will only ensure that the regime will develop in a direction inimical to Chinese interests. Asian countries understand this point. They have admitted China into the Association of Southeast Asian Nations Regional Forum and the Asia-Pacific Economic Cooperation forum because they understand that a Chinese commitment to these institutions requires a Chinese voice in their development. The same truth holds for the WTO. By incorporating China, the WTO will develop in a direction that reflects a consensus of all the major powers. This is the prerequisite to global economic stability. The alternative is a trade regime that encourages Chinese policies that are likely to destabilize a system that does not reflect its interests.

Chinese membership in the WTO will also strengthen the hand of Chinese policymakers who want to promote a more liberal Chinese trading system. Prior to Chinese membership in the World Bank and the International Monetary Fund,

many analysts argued that China would be a destructive force—that its communist bureaucrats would undermine these institutions' commitments to international norms. Just the opposite occurred. Not only did China become a constructive member of these institutions, but its membership has allowed implicit alliances to develop between the institutions and proreform policymakers, strengthening their hand within China. Chinese membership in the WTO could create similar partnerships.

Finally, Chinese membership in the WTO would serve American bilateral interests with China. The United States has assumed the burden of obtaining Chinese compliance with international economic norms. This is the case in intellectual property rights negotiations. The primary causes of Chinese intellectual property rights violations are the political and economic decentralization of post-Mao China, the lack of an effective legal system to enforce government regulations, and the corruption of those authorities who participate in the piracy of intellectual property. Copyright infringement is rampant in China, affecting domestic producers of cigarettes, drugs, and food products as well as the profits of China's own software and entertainment industries, and the regime's legitimacy has suffered. By all appearances, the Chinese government would like to end much of the piracy in the Chinese economy. It simply lacks the authority.

There seems to be little that U.S. policymakers can do to fundamentally improve Chinese enforcement of intellectual property rights violations—foreign economic sanctions will not enhance central Chinese government authority over local activities. The threat of sanctions has only encouraged Chinese leaders to commit to improved intellectual property protection by local officials who are not susceptible to government policy, creating periodic crises with Washington when agreements are not fulfilled. Moreover, when Beijing shuts down factories that pirate intellectual property, they often quickly reopen elsewhere in connivance with corrupt local officials. The economics of piracy almost guarantees it; the cost of new duplicating facilities is significantly less than the potential profit. Focusing on Chinese policy toward these high-profile factories merely creates the illusion that rapid progress is possible and heightens American acrimony when expectations are unmet.

As with Chinese protectionism, the issue is how to encourage constructive Chinese behavior. Current U.S. policy has failed. Multilateral WTO sanctions would impose costs on the central government for its failure to control localities, while removing the burden on Sino–U.S. relations for inevitable Chinese infractions. Moreover, the WTO could be an effective channel for technical assistance in developing a Chinese system for regulating intellectual property. Over the long run, a better Chinese regulatory and legal system will do the most to promote global interests.

Without doubt, Chinese foreign economic practices will remain troubling for many years to come. The evolution of the Chinese political and economic systems will primarily reflect long-term domestic trends—a growing respect for law and the institutionalizaton of political authority. International pressures will not fundamentally affect the pace of change. Whether or not China is admitted into the WTO, it will remain a problematic trading partner.

In these circumstances, foreign policies can only help to ameliorate a difficult situation; they cannot resolve it. Moreover, Chinese membership in the WTO entails some risk—allowing a blatant violator of international economic norms to join the WTO may well erode the organization's credibility. Nonetheless, Chinese membership in the WTO sooner rather than later remains the best option for improving a difficult situation.

China's admission to the WTO will subject it to multilateral pressures for adherence to a self-imposed agreement to adopt liberal trading practices within a specified time. Currently, China has not agreed to any multilateral commitments to reform its trading system. Isolating China will not compel China to change nor will it protect the international economic system from counterproductive Chinese trade practices. Rather, it will ensure that China's gap with WTO standards will grow, along with Chinese resentment and the incentive to adopt destabilizing trade policies.

Current American policy fails either to minimize the likelihood of international economic instability or to improve Chinese trading practices. There is no more opportune time than now to promote China's support for a liberal trade order that can endure into the twenty-first century.

NO

Greg Mastel

BEIJING AT BAY

With the Sino-American relationship under much stress, many "China hands" have viewed China's application to join the World Trade Organization (WTO) as an issue on which the United States could compromise in order to keep the peace. The United States, with the support of other major countries, has been delaying China's entry into the WTO until China commits to sufficient trade and market reforms. Arguing, however, that the Clinton administration is too legalistic in its approach to China's application, some China experts have urged that the administration put aside its concerns and support China's immediate entry into the WTO.

This view places political and security concerns above economic concerns. It has the ring of classic U.S. Cold War foreign policy decision making, a paradigm that has dominated U.S. policy toward China for decades. This viewpoint is dated and out of touch with current realities. China is an important player in the global economy. It is already one of the world's top 10 exporters and is expected to be the world's largest economy early in the next century. As a result, economic and trade issues with China are at least as important as security and political issues.

More importantly, the integrity of the WTO would be severely damaged if China were admitted without significant legal and economic reform. The WTO is more than a simple club of trading partners. The WTO—originally the General Agreement on Tariffs and Trade (GATT)—is a postwar institution founded to establish and promote the principles of free markets and free trade. Thus, simply being a big player in international commerce does not warrant WTO membership. The acceptance of key market principles—even if they are not always rigorously applied—should be the key test for WTO membership. Viewed in this light, China's compatibility with the WTO is open to question. In fact, there are three basic reasons to question China's current compatibility with the organization.

Chinese trade barriers. The most visible impediments to China's membership in the WTO are its formal trade barriers, including tariffs, import licenses, and subsidies. In recent years, these formal trade barriers have been

From Greg Mastel, "Beijing at Bay," *Foreign Policy,* no. 104 (Fall 1996). Copyright © 1996 by The Carnegie Endowment for International Peace. Reprinted by permission.

lowered; however, others have appeared, and China still has considerably more formal trade barriers that are inconsistent with WTO membership than any other major country. These barriers have been the focus of WTO accession negotiations so far.

The negotiations on formal trade barriers have already proven contentious. In theory, however, the issues under discussion—tariffs, investment policy, etc.—have been addressed in previous negotiations (NAFTA [North American Free Trade Agreement], Uruguay Round). Thus, if the political will exists to reach an agreement, traditional trade barriers do not pose a conceptual obstacle to China's accession.

Rule of law. The formal trade barriers, however, are only the tip of the iceberg. It is very difficult to ensure that any trade agreement will translate into changes in Chinese policy. China simply does not yet have a reliable rule of law. The current generation of leaders frequently pronounces that establishing the clear and consistent rule of law is a primary goal. The... leader of the National People's Congress, Qiao Shi, ... spoke of the importance of establishing the rule of law, as opposed to the rule of a strong leader, which has led to tragedies like the Cultural Revolution.

This issue may seem initially to have little to do with international trade negotiations, but China's lack of a rule of law presents almost insurmountable problems for WTO membership. In China, trade regulations and tariffs are set by national policy, but their implementation in different provinces and ports is inconsistent. Officials often are open to bribes, a practice that results in further inconsistency. Some laws are simply not enforced,

particularly if it is profitable not to enforce them.

The severity of this problem was brought into sharp focus in a recent dispute over the protection of intellectual property. The United States has criticized China for not enforcing the bilateral understanding, struck last year, on the protection of intellectual property rights. In defense, Chinese officials cite the lack of central government control over provincial governments—and even over some operations affiliated with the People's Liberation Army.

The lack of a reliable rule of law governing Chinese behavior in international commerce raises serious concerns about China's readiness for WTO membership. After all, it does little good to negotiate trade agreements with a government that, by its own admission, is unable or unwilling to live by the agreements it negotiates. Before China can be considered a serious applicant for WTO membership, it must establish a reliable rule of law, at least in relation to trade and investment.

The Communist system. Another difficulty, closely related to the lack of a rule of law, is the presence of a still nearly totalitarian government. One of the issues that illustrates the problem, and is currently under discussion in the context of WTO membership for China, is the issue of "trading rights." Essentially, trading rights are granted to private enterprises to enable them to engage in foreign commerce without governmental approval. But Chinese citizens, or enterprises operating in China, do not automatically enjoy these rights. In WTO negotiations, China has proposed granting these rights, in a limited sense, to foreign entities operating in China but has been silent on extending similar rights to Chinese citizens. This issue highlights the expansive role of the Chinese government in commercial decision making. After all, if consumers do not have the right to purchase imports, what sense does it make to negotiate on tariffs and quotas?

The WTO, like the GATT before it, normally ignores the degree of political freedom a government permits: A number of WTO members have authoritarian governments. But now there is an increasing focus on the link between social freedom and the potential for conducting normal commerce. In the debate over congressional approval of the North American Free Trade Agreement, Senator Patrick Moynihan (D-New York) posed the question, "How can you have free trade with a country that is not free?" In his argument, Moynihan focused on the absence of both an independent judiciary and a corruption-free government to enforce trade and commercial regulations in Mexico, but an even more compelling argument can be made with regard to China.

There are several problems caused by the expansive powers and influence of the Chinese government. The first and most obvious is the continuing role of government planning in the Chinese economy. Since the late 1970s, China has undertaken considerable economic reforms and has moved toward creating a more market-oriented economy. Yet China is still—and intends to remain —largely a centrally planned economy. Although China is undertaking reforms, state-run industries are still responsible for a significant portion of China's gross domestic product, and they employ an enormous number of people and provide a major source of exports. China recently adopted another five-year economic plan and maintains extensive plans to support what it calls "pillar industries." Reaching beyond those industries directly owned by the state, new sectoral guidelines have been issued for the automotive and pharmaceutical industries, and there is reportedly a similar blueprint for the electronics industry.

CHINA SIMPLY DOES NOT HAVE A RELIABLE RULE OF LAW

These plans contain many policy elements inconsistent with the WTO, including import-substitution directives, local-content requirements, onerous investment requirements, and foreign-exchange balancing requirements. Even more troubling is the fact that the Chinese government clearly has no intention of ending the issuance of industrial guidelines. Despite assurances that future plans would be WTO-consistent, there is no evidence that recent industrial plans are moving in that direction.

Beyond the formal role of central planning, the pervasive presence of the government in Chinese society raises serious questions about the possibility of establishing a normal trading relationship with China. A large percentage of trading decisions, particularly with regard to infrastructure projects and agriculture, are made directly by government agencies, and the Chinese government has explicitly used foreign purchases and business deals as tools to promote foreign policy objectives.

Where the government's role in commercial decisions is direct, perhaps WTO provisions regulating government procurement and state trading could be of some help in regulating Chinese trading decisions. The Chinese government, however, has innumerable opportunities to tilt regulatory decisions in favor of, or against, any enterprise. The opportunities to harass foreign businesses are numerous, and the opportunities for WTO policing are limited, because there is rarely any formal paper trail, and there is often no formal decision.

More difficult still is moderating the informal role the government plays throughout society. The official Chinese press has been pounding away regularly at the United States on a variety of foreign policy issues, accusing the United States of seeking to "contain" China. In such a political environment, and given the need for government approval to thrive and even survive, can any Chinese citizen ignore government rhetoric when selecting business partners? With memories of the Cultural Revolution and Tiananmen Square very much in mind, the answer is almost certainly "no."

Historically, the GATT/WTO was conceived in part as an organization of market economies convened to assist the market world in its competition with the nonmarket world. Viewed in this context, the problem presented by the fact of the world's largest nonmarket economy seeking to join the WTO comes into focus. The Chinese government's influence over its economy may be so pervasive that the WTO trading rules will prove inadequate to create a "level playing field." Simply put, China retains too many features of the communist system to be easily married with the WTO.

The U.S. Interest

Ultimately, China's membership in the WTO seems clearly to be in the best interest of the United States, China, and the world. Assuming China is enticed to operate its economy within the terms of the WTO, membership would commit China to further economic reform. Such reform is likely to improve the life of the average Chinese citizen, make China a more reliable trading partner, increase trade opportunities, and stimulate economic growth worldwide.

China's membership is not, however, urgently required. Currently, the United States can regulate trade with China through bilateral negotiations and the application of domestic laws. Other countries can and have taken similar steps. For its part, China's trade with the world is already growing at an astounding rate. Over the last 15 years, Chinese exports have grown at three times the world average rate. In short, all parties have alternatives to China's immediate membership, and, even if China is not able to join the WTO for some time, no serious problems will result.

Unfortunately, if China were allowed to enter the WTO without undertaking substantial reforms, the fallout *would* be serious. Under the accession agreement, China has suggested it would make no additional, immediate reforms and would do the minimum required of the world's weakest trading countries in order to join the WTO—while immediately gaining all the benefits of membership.

From the American perspective, the immediate implication of China's entry into the WTO is that the United States would have dramatically less leverage with which to address trade concerns. Currently, the United States can negotiate with China to improve the protection of intellectual property, to enhance market access, or to address other trade problems under threat of imposing sanctions on Chinese exports if the negotiations do not succeed. If China were a WTO member, WTO rules would bar sanctions on Chinese exports unless the WTO ruled in favor of the United States in the matter being disputed. Since China presumably would be bound only to the WTO's minimum standards and would be entitled to special treatment as a developing country, it is unlikely that the WTO would rule in any major country's favor.

The difference between what can be achieved bilaterally and what would be possible under the WTO is dramatic. For example, the bilateral commitments for the protection of intellectual property are in many respects superior to those required by the WTO. Of course, there have been serious problems in convincing China to abide by these bilateral commitments, but it is unlikely that China would be any more enthusiastic about honoring WTO commitments. Bilaterally, the United States has negotiated strong trade reforms that have benefited U.S. trading interests and Chinese economic reforms.

The negative consequences of allowing China to enter the WTO without committing to substantial reform go beyond harming the economic interests of China's trading partners and slowing the pace of reform in China. Another negative consequence is the precedent China's application would establish for other countries seeking WTO membership, including Russia, Saudi Arabia, Taiwan, and Vietnam.

In practice, these applications are not likely to proceed until after disputes over China's application are resolved. As a result, the terms of China's accession are likely to set a powerful precedent for these negotiations. Given the success of Chinese industry in world markets and the strength of the Chinese economy, WTO rules bent or broken to allow China's entry would almost certainly be bent or broken for weaker economies. As

a result, the credibility of the WTO as the policeman of world trade would be severely damaged. The immediate effect would be that many countries would emulate China and refuse to dismantle their trade barriers. After all, if such a major trading country can successfully ignore WTO discipline, certainly smaller countries can keep their trade barriers in place. The longer-term result could be an increase in the already significant political dissatisfaction with the global trading system—in the United States and perhaps elsewhere—which threatens the system itself.

In the past, the trading community allowed a number of countries, notably Japan, to join the world trading system without demanding substantial adherence to its principles. The result was an erosion of the trading system's credibility, which the negotiations that created the WTO aimed to restore. Clearly, allowing countries to enter the world trading system without opening their markets has hurt the system in the past, and allowing China to follow suit risks placing the exception above the rule.

The global trading system is far from perfect. Despite flaws, however, the WTO provides discipline in international trade and has created some order where anarchy would otherwise prevail. Trade liberalization created under the GATT/WTO system has been one of the great engines of global growth in the postwar era, and there is the potential for further progress for decades to come. Weakening or destroying the system as a political favor to China would be an enormous economic and political mistake.

A Transitional Mechanism

The decision on China's accession need not come down to a black-or-white choice of either allowing China's immediate entry into the WTO or permanently blocking its membership. The challenges that must be confronted to integrate China into the WTO are larger than those faced in other accession agreements, such as those with Japan and Mexico. Nonetheless, in the 1960s there was an effort to integrate three non-market economies—Hungary, Poland, and Romania. This experience suggests some possible elements of a transitional arrangement to do the same for China.

A three-part transitional arrangement could be devised for China's WTO accession. First and foremost, China would agree to accept WTO discipline within a fixed period of time. Second, since during the phase-in China would continue to maintain WTO-inconsistent policies, other WTO members would retain the right to unilaterally limit China's exports to their markets, either to prevent a market disruption or to retaliate for China's failure to fulfill its commitments. Finally, to ensure that the Chinese market would continue opening to imports, China would be obligated to increase imports by a fixed percentage each year. A similar approach was used both with Poland and, more recently, as part of the effort to open agricultural markets worldwide. With vigorous oversight and a real effort by China, such an approach could integrate China into the WTO.

It is certainly possible that negotiation of such an arrangement would take years. However, the trade relationship between China and the world has advanced over the last two decades without China's admission to the GATT/WTO. China's exports have grown strongly, its imports have increased, and many trade issues have been dealt with bilaterally. It is also possible that China may decide that it is not prepared to undertake such a negotiation at this time. Far from being a disaster, either outcome is preferable to allowing China to enter the WTO without making meaningful reforms.

Most of the "China hands" who suggest that China be allowed immediate entry into the WTO unfortunately are not "WTO hands," or even "trade hands." The more one understands the cost of such a gesture, the clearer it becomes that it would amount to granting an enormous trade concession in order to achieve ill-defined political benefits. Both the United States and China have compelling interests in developing a stable and mutually beneficial economic, security, and political relationship, and both must work to establish that relationship. Sacrificing a sound economic and trade relationship in the hope of achieving some temporary gains in other areas would be unwise policy. China should become a full-fledged member of the world trading system, but it should do so in a way that strengthens the system instead of undermining it.

POSTSCRIPT

Should China Be Admitted to the World Trade Organization?

There was a great deal of activity between the United States and China over its bid to enter the WTO as a charter member in 1995. The bid failed, and while negotiations continued, the tempo of the diplomacy declined. In 1999 the urgency of negotiations picked up because China is again anxious to join the WTO so that it can participate in the next general round of trade talks that will begin in Seattle, Washington, in 2000. These important talks will almost certainly take several years and will be aimed at further changing the rules of trade and other forms of international interchange.

For this reason, among others, China is pressing once again for membership. For its part, the United States is also feeling pressed to allow China to be admitted. The view of the Clinton administration is that it has an opportunity to use membership to wring trade concessions (justified or not, depending on one's point of view). Moreover, the administration believes that membership in the WTO will give it leverage to insist that China not only agree to but abide by international commercial law and treaties. For China's political and economic changes, see Andrew Nathan, *China's Transition* (Columbia University Press, 1998).

Chinese and American negotiators met in early 1999, and while each side expressed some optimism, each also indicated that many difficult issues remained. U.S. trade representative Charlene Barshefsky noted the progress but said that while China had faced a "pivotal opportunity" to advance its bid to join the WTO, "China's WTO accession can and will only occur on commercially meaningful terms. There is no possibility of a political settlement."

China contends, in the words of its chief trade negotiator, Wu Yi, that it has a "fundamental right" to join the WTO and that "no country should expect China to offer so many concessions to the point that our country's economic stability is being undermined." Echoing the basic argument that China should not be treated as an industrialized nation, Dai Xianglong, head of China's central bank, asserted, "China has made considerable compromises to promote its entry into the World Trade Organization. Some countries are too demanding on this matter." With some justification, Wu also argues that "the WTO will be incomplete without China's participation, and long-term exclusion of China from the organization will not help the improvement and implementation of the world multilateral trade system."

While the thrust of the negotiations have been involved with economic issues, international relations between any two countries are not neatly separable into isolated issues. Therefore, general political relations between Washington and Beijing are a factor. The Clinton administration had succeeded in improving relations with China, but 1999 saw a sharp downturn. Some of this was caused by long-standing issues, such as the mounting U.S. trade deficit with China and its continued suppression of political dissidents. These were joined by new issues. Americans were appalled to find that China successfully managed to steal top secret plans for some of the most modern U.S. nuclear warheads. The Chinese were apoplectic when U.S. warplanes mistakenly (according to Washington) bombed the Chinese embassy in Belgrade, Yugoslavia, during the conflict related to Kosovo. Additional information on Clinton's policy toward China can be found in John Rourke and Richard Clark, "Making U.S. Foreign Policy Toward China in the Clinton Administration," in James M. Scott, ed., *After the End: Making U.S. Foreign Policy in the Post–Cold War World* (Duke University Press, 1998).

For all of this, President Clinton remained optimistic that an agreement should and would soon be reached. According to deputy White House press secretary Jake Siewert, in late May 1999 the president predicted to a group of Democratic senators that he could reach a deal that would allow China's entry into the WTO. In Siewert's words, "Clinton spoke about China and contrary to the conventional wisdom, he thinks we can get this done. He said it is very important and that it would be a great mistake to walk away from a strong deal."

That may be true, but whether or not Washington and Beijing can agree on what a strong deal is remains to be seen. Furthermore, Clinton has to deal with Congress, and it is very skeptical. Senate majority leader Trent Lott has said, "From what I have seen, I don't think you can trust the Chinese to live up to an agreement they would make on trade" in order to enable their entry into the WTO. Lott went on to say, "We should demand that it be a good trade deal for us and, this is more important, that it be enforced." To keep up with the latest on the issue, go to the Web site `http://lateline.muzi.net/topics/China_WTO/index.shtml`.

On the Internet . . .

http://www.dushkin.com

International Development Exchange (IDEX)

This is the Web site of the International Development Exchange (IDEX), an organization that works to build partnerships to overcome economic and social injustice. The IDEX helps people gain greater control over their resources, political structures, and the economic processes that affect their lives. *http://www.idex.org*

United Nations Development Programme (UNDP)

This United Nations Development Programme (UNDP) site offers publications and current information on world poverty, the UNDP's mission statement, information on the UN Development Fund for Women, and more. Be sure to see the "poverty clock." *http://www.undp.org*

U.S. Trade Representative

The Office of the U.S. Trade Representative (USTR) is responsible for developing and coordinating U.S. international trade, commodity, and direct investment policy and leading or directing negotiations with other countries on such matters. The U.S. trade representative is a cabinet member who acts as the principal trade adviser, negotiator, and spokesperson for the president on trade and related investment matters. *http://www.ustr.gov*

U.S. Agency for International Development (USAID)

This is the home page of the U.S. Agency for International Development (USAID), which is the independent government agency that provides economic development and humanitarian assistance to advance U.S. economic and political interests overseas. *http://www.info.usaid.gov*

World Trade Organization (WTO)

The World Trade Organization (WTO) is the only international organization dealing with the global rules of trade between nations. Its main function is to ensure that trade flows as smoothly, predictably and freely as possible. This site provides extensive information about the organization and international trade today. *http://www.wto.org*

International Monetary Fund (IMF)

This Web site of the International Monetary Fund (IMF) offers a highly detailed description of the organization and its activities. *http://www.imf.org*

PART 2

Economic Issues

International economic and trade issues have an immediate and personal effect on individuals in ways that few other international issues do. They influence the jobs we hold and the prices of the products we buy—in short, our lifestyles. In the worldwide competition for resources and markets, tensions arise between allies and adversaries alike. This section examines some of the prevailing economic tensions.

■ Is the Current Trend Toward Global Economic Integration Desirable?

■ Should Multinational Corporations Be Concerned With the Global Public Good?

■ Should the Developed North Increase Aid to the Less Developed South?

ISSUE 5

Is the Current Trend Toward Global Economic Integration Desirable?

YES: Murray Weidenbaum, from "American Isolationism Versus the Global Economy: The Ability to Identify With Change," *Vital Speeches of the Day* (January 15, 1996)

NO: Gregory Albo, from "The World Economy, Market Imperatives and Alternatives," *Monthly Review* (December 1996)

ISSUE SUMMARY

YES: Business professor Murray Weidenbaum argues that the integration of the American economy with the world is both inevitable and desirable.

NO: Professor of political science Gregory Albo maintains that globalization is neither irreversible nor, in its present form, desirable.

One of the important political and economic changes during the twentieth century has been the rapid growth of economic interdependence between countries. The impact of international economics on domestic societies has expanded rapidly as world industrial and financial structures have become increasingly intertwined. Foreign trade wins and loses jobs; Americans depend on petroleum and other imported resources to fuel cars, homes, and industries; inexpensive imports help keep inflation down and the standard of living up; the very shirts on our backs and the televisions we watch were probably made in another country. Global exports grew from $53 billion in 1948 to $6.5 trillion in 1997.

The world's largest trader is the United States, which in 1997 exported $959 billion in goods and services and imported $1.1 trillion in goods and services. Export production that year employed approximately 17.5 million Americans, about one of every eight U.S. workers.

In addition to trade, the trend toward globalization also includes factors such as the growth of multinational corporations (MNCs), the flow of international investment capital, and the increased importance of international exchange rates. There are now at least 40,000 MNCs that conduct business (beyond just sales) in more than one country. Of these, just the 50 largest global corporations in 1997 had assets of $8.8 trillion, produced $2.7 trillion in goods and services, and employed over 8 million workers.

Foreign investment is also immense. Americans alone own over $1.5 trillion in foreign stocks and bonds, and people outside of the United States own over $1.2 billion in U.S. stocks and bonds. Such holdings are often seen as the province of the rich, but, in reality, an ever-increasing number of less wealthy people are involved in overseas investment through their pension plans and mutual funds.

The issue here is whether this economic globalization and integration is a positive or negative trend. For more than 50 years, the United States has been at the center of the drive to open international commerce. The push to reduce trade barriers that occurred during and after World War II was designed to prevent a recurrence of the global economic collapse of the 1930s and the war of the 1940s. Policymakers believed that protectionism had caused the Great Depression; that the ensuing human desperation had provided fertile ground for the rise of dictators who blamed scapegoats for what had occurred and who promised national salvation; and that the spawning of fascism had set off World War II. In sum, policymakers thought that protectionism caused economic depression, which caused dictators, which caused war. Free trade, by contrast, would promote prosperity, democracy, and peace.

Based on these political and economic theories, American policymakers took the lead in establishing a new international economic system. As the world's dominant superpower, the United States played the leading role at the end of World War II in establishing, among other things, the International Monetary Fund (IMF), the World Bank, and the General Agreement on Tariffs and Trade (GATT). The latest GATT revision talks were completed and signed by 124 countries (including the United States) in April 1994. Among the outcomes was the establishment of a new coordinating body, the World Trade Organization (WTO).

The movement during the entire latter half of this century toward economic globalization has been strong, and there have been few influential voices opposing it. Most national leaders, business leaders, and other elites continue to support economic interdependence. The people in various countries have largely followed the path set by their leaders.

More recently, the idea that globalization is either inevitable or necessarily beneficial has come under increasing scrutiny. Some analysts question how widely the benefits are distributed in a society. What is the morality of buying products manufactured by MNCs in countries where businesses are free to pay workers almost nothing, give them no benefits, and perhaps even use child labor? Is there a benefit if MNCs avoid environmental laws by moving to a country with less strict requirements? If global warming is really a threat, does it make any difference whether the industrial emissions come from the United States or Zimbabwe?

Murray Weidenbaum and Gregory Albo take up the issue in the following two selections. Weidenbaum maintains that the world is on the globalization track, which is going in a positive direction. Albo argues that it is wrong to assume that history is on the side of a tired, destructive economic system that values profit over human and ecological needs.

YES

Murray Weidenbaum

AMERICAN ISOLATIONISM VERSUS THE GLOBAL ECONOMY

Delivered to the Fourteenth Annual Monetary and Trade Conference in Philadelphia, Pennsylvania, November 13, 1995

A growing paradox faces the United States. It is the simultaneous rise of a new spirit of isolationism amid the increasing globalization of business and economic activity. Viewed independently, each of the two trends possesses a certain logic. In juxtaposition, however, isolationism amid globalization is simply unachievable. Some explanation may help.

The end of the Cold War brought on a widespread expectation that the United States could safely and substantially cut back its military establishment. The threat from a powerful Soviet Union was a fear of the past. Moreover, government leaders could shift their attention from foreign policy to the host of domestic problems that face the American people. Surely, there is no shortage of urgent national issues to occupy our attention, and they are all inwardly oriented—welfare reform, health care, immigration, environmental cleanup, crime control, deficit reduction, and tax reform. The isolationist tendency is visible and apparent.

But, in a far less dramatic way, it is also becoming clear that the rest of the world is not content with going its separate way. Overseas forces, institutions, and people increasingly affect the workers and managers of America's business and their families. The global marketplace has rapidly shifted from just being a simple minded buzzword to complex reality. International trade is growing far more rapidly than domestic production. That's true all around the globe. It is hardly a matter of a company or an investor deciding to participate or not. The days of agonizing over whether to go global are over. Eight basic points illustrate the changing external environment for public sector and private sector decisionmakers.

1. Americans do not have to do anything or change anything to be part of the global marketplace. Even if a business does not export a thing and has no overseas locations, its owners, managers, and employees are still part of the world economy. The same goes for the many companies and individuals that supply it with goods and services. The issue has been decided by technology. The combination of fax machines, universal telephone service (including cellular), low-cost, high-speed copiers and computers, and speedy jet airline service enables money, goods, services, and people to cross most borders rapidly and often instantly. And that goes especially for what is the most strategic resource—information.

A dramatic example of the ease of business crossing national borders occurred during the Gulf War. On the first day of the Iraqi attack on Kuwait, a savvy Kuwaiti bank manager began faxing his key records to his subsidiary in Bahrain. Every once in a while the shooting got close and transmission was interrupted. By the end of the day, however, all of the key records had been transferred out of Kuwait. The next morning, the bank opened as a Bahraini institution, beyond the reach of the Iraqis—and also not subject to the U.S. freeze on Kuwaiti assets. Literally, a bank was moved from one country to another via a fax machine.

No American business of any consequence remains insulated from foreign producers because of vast distances. Every American is subject to competition from overseas. If that force has not hit a region yet, it probably is on its way.

2. Employees, customers, suppliers, and investors in U.S. companies are increasingly participating in the international economy. That is not just a matter of sales or even earnings originating from for-

eign operations. Increasingly, U.S. firms are establishing factories, warehouses, laboratories, and offices in other countries. As a result, one-half of Xerox's employees work on foreign soil. The pharmaceutical firm Pfizer is exceedingly blunt on this subject:

> Pfizer does not have a choice about whether to manufacture in the EC [European Community] or not.
>
> If we are going to sell to Europe, we have to manufacture there.

Surprisingly large numbers of American companies have already deployed a majority of their assets overseas. Here are a few important examples: Citicorp (51 percent), Bankers Trust (52 percent), Chevron (55 percent), Exxon (56 percent), Digital Equipment (61 percent), Mobil (63 percent), Gillette (66 percent), and Manpower Inc. (72 percent). To underscore the point, a recent Conference Board survey of American manufacturing companies shows that becoming an internationally oriented company usually pays off. Sales by firms with foreign activities grow at twice the rate of those with no foreign operations. Firms with international activities grow faster in every industry —and profits are higher. Geographic diversification is especially important for profitability. Companies with factories in North America, Europe, and the Asian rim outperform companies that stay in one region.

3. The transnational enterprise is on the rise. It is far more than merely a matter of which country to choose to locate a manufacturing or marketing operation. For the dominant companies, the locus of executive decision-making is shifting. "Think global but act local" is not just a slogan. It is a competitive necessity. The larger business firms operating in several regions of the world have been setting up multiple locations for decision-making. For those domestic firms that sell goods or services to other American companies, increasingly their customers are located in one or more decentralized divisions, some of which are now based overseas. That works two ways for Americans. DuPont has shifted the headquarters of its electronic operation to Japan. Germany's Siemens has moved its ultrasound equipment division to the United States.

Moreover, cross-border alliances have become commonplace. It is the rare business of any considerable size that has not entered into some form of cooperative arrangement with one or more companies located overseas—companies that they still often compete against in many markets. The concept of strategic alliances has moved from the classroom to the boardroom. A new set of international business relationships has arisen: joint ventures, production sharing, cross-licensing agreements, technology swaps, and joint research projects.

Increasingly, the successful business looks upon its entire operation in a global context. It hires people, buys inputs, and locates production, marketing, and decision-making centers worldwide. An example helps to convert theory to reality. Here is a shipping label used by an American electronics company:

> Made in one or more of the following countries: Korea, Hong Kong, Malaysia, Singapore, Taiwan, Mauritius, Thailand, Indonesia, Mexico, Philippines. The exact country of origin is unknown.

Any comprehensive and balanced analysis also tells us that not every aspect of the international economy has a positive impact on Americans. Of course,

a similar warning applies to the business environment here at home.

4. *Some overseas markets are more profitable than domestic sales, but high risk and high rewards tend to go together.* The attraction of overseas locations is increasing. Southeast Asia is the faster growing part of the world. Any observant visitor to Hong Kong, Singapore, Malaysia, or Thailand will see that the 8 percent real growth they have been reporting is no statistical mirage. Each of those economies is booming. Mainland China has been experiencing double-digit expansion year after year. Only the most modest slowdown is in sight. Of course, starting off from a small base makes it easier to achieve large percentage gains than is the case for an advanced industrialized country like the United States. But far more than that is involved.

Government policy in each of those countries welcomes foreign investment. With the inevitable exceptions, they encourage the formation of new private enterprises. The contrast with the United States is striking—and ironic. While these present or former communist and totalitarian countries are moving toward capitalism and trying to reduce the role of the public sector, we have been moving in the opposite direction. Despite efforts by the House of Representatives, the United States is still expanding government regulation of business. The result is to make it more difficult and certainly more costly for private enterprise to prosper. Under these circumstances, it is not surprising that so many American companies are doing their expansion overseas.

Take the energy company that explores in faraway Kazakhstan, or the mining enterprise that moves to Bolivia, or the medical devices firm that sets up a laboratory in the Netherlands, or the manufacturing corporation that builds a new factory in Guangdong. To a very considerable extent, these companies are responding to adverse domestic policies as much as to the attractions of overseas markets. The villains of the piece are the government officials in the United States who lock up much of the nation's natural and labor resources in fear that somebody somewhere may make a profit.

Nevertheless, the risks overseas may be great. Over the years, many companies have suffered the expropriation of their foreign assets. You do not have to go farther than Mexico to recall a vivid, although not recent, instance. Iran furnishes a more current and dramatic example. The dangers are not just political. Wars and insurrections are more likely in the regions of the world with less strongly established political institutions. There is no shortage of examples —Croatia, Bosnia, Armenia, Azerbaijan and Chechnya currently make the headlines. Civil wars and large scale violence occurred in recent decades in Indonesia, Malaysia, Thailand, Sri Lanka (Ceylon), and Myanmar (Burma).

Less dramatic but still noteworthy are the difficulties experienced by some Western enterprises in collecting on their debts in China. Moreover, many companies operating in that region report that the special expenses of doing business there make it difficult to convert sales into profits. One large American law firm expects to show its first profit only after six years of doing business on the mainland.

The special risks are numerous. Differences in language, culture, and business practices are pervasive. Our notions of personal honesty are not exactly universal. My purpose is not to scare anyone away from foreign markets, but to emphasize the often painfully close relationship between high profits and high risk. But there is a new positive side to all this.

5. *The rise of the global market place provides vast new opportunity for Americans to diversify their investments and—of course —to broaden business risk.* The last half dozen years provide a cogent example in terms of the global business cycle. At first, the AngloSaxon economies lost momentum. Remember when our friends in continental Europe needled us about the odd phenomenon of an English-speaking recession? That was the time when the economies of the United States, the United Kingdom, Canada, Australia, and New Zealand all were in decline simultaneously.

But, as we were coming out of recession, Japan and most of Western Europe started to experience slowdowns and then downturns in their economies. The American economy has been coming off a cyclical peak and is now slowing down. At the same time, Western Europe has turned the corner and is on an expansion path once again.

In the case of the developing countries, it is hazardous to forecast which one of them will get unglued. There is no certainty that any of them will. But the odds are that at least one of those rapidly growing nations will be derailed from the path of continued progress. Military coups and domestic insurrections do occur. The biggest uncertainties are what will happen to China [now that Deng Xiaoping has died] and how well... the integration of Hong Kong [is going].

6. *The rise of China and Southeast Asia is a new and durable force in the world economy that Americans will have to recognize.* Depending how you measure national economies, China is in the top 10 or top

three, or top two. That is an interesting range of variation.

Even the most experienced Asia experts candidly tell you that they do not know what will happen [in the post-Deng era]. There is already considerable pressure in China to reverse course, to move back to a more authoritarian society with less opportunity for private ownership. China also has a history of internal dissension, of splitting up into several regions each of which is the size of several major Western European countries. So far, the ability of the economic reforms to create tremendous amounts of income and wealth is the best guarantee of their being continued. But, the many misunderstandings between China and the United States constitute a very real dark cloud on the political as well as economic horizon.

The economies of several other countries in Southeast Asia are also growing rapidly at about 8 percent a year, compared to China's 10–12 percent. They seem to be welcoming American and other Western businesses with more enthusiasm than the Chinese.

Malaysia is a good example of a fairly stable nation with a sound economic policy, notably a balanced budget—and an 8 percent overall growth rate. Other opportunities for geographic diversification exist in Thailand, Indonesia, and now the Philippines, whose economy has turned around. To the surprise of some, Vietnam welcomes American businesses as well as tourists.

A decade from now, Southeast Asia will be one of the major economic regions of the globe—along with Japan, North America, and Western Europe. Americans must face the fact that the economies of Southeast Asia are potentially both customers and competitors for our companies. To think of that area as just low-cost labor is misleading. The level of technology is high in Taiwan, Singapore, and Malaysia. The amount of education is also impressive. Intelligent and productive work forces are available in substantial quantities—and they also constitute a substantial and rapidly rising consumer base.

The $1\frac{1}{2}$ billion people in Southeast Asia constitute the major new market area of the world. A noteworthy although not particularly welcome trend is for the nations of Southeast Asia increasingly to trade with each other. That is not surprising when you examine the investment patterns. Who are the major investors in China, Malaysia, Indonesia, Thailand, and Vietnam? The answer is neither the United States nor Western Europe. It is Hong Kong, Taiwan, South Korea, and Japan.

As a result, the major sources of imports into Southeast Asia are Hong Kong, Taiwan, South Korea, and Japan. Likewise, those same four nations are the major markets for Southeast Asia's products. As Southeast Asia continues to grow rapidly, it will be a major challenge to Western businesses to participate in that key market.

7. *Despite the military and political issues that divide Western Europe, the economic unification is continuing full bore.* With a minimum of fanfare, Sweden, Finland, and Austria are entering the European Union. Note the successive changes in terminology as the nations of Western Europe move closer together while increasing their membership. The six-nation European Common Market became the 12-nation European Community. Now we have the 15 member European Union.

As in every major change, there are winners and losers—for Americans as well as for Europeans. With the elimination of internal trade barriers, the stronger European companies can now compete in a continent-wide market. They enjoy considerable economies of scale. American companies well established in Western Europe—such as Ford —are included in that category. The losers are the high-cost European producers who were accustomed to the protections afforded by a restricted national market. The loser category also contains those American producers who have been taken by surprise by the reinvigorated European competition.

Fifteen member nations are not going to be the end of the line for the European Union. The entrance of Austria is a strategic move because Vienna is a major gateway to Eastern Europe. Hungary, Poland, and the Czech Republic are anxious to develop closer economic and business relations with Western Europe.* They can become low-cost suppliers or low-cost competitors—likely both.

Perhaps the most important positive development in that continent in the coming decade will be the new economic strength of the largest member, Germany. It is taking more time than expected to fully consummate the integration of the "new provinces" (neuer Under), as East Germany is now referred to. Any visitor is struck by the substantial amount of physical investment that the national government is making in the East. That is bound to result in a strong and newly competitive region. All in all, we should not forget Europe in our attention to the Orient.

*[Hungary, Poland, and the Czech Republic were invited to join in the North Atlantic Treaty Organization in 1997.—Ed.]

Let us end on an upbeat and realistic note.

8. The American economy is still the strongest in the world and our prospects are impressive. We are not a weak or declining nation in the world marketplace. Legislation and political pressures to "buy local" may be popular, but they fly in the face of economic reality.

Our concern for the losers in the domestic marketplace requires a constructive response; make the United States a more attractive place to hire people and to do business.

After all, in a great many important industries, American firms are still the leaders. U.S. firms rank number one (in sales volume) in 13 major industries— aerospace, apparel, beverages, chemicals, computers, food products, motor vehicles, paper products, petroleum, pharmaceuticals, photographic and scientific equipment, soap and cosmetics, and tobacco.

What about the future? Recall that the first of these eight points began with an illustration of the awesome power of technology. Nobody can forecast which specific technologies will succeed in the coming decade. But the prospects for American companies being in the lead are very bright. There is a special reason for optimism.

Although in the 1990s, America will be benefiting from the upsurge of industrial research and development (R&D) during the 1980s. A key but undramatic crossover occurred in the early 1980s. For the first time in over a half century, the magnitude of company-sponsored R&D exceeded the total of government-financed R&D. That primary reliance on private R&D continues to this day.

Few people appreciate the long-term impact of that strategic crossover. The new and continued dominance of the private sector in the choice of investments in advanced technology makes it more likely that there will be an accelerated flow of new and improved civilian products and production processes in the years ahead. A progression of innovation may be forthcoming comparable to the advent of missiles and space vehicles following the massive growth of military R&D in the 1950s and 1960s. Just consider how the fax machine has altered our customary work practices.

There is a positive macroeconomic aspect to continued technological progress. When the persistent trade deficit of the United States is disaggregated, we find some surprisingly good news: our exports of high-tech products steadily exceed our high-tech imports. We more than hold our own. This country does indeed enjoy a comparative advantage in the production and sales of goods and services that embody large proportions of new technology.

Of course, these are not laurels to rest on. The point is that there is no need to take the low road of economic isolationism—which is protectionism—to deal with foreign competition. We should take the necessary actions, in both the public and private sectors, which make American business and labor more productive and hence more competitive in what is increasingly a globalized marketplace. The ingredients are well known—tax reform, regulatory reform, and a modern labor policy.

Perhaps the most basic development since the end of the Cold War has been missed by all observers and analysts because it is so subtle. During the Cold War, the two military superpowers dominated the world stage. It is currently fashionable to say that in the post–Cold War period, three economic superpowers have taken their place—the United States, Japan, and Germany. That is technically accurate but very misleading.

During the Cold War, government was the pace-setting player on the global stage. Governments made the strategic decisions. Businesses were important, but they were responding to government orders, supplying armaments to the superpowers. In the process, of course, business created substantial economic wealth. But the shift from military to economic competition is fundamental. It means that the business firm is now the key to global economic competition. Governments, to be sure, can help or hinder, and in a major way. But they are supporting players, at best.

The basic initiative in the global marketplace has shifted to private enterprise. Individual entrepreneurs and individual business firms now make the key decisions that will determine the size, composition, and growth of the international economy. That makes for an extremely challenging external environment for the competitive American enterprise of the 1990s. It also requires greater degrees of understanding and forbearance on the part of U.S. public policymakers.

The rapidly growing business-oriented global marketplace is a source of great actual and potential benefit to American entrepreneurs, workers, and consumers. Because the international economy is changing so rapidly, Americans face both threats and opportunities.

Those who identify with the change are likely to be the winners; those who resist will be among the losers.

History tells us that trying to shut ourselves off from these "foreign" influences just does not work. When imperial China tried to do that some 500 years ago, it fairly quickly went from being the world's most advanced and powerful nation to becoming a very poor backwater of the globe.

One thing is certain; it is futile to say, "Stop the world, I want to get off!"

NO

Gregory Albo

THE WORLD ECONOMY, MARKET IMPERATIVES AND ALTERNATIVES

In the crisis after 1974, social democratic governments like Sweden's and technologically ascendant countries such as Germany seemed to be moving in very different directions from other capitalist countries. Today, these divergent economic paths seem to be only alternate routes converging in neoliberalism. The world economy in the 1990s, everyone now seems to agree, accommodates only one model of development: export-oriented production based on flexible labor markets, lower real and social wages, less environmental regulation and freer trade. Neoliberal economic strategies are proposed for conditions as vastly different as those faced by the new ANC government in South Africa, the transitional economies of Eastern Europe, and the new center-Left coalition in Italy.

The Right, of course, has greeted these developments triumphantly. The Left has responded less with triumph than with resignation, but it still accepts them as inevitable. A stalwart American Liberal such as [Secretary of Labor] Robert Reich baldly concludes that "as almost every factor of production... moves effortlessly across borders, the very idea of an American economy is becoming meaningless." Fritz Scharpf, a leading strategist of the German SDP [Social Democratic Party], voices what is often a convention on the Left, that "unlike the situation of the first three postwar decades, there is now no economically plausible Keynesian strategy that would permit the full realization of social democratic goals within a national context without violating the functional imperatives of a capitalist economy. Social democracy must rethink its traditional goals to accommodate the new imperatives. And from outside the traditions of social democracy, [one analyst] despondently reports that "the future belongs to the set of [capitalist] forces that are overtaking the nation-state."

Across a broad political spectrum, then, economic strategies have come to be based on the common premise that "there is no alternative," that "globalization is irreversible," and that economic success depends upon encouraging and enhancing this process. Neoliberals have fostered the movement to

From Gregory Albo, "The World Economy, Market Imperatives and Alternatives," *Monthly Review* (December 1996). Copyright © 1996 by Monthly Review Press. Reprinted by permission of The Monthly Review Foundation. Notes omitted.

freer trade and deregulation of labor markets, arguing that overcoming the constraint of limited markets is the means to increase growth, remedy trade imbalances, and lower unemployment. The state needs to be forced to comply with the "laws" of the market. Social democrats differ from neoliberals only in their belief that there are specific constraints on the market that need to be surmounted—for instance, the constraints imposed by an insufficiently skilled workforce, which can be surmounted by training policies—to allow the harvest of globalization to be reaped.

On empirical grounds alone it is quite clear that the result of policies which advance globalization has been a series of economic failures, particularly increasing trade imbalances and mass unemployment. But the various proposals for correcting these failures and imbalances are deeply flawed not only empirically but also in their theoretical foundations —from neoliberal assumptions about the market, to Keynesian conceptions of market regulation, and social democratic variations on the theme of "shaped advantage." The problems of neoliberal theories are well known after two decades of these policies. The flaws in social democratic proposals have been less widely discussed. I want first to outline the theoretical flaws in the social democratic version of market regulation and then to argue that there are, in fact, alternatives for socialists even in capitalist societies.

The common view that there is no alternative, that we must submit to the market and that the autonomous agency of the state has been diminished, is really based on circular reasoning. It is true only if we begin by accepting the social property and power relations that impose global market imperatives

in the first place. But if we challenge this presumption, there are alternatives even within the existing social relations of power in capitalism.

THE ILLUSION OF SOCIAL DEMOCRACY

Economic processes occur in real historical time, not in the timeless space of neoliberal equilibrium models. These models assume that, for every economic imbalance, there is an immediate correction that will bring the economy back into balance. But in the real world, capitalist techniques and workers wage demands do not change instantly, as soon as there is excess labor supply; and a change in the value of currency does not necessarily bring about greater export demand or cause expenditures to be shifted from exports to domestic industry.

If Left economists generally acknowledge these flaws in the equilibrium model, beyond this very general agreement various stands of the Left part company. For Marxists these market instabilities arise from the inherent contradictions of capitalism, and they can be resolved only by transitional strategies of disengagement from market relations. Social democratic Keynesians on the other hand, believe that the market simply needs to be regulated to remove certain *specific* constraints which present capitalism from reaching the volumes of output associated with full employment.

If economic openness is irreversible and trade expansion is a foundation for prosperity, as the new conventional wisdom insists, social democratic economic policy is left with only one central question: how should national (or regional) competitiveness be created and maintained? Everything else—from macroeconomic policies to strategies for training and welfare—flows from this question.

Since markets are not perfect, social democratic theorists argue that the economy cannot be left to work itself out through free trade: states can and must help "shape advantage" to improve trade balances and competitiveness. New industries, for example, often require protection before they can face import competition. Early entry into the market and increasing economies of scale can "lock in" market share before rivals gain a chance to develop. In this way, the technically superior BETA recorders lost out in the capitalist marketplace to the less capable VHS in the early 1980s.

In the social democratic view, then, it is imperative to have a strategic trade policy to get new products developed and into markets as quickly as possible. Since technological change is a continual process of building up technical skills, capacity, and entrepreneurship, a "technological dynamism" needs to be nourished. Countries that lose technological capacity suffer the economic misfortunes vividly exemplified by Britain's fall in world standing. In this case, every attempt to expand demand, instead of raising domestic output, has simply sucked in imports, and the economy has been forced to slow down in order to avert a balance-of-payments crisis. The result has been a vicious stop-go cycle, and this has discouraged investment, which requires stable growth. As a result, in the absence of new technical capacities, competitiveness has increasingly come to depend upon low cost production. In contrast, stronger competitors can continue to keep investment high in new techniques, thereby enhancing output capacity and competitive advantage.

The social democratic case for an industrial policy of shaped advantage has found particularly strong advocates in the economically declining powers of Britain, Canada, and the United States, as with popular writers like Will Hutton, Jim Laxer, Lester Thurow, and Robert Reich. In their view, a world economy of ever-increasing trade volumes affords ample market opportunities if the industrial successes of Japan, Germany, and Sweden can be replicated (and their failures ignored). Shaped advantage can resolve the problems of external trade imbalances and create a stable capitalism.

There are several competing social democratic positions—though to some extent they complement each other—on how shaped advantage can also resolve the internal imbalances of employment. The "progressive competitiveness" strategy emphasizes the effects of *external* constraints imposed by globalization. In a globalized market, what distinguishes one economy from another is the skills of its labor force and the nature of workplace relations. Training policies should, therefore, be the central component of a jobs and welfare strategy, while relationships of "trust" and co-operation should be fostered within enterprises.

The "shared austerity" strategy stresses the *internal* constraint of distribution relations. Full employment requires severe restraint on workers pay and consumption to keep exports competitive, investment high, and the state budget under control. Incomes policy has a role to play in spreading work through wage restraint and keeping unit labor costs down for exports.

Finally, the "international Keynesian" view maintains that removing constraints on the market simply requires the *political will* to shift expansionary policies from the national to the supranational level, where leakages to exports and capital outflows would be irrelevant. What is needed, according to this view, is international co-ordination of economic policy; and a "cosmopolitan democracy" imposed on global governance structures would legitimate that kind of international co-ordination.

All these variants of social democratic Keynesianism avoid the neoliberal illusion that free trade and deregulation of labor markets will resolve trade and employment imbalances. But they also have in common the conviction that constraints on the market are not general barriers to capital accumulation but just specific problems that can be resolved by judicious policy. This conviction is simply unsustainable for several reasons and cannot be the basis of an economic strategy for socialists.

THE MARKET IN THE REAL WORLD

First, let us consider the problem of "internal" balance, the growing reserve army of the unemployed. Unemployment is regarded as a result of the relation between competitive capacity and the level of demand: the more "competitive" an economy becomes by improving its technical capacities, specifically by means of labor-saving technology, the less labor it needs to meet the same demand. So shaping advantage to improve technical capacity will *create* unemployment, unless there is an increase in total income—and hence an increase in demand—which would create a need for increasing total hours of work; yet unemployment itself tends to reduce total income and hence reduces demand. The strategy of "shaping advantage" to maintain high employment depends on increasing external trade in relation to domestic output, in order to make up for shortfalls in domestic demand by seeking markets elsewhere, so that employment can be created to meet these external demands. And as technological change continues, trade must continue to grow at an accelerating rate to generate a given level of employment and hours of work.

This strategy therefore requires some very delicate maneuvering, but such "knife-edge" balance becomes difficult to maintain when the strategy must be implemented in real historical conditions and in real historical time. Even in a stable world economy it would be quite fanciful to expect it all to work out. In a capitalism that is exhibiting the trade asymmetries and currency instability that exist today, it is quite impossible. Shaped trade advantage is no substitute for national and local employment policies that would constrain the capitalist market to deal with the unemployment crisis.

Second, it is just as unrealistic to assume that shaped advantage can resolve *external* imbalances. Indeed, the reliance on market adjustment may well make matters worse. Countries that succeed in maintaining export-led growth may be able to sustain the necessary balance between technological advance, external demand, and internal growth in employment. But deficit countries will have listless investment and faltering technological capacity. They will be forced to rely on "competitive" wages in order to try to resolve their trade imbalance. The pressures to compete by lowering labor costs are obvious in countries such as Britain and the United States, which have been suffering from structural deficits; but they also have become increasingly visible in cases like Germany and Japan which have enjoyed relatively constant trade surpluses. In Germany, for instance, the relatively "uncompetitive" costs of labor have in recent years been accompanied by unusually high levels of unemployment. In other words, uneven development and trade imbalances can be expected to persist. Countries (or regions) in this kind of competitive world economy must inevitably enter into an ever more intense battle over unit labor costs and employment.

Third, if shaped advantage has drawbacks for individual national economies, there are even greater contradictions in the system as a whole. As Marxists have often insisted, capitalism must be evaluated as a total system, not just by the relative success of some piece of the system which succeeds at the expense of others. Shaped advantage relies on export-led growth. Trading partners must leave their economies open while the country engaging in policies of shaped advantage improves its competitive position. An immediate problem arises: if the country whose market is to be penetrated responds with protectionism or its own shaped advantage policies, any trade and employment gains are wiped out.

If the actions of a single trading partner can create problems for the theory of shaped advantage, a world of many, if not all, countries seeking to shape advantage makes a shambles of social democratic economic policy. It is obvious that not all countries can have successful export-led economic strategies. As all countries cannot run trade surpluses to improve employment: some must incur deficits. Trade imbalances and unemployment will necessarily co-exist. Indeed, this has been the norm for the world economy over the economic history of capitalism. This is, in effect, what happened in the great crisis of the 1930s.

As the strategy of shaped advantage is pursued over time, and more countries are forced to adopt it or face balance-of-payments problems, everyone can be left worse off. Indeed, as trade imbalances persist, there is every incentive for competition over unit labor costs to spread from improving productivity to more general austerity programs, *even* in technologically leading countries. Technological laggards must compete by means of lower wages to reduce unit costs or face a growing trade deficit. Paradoxically, this tends to undermine the foundations on which the successful policies of the *leading* economies are based: lower incomes in other countries deprive successful economies of growing markets, while their capacity to produce more output is increasing because of their technical advances and growing productivity. This means that technological leaders are eventually obliged to follow the losers or they will lose their own surpluses and suffer increased unemployment.

So even technologically advanced countries with an explicit policy of shaping advantage like Japan and Germany begin to feel the sting of "competitive austerity," while peripheral economies such as Ghana and Newfoundland eventually buckle and collapse from the exhaustion of a never-ending competitive spiral. The only possible winners are the fortunate few capitalists in societies which can combine cheap labor with technological capacity so that rates of exploitation can be maintained. But social democrats would concede that Korea and Malaysia are not particularly desirable economic models. For the capitalist system as a whole, therefore, the social democratic strategy of unplanned external trade based on shaped advantage policies is not much better than neoliberal free trade, and equally capable of increasing economic instability.

Fourth, if we add the real world condition of massive capital mobility, the social democratic case for shaped advantage is weakened even further. Shaped advantage requires long-term planning and thus what social democrats call "patient capital." Yet the more global the economy becomes, the greater will be the uncertainty and risk of investment, so financial capital in a global market is increasingly driven by short-term demands for profit and liquid assets as a hedge against risk. Global financial markets therefore pose an obstacle to industrial policy. If there is instability and thus increasing risk and uncertainty, financial capital will be even less willing to be tied to the long-term investments necessary to increase capacity in export industries.

Keynesian economics has always acknowledged that there is a mismatch between the time horizons of financial and industrial capital: where the latter requires long-term investment, the former thrives on short-term profit. Capital mobility and floating exchange rates in a world economy raise this problem to an entirely new level. So the traditional socialist argument that democratizing financial capital is a necessary condition for political alternatives is now more important than ever.

But something more, and different, is needed than the "democratic" structures of international governance advocated by social democrats of the "international Keynesian" variety. These structures would not go to the heart of the problem. They are not, for example, designed to restrict capital mobility. More democratic international institutions of the kind envisaged by international Keynesians would do little more than confer a greater political legitimacy on the existing global economy formed by internationalized capital movements. To do more than that would require giving up the very assumptions on which the social democratic strategy of shaped advantage is based. It would require abandoning the consensus that globalization is irreversible and that the capitalist market is essentially efficient.

Similarly, international Keynesianism must assume that the world market suffers only from a specific, and soluble, problem of adequate demand. Yet stimulating global demand to reduce unused capacity is likely only to compound existing trade imbalances. It will do nothing to clear these imbalances. Neither will it reverse unemployment in economically declining regions such as Atlantic Canada which lack industrial capacity (or whose advantage in natural resources has already been wiped out by the competitive game, as in the Atlantic fishery), nor reverse the cheap labor strategies adopted in, say, Alabama.

Moreover, the capitalist market imperatives of competition prevent the co-operation necessary for international relations. How do you encourage co-operation when it is always possible to achieve better trade balances and rates of employment by cheating—through import restraints, cheap currency, or austerity—before your competitor does? The world can stand only so many Swedens of competitive devaluations, Japans of import controls, or Germanys of austerity shaping advantage to prop up export surpluses and employment.

If economic efficiencies can be achieved by industrial policy, it can only be by means of trade regimes that plan trade and control capital mobility. Social democratic economic policy for national competitiveness through shaped advantage simply rests on the indefensible assumption that globalization is irreversible, that market imperatives require the global economy to be maintained as it is, and that, even if the planet is ravaged by endless economic growth, there is no other way of sustaining employment. These assumptions cannot be the basis of a socialist economic strategy.

THE MYTHS OF GLOBALIZATION

The internationalization of capitalism no doubt accentuates the imperatives of the market and places certain limits on socialist economic policy. Yet the only thing that obliges us to conclude that there is no alternative to international competitiveness is the *a priori* (and unexamined) assumption that existing social property relations—and hence the structural political power sustained by these relations—are sacrosanct.

Even *The Economist* seems to concede this point. This highly respected mouthpiece of neoliberal dogma has said that the "powerless state" in the global economy is simply a "myth" and that governments have "about as many economic powers as they ever had." The notion that the nation-state at one time, before globalization, acted as the center of social power and the regulator of economic activity, and that it is no longer capable of doing so today, is fundamentally misleading. The process of world market formation together with the "international constitutionalism of neoliberalism has taken place through the agency of states."

This does not mean that the imperatives of competition in a world market have not lessened the autonomous agency of individual capitalists or states. The NAFTA [North American Free Trade Agreement], Maastricht, and WTO [World Trade Organization] agreements all have restricted the capacity of nation-states (or regions) to follow their own national (or local) development strategies. It does mean, however, that the limits on state policy are to a significant extent self-imposed. Market imperatives certainly place limits on state policy, but there is no obligation to accept those imperatives. If we are prepared to question the social property and power relations that imposed global market imperatives in the first place, the scope of state action increases and there are indeed alternatives.

Globalization has to be considered not just as an economic regime but as a system of social relations, rooted in the specific capitalist form of social power, which is concentrated in private capital and the nation-state. What globalization basically means is that the market has become increasingly universal as an economic regulator; and as the scope of the market widens, the scope of democratic power narrows: whatever is controlled by the market is not subject to democratic accountability. The more universal the market becomes as an economic regulator, the more democracy is confined to certain purely "formal" rights, at best the right occasionally to elect our rulers; and this right becomes less and less important as the domain of political action is taken over by market imperatives. So the more globalized the economy becomes, the less possible it is for socialists just to tinker with economic policies. The more global the economy, the less possible it is for socialist *economic* policy to avoid *political* contestation over the social property relations of capitalism.

Finding an alternative to globalization, then, is as much a question of democracy in opposition to the imperatives of the market as it is of alternate development models. The alternative to globalization is democracy, not just in the sense of civil liberties or the right to vote but also the capacity to deliberate collectively as social equals about societal organization and production, and to develop self-management in workplaces and communities. Democracy in this sense is both a form of political organization and an alternative to the market as an economic regulator.

The geographic expansion of production prompts, then, challenging questions for socialists about the space and scale of both economic activity and democracy. The replacement of market imperatives by democratic regulation means more than just the "democratization" of institutions like the EC [European Community], NAFTA or even the IMF [International Monetary Fund]. It is quite clear that the "rational interest" of workers, peasants, and ecologists, North and South, entails taking a stand against globalization as it actually exists: globalization is an internationalism only of the capitalist class which is disrupting local communities and environments at a breathtaking pace. Progressives who call for international strategies to remedy the democratic deficits of existing international economic institutions have yet to demonstrate how this could possibly be anything but productivist and socially polarizing if the market itself is untouched.

Indeed, the imperatives of a capitalist market at the global level makes such an outcome inevitable *unless* the spatial expansion of democracy is matched by capital controls which more firmly embed production in national and local economies. How, then, can we plan production or begin a process of transition to democratic organizational forms at the global level?

SOCIALIST ALTERNATIVES: EXPANDING DEMOCRACY, CONTROLLING PRODUCTION

The answer may be a dual, and somewhat paradoxical, strategy: expanding the scale of democracy while reducing the scale of production. Expanding the scale of democracy means changing the governance and policy structures of international agencies and fora, but also of extending the basis for democratic administration and self-management nationally and locally. Let us be clear here. Expanding the scale of democracy in any meaningful sense will entail a challenge to the social property relations of capitalism. To make collective decisions implies some democratic capacity, backed by the coercive sanctions of the state, to direct capital allocation and thus to establish control over the economic surplus. The point is to enhance, with material supports, the capacities of democratic movements (which will vary tremendously according to the class relations and struggles in specific places), at every level, from local organizations to communities up to the nation-state—so as to challenge the power of capital.

Reducing the scale of production means shifting towards more inward-oriented economic strategies, but also forming new economic relations of cooperation and control internationally. The logic of the capitalist market creates a need for large-scale production, an obsession with quantity and size, to which all other considerations—of quality, of social need, and so on—are subordinated. The general objective of socialist policy should be to reduce the scale of production runs as the central economic objective putting other social considerations before quantity and size. Of course the massive material inequalities between nations mean that the general principle of reducing the scale of production will have to vary between developed and developing countries. Certain major industrial sectors necessary to produce adequate levels of welfare will obviously need to be put in place. Scale economies will also be important in some sectors to achieve the most efficient plant size, to reduce inputs and environmentally damaging outputs. But the reduction of scale should remain the general guiding principle, in keeping with the socialist conviction that production should above all meet basic needs, foster self-management capacities, and adopt more labor-intensive techniques when capital-intensive ones, like chemicalized agriculture, have large negative environmental consequences. The present desperate levels of economic insecurity, the volume of contamination and resource use, and degradation of local ecologies in the developed countries have surely made clear that economic growth cannot be equated with human welfare in any simple manner.

This implies that socialist economic policy must take a strong stand in support of those institutional structures at the level of the world economy which favor alternative development models. There is a sound basis for this approach. The postwar period displayed a variety of models of economic development, in the diversity of Fordism in the North, import-substitution industrialization in the South, and the various "socialist ex-periments." Even the attempt to impose a neoliberal homogeneity of development confirms that there is no single economic path: there is now a diversity of disasters across the North, the East, and the South. It is impossible for socialists to put forward alternatives unless it is insisted that there are variable ways of organizing economic and ecological relations, if only we create the political space for them.

The objective of such a solidaristic economic policy can be summed up like this: to maximize the capacity of different national collectivities democratically to choose alternate development paths (socialist or capitalist) that do not impose externalities (such as environmental damage) on other countries, by re-embedding financial capital and production relations from global to national and local economic spaces.

Such an objective would entail, broadly speaking, control of open trade and diversity of inward-oriented economic policies. This strategy obviously does not do away with international fora or the need to democratize them. But democracy at this level would not be just a place where more accountable elected representatives meet to enlarge the space of the market. Instead, the purpose of international bodies would be to constrain capitalist social property relations and widen the space for democratic organizational forms and capacities.

For example, it is quite easy to envision these democratized agencies being mandated to co-ordinate and plan the institutional and material supports for alternate development models, planned trade, control of capital, and enforcement of ecological standards. This cannot be accomplished by some kind of "international civil society" or a "cosmopolitan democracy"—as some currently fashionable and rather vague formulations of the Left suggest. It can only be the result of specific national and local struggles for democratic control of space, solidaristically supported by international movements.

Alternate development equally requires a coherence between tax and welfare policies, collective agreements, the enforcement of environmental regulations and, to the maximum extent possible for ecological reasons, the maintenance of bio-regional zones. Neoliberalism and globalization have seriously damaged the internal coherence of virtually all national and local economies and ecologies. This is the madness in which mono-culture crops for export flourish while peasants starve and the bio-diversity of plant life is lost; national exports of computers attain record volumes but local schools cannot afford them; and long-established cultural institutions lack resources while global advertising budgets flourish.

Socialist economic policy has always been—or ought to have been—redistributive not just in apportioning incomes among social classes but also in sharing out political power, the democratic capacity to direct sustainable economic activity. It is possible here, too, to identify strategies that re-orient institutions and resources against market imperatives. The redistribution of work simply to expand demand will neither absorb the unemployed nor be ecologically sound. A socialist policy should be directed at productivity advances that take the form of reducing work-time, spreading work, and equalizing incomes; a tax regime that will expand democratically controlled and egalitarian services where most job growth will occur; an industrial policy that expands employment on the

basis of increased worker input and quality products; and market-modifying policies that control capital movements and plan capital allocation. The radical reduction of work-time, for example, might enhance ecological health and spread work within the existing power relations of capitalism. But if some of that reduced worktime is allocated to the administrative work of self-management it will also contribute to the long revolution toward socialism.

UTOPIAN CAPITALISM, REALISTIC SOCIALISM

This is a long way from where we are now. The configuration of the world economy that has evolved since the end of the postwar boom remains unstable: the structural asymmetries in the world payments system, the debt burden weighing down governments North and South, the uncertainty of currency markets, the strengthened hand of speculative rentier interests over state policies, and marginalization of large geographic zones form the ruined economic landscape of the 1990s. The policy of restraint adopted by OECD [Organization for Economic Co-operation and Development] governments in the 1970s, in the initial response to the economic crisis, was meant to be only a minor period of correction in a quick return to a high-growth path; and the Volcker-Reagan shocks of the 1980s were supposed to inflict the short-term pain of adjustment in exchange for long-term gains of jobs and income. Now, under governments of varied political stripe, the long-term pain of austerity will only yield more long-term pain of austerity.

The market imperatives in the world economy to compete or join the marginalized—for individuals, companies, state governments and, indeed, nation-states —have not yet led to depression and war like the "beggar-thy-neighbor" policies of the 1930s; that was how the last appearance of an unregulated world market ended. The multilateral trade agreements at least prevent this disaster from unfolding today. Yet the same competitive dynamic is being transferred to the "beggar-thy-working-class" cost-cutting policies that are actively being pursued by virtually all governments.

The imperative of "competitive austerity" leaves the world economy stagnant and, as every quiver of the stock exchange reveals, full of potential for rapid deflation. This imperative is what lies behind the spread of the North American model of development, with its income-splitting, insecure jobs, longer hours of work, and impoverishment of the public sector. It also means that the post-Fordism of the Japanese, Swedish, or German models advocated by social democrats are little more than intellectual phantoms.

In Raymond Williams's novel, *The Fight for Manod*, one of the characters grapples with the question of political alternatives to social decay, and decries the impasse which he presents as a specifically British disease but which today seems universal:

> The whole of public policy is an attempt to reconstitute a culture, a social system, an economic order, that have in fact reached their end, reached their limits of viability. And then I sit here and look at this double inevitability: that this imperial, exporting, divided order is ending, and that all its residual forces, all its political formations, will fight to the end to reconstruct it, to re-establish it, moving deeper all the time through crisis after crisis in an impossible attempt to regain a familiar world. So then a double inevitability: that they will fail, and that they will try nothing else.

In just this way, neoliberal and social democratic economic polices are today utopian in the bad sense of the word: attempting to fashion an unregulated laissez-faire capitalism at the world level on the one hand, or trying to recapture the human side of capitalism of the postwar period on the other. The only alternative that is realistic, in the good sense of the word, is to try something else that begins with the actual social relations of power in capitalism while challenging them from within. History can hardly be on the side of an old tired social order which still imposes the imperatives of the market against all other needs, human and ecological.

POSTSCRIPT

Is the Current Trend Toward Global Economic Integration Desirable?

The latest strengthening of free trade and investment under GATT and the creation of the WTO in 1994 was just one of many significant steps toward globalization in recent years. In the short term, the forces of economic integration carried the day. Regional economic organizations are also rapidly growing. The European Union has expanded and is set to create a single currency. The North American Free Trade Agreement will eventually commingle the American, Canadian, and Mexican economies; by the year 2005 the Free Trade Agreement of the Americas (FTAA) will include virtually all countries in the Western Hemisphere. The Association of Southeast Asian Nations (ASEAN) is adding new members. To explore the various aspects of international economy and business, a good place on the Internet to start is "The WWW Virtual Library: International Affairs Resources" at `http://www.etown.edu/home/selchewa/international_studies/intlbus.htm`.

Now, however, an increasing number of voices are being raised against the trend toward integration. Countries may lose their ability to control their own economies and may even become strategically vulnerable. Japan, for example, worries about being flooded with cheap agricultural imports and losing the ability to feed itself independently. There is also something of a strange alliance between those on the right wing and left wing based on the sovereignty issue. Among Americans, for example, the right wing takes the nationalist view that the United States should not surrender its unilateral decision-making ability to the WTO or any other international organization. The left worries that the United States can no longer restrict the sale of imported products that are produced by child labor, produced in ways that damage the environment, or produced in some other socially unacceptable way.

It is important to avoid being too concerned about the labels of those who favor or oppose free economic exchange. Albo writes against free economic interchange from a socialist perspective, but you should think about his arguments regardless of the perspective he takes. For further investigation, read William Greider, *The Manic Logic of Global Capitalism* (Simon & Schuster, 1997). For another perspective on global integration, read Dani Rodrik, *Has Globalization Gone Too Far?* (Institute for International Economics, 1998).

ISSUE 6

Should Multinational Corporations Be Concerned With the Global Public Good?

YES: Dominic A. Tarantino, from "Principled Business Leadership: Global Business and the Caux Round Table at a Crossroads," *Vital Speeches of the Day* (July 1, 1998)

NO: Manuel Velasquez, from "International Business, Morality and the Common Good," *Business Ethics Quarterly* (January 1992)

ISSUE SUMMARY

YES: Dominic A. Tarantino, former chairman of Price Waterhouse World Firm, Ltd., contends that business leaders should take personal responsibility for the well-being of the entire globe.

NO: Professor of business ethics Manuel Velasquez argues that since there is no way to enforce morality, and since some corporations will not act ethically, then those companies that do so will be disadvantaged and therefore cannot be expected to do so.

Multinational corporations (MNCs) are companies that produce agricultural products, mine, manufacture, conduct banking, insure lives and property, or otherwise operate (beyond just selling products) in more than one country. Today there are about 2,000 large MNCs (those that operate in six or more countries) and over 8,000 smaller MNCs. It is important to stress that these MNCs are both economically and politically powerful because of the vast financial resources they control. In 1997 the world's 500 largest MNCs, the so-called Global 500, had a combined gross corporate product (GCP, or gross revenue) of $21.9 trillion and a profit of $810 billion. They were valued at $12.2 trillion, controlled assets of $35.6 trillion, and employed 84.5 million people. It is hard to overestimate the significance of these numbers. For example, the GCP of the Global 500 accounted for about 61 percent of the world economic production—the combined gross domestic products (GDPs)—of the world's countries. It is also worth noting that control of this vast wealth and economic muscle is not spread evenly around the world. Of the 500 largest MNCs, 93 percent are headquartered in the United States, Western Europe, or Japan. Moreover, all of the top 50 MNCs are located in the industrialized countries; the United States alone has 27 of the top 50.

It is clear, then, that MNCs are important international actors. What is debatable is whether their role is positive or negative and what standards they should follow in their business practices. Supporters contend that MNCs are a natural outgrowth of the expanding and interdependent world economy and that MNCs provide their home countries with important advantages, such as securing new markets and resources and finding new and profitable outlets for investment. MNC supporters also cite advantages for the host countries in which the MNCs operate. The host countries, they say, gain development capital, an infusion of technology, managerial skills, worker training, and jobs. Some even maintain that MNCs further international political cooperation by increasing international contact and economic interdependence.

MNCs also have strong critics. Among other things, they accuse MNCs of exploiting the resources and workers of host countries, of taking out more in profits than they invest, and of engaging in manufacturing practices that harm the environment and endanger the health and social welfare of the citizens of the host country. Another charge is that MNCs promote products that are unsafe.

Globalization has allowed businesses, at least in the industrialized countries, to escape much of the regulation that has been established to protect workers, children, the environment, and others. An American company can, for instance, avoid paying the minimum wage rate in the United States by moving some or most of its operations to a less developed country (LDC), where the daily wage might be equal to the U.S. hourly wage. A British company can avoid restrictions on dumping waste chemicals by moving its operations to an LDC that has less stringent laws. Child labor is not allowed in France, but many French soccer players kick balls made in Asia by children working in awful conditions. Certainly, LDCs could enact more stringent wage, environmental, child labor, and other laws. But many of the LDCs are desperate for economic betterment, and they fear that if they enact stricter laws, the MNC will abandon the country.

It would be wrong to imply that corporations are all run by ruthless people who are willing to exploit children, suppress wages, and pollute in order to maximize profits. But it would be naive to deny that companies, domestic and international, exist to make a profit. The profit motive is what persuades investors to risk their capital and the standard by which corporate executives are judged. The issue, then, is one of balance. When "doing the right thing" either prevents a company from making a profit or substantially reduces that profit, what should a corporate executive do?

In the first of the following selections, Dominic A. Tarantino answers this question by contending that business must take the lead to identify and promote solutions of the world's economic, social, and environmental problems. In the second selection, Manuel Velasquez contends that in the intense competitive economic world, corporations that attempt to operate in the public interest will be disadvantaged.

YES

Dominic A. Tarantino

PRINCIPLED BUSINESS LEADERSHIP

Delivered to the Keidanran Subcommittee on the Charter for Good Corporate Behavior, Tokyo, Japan, March 4, 1998

Let me begin by asking... a question. Recently, scandals have plagued the financial giants of Japan. Global organizations and foreign investors wanting to do business in Japan are asking:

Why do companies in Japan pay the "sokaiya" [payoffs]?

Clearly this question is at the heart of the issue widely reported in the media, focusing attention on several leading financial service industry enterprises. I use payments to the "sokaiya" only to highlight the contrast between the business ethics that shaped Japan's financial world during the post-war era, and the demands of the era of financial globalization. The global financial marketplace operates on the basis of transparency and disclosure. Consequently, Japanese businesses cannot be surprised when international investors demand to know why so called antisocial forces seem to have such a hold on these important Japanese companies. The efforts of the Keidanren with its Charter for Good Corporate Behavior and its members' efforts to make the spirit of the Charter their criterion for corporate behavior should have a salutary effect.

Nevertheless, the question hanging over Tokyo, as it prepares for Big Bang deregulation, is whether Japan can now adapt to the new demands of business globalization.

I believe the answer to this question is yes. In fact, Japanese businesses have no real choice. More importantly, because Japan is a financial superpower in Asia, it will need to drive similar changes in the way business is done throughout the region.

How is business done throughout the region? The perception is that business is done in a secretive manner, and that the lack of adequate disclosure was a major cause for the "Asian meltdown" that sent stocks plunging all over the world. To be fair, reality may in some ways differ from perception. But in the accounting profession, we follow the rule that perception is reality as far as shareholders and other stakeholders are concerned.

As a result of the economic crisis, some Asian countries and their businesses are being subjected to what they consider unwarranted outside interference in their affairs. The International Monetary Fund is imposing conditions on bailout packages, and international bodies are calling for an end to unacceptable business practices.

Do these demands really constitute unwarranted interference? So long as they are fair and reasonable, they do not. They are the quid pro quo for tapping global capital markets, global consumer markets, and global labor markets. When one country's financial crisis is every country's financial crisis, national boundaries become irrelevant.

I am not speaking as a Westerner, preaching redemption to the East. Western companies have had to learn this same lesson. We have not been especially good pupils. We have supported open trade and investment policies when they suited us, and pressured our governments to invoke national sovereignty when they did not. We have done our share to perpetuate corrupt practices in other countries by acquiescing to them. We have behaved irresponsibly towards the environment. Our record on labor practice is far from spotless. Publicly owned corporations have not always been responsive to demands for increased financial disclosure.

But I believe that businesses around the world are beginning to recognize the full implications of globalization. I also believe that business, rather than government, must accept primary responsibility for addressing those implications.

Let me quote from the Caux Round Table [(CRT) on principled business leadership] Position Paper.

"Global business stands at the crossroads of the fundamental changes taking place in the world. The CRT believes that business has a crucial role in helping to identify and promote solutions to issues that indeed the development of a society that is more prosperous, sustainable and equitable."

I agree 100 percent.

The paper goes on to say that "Corporations cannot act alone but should seek to address key societal issues through cooperative efforts with governments, other institutions and local communities."

I also endorse a cooperative effort. But I strongly believe that business must lead this effort. Governments still place national agendas above global interests. Local communities often fail to see the strong link between global prosperity and their own prosperity. Many other institutions pursue one goal to the exclusion of others. Preserving the environment. Protecting worker rights. Ending corruption.

One business that has taken such a lead is 3M. The company's commitment to strong environmental policies is based on the belief that such policies make sense for social, environmental and business reasons. For example, by decreasing its use of solvents, 3M not only reduces its air emissions; it also improves its responsiveness and cuts costs. You might wonder how? The answer: less solvents used result in less regulatory oversight and approval. 3M's strategy is based on a straightforward premise: stop pollution at the source to avoid the expense and effort of cleaning it up or treating it after the fact.

As an article I read recently put it, business ethics comes down to personal responsibility and critical mass. We need plenty of both. Global business ethics is no longer just a matter of playing by the rules. It's matter of making the rules to ensure that the global economy reaches its full potential and everyone gets a piece of the pie or sushi as the case may be. Enough business leaders must take personal responsibility to create the critical mass to get this job done.

The Caux Principles call on business to make the rules, to be an agent of positive social change. The principles must have struck a responsive chord, because they are now the most widely-accepted code of business standards in the world. And I don't need to remind anyone... of the important role Japanese business and Japanese principles played in the development of the CRT standards.

The Caux principles are a significant achievement. But this achievement poses its own challenge. Principles become meaningless if they do not lead to action. The time has come to act on the Caux principles.

Carl Bro is a consultancy firm based in Denmark. In 1996, a new generation of management and co-owners took over the company. As part of this change, the new management team set out to define the company's mission, vision and values. Behind the quest for a company philosophy was the belief that "consultants should take a holistic view of their role in society." However, the question they asked themselves was: "Is it reasonable for a (relatively) small company to involve itself with global social responsibility and try to tackle issues such as corruption?" Carl Bro's management group used a business principles document drawn up by business people to reach agreement on a mission, vision and values statement for their firm. The business principles document Carl Bro's man-

agement used as a basis for developing their own global view, was none other than the CRT Principles for Business.

In the global environment, ethical activism is not always greeted with open arms. We have all heard objections to moral absolutism and defenses of cultural relativism. But there are certain moral absolutes that cut across all cultures. Respect for human dignity. Freedom from pain, want, suffering and oppression. Integrity. Honor. Compassion. Generosity. These are just a few of the basic values that define a civilized society. You may encounter different interpretations and applications of these values in different cultures. But, you won't encounter disagreements about their desirability.

Experts in the field of global business ethics believe "when you dig deeply enough and scrape away all the trappings, the real ethical solid building blocks or principles of most cultures are the same."

There's also the school of thought that says the business of business is to make a profit for the shareholders. Leave ethics to philosophers and the clergy. That view fails to recognize that business cannot flourish in the midst of poverty, ignorance, disorder, disease, oppression, and lawlessness. I think former Dayton Hudson CEO, William Andres, summed it up perfectly when he said "A stable, healthy community is not just good for the bottom line. It is the bottom line."

Or put another way, as James W. Rouse, founder of The Rouse Company said "Profit is not the legitimate purpose of business. Its purpose is to provide a service needed by society. If this is done efficiently, companies will be profitable."

Clearly, these men felt there is no tension between responsible behavior and business success. Companies that effectively exercise their social responsibility, in fact, maximize their stake holder value in the long term.

Global scandals make headlines daily. Many of the recent incidents have one thing in common: they're a matter of ethics—or a lack thereof. To combat this, many global businesses are creating codes of conduct, like the ones such companies as IBM, Xerox and Shell Oil have had for years. These three companies, and others, including Levi Strauss, Honeywell, Digital Equipment, Siemens, Nortel, IIT Corporation, Matsushita Electric, and Canon are taking their efforts further—by incorporating their messages into everyday business practices and making them living documents with global applicability.

Defining ethical behavior in a domestic setting is tricky enough. Not only do people respond differently to moral questions, but individuals interpret morality differently. Some even say the term "global ethics" is an oxymoron. Is it?

BT's chairman, Sir Lain Vallance says it well, "a good reputation is a real asset for a business; it can improve a company's competitiveness, with all the advantages that can bring." He says, "so it is not for altruistic motives alone that we have been active in these areas. It makes sound business sense."

Pricing, products and services are no longer the sole arbiters of commercial success.

Many companies are now developing credos, brief statements of their corporate philosophies, and articulating basic company values, including ethical values. Lucent Technologies uses its corporate values statement as a guide for responsible decision making. One of Lucent Technologies' values is "A strong sense of social responsibility."

Is corporate social responsibility catching on? I believe it is. More and more mutual-fund companies are offering what they call "socially responsible" investments. Cash coming in to socially responsible funds is growing—slowly, but growing nonetheless. I recently learned of an index called the Domini 400 Social Index created by a U.S. company called Kinder, Lydenberg, Domini and Co. The index reflects the behavior of a portfolio of stocks in companies that meet socially responsible criteria. The index has outperformed the S&P 500 on a total return basis and on a risk-adjusted basis since its inception in May 1990! For those of you who are interested in learning more about this index, you can do so by visiting their website.

So, is a broader corporate responsibility agenda catching on? Avon Cosmetics, Toys R Us, Eileen Fisher—a small upscale clothier, and the world's biggest mail order company, based in Germany, called Otto-Versand, are the first signatories to Social Accountability 8000—the first ever universal standard for ethical sourcing. SA8000 is an initiative of the Council On Economic Priorities, a New York based research organization. It provides a common framework for ethical sourcing for companies of any size and any type, anywhere in the world. SA8000 sets out provisions for issues such as trade union rights, the use of child labor, working hours, health and safety at work, and fair pay.

This initiative builds on the earlier efforts of Levi Strauss, Nike, and other leading companies who developed global sourcing and operating guidelines to select business partners who will manufacture their products.

Now global companies can request SA8000 certification for themselves and their suppliers from around the world by using a common framework. I am excited to see that an increasing number of global companies are recognizing the value to the bottom line by taking a lead on issues of ethical sourcing.

So what is our mission? Our mission is to create a stable, healthy global community out of an untamed global frontier. Perhaps I should say frontiers. Each emerging market is a new frontier. And cyberspace is the wildest frontier of all. Should we accept this mission? Enlightened self-interest dictates that we do not have a choice. In the western United States there are many abandoned towns that flourished when gold and silver were discovered, and then died when the mines were depleted. The people who made their fortunes in these frontier towns took their money and ran rather than using their new found wealth to expand the boundaries of civilized society.

Global businesses cannot abandon the global frontier. It's all around us. It's sitting in our laps or perhaps I should say, in our laptops. We are no longer insulated by distance. What happens on another continent or in another country is as important as what happens next door. We see this very clearly today.

Business will have to cross some frontiers of its own in order to successfully complete its mission.

We will have to think in radically different terms. Some call it "thinking out of the box." I see it as thinking beyond boundaries—national, cultural and corporate boundaries, the boundaries between the public and private sectors, and the boundaries of "It's never been tried" and "It can't be done."

Frontier-style thinking will be needed to address four challenges:

- Establish "rule of law" in emerging markets;
- End business bribery;
- Police cyberspace; and
- Confront the have/have not dilemma.

Of these four challenges,... I will elaborate on only one—ending business bribery.

Business bribery is bad for the givers, bad for the receivers, and bad for the global economy. It tilts the level playing field, institutionalizes corruption, and takes billions of dollars out of productive use. It transforms market access into a question of who can pay the most. It can mire developing countries in debt by encouraging huge expenditures on unnecessary procurements. Even grease payments are a bad idea because they perpetuate the red tape and bureaucratic fiefdoms that give rise to them in the first place.

Good steps to combat business bribery are being taken under the auspices of the OECD [Organization for Economic Cooperation and Development], the World Bank, the OAS [Organization of American States], the European Community, and various international business and professional organizations, like Transparency International. Progress will likely be slow and inconsistent. Citizens in many developing countries are finally beginning to recognize the costs and consequences of this institutionalized corruption. But it is deeply entrenched.

Business itself must accept a share of the blame. To quote some remarks I read about another Asian country where the economic boom has been replaced by an economic crisis, "Too often foreigners arrive . . . to do business with expectations that the country is corrupt, even before they've seen the way things are done here. They come here already planning to pay bribes."

Business leaders can increase the momentum of change. They can take personal responsibility and "just say no" to business bribes. That includes "just saying no" both in their own countries and abroad. Most countries do not yet outlaw foreign bribery. On the other hand, even countries where bribery is rampant have laws against it. One way or another, business bribes are illegal in just about every country. Global companies cannot preach rule of law in emerging markets and simultaneously ignore laws which they regard as inconvenient.

As you have heard, I believe it is business that must take the lead in taming the global frontier. Business must take the lead in establishing the rule of law in emerging markets. Business must take the lead in stopping bribery. Business must take the lead in bringing order to cyberspace. Business must take the lead in ensuring that technology does not split the world into haves and have nots.

But global business is conspicuously absent from the roster of non-governmental organizations [NGOs] that take the lead in filling the leadership void left by the public sector. Yet, if you took the combined resources of only the multinational companies in the Caux Round Table, you would dwarf the resources and clout of even the largest and best financed non-business NGOs. It's true that individual companies and groups of companies are attacking global problems, but the approach has been largely ad hoc and random. Training is provided here, development assistance there.

A "superbusiness" NGO composed of large global companies could set the priorities, develop the plans, and marshall the resources required to address global challenges systematically. It could act in alliance with national governments and multigovernmental organizations, national and international business groups, international funding agencies, and other NGOs. But, as I emphasized at the beginning . . . , the business NGO should not regard action by any of these groups as a prerequisite for taking action itself. Nor should it depend on achieving consensus among these groups. That would simply leave us where we are now—bogged down in endless negotiations to achieve watered-down solutions to problems that grew more serious while we were talking.

So, I would say:

Business must:

- Develop a coherent strategy for addressing global problems,
- Establish a constructive business network embracing its principal world centers,
- Develop a dialogue with relevant public institutions,
- Mount and fund agreed initiatives and action programs, and finally.
- Monitor progress and outcomes.

It all comes back to personal responsibility. The business leaders represented in the Caux Roundtable are no strangers to taking personal responsibility for the economic success of their companies and the well-being of their stakeholders and their communities. They just have to enlarge their stakeholder population and expand their concept of community to include the entire globe.

NO
Manuel Velasquez

INTERNATIONAL BUSINESS, MORALITY AND THE COMMON GOOD

During the last few years an increasing number of voices have urged that we pay more attention to ethics in international business, on the grounds that not only are all large corporations now internationally structured and thus engaging in international transactions, but that even the smallest domestic firm is increasingly buffeted by the pressures of international competition....

Can we say that businesses operating in a competitive international environment have any moral obligations to contribute to the international common good, particularly in light of realist objections? Unfortunately, my answer to this question will be in the negative....

INTERNATIONAL BUSINESS

... When speaking of international business, I have in mind a particular kind of organization: the multinational corporation. Multinational corporations have a number of well known features, but let me briefly summarize a few of them. First, multinational corporations are businesses and as such they are organized primarily to increase their profits within a competitive environment. Virtually all of the activities of a multinational corporation can be explained as more or less rational attempts to achieve this dominant end. Secondly, multinational corporations are bureaucratic organizations. The implication of this is that the identity, the fundamental structure, and the dominant objectives of the corporation endure while the many individual human beings who fill the various offices and positions within the corporation come and go. As a consequence, the particular values and aspirations of individual members of the corporation have a relatively minimal and transitory impact on the organization as a whole. Thirdly, and most characteristically, multinational corporations operate in several nations. This has several implications. First, because the multinational is not confined to a single nation, it can easily escape the reach of the laws of any particular nation by simply moving its resources or operations out of one nation and transferring them to another nation. Second, because the multinational is not confined to a single nation,

From Manuel Velasquez, "International Business, Morality and the Common Good," *Business Ethics Quarterly* (January 1992). Copyright © 1992 by Manuel Velasquez. Reprinted by permission of *Business Ethics Quarterly*. Notes omitted.

its interests are not aligned with the interests of any single nation. The ability of the multinational to achieve its profit objectives does not depend upon the ability of any particular nation to achieve its own domestic objectives....

THE TRADITIONAL REALIST OBJECTION IN HOBBES

The realist objection, of course, is the standard objection to the view that agents —whether corporations, governments, or individuals—have moral obligations on the international level. Generally, the realist holds that it is a mistake to apply moral concepts to international activities: morality has no place in international affairs. The classical statement of this view, which I am calling the "traditional" version of realism, is generally attributed to Thomas Hobbes....

In its Hobbsian form, as traditionally interpreted, the realist objection holds that moral concepts have no meaning in the absence of an agency powerful enough to guarantee that other agents generally adhere to the tenets of morality. Hobbes held, first, that in the absence of a sovereign power capable of forcing men to behave civilly with each other, men are in "the state of nature," a state he characterizes as a "war...of every man, against every man." Secondly, Hobbes claimed, in such a state of war, moral concepts have no meaning:

> To this war of every man against every man, this also is consequent; that nothing can be unjust. The notions of right and wrong, justice and injustice have there no place. Where there is no common power, there is no law: where no law, no injustice.

Moral concepts are meaningless, then, when applied to state of nature situations. And, Hobbes held, the international arena is a state of nature, since there is no international sovereign that can force agents to adhere to the tenets of morality.

The Hobbsian objection to talking about morality in international affairs, then, is based on two premises: (1) an ethical premise about the applicability of moral terms and (2) an apparently empirical premise about how agents behave under certain conditions. The ethical premise, at least in its Hobbsian form, holds that there is a connection between the meaningfulness of moral terms and the extent to which agents adhere to the tenets of morality: If in a given situation agents do not adhere to the tenets of morality, then in that situation moral terms have no meaning. The apparently empirical premise holds that in the absence of a sovereign, agents will not adhere to the tenets of morality: they will be in a state of war. This appears to be an empirical generalization about the extent to which agents adhere to the tenets of morality in the absence of a third-party enforcer. Taken together, the two premises imply that in situations that lack a sovereign authority, such as one finds in many international exchanges, moral terms have no meaning and so moral obligations are nonexistent....

REVISING THE REALIST OBJECTION: THE FIRST PREMISE

... The neo-Hobbsian or realist... might want to propose this premise: When one is in a situation in which others do not adhere to certain tenets of morality, and when adhering to those tenets of morality will put one at a significant competitive disadvantage, then it is not immoral for one to like-wise fail to adhere to them. The realist might want to argue for this claim, first, by pointing out that in a world in which all are competing to secure significant benefits and avoid significant costs, and in which others do not adhere to the ordinary tenets of morality, one risks significant harm to one's interests if one continues to adhere to those tenets of morality. But no one can be morally required to take on major risks of harm to oneself. Consequently, in a competitive world in which others disregard moral constraints and take any means to advance their self-interests, no one can be morally required to take on major risks of injury by adopting the restraints of ordinary morality.

A second argument the realist might want to advance would go as follows. When one is in a situation in which others do not adhere to the ordinary tenets of morality, one is under heavy competitive pressures to do the same. And, when one is under such pressures, one cannot be blamed—i.e., one is excused—for also failing to adhere to the ordinary tenets of morality. One is excused because heavy pressures take away one's ability to control oneself, and thereby diminish one's moral culpability.

Yet a third argument advanced by the realist might go as follows. When one is in a situation in which others do not adhere to the ordinary tenets of morality it is not fair to require one to continue to adhere to those tenets, especially if doing so puts one at a significant competitive disadvantage. It is not fair because then one is laying a burden on one party that the other parties refuse to carry.

Thus, there are a number of arguments that can be given in defense of the revised Hobbsian ethical premise that when others do not adhere to the tenets of morality, it is not immoral for one to do likewise....

REVISING THE REALIST OBJECTION: THE SECOND PREMISE

Let us turn, to the other premise in the Hobbsian argument, the assertion that in the absence of a sovereign, agents will be in a state of war. As I mentioned, this is an apparently empirical claim about the extent to which agents will adhere to the tenets of morality in the absence of a third-party enforcer.

Hobbes gives a little bit of empirical evidence for this claim. He cites several examples of situations in which there is no third party to enforce civility and where, as a result, individuals are in a "state of war." Generalizing from these few examples, he reaches the conclusion that in the absence of a third-party enforcer, agents will always be in a "condition of war."...

Recently, the Hobbsian claim... has been defended on the basis of some of the theoretical claims of game theory, particularly of the prisoner's dilemma. Hobbes' state of nature, the defense goes, is an instance of a prisoner's dilemma, and *rational* agents in a Prisoner's Dilemma necessarily would choose not to adhere to a set of moral norms....

A Prisoner's Dilemma is a situation involving at least two individuals. Each individual is faced with two choices: he can cooperate with the other individual or he can choose not to cooperate. If he cooperates and the other individual also cooperates, then he gets a certain payoff. If, however, he chooses not to cooperate, while the other individual trustingly cooperates, the noncooperator gets a larger payoff while the cooperator suffers a loss. And if both choose not to cooperate, then both get nothing.

It is a commonplace now that in a Prisoner's Dilemma situation, the most rational strategy for a participant is to choose not to cooperate. For the other party will either cooperate or not cooperate. If the other party cooperates, then it is better for one not to cooperate and thereby get the larger payoff. On the other hand, if the other party does not cooperate, then it is also better for one not to cooperate and thereby avoid a loss. In either case, it is better for one to not cooperate.

... In Hobbes' state of nature each individual must choose either to cooperate with others by adhering to the rules of morality (like the rule against theft), or to not cooperate by disregarding the rules of morality and attempting to take advantage of those who are adhering to the rules (e.g., by stealing from them). In such a situation it is more rational ... to choose not to cooperate. For the other party will either cooperate or not cooperate. If the other party does not cooperate, then one puts oneself at a competitive disadvantage if one adheres to morality while the other party does not. On the other hand, if the other party chooses to cooperate, then one can take advantage of the other party by breaking the rules of morality at his expense. In either case, it is moral rational to not cooperate.

Thus, the realist can argue that in a state of nature, where there is no one to enforce compliance with the rules of morality, it is more rational from the individual's point of view to choose not to comply with morality than to choose to comply. Assuming—and this is obviously a critical assumption—that agents behave rationally, then we can conclude that agents in a state of nature

will choose not to comply with the tenets of ordinary morality....

Can we claim that it is clear that multinationals have a moral obligation to pursue the global common good in spite of the objections of the realist?

I do not believe that this claim can be made. We can conclude from the discussion of the realist objection that the Hobbsian claim about the pervasiveness of amorality in the international sphere is false when (1) interactions among international agents are repetitive in such a way that agents can retaliate against those who fail to cooperate, and (2) agents can determine the trustworthiness of other international agents.

But unfortunately, multinational activities often take place in a highly competitive arena in which these two conditions do not obtain. Moreover, these conditions are noticeably absent in the arena of activities that concern the global common good.

First, as I have noted, the common good consists of goods that are indivisible and accessible to all. This means that such goods are susceptible to the free rider problems. Everyone has access to such goods whether or not they do their part in maintaining such goods, so everyone is tempted to free ride on the generosity of others. Now governments can force domestic companies to do their part to maintain the national common good. Indeed, it is one of the functions of government to solve the free rider problem by forcing all to contribute to the domestic common good to which all have access. Moreover, all companies have to interact repeatedly with their host governments, and this leads them to adopt a cooperative stance toward their host government's objective of achieving the domestic common good.

But it is not clear that governments can or will do anything effective to force multinationals to do their part to maintain the global common good. For the governments of individual nations can themselves be free riders, and can join forces with willing multinationals seeking competitive advantages over others. Let me suggest an example. It is clear that a livable global environment is part of the global common good, and it is clear that the manufacture and use of chlorofluorocarbons is destroying that good. Some nations have responded by requiring their domestic companies to cease manufacturing or using chlorofluorocarbons. But other nations have refused to do the same, since they will share in any benefits that accrue from the restraint others practice, and they can also reap the benefits of continuing to manufacture and use chlorofluorocarbons. Less developed nations, in particular, have advanced the position that since their development depends heavily on exploiting the industrial benefits of chlorofluorocarbons, they cannot afford to curtail their use of these substances. Given this situation, it is open to multinationals to shift their operations to those countries that continue to allow the manufacture and use of chlorofluorocarbons. For multinationals, too, will reason that they will share in any benefits that accrue from the restraint others practice, and that they can meanwhile reap the profits of continuing to manufacture and use chlorofluorocarbons in a world where other companies are forced to use more expensive technologies. Moreover, those nations that practice restraint cannot force all such multinationals to discontinue the manufacture or use of chlorofluorocarbons because many multinationals can escape the reach of their laws. An exactly parallel,

but perhaps even more compelling, set of considerations can be advanced to show that at least some multinationals will join forces with some developing countries to circumvent any global efforts made to control the global warming trends (the so-called "greenhouse effect") caused by the heavy use of fossil fuels.

The realist will conclude, of course, that in such situations, at least some multinationals will seek to gain competitive advantages by failing to contribute to the global common good (such as the good of a hospitable global environment). For multinationals and rational agents, i.e., agents bureaucratically structured to take rational means toward achieving their dominant end of increasing their profits. And in a competitive environment, contributing to the common good while others do not, will fail to achieve this dominant end. Joining this conclusion to the ethical premise that when others do not adhere to the requirements of morality it is not immoral for one to do likewise, the realist can conclude that multinationals are not morally obligated to contribute to such global common goods (such as environmental goods).

Moreover, global common goods often create interactions that are not iterated. This is particularly the case where the global environment is concerned. As I have already noted, preservation of a favorable global climate is clearly part of the global common good. Now the failure of the global climate will be a one-time affair. The breakdown of the ozone layer, for example, will happen once, with catastrophic consequences for us all; and the heating up of the global climate as a result of the infusion of carbon dioxide will happen once, with catastrophic consequences for us all. Because these environmental disasters are a one-time affair, they represent a non-iterated prisoner's dilemma for multinationals. It is irrational from an individual point of view for a multinational to choose to refrain from polluting the environment in such cases. Either others will refrain, and then one can enjoy the benefits of their refraining; or others will not refrain, and then it will be better to have also not refrained since refraining would have made little difference and would have entailed heavy losses.

Finally, we must also note that although natural persons may signal their reliability to other natural persons, it is not at all obvious that multinationals can do the same. As noted above, multinationals are bureaucratic organizations whose members are continually changing and shifting. The natural persons who make up an organization can signal their reliability to others, but such persons are soon replaced by others, and they in turn are replaced by others. What endures is each organization's single-minded pursuit of increasing its profits in a competitive environment. And an enduring commitment to the pursuit of profit in a competitive environment is not a signal of an enduring commitment to morality.

POSTSCRIPT

Should Multinational Corporations Be Concerned With the Global Public Good?

The growth and impact of MNCs have occasioned increasing international concern with the standards by which they operate. Realistically, given the growth of the world economy and the trend toward economic concentration, it is extremely unlikely that MNCs will be broken up. It is also somewhat unrealistic to expect capitalist corporations not to do what they are created for: to seek profits by expanding old markets and promoting new ones. They are not social welfare agencies. For more about MNCs and the international political economy (IPE), see Leon Gruenberg, "The IPE of Multinational Corporations," in David N. Balaam and Michael Veseth, eds., *Introduction to International Political Economy* (Prentice Hall, 1996). A Web site that is a joint project of the Interhemispheric Resource Center and the Institute for Policy Studies and that focuses on MNCs and their control can be found at http://www.foreignpolicy-infocus.org/briefs/vol1/TNCS.html.

The question, therefore, is how to manage MNCs. Home countries find such management difficult because MNCs operate in part outside their home countries' legal boundaries. Also, the MNC is an important economic asset to its home country. In the world's mightiest economy, the United States, foreign MNCs employ 4.9 million people, or about 4 percent of the U.S. workforce. The presence of MNCs in most LDCs is much more substantial, and the departure of one or more large MNCs might devastate an LDC's economy. The power of MNCs is discussed in Richard J. Barnet and John Cavanagh, *Global Dreams: Imperial Corporations and the New World Order* (Institute for Policy Studies, 1994).

Self-regulation is one answer to the question of how MNCs should be managed. This approach, advocated by Tarantino, would require companies to take the lead in regulating themselves so that they operate in a socially and environmentally sustainable way. Tarantino maintains that business, not government, should take the primary responsibility. To learn more about one business-based organization that is promoting responsible business behavior, see the home page of the International Business Ethics Institute at http://www.business-ethics.org/index.htm.

Most analysts do not believe that business can or will regulate itself satisfactorily. An ideal answer, of course, would be international regulation that harnesses the capital, technical, and training potential of MNCs while curbing abuses and limiting the LDCs' self-destructive competition for MNC investment. To this end, the UN has established the Center on Transnational Corporations, and the industrialized nations' Organization for Economic Co-operation and Development (OECD) has set up a Committee on International Investment and Multinational Enterprises to monitor MNCs and to suggest regulations. Velasquez does not address this, but international regulation would solve the problem of companies that do try to regulate themselves being at a competitive disadvantage with companies that do not consider the public good in their operations. The problem is that organizations such as the UN and the OECD do not have the authority to establish meaningful regulations and, so far, efforts through these organizations have been slow.

ISSUE 7

Should the Developed North Increase Aid to the Less Developed South?

YES: James P. Grant, from "Jumpstarting Development," *Foreign Policy* (Summer 1993)

NO: Editors of *The Economist*, from "The Kindness of Strangers," *The Economist* (May 7, 1994)

ISSUE SUMMARY

YES: James P. Grant, executive director of the United Nations Children's Fund (UNICEF), contends that many world problems stem from the impoverished conditions found throughout much of the world and that one way to jumpstart solutions to these problems is to extend more assistance to the poor countries.

NO: The editors of the *Economist*, a well-known British publication, suggest that the way that aid is typically given and spent makes it a waste of resources and may even have a negative impact on the recipients.

One stark characteristic of the world system is that it is divided into two economic classes of countries. There is the North, which is industrialized and relatively prosperous. Then there is the South, which is mostly nonindustrial and relatively, and sometimes absolutely, impoverished. The countries that compose the South are also called the less developed countries (LDCs) or the developing countries and were once known in a cold war context as the Third World. By whatever name they are known, however, LDCs have social conditions that are unacceptable. At a macroeconomic level, approximately three-quarters of the world's people live in the LDCs, yet they possess only about one-seventh of the world's wealth (measured in gross national products, or GNPs). On a more personal level, if you compare the lives of the average citizens of Japan and the average citizens of Nigeria, the Nigerians die 27 years earlier, earn an income that is 88 times smaller, are half as likely to be literate, are 53 times more likely to die during childbirth, and will find it 82 times more difficult to find a physician for medical help.

Despite the rhetoric of the North about the LDCs' plight, the countries of the North do relatively little to help. For example, U.S. economic foreign aid in 1994 was approximately $15 billion, which amounted to only about half of what Americans spent annually in retail liquor stores. Canada's foreign aid, about $2.8 billion, is equivalent to only about one-third of what its citizens spent in 1994 on tobacco. Foreign investment in the LDCs is also extremely limited, and what increases there are go to the relatively few countries, such as South Korea, that have been able join the ranks of what are called newly industrializing countries (NICs). Furthermore, loans to the LDCs have declined, and repayment of existing loans is draining much-needed capital away from many less developed countries. Trade earnings are another possible source of development capital, but the raw materials produced and exported by most LDCs earn them little compared to the cost of importing the more expensive finished products manufactured by the North.

There are a number of ways of approaching this issue of greater aid by the North for the South. One approach focuses on morality. Are we morally obligated to help less fortunate humans? A second approach explores more aid as a means of promoting the North's own self-interest; some analysts contend that a fully developed world would mean greater prosperity for everyone and would be more stable politically. A third avenue pursues the causes for the LDCs' poverty and lack of development in order to assess who or what is responsible.

It is possible to divide views on the origins and continuance of the North-South gap into three groups. One believes that the uneven (but unintended) spread of the Industrial Revolution resulted in unequal economic development. From this point of view, the answer to the question "Who is at fault?" is, "Nobody; it just happened." A second group finds the LDCs responsible for much of their continuing poverty. Advocates of this view charge the LDCs with failure to control their populations, with lack of political stability, with poor economic planning, and with a variety of other ill-conceived practices that impede development. This group believes that foreign aid is wasteful and is destructive of the policies needed to spur economic development.

A third group maintains that the North bears much of the responsibility for the South's condition and, therefore, is obligated to help the LDCs. Those who hold this view contend that the colonization of the LDCs, especially during the 1800s, when the Industrial Revolution rapidly took hold in the North, destroyed the indigenous economic, social, and political organizations needed for development. These powers then kept their colonial dependencies underdeveloped in order to ensure a supply of cheap raw materials. Even though virtually all former colonies are now independent, this view persists; the developed countries continue to follow political and economic strategies designed to keep the LDCs underdeveloped and dependent.

In the following selections, James P. Grant takes the position that, notwithstanding the poor media image of the LDCs as a lost cause, there is real momentum for change. He recommends focusing on the children of the LDCs—that if educated, kept healthy, and given other basic advantages, they can be the force for rapid positive change in the LDCs. The editors of the *Economist* argue that aid is ill-managed today and that, even if aid were vastly increased and managed well, it is not certain that the recipient countries would do much better.

YES

James P. Grant

JUMPSTARTING DEVELOPMENT

Anyone who thought, amidst the euphoria of dizzying change starting in 1989, that the end of the Cold War would usher in an age of global harmony and easy solutions has long since been disabused of the notion. Every day we open our newspapers to dark headlines confirming that the world is still a very dangerous place—in some ways more dangerous than before. We are confronted with a host of problems, both old and new, that are reaching crisis proportions. Is there a way of "jumpstarting" solutions to many of those problems? In fact, there is.

To many, it may not seem so. Ethnic conflict, religious hatred, failed states, economic devastation in Eastern Europe and the former Soviet Union, AIDS, and environmental degradation all seem intractable problems. Meanwhile, the number of poor in the world continues to increase at about the same rate as the world's population. The World Bank put their number at 1.1 billion in 1990. A fifth of the world's population is living on less than one dollar a day, and during the 1980s the poor actually lost ground. The 1990s show little evidence that the world economy will return anytime soon to a high growth trajectory.

The negative trends have even begun to afflict the rich. In the last decade, poverty increased in a number of industrialized countries, most notably in the United States and the United Kingdom and, of course, in the former communist countries of Europe. In most of those countries, children bore the brunt of the reversal. In America today, one in five children is poor, the highest level of child poverty in a quarter century in the world's richest country. In both the United Kingdom and the United States, child poverty has nearly doubled in a decade.

Small wonder that the lead article in this journal's spring issue contended that "all the trends" are in the wrong direction and that the world "appears to be at the beginning, not of a new order, but of a new nightmare." Such pessimism, however, can be misplaced. The world is in fact on the threshold of being able to make vastly greater progress on many problems that have long seemed intractable. Rather than merely reacting to situations after they have become critical, as in Somalia, the world has an opportunity in the 1990s

From James P. Grant, "Jumpstarting Development," *Foreign Policy,* no. 91 (Summer 1993).

to make an effective—and efficient—social investment to convert despair into hope and go a long way toward preventing future crises and building healthy societies.

The situation today may be analogous to that of Asia in the mid 1960s, when population growth seemed set to outrun the food supply. Many predicted widespread famine, chaos, and instability for the last third of this century. But then, quite suddenly, within four or five years, the Green Revolution took hold in Asia, extending from the Philippines through South Asia to Turkey. In country after country, wheat and rice production increased at annual rates unprecedented in the West. The immediate cause was not so much a scientific breakthrough—strains of the miracle wheats had been around for as many as 15 years—as a political and organizational one. Only by the mid 1960s had fertilizer, pesticides, and controlled irrigation become widely used, thanks in large part to earlier aid programs. At the same time, the combination of Asian drought and increasing awareness of the population explosion created the political will to drastically restructure price levels for grains and agro-inputs, and to mobilize the multiple sectors of society—rural credit, marketing, transport, foreign exchange allocations, media—required for success. U.S. president Lyndon Johnson deserves credit for his leadership contribution to that effort, though his deep personal involvement remains a largely untold story.

We may be in a similar position today, but on a much broader front—poised for advances in primary health care, basic education, water supply and sanitation, family planning, and gender equity, as well as food production—and covering a much wider geographical area, including Africa and Latin America as well as Asia. With an earnest effort from the major powers, the 1990s could witness a second green revolution—extending, this time, beyond agriculture to human development.

Frequent illness, malnutrition, poor growth, illiteracy, high birth rates, and gender bias are among poverty's worst symptoms. They are also some of poverty's most fundamental causes. We could anticipate, therefore, that overcoming some of the worst symptoms and causes of poverty would have far-reaching repercussions on the national and global level. The recent experiences of such diverse societies as China, Costa Rica, the Indian state of Kerala, Sri Lanka, and the Asian newly industrializing countries (NICs) suggest that high population growth rates, which wrap the cycle of poverty ever tighter, can be reduced dramatically. Reducing poverty would give a major boost to the fragile new efforts at democratization that will survive only if they tangibly improve the lives of the bottom half of society. As we know from the experience of Singapore, South Korea, Taiwan, and the other Asian NICs, such progress would in turn accelerate economic growth. By breaking the "inner cycle" of poverty, we would increase the capacity of the development process to assault poverty's many external causes, rooted in such diverse factors as geography, climate, land tenure, debt, business cycles, governance, and unjust economic relations.

We are uniquely positioned to succeed in the 1990s. Recent scientific and technological advances—and the revolutionary new capacity to communicate with and mobilize large numbers of people—have provided us with a host of new tools. The world's leaders can now use them together to produce dramatic, even unprecedented, results.

For example, the universal child immunization effort—the largest peacetime international collaboration in world history—has since the mid 1980s established systems that now reach virtually every hamlet in the developing world and are saving the lives of more than 8,000 children a day—some 3 million a year. Here, too, the technology was not new; vaccines had been available for some 20–30 years. Success has been the result of applying new communication and mobilization techniques to the immunization effort, often led personally by heads of state, making use of television and radio advertisements, and supported by a wide range of local leaders. School teachers, priests, imams, local government officials, nongovernmental organization (NGO) workers, and health personnel all joined the effort. By 1990, more than 80 per cent of the developing world's children were being brought in four or five times for vaccinations even before their first birthdays. As a result, Calcutta, Lagos, and Mexico City today have far higher levels of immunization of children at ages one and two than do New York City, Washington, D.C., or even the United States as a whole.

A similar effort is now being made to spread the use of oral rehydration therapy (ORT) to combat the single greatest historical killer of children, diarrhea, which takes the lives of some 8,000 children every day, down from 11,000 daily a decade ago. ORT was invented in the late 1960s, but only recently have leaders mobilized to use this lifesaver on a national scale. Every year it now saves the lives of more than 1 million children, a figure that could easily more than double by 1995 with increased national and international leadership.

The arsenal is now well stocked with other new technologies and rediscovered practices that can bring tremendous benefits with inspired leadership and only modest funding. Thus, the simple iodization of salt—at a cost of five cents annually per consumer—would prevent the world's single largest cause of mental retardation and of goiter, which affect more than 200 million people today as a result of iodine deficiency. Universal access to vitamin A through low-cost capsules or vegetables would remove the greatest single cause—about 700 cases per day—of blindness while reducing child deaths by up to a third in many parts of the developing world. The scientific rediscovery of the miracles of mother's milk means that more than a million children would not have died last year if only they had been effectively breast-fed for the first months of their lives, instead of being fed on more-costly infant formula. In such diverse countries as Bangladesh, Colombia, Senegal, and Zimbabwe, it has proven possible to get poor children, including girls, through primary education at very little cost. Recent advances have shown how to halve the costs of bringing sanitation and safe water to poor communities, to less than $30 per capita. New varieties of high-yield crops—from cassava to corn—are now ready to be promoted on a national scale in sub-Saharan Africa.

Meanwhile, with such tools in hand, the new capacity to communicate—to inform and motivate—empowers families, communities, and governments to give all children a better chance to lead productive lives. In short, we are now learning to "outsmart" poverty at the outset of each new life by providing a "bubble of protection" around a child's first vulnerable months and years. Strong international leadership and cooperation—facilitated enormously by the end of the Cold War and the expansion of democracy—could leverage that new capacity into wide-ranging social progress.

A CHILDREN'S REVOLUTION

Notwithstanding the media image of the Third World as a lost cause, there is real momentum there for change. In fact, for all the difficulties and setbacks, more progress has been made in developing countries in the last 40 years than was made in the previous 2,000, progress achieved while much of the world freed itself from colonialism and while respect for human and political rights expanded dramatically. Life expectancy has lengthened from 53 in 1960 to 65 today, and continues to increase at a rate of 9.5 hours per day. Thirty years ago, approximately three out of four children born in the developing countries survived to their fifth birthdays; today, some nine out of ten survive.

At the same time, the birth rates in countries as disparate as Brazil, China, Colombia, Cuba, Korea, Mexico, Sri Lanka, Thailand, and Tunisia have been more than halved, dramatically slowing population growth and the inherent strains it places on limited natural resources and social programs. Among the factors that have helped contain population growth, improving children's health is undoubtedly the least well-known and appreciated. As the United Nations Population Division puts it, "Improvements in child survival, which increase the predictability of the family building process, trigger the transition from natural to controlled fertility behavior. This in turn generates the need for family planning." While they are important priorities them-selves, reductions in child mortality, basic education of women, and the availability of family planning make a strong synergistic contribution to solving what Yale historian Paul Kennedy calls, in *Preparing for the Twenty-First Century* (1992), the "impending demographic disaster." As population specialist Sharon Camp noted in the Spring 1993 issue of FOREIGN POLICY:

> Measures like quality reproductive health care, greater educational and economic opportunities for women, and reductions in infant and child death rates can and will bring about rapid birthrate declines. If all developing countries were to emulate the most effective policies and programs and if donor governments such as the United States were to provide adequate levels of assistance, the population problem could be resolved in the lifetime of today's children.

In fact, a children's revolution is already under way in the developing world, often led by those in power. Developing country leaders took the lead in seeking history's first truly global summit—the 1990 World Summit for Children—with an unprecedented 71 heads of state and government participating. They also pressed for early action on the Convention on the Rights of the Child, which was adopted by the [UN] General Assembly in November 1989 and which has since been signed or ratified in record time by more than 150 countries—with the United States now being the only major exception.

The experience of the past decade showed it possible—even during the darkest days of the Cold War and amid the Third World economic crisis of the 1980s—to mobilize societies and the international community around a package of low-cost interventions and services, building a sustainable momentum of human progress. The United Nations Children's Fund (UNICEF) and NGOs called it the Child Survival and Development Revolution, and as a result more than 20 million children are alive today who would not otherwise be; tens of millions are healthier, stronger, and less of a burden upon their mothers and families; and birth rates are falling.

Leaders are learning that productive things can be done for families and children at relatively low cost, and that it can be good politics for them to do so and bad politics to resist. More than 130 countries have issued or are actively working on National Programmes of Action to implement the goals set by the World Summit for Children, all of which were incorporated into Agenda 21 at the June 1992 Earth Summit in Rio de Janeiro. Those ambitious goals—to be met by the year 2000—include controlling the major childhood diseases; cutting child malnutrition in half; reducing death rates for children under five by one-third; cutting in half maternal mortality rates; providing safe water and sanitation for all communities; and making family planning services and basic education universally available. In 1992, most regions of the developing world took the process a step further by selecting a core of targets for 1995, when the first World Social Summit will review children's progress within the broader development process. For the first time since the dawn of history, humankind is making long-term plans for improving the lives of the young.

In part, that new concern has its roots in the communications revolution that brings daily pictures of large-scale famine or violence into our homes. At the same time, the new communications capacity has permitted deprived populations everywhere to see how much better people can live, firing grassroots movements for reform and democracy. But most of the Third World's suffering remains invisible. Of the 35,000 children under age five who die every day in the developing countries, more than 32,000 succumb to largely preventable hunger and illness. No earthquake, no flood, no war has taken the lives of a quarter million children in a single week; but that is the weekly death toll of the invisible emergencies resulting from poverty and underdevelopment. In 1992, 500,000 children under the age of five died in the kind of dramatic emergencies that attract media attention, but that is a small portion of the nearly 13 million children under five who are killed every year by grinding poverty and gross underdevelopment. The tragic deaths of 1,000 children per day in Somalia last year captured far more public attention than those of the 8,000 children around the world who die every day from the dehydration caused by ordinary diarrhea, which is so easily treated and prevented.

As the international community assumes greater responsibility for proliferating civil strife and other emergencies, it must come to terms with the realities of limited resources. How many operations to rescue failed states like Somalia can the international community afford? It is estimated that the U.S. component of the Somalia operation alone will cost more than $750 million for just four months' involvement, nearly comparable to UNICEF's average annual global budget of recent years, much of which is used to prevent future crises. There are now 48 civil and ethnic conflicts in progress around the globe. The United Nations is involved in 14 peacekeeping operations on five continents. Last year, those operations cost more than $3 billion, about four times higher than the previous record. Those operations are the most expensive way to relieve suffering, and it is clearly time to invest far more in *preventing* emergencies and conflicts, and in buttressing the new democracies, even as we put out the world's fires. As U.N. secretary-general Boutros Boutros-Ghali argues in his *Agenda for Peace,* prevention can prove far less costly—and produce far greater results—than relying on expensive and sometimes ineffective rescue operations.

As the international community shifts toward prevention—as it must—it makes the most sense to focus on eradicating poverty's worst manifestations early in the lives of children, breaking the cycle of poverty from generation to generation. At the World Summit for Children, the international community identified the basic package of high-impact, low-cost interventions that can make a difference in the short and medium term, while helping to build long-term development. Now it has only to make them work, albeit on a massive scale.

The overall price tag for reaching all the year 2000 goals for children and women, which would overcome most of the worst aspects of poverty, would be an extra $25 billion per year. The developing countries themselves are trying to come up with two-thirds of that amount by reordering their domestic priorities and budgets, while the remaining third—slightly more than $8 billion per year—should come from the industrialized world in the form of increased or reallocated official development assistance (ODA) and debt relief. That is a small price for meeting the basic needs of virtually every man, woman, and child in the developing world in nutrition, basic health, basic education, water and sanitation, and family planning within this decade.

In Russia and the other former Soviet republics, such aid could produce rapid grassroots results at an affordable cost, easing pain and helping to buy time until democratic and macroeconomic reforms show concrete progress. Plans for restoring democracy to Cambodia, Haiti, and Mozambique will need to alleviate suffering among the poor quickly; and targeting the essential needs of children and women can produce the biggest impact at the lowest cost. International relief programs for Somalia must rapidly give way to assistance that constitutes an investment in human development, and no such investment has been found to be more cost-effective than primary health care, nutrition, and basic education for children and women. The road to power for many of the world's extremist movements—whether based in religion or political ideology—is paved with the unmet needs of the poor.

Sadly, the U.S. has stagnated or regressed over the past decade with respect to children, even while much of the developing world has been making impressive progress. The United States has provided little leadership for that progress, except for that provided by the bipartisanship of Congress, which actively encouraged U.S. support to child survival and development programs abroad. But by increasing investment in American children and strengthening American families, and by reordering foreign assistance to reflect that new priority, the United States, the world's sole superpower, could once more set the global standard and give a major boost to human development and economic growth.

First, few actions would have more immediate impact than the signature and ratification this year of the historic Convention on the Rights of the Child. President Bill Clinton's signature of the convention and its submission to the U.S. Senate for early ratification (as has been urged by bipartisan leadership) would send an important message to the world, bringing the rights of children close to becoming humanity's first universal law.

Second, the United States needs to demonstrate a new culture of caring for its own children. The much-needed reordering of priorities for American children, women, and families is already under way, with initiatives on Head Start, universal immunization, parental leave, family planning, and health services for all. A "Culture of Caring," the American plan in response to the World Summit for Children that was issued at the end of the Bush administration—in January 1993 —provides a useful base for bipartisan action.

Third, the United States needs "20/20 vision." It should support the May 1991 proposal of the United Nations Development Programme, which had two components: It called on developing countries to devote at least 20 per cent of their budgets to directly meeting the basic human needs of their people, roughly double current average levels. It also argued that 20 per cent of all international development aid should go to meet those same basic needs: primary health care, nutrition, basic education, family planning, and safe water and sanitation. Today, on average, less than 10 per cent of already inadequate levels of ODA are devoted to that purpose. Different ways of defining and reporting social sector allocations within national and ODA budgets make precise quantification of those proportions somewhat difficult, and efforts are therefore underway to achieve a common form of reporting. But even if subsequent research changes the target percentages, the "20/20 vision" concept underscores the importance of restructuring both sets of budgets in line with the priorities established at the World Summit for Children, which may require—on average—a doubling of existing allocations.

On the ODA side, the United States today devotes less than $1 billion to basic human needs. Of the projected $25 billion extra annually that will be required globally by mid-decade to meet the World Summit year 2000 goals, the U.S. share would be $2 billion. The roughly $3 billion total would then still be less than 20 per cent of all U.S. foreign and military assistance. It is a small price to pay for jumpstarting solutions to so many of the overwhelming problems of population, democracy, and the worst aspects of poverty, to say nothing about saving tens of millions of young lives this decade. The additional funds can be obtained from reductions in the military and security component of the U.S. international affairs budget.

Fourth, the new spirit of democratic change and economic reform in Africa will not survive if its creditors do not give it some debt relief: Together, the sub-Saharan African countries pay $1 billion in debt service to foreign creditors every month, and its debt is now proportionally three or four times heavier than that of Latin America. At the November 1992 Organization of African Unity–sponsored International Conference on Assistance to African Children, donor countries and lending agencies alike pledged to promote more debt relief while expanding or restructuring ODA in order to help Africa protect and nurture its children. Here again the

United States could help lead the way, preventing Africa from deteriorating into a continent of Somalias. The G-7 Summit in Tokyo in July 1993 should make a definitive commitment to debt relief, with much of the local currency proceeds going to accelerate programs for children, women, and the environment through a variety of debt-swapping mechanisms. With the right mixture of domestic and international support, and with apartheid ending in South Africa, we could see dramatic progress in most of Africa by the year 2000. That could include a food revolution every bit as green as Asia's—but African countries will need help. The alternative could be a return to authoritarian rule, corruption, and conflict throughout large parts of the continent.

Fifth, the United States must actively support multilateral cooperation. With human development and poverty alleviation increasingly accepted as the focus for development cooperation in the 1990s, the United States has an opportunity to transform rhetoric into reality. Active U.S. support and leadership along those lines in the World Bank, the International Monetary Fund, the regional banks, and throughout the U.N. system will go a long way toward overcoming, in our time, the worst aspects of poverty in the South, where it is most acute. Land-mark U.N. conferences have been scheduled on human rights (1993), population (1994), and women (1995); U.S. leadership at those conferences and at the U.N. summit on social development in 1995 will strengthen their impact. The U.S. role will also be critical in reducing poverty in the North and in the transitional societies of Eastern Europe and the former Soviet Union.

Finally, the United States must strengthen its commitment to the United Nations. The new administration's initiative to seek restoration of U.S. funding for the United Nations Population Fund is a welcome step—a step that Congress should rapidly implement. That and a decision to rejoin the United Nations Educational, Scientific, and Cultural Organization (UNESCO) would not only give an important boost to family planning and global education, but—together with full payment of its U.N. arrears—it would signal long-term U.S. commitment to the United Nations as the global village's central vehicle for development cooperation and safeguarding the peace.

Focusing on children as a means of attacking the worst aspects of poverty will not solve all the world's problems, but it would make a historic contribution—at this all-too-brief juncture of opportunity —to the better world we all seek. It could change the course of history.

NO

Editors of *The Economist*

THE KINDNESS OF STRANGERS

The old jibe about aid—"poor people in rich countries helping rich people in poor countries"—has plenty of truth in it. Donors need to learn from past mistakes if they want to help poor countries grow.

Anybody who tried to see the case for aid by looking merely at the way it is allotted would quickly give up in despair. The richest 40% of the developing world gets about twice as much per head as the poorest 40%. Big military spenders get about twice as much per head as do the less belligerent. El Salvador gets five times as much aid as Bangladesh, even though Bangladesh has 24 times as many people and is five times poorer than El Salvador.

Since 1960, about $1.4 trillion (in 1988 dollars) has been transferred in aid from rich countries to poor ones. Yet relatively little is known about what that process has achieved. Has it relieved poverty? Has it stimulated growth in the recipient countries? Has it helped the countries which give it? Such questions become more pressing as donor governments try harder to curb public spending. This year, two of the biggest players in the international aid business are looking afresh at their aims and priorities.

Brian Atwood, appointed by the Clinton administration to run America's Agency for International Development (AID), inherited an organisation encumbered over the years with 33 official goals by a Congress that loved using aid money to buy third-world adherence to its pet ideas. Now, faced with a sharp budget cut, Mr Atwood is trying to pare down to just four goals: building democracy, protecting the environment, fostering sustainable economic development and encouraging population control. Not, however, anything as basic as the relief of poverty.

A few blocks away from Mr Atwood's Washington office, the World Bank is going through a similar exercise. Set up in 1946, the Bank has become the most powerful of all the multilateral development organisations. But a critical internal report recently accused the Bank of caring more about pushing out loans than about monitoring how well the money was spent. Now the Bank hopes to improve the quality of its lending. It is also wondering about its future. Some of its past borrowers in East Asia are now rich enough to turn lenders themselves. More should follow. The Bank is trying to move into new

From "The Kindness of Strangers," *The Economist* (May 7, 1994). Copyright © 1994 by The Economist Newspaper Group, Inc. Reprinted by permission. Further reproduction prohibited.

areas, such as cleaning up the environment and setting up social-welfare systems. But some people wonder how long it will really be needed.

AID and the World Bank are unusual (although their critics rarely admit as much) in their openness and in the rigour with which they try to evaluate what they do. But other donors will also have to think about which kinds of aid to abandon as their budgets stop expanding. In the 1980s the official development assistance[1] (ODA) disbursed by members of the OECD's [Organization for Economic Cooperation and Development's] Development Assistance Committee (DAC)—21 rich countries plus the European Commission—increased by about a quarter in real terms; but between 1991 and 1992, the DAC's disbursements rose by just 0.5%. Development Initiatives, an independent British ginger group [a driving force within a larger group], believes "the end of an era" may have come; it reckons that aid budgets around the world are ceasing to grow at all. Almost the only exception is Japan, which provides a fifth of DAC aid and plans a substantial increase over the next five years.

Most multilateral donors, such as the UN agencies, also have budgets frozen. A rare exception is the European Development Fund [EDF], the aid arm of the European Union, which is taking a rapidly rising share of member-states' aid budgets. The EDF's secrecy and its mediocre reputation with recipient countries make some bilateral donors unhappy. "British officials are concerned about having to devote increasing quantities of their aid, which they regard as successful, to the European programme," reports Robert Cassen, a British aid expert.

Figure 1

More from the Market: Net Resource Flows to Developing Countries [in] $bn, Constant 1991 Prices and Exchange Rates

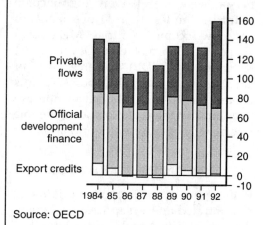

Source: OECD

NEEDED: A CASE FOR GIVING

Some developing countries—mainly the faster-growing ones perceived as "emerging markets"—have found the international capital markets to be increasingly willing suppliers of finance (see Figure 1). But demands for ODA are still appearing in new forms and from new sources. Astute third-world countries are giving old projects a green tinge to profit from fashionable enthusiasm for the environment. The countries of Eastern Europe and the former Soviet Union are competing with the third world for help. And the proportion of aid spent on relieving disasters has soared from 2% five years ago to around 7% today.

But with the clamour for more money goes increasing uncertainty about what aid is for and what it has achieved. The naive taxpayer might imagine that aid's main purpose was to relieve poverty. Yet only relatively small amounts of ODA go to the poorest of countries or to projects that benefit mainly the poorest of people. A study of America's aid programme conducted by the Overseas Development Council (ODC), a Washington, DC, think-tank, found that more than $250 per person went to relatively high-income countries, but less than $1 per person to very low-income countries. Mahbub ul Haq of the United Nations Development Programme (UNDP), a fierce critic of aid's failure to reach the poorest, points out that the ten countries that are home to two-thirds of the world's poorest people receive only one-third of world aid.

NOT HELPING THE POOR

Within poor countries, too, aid is rarely concentrated on the services that benefit the poorest. The World Bank reckons that, of all the aid going to low-income countries in 1988, a mere 2% went on primary health care and 1% on population programmes. Even the aid that is spent on health and education tends to go to services that benefit disproportionately the better-off. Aid for health care goes disproportionately to hospitals (in 1988–89, for instance, 33% of Japan's bilateral aid for health went on building hospitals); aid for education, to universities. In sub-Saharan Africa in the 1980s, only $1 of ODA went on each primary pupil; $11 on each secondary pupil; and $575 on each university student.

Such spending patterns often reflect the priorities of the recipient governments. Some donors have tried to persuade governments to distribute aid differently. They have had mixed success —not surprisingly, for their own motives in aid-giving often override the goal of poverty relief.

One such motive, powerful even since the end of the cold war, is the pursuit of national security. Most governments are coy about the role that national security plays in their aid budgets, but the biggest donor of all, the United States, is blatant: roughly a quarter of its $21 billion foreign-aid budget takes the form of military assistance, and roughly a quarter of the total budget goes to Israel and Egypt alone. "The United States has spent a lot less money on development than on advancing political and military goals," says John Sewell of the ODC. This year, America's aid budget protects the shares of Israel and Egypt. America also sees aid to Eastern Europe and to the countries of the former Soviet Union primarily in strategic terms.

"National security" is also now being used as an argument for giving more weight to all sorts of other goals in the drawing-up of aid budgets. Environmentalists claim that some types of environmental damage, such as global warming and the thinning of the ozone layer, may be worsened by poor-country growth, and they argue that rich-country aid donors should in their own interests take special care to minimise such risks. Others say aid should be used to parry the threats to rich countries posed by the trade in illegal drugs, by population growth and by third-world poverty.

If the goal of national security can conflict with that of poverty relief, then the commercial interests of aid donors can do so even more. Japan's approach has at least the merit of simplicity: its development assistance goes mainly to countries that are most likely to become its future customers. All DAC countries tie some aid—the average is about a quarter—to the purchase of their own goods and services. One problem with tying is that it forces countries to pay over the odds for imports: on average, some estimates suggest, recipients pay 15% more than prevailing prices. Another is that it often distorts development priorities. It is easier to tie aid to a large item of capital spending, such as a dam, road or hospital, than to a small rural project that may do more good. Not surprisingly, tying is especially common in transport, power generation and telecommunications projects.

Aid recorded as tied has been falling as a proportion of bilateral ODA, according to the OECD, which monitors the practice. That may be partly because of the rise in spending on disaster relief. It may also reflect an international agreement on guidelines for tied aid. But governments are clever at finding ways to use aid to promote exports. It has, for example, taken two official investigations to uncover some of the links between British aid to Malaysia and British arms sales to that country.

Some kinds of ODA are given in the sure knowledge that the money will be spent mainly in the donor country, but without explicit tying. One example is technical assistance. Of the $12 billion or so which goes each year to buy advice, training and project design, over 90% is spent on foreign consultants. Half of all technical assistance goes to Africa —which, observes UNDP's Mr Haq, "has perhaps received more bad advice per capita than any other continent". Most thoughtful people in the aid business regard technical assistance as one of the least effective ways to foster development.

Stung by the claims of their aid lobbies that too little help goes to the poor, some governments are trying to steer more money through voluntary bodies, such as charities and church groups. Such bodies, known in the trade as non-governmental organisations or NGOs, have proliferated at astonishing speed in both the rich and poor worlds. The OECD counted 2,542 NGOs in its 24 member countries in 1990, compared with 1,603 in 1980. The growth in the south may have been faster still. Roger Riddell, of the Overseas Development Institute in London, who has made a special study of NGOs and development, talks of a "veritable explosion" in their numbers; he mentions 25,000 grassroots organisations in the Indian state of Tamil Nadu alone. The public and private money dispensed by NGOs amounted to 13% of total net ODA flows in 1990, and the share has been creeping up.

NGOs may be better than central governments at handling small projects and more sensitive to what local people really need. But even NGOs, according to Mr Riddell, usually fail to help the very poorest. "If government and official aid programmes fail to reach the bottom 20% of income groups, most NGO interventions probably miss the bottom 5–10%," he guesses. And, as more aid is channelled through NGOs, some groups may find it harder to retain the element of local participation which is their most obvious strength. More searching questions might be asked about whether they are efficiently run, or achieve their purported goals: a study of projects supported by the Ford Foundation in Africa in the late 1980s found "very few successes to talk about, especially in terms of post-intervention sustainability".

AND WHAT ABOUT GROWTH?

When the modern panoply of official aid institutions grew up after the second world war, the intention was not to relieve poverty as such but to promote economic growth in poor countries. Aid was seen as a transitional device to help countries reach a point from which their economies would take off of their own accord. Its use was to remove shortages of capital and foreign exchange, boosting investment to a point at which growth could become self-sustaining.

In their baldest form, such views sit oddly beside the fact that, in many of the countries that have received the most aid and have the highest levels of capital investment, growth has been negligible. For at least 47 countries, aid represented more than 5% of GNP [gross national product] in 1988. Many of those countries were in sub-Saharan Africa, where GDP [gross domestic product] per head has been virtually flat for a quarter of a century. Yet, as David Lindauer and Michael Roemer of the Harvard Institute for International Development point out in a recent study, some of them were investing a share of GDP almost as large as that of much faster growing South-East Asian countries: Cameroon, Côte d'Ivoire, Kenya, Tanzania and Zambia all invested at least 20% of GDP, a figure comparable with that for Indonesia or Thailand.

Such rough comparisons may prove little, but they draw attention to an awkward point. Some third-world countries have enjoyed fast economic growth with relatively little aid per head. In particular, some Asian success stories, such as China and Vietnam, had little or no aid at a time when donors were pouring money into Africa (although China is now the World Bank's largest single customer). If some countries can achieve economic growth with little aid, while other countries which get a great deal of aid do not grow at all, what if anything is aid good for?

One way to try to answer that question is to review the experience of individual countries and aid projects. In the late 1980s there were two valiant attempts to do just this: one conducted by a team led by Mr Cassen, the other on a more modest scale by Mr Riddell. Mr Cassen's team argued that "the majority of aid is successful in terms of its own objectives", but added that "a significant proportion does not succeed." Aid had worked badly in Africa; better in South Asia. Where aid did not work, the reason was sometimes that donors failed to learn from their mistakes or the mistakes of other donors; and sometimes that a recipient country failed to make the most of what was offered to it.

As for the impact of aid on economic growth, Mr Cassen concluded cautiously that one could not say that aid failed to help. In some countries, indeed, he found evidence that it did increase growth. Mr Riddell was similarly tentative. Aid, he concluded, "can assist in the alleviation of poverty, directly and indirectly" and "the available evidence... fails to convince that, as a general rule, alternative strategies which exclude aid lead in theory or have led in practice to more rapid improvements in the living standards of the poor than have been achieved with aid."

These are hardly ringing endorsements. But these evaluations of individual aid programmes and projects are more positive in their findings than attempts to establish broader links between aid and growth, which have usually failed entirely. Plenty of economists have picked holes in the original idea that aid would boost investment: why should it, some ask, when governments may simply use income from aid as an excuse to spend tax revenues in other, less productive ways?

Other economists, such as Howard White of the Institute of Social Studies at The Hague, who has reviewed many of the economic studies of the effects of aid on growth, point to the difficulties of generalising. Given the various transfers that count as "aid", the many conditions that donors attach, the differing importance of aid in national economies and the complexity of economic growth, there are simply too many variables to say much that is useful.

THIRD-WORLD DUTCH DISEASE

Since the start of the 1980s, many donors have come to believe that the quality of a country's economic management will do most to determine whether aid will do some good. Aid in the 1980s was frequently used, especially by the World Bank, as a prod to encourage countries to begin "structural adjustment" programmes. In some cases, the economic performance of these countries did improve—Ghana is one of the Bank's favourite examples. In other cases, it did not. A review by the IMF [International Monetary Fund] of 19 low-income countries which had undergone structural adjustment found that their current-account deficits averaged 12.3% of GDP before adjustment and 16.8% in the most recent year; and that their external debt had grown from 451% of exports to 482%.

Why was this? Were countries encouraged to adopt the wrong policies? Did they ignore the advice they were given? Or did the aid itself do some damage? Stefan de Vylder, a Swedish economist, argued for the last of these explanations at a conference in Stockholm in March. He argued that large volumes of aid

Figure 2

Friends in Need: Aid* as % of GDP, 1992

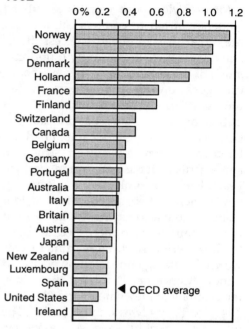

*Net official development assistance
Source: OECD

(such as those associated with structural adjustment programmes) could damage an economy's international competitiveness; and countries where export performance was especially bad tended to be "rewarded" with low-interest loans and grants.

The damage to competitiveness, Mr de Vylder believes, is a version of "Dutch disease". This was the term coined in the 1970s to describe how Holland's exports of natural gas boosted its real exchange rate and thereby harmed its export competitiveness. Mr White thinks something similar happened in Sri Lanka between 1974 and 1988, when a sharp increase in aid contributed to a divergence between the nominal and real exchange rates; this hurt the growth of the country's manufactured exports.

Mr de Vylder also worries about the tendency of aid to compensate for failure rather than to reward success. Bilateral donors have increasingly found that much of the aid they give to some countries goes towards paying back money unwisely lent by international financial institutions. Take Zambia as an example. Between 1974 and 1987, Zambia had entered into seven stand-by or structural agreements with the IMF—one every two years. Each was broken by the Zambian government. When, in 1987, Mr de Vylder visited Zambia to assess the latest bout of economic disaster, he asked a minister how seriously the government was worried at being lambasted by every aid donor. "Concerned?" mused the minister, seeming somewhat surprised. Then: "Oh no. They always come back." The minister was right, says Mr de Vylder. Shortly afterwards, the international financial institutions were again knocking on the door, asking for a new agreement.

It is easy, with aid, to find examples of individual projects that do some good. Most of those who criticise aid argue that if the quality were better—if donors tried harder to learn from each other's mistakes, if they were less keen to reap commercial gain, if they concentrated harder on meeting basic human needs—then there would be far fewer failures. All that is true; but—other things being equal—there would also be much less aid. Will poor countries do worse, over the next 30 years, if rich countries decline to give or lend them another $1.4 trillion? At that price, the answer should be "Yes". Given the way that aid works at present, it is only "Maybe".

NOTES

1. Defined as aid administered with the promotion of economic development and welfare as the main objective; concessional in character; and with a grant element of at least 25%.

POSTSCRIPT

Should the Developed North Increase Aid to the Less Developed South?

There can be no argument that most of the people in most of the countries of the South live in circumstances that citizens in the developed countries of the North would find unacceptable. There is also no question that most of the LDCs were subjugated and held in colonial bondage by the developed countries. Apart from these points, there is little agreement on the causes and the solutions to the plight of the South.

Many LDC specialists blame colonialism for the LDCs' lack of development, past and present. This view is held in many of the LDCs and is also represented widely in Western scholarly opinion. Johan Galtung's "A Structural Theory of Imperialism," *Journal of Peace Research* (1971) is a classic statement from this perspective. This belief has led to the LDCs' demand for a New International Economic Order (NIEO), in which there would be a greater sharing of wealth and economic power between the North and the South. More on the common views and efforts of the LDCs can be found in Darryl C. Thomas, *The Theory and Practice of Third World Solidarity* (Praeger, 1994). It is also possible to argue that continued poverty in the LDCs, especially amid the general prosperity of the economically developed countries, will increase anger among the people of the economically less developed countries, decrease global stability, and have a variety of other negative consequences. For a discussion of the growing military capabilities of the LDCs, consult Donald M. Snow, *Distant Thunder: Third World Conflict and the New International Order* (St. Martin's Press, 1993).

Other analysts argue that colonialism actually benefited many dependencies by introducing modern economic techniques and that those former colonies that have remained close to the industrialized countries have done the best. Still others have charged that some LDCs have followed policies that have short-circuited their own development. This point of view sees calls for an NIEO as little more than an attempt by the countries of the South to increase their power and to reorder the international system. Steven D. Krasner's *Structural Conflict: The Third World Against Global Liberalism* (University of California Press, 1985) is written from this point of view. There are also disagreements about how much the North should aid the South, irrespective of who has caused the South's problems. Humanitarian concerns, as well as a sense that all the world's people will eventually be more prosperous if the 80 percent who live in poverty in the South can develop, argue for greater aid, a view represented in David Aronson, "Why Africa Stays Poor and Why It Doesn't Have To," *The Humanist* (March/April 1993).

On the Internet . . .

Center for Security Policy
The Web site of this Washington, D.C.–centered "think tank" provides a wide range of links to sites dealing with national and intenational security issues.
http://www.security-policy.org/links.html

Jane's Electronic Information System
This is an online demonstration of the Jane Information Group's electronic information system. For nearly 100 years, Jane's has published accurate and impartial books on the subjects of defense, weaponry, civil aviation, and transportation. *http://www.janes.com*

United Nations Department of Peacekeeping Operations
This UN site provides access to descriptions of current and past peacekeeping operations, maps, lists of contributing countries, and other data related to UN military, police, and observer missions.
http://www.un.org/Depts/dpko/

U.S. Arms Control and Disarmament Agency (ACDA)
This is a good place to begin research on arms control and disarmament, especially as they relate to nuclear weapons and the views and efforts of the United States.
http://www.acda.gov

PART 3
Military Security Issues

Whatever we may wish, war, terrorism, and other forms of physical coercion are still important elements of international politics. Countries calculate both how to use the instruments of force and how to implement national security. There can be little doubt, however, that significant changes are under way in this realm as part of the changing world system. Strong pressures exist to expand the mission and strengthen the security capabilities of international organizations and to reduce or eliminate nuclear weapons worldwide. This section examines how countries in the international system are addressing these issues.

■ Does the World Need to Have Nuclear Weapons at All?

■ Should a Permanent UN Military Force Be Established?

ISSUE 8

Does the World Need to Have Nuclear Weapons at All?

YES: Tom Bethell, from "No Nukes America," *American Spectator* (December 1996)

NO: George Lee Butler, from "Eliminating Weapons of Mass Destruction: The Scourge of Nuclear Weapons," *Vital Speeches of the Day* (February 1, 1997)

ISSUE SUMMARY

YES: Tom Bethell, Washington correspondent for the *American Spectator*, contends that the drive toward denuclearization is likely to leave the United States exposed to its enemies.

NO: George Lee Butler, a retired U.S. Air Force general and former commander of the Strategic Air Command, advocates the elimination of all nuclear weapons.

Efforts to control weapons of war go back to nearly the beginning of written history. Although progress was rarely made, it can be argued that the limited killing power of weapons made arms control agreements seem a low priority. That changed rapidly as the destructive capability of weapons grew exponentially during the industrial and then the technological ages. The first, albeit ineffective, multilateral arms negotiations were the Hague Conferences (1899, 1907). The awful toll and fearsome weapons of World War I prompted renewed arms control efforts. Conferences in Washington and London set limits to battleship tonnage among the world's leading naval powers.

The arms control efforts were spurred yet again by the horror of World War II and then by the existence—and use on Hiroshima and Nagasaki, Japan, in 1945—of atomic weapons that had the potential to end civilization. In January 1946 the UN established the International Atomic Energy Agency to try to limit the use of nuclear technology to peaceful purposes. Later that year, the UN also called for the "general regulation and reduction of armaments and armed forces" and established a Commission for Conventional Armaments.

Still, for almost 20 years nuclear weapons building and testing mushroomed unimpeded. Then, in 1963, the first major nuclear arms control agreement was signed, and by its terms most countries agreed to cease testing nuclear weapons in the atmosphere. Arms control efforts strengthened in the 1970s and continued to speed up. The cost of weaponry; the huge arsenals that each superpower had; the ever-increasing speed, power, and accuracy of those weapons; and the moderation of the cold war all prompted this acceleration.

Several of the arms control agreements are worth noting: the two Strategic Arms Limitation Talks treaties (SALT I and II, 1972 and 1979); the Intermediate-range Nuclear Forces (INF) Treaty (1987); and the two Strategic Arms Reduction Talks treaties (START I and II, 1991 and 1993). The SALT treaties limited the number of weapons systems that each superpower could possess. The INF Treaty eliminated an entire type of missile—those missiles with an intermediate range (500–5,500 km). It was the first step toward actually reducing the number of nuclear weapons. The START treaties took up the abolition of the intercontinental-range (over 5,500 km) U.S. and Soviet weapons, now all held by Russia. Like the INF Treaty, the START treaties pledged the signatories to reduce their nuclear arsenals. Unlike the INF Treaty, the reductions that were agreed to are substantial.

Under START II, which superseded START I, Russia will possess all the former Soviet intercontinental-range nuclear weapons delivery systems (missiles, bombers) and their associated weapons (warheads, bombs). Arsenals will be slashed to 3,500 weapons for the United States and 2,997 for Russia by the year 2003. The two sides agreed to eliminate all multiple-warhead, land-based missiles. The treaty has been ratified by the United States but not, to date, by Russia.

The question before us here is, If the two nuclear behemoths can slim down their nuclear systems by approximately 75 percent, as they did comparing the SALT II and START II limits, then why not reduce the two sides' weapons (including both long-range weapons and the still-formidable short-range systems of bombs and artillery shells) to zero? Before we move to that debate, it is important to note that the closer one comes to zero, the more important others' nuclear arsenals become. Three countries (and their number of weapons) that have substantial arsenals are China (284), France (534), and Great Britain (200). Israel, India, Pakistan, and perhaps North Korea also have nuclear weapons.

The following selections carry the debate over nuclear weapons into the future. Tom Bethell outlines a number of reasons why it would not be wise for the United States to take the lead in eliminating nuclear weapons in the foreseeable future. George Lee Butler contends that attaining a nuclear-free world is neither wishful thinking nor a perilous path but, rather, attainable and desirable.

YES

Tom Bethell

NO NUKES AMERICA

Over a period of several decades, the weapons in the U.S. nuclear arsenal were assembled at the Pantex plant, a few miles northeast of Amarillo, Texas. The components were fabricated elsewhere—at Rocky Flats, near Denver; at Hanford reservation, in Washington state; at the Savannah River reactor in South Carolina—but they were finally all put together at Pantex, 16,000 acres of parched scrub surrounded by steel fences and coils of razor wire. The plant is dotted with infrared motion detectors and armed guards in desert camouflage.

Today, the entire U.S. nuclear weapons assembly line is running in reverse. All the nuclear-weapons production facilities are closed down, and the bombs themselves, having been retrieved from silos and Air Force bases, are being brought back to the same Pantex plant at a rate of about 35 or 40 a week. They are transported across U.S. highways in unmarked, heavily guarded tractor-trailers; at Pantex they are disassembled, and their plutonium "pits" stored in bunkers. State officials have expressed concern that Pantex is fast becoming "an unlicensed plutonium dump." The U.S. is said to be dismantling its arsenal at a rate of about 2,000 weapons a year.

The planned final size of the arsenal is secret, but some say the total may be no more than 1,000 weapons. Anti-nuke groups stationed outside the Pantex gates monitored the trucks as the completed weapons left the plant, and they continue to monitor them as they return.

In the postwar period, the U.S. produced some 70,000 nuclear weapons, of about 75 different types. Annual production rates in the early 1960's reached about 5,000 a year, and a maximum stockpile of over 32,000 warheads was reached in 1967. Information provided by Boris Yeltsin and Mikhail Gorbachev implied that the Soviets' arsenal at its peak exceeded 40,000 warheads. France today has about 480 nukes, China about 450, Britain 200, Israel "probably 100 plus devices," India 60-odd, and Pakistan 15–25, according to a guide published by the Carnegie Endowment for International Peace, *Tracking Nuclear Proliferation*.

It seems undeniable that the quantity of Soviet and U.S. nukes at their peak defied logic on both sides. Misleading "perceptions," inter-service rivalry, and the skewed incentives of government agencies contributed to a build-up that was vastly in excess of whatever could have been used. The elimination of superfluous arsenals by definition does not jeopardize security, and there is much to be said for the current "build down." But it also has its disquieting aspects. Above all, it will be difficult to reverse the present course. In an emergency it could be done, but by then it would be too late, in view of the time required to build or re-start the industrial infrastructure. It is safe to say that the existing atomic-weapons production facilities will never be reopened. The enduring superstition surrounding all things nuclear will see to that: Not in my back yard, or anyone else's.

* * *

As the Cold War was coming to an end, the environmentalists gained a crucial and little remarked ascendancy over the military in the ordering of government priorities. It helped that George Bush was president when this happened, for he was willing to do almost anything to ward off accusation from environmentalists. Weapons plants were stigmatized as contaminated sites, "hot spots," sources of hazardous waste. All of the major nuclear weapons facilities have since then been included on the Environmental Protection Agency's "Superfund" National Priorities List of the worst contaminated sites in America. "In preparing to fight a nuclear war with the former Soviet Union," according to the Center for Defense Information's *Defense Monitor*, "America succeeded in 'nuking' itself." It is an irony, surely, that the plants that arguably yielded a 50-year stretch of domestic peace rarely enjoyed by any nation should in the end have been so condemned.

The symbolic moment came in June, 1989, when Rocky Flats was raided by FBI agents. The nation's only source of purified plutonium for nuclear weapons, Rocky Flats manufactured the softball-sized plutonium cores at the heart of the weapon. The raid came as a surprise to the Department of Energy, which has responsibility for the production and maintenance of nuclear weapons. Until the mid 1980's the department successfully argued that the practices of weapons-plant contractors were exempt from federal environmental laws. But by 1992 it had in effect become a loyal subsidiary of the Environmental Protection Agency. In that year, Rockwell International, the Rocky Flats contractor, pleaded guilty to charges that it had violated hazardous waste and clean-water laws. The company was fined $18.5 million. Today, according to the General Accounting Office, nuclear weapons facilities all across the country are closed "for environmental, health and safety reasons." The Department of Energy has estimated that cleaning up these sites will cost $300 billion—more than the annual defense budget.

In order to gain insight into future nuclear-weapons policy, it is worth studying the tracts of the anti-nukes, the bulletins of atomic scientists, and the pug-wash of "responsible" physicists and physicians. Their goal is unmistakable: America as a nuclear-free zone. The present deconstruction of America's nukes was prescribed in their earlier manifestos. But abolition is the goal. In 1992 the *Bulletin of the Atomic Scientists* published its "Agenda 2001." Among the contributors was Daniel Ellsberg of Harvard Medical School, earlier the publicist of the *Pentagon Papers*. It is fair to say that the present (anti) nuclear policies of the U.S., if not of the other nuclear states, are currently in line with his recommendations: No nukes are being built, production facilities are shut tight, the current arsenal is being deconstructed, and the U.S. has signed the Comprehensive Test Ban Treaty.

If ridding the whole world of nukes cannot quite be achieved, eliminating America's may be manageable. At the signing ceremony for the United Nations test-ban treaty this September, Clinton expressed the hope that the "role" of nuclear weapons could be "ultimately eliminated." Signatories include the *declared* nuclear powers (the U.S., Russia, China, France, Britain). The treaty has not taken effect, one reason being that India has refused to sign. (Gandhi must be turning in his sainted grave.) But the U.S. will respect its own signature and abide by its own gentleman's agreement. The effect will be to deny the benefits of modernization to just those countries that can be most trusted with nuclear weapons. Only those countries whose diplomats believe in the efficacy of such mantras as "trust but verify" will in the end sign on the dotted line.

The modernization of weapons without testing them is still permitted, and the U.S. is doing so. Innards are being removed, and old technology is being replaced by modern electronics. But the bombs can no longer be detonated, whether under the ground or above it, and so computer simulations must replace explosions. Will the new mechanisms actually work as intended? Nuclear weapons have a stockpile life of twenty years, and the U.S. arsenal is aging rapidly. Former Defense and Energy Secretary James Schlesinger says that the Clinton administration is hiding the reality that "with an end to testing, confidence in the nuclear stockpile must decline." He adds that if we are determined not to "design, test, manufacture or stockpile nuclear weapons," then perhaps shutting down our production facilities "makes logical sense."

* * *

Bill Clinton adopted a policy of no more testing against the advice of the director of the Los Alamos National Laboratory, Sigfried Hecker. In May 1993, he told Clinton that testing was the best way to maintain a reliable deterrent. Two months later, Clinton nonetheless ordered an end to testing. When China proceeded with an atmospheric test a few weeks later, U.S. policymakers chose to pay no attention. (Why make trouble with the big boys?) Russia is reliably reported to be maintaining its production lines, perhaps assembling as many nuclear weapons a year as we are disassembling. Even the humble Brits continue with a slow but active weapons production cycle to keep their hand in. But the U.S. has produced no weapons since 1990.

Tritium, a hydrogen isotope that is an essential ingredient of all American nukes, has not been produced anywhere in the U.S. since 1988, when the Savannah River reactor was shut down. With a half life of 12.6 years, most of the installed tritium will have vanished into thin air by the year 2015. At that point the U.S. arsenal will have a short half-life indeed. Tritium could be manufactured by electricity-generating nuclear reactors, but here we encounter the popular ignorance that has been both nurtured and exploited by the anti-nukes. Tritium-production would expose power plants to the charge that they are "hydrogen bomb plants." A recent editorial in *Science* suggested that maybe we could buy some tritium from Canada. Or, er, the Russians. That would "improve our relations" with them, and, in case you hadn't thought of it, "help alleviate their need for hard currency."

The main concern of those who are responsible for maintaining the nuclear arsenal today is that the needed human capital, experience, and knowledge will dwindle away along with the tritium. Automobile mechanics who know how to rebuild a 1933 Jaguar S-type sports coupe are difficult to find today. The refusal to allow further testing ensures that nuclear weapons technology will become increasingly outdated. It will require the expertise of those who understand and know how to maintain the nuclear equivalent of cathode ray tubes. The best minds will not be attracted by the prospects of working with museum technology in a dying industry.

The blueprints of nuclear weapons are now widely diffused throughout the world, and the knowledge they embody can never be eradicated from human consciousness. Because crude bombs can be assembled without the need for testing—the Hiroshima bomb was of a type that had not been tested—an end to testing enhances global security only in the minds of those who think the U.S. is the great threat to it. The main constraint on proliferation is the difficulty of obtaining weapons-grade fissile material: highly enriched uranium and plutonium. Neither occurs in nature —the main reason why all things nuclear are regarded with dread and horror by *homo sapiens*-hating enviros—and both depend for their production upon an advanced industrial capacity that itself has not yet proliferated much beyond the Western world.

The uncomfortable fact is that the U.S. has pursued its undeclared policy of unilateral denuclearization at just the time when this material has become more available than ever before, thanks to the breakup of the former Soviet Union. More than 100 cases of smuggling of weapons grade material have been detected, and it seems only a matter of time before a sufficient quantity of it finds its way into the hands of people who pay only lip service to the sleep-inducing diplomatic formulae. Will we feel more secure, let us say ten years from now, when more countries have acquired nuclear weapons, and it sinks in that our own dwindling arsenal is untested and of questionable reliability?

NO

George Lee Butler

ELIMINATING WEAPONS OF
MASS DESTRUCTION

Delivered to the Stimson Center Award Remarks, Washington, D.C., January 8, 1997.

Permit me to quote briefly from a memorandum that many of you will find familiar. It is from Secretary [Stimson] to President Truman, dated September 11, 1945:

"If the atomic bomb were merely another, though more devastating, military weapon to be assimilated into our pattern of international relations, it would be one thing. We could then follow the old custom of secrecy and military superiority relying on international caution to prescribe the future use of the weapon, but I think the bomb instead constitutes merely a first step in a new control by man over the forces of nature too revolutionary and dangerous to fit into the old concepts. I think it really caps the climax of the race between man's growing technical power for destructiveness and his psychological power of self-control, his moral power."

This prescient insight gives perfect expression to the growing sense of alarm, which over the course of my long experience in the nuclear arena, evolved ultimately to a singular goal: to bend every effort, within my power and authority, to promote the conditions and attitudes which might someday free mankind from the scourge of nuclear weapons.

To my utter astonishment and profound gratitude, the opportunity to advance that agenda came in the form of two wholly unanticipated and unlikely eventualities. One, of historic consequence, was the end of the Cold War; the other, of little moment, was my appointment as the commander of America's strategic nuclear forces. I was electrified by the prospects presented by the sudden shattering of the Cold War paradigm. And on entering my new office, I was seized by the opportunity to promote fundamental changes in nuclear weapons policy, force structure, planning and operational practice.

Two days after taking the helm of Strategic Air Command, I called together my senior staff of 20 generals and one admiral, and over the course of what I am sure for all of them was a mystifying and deeply unsettling discussion,

I presented my case that with the end of the Cold War, SAC's mission was effectively complete. I began to prepare them for a dramatic shift in strategic direction, to think in terms of less rather than more, to argue for smaller forces, fewer targets, reduced alert postures and accelerated arms control agreements. This was a wrenching readjustment. It prompted angry debate, bruised feelings and the early termination of a dozen promising careers. But in the final analysis, I could have not been prouder of a staff that over the course of a few short months endorsed the cancellation of $40 billion of strategic nuclear force modernization programs; that supported my recommendations to convert the B-2 to a primarily conventional role and to stand the entire bomber force down from 30 years of alert; that did pioneering analysis in developing national nuclear war plans numbering down to hundreds of targets; and perhaps most notably, unanimously supported my decision to recommend that Strategic Air Command itself be dis-established after 46 years at the nuclear ramparts.

This was an extraordinary period, a promising start to a wholesale realignment of America's national security policy and practice. And in the ensuing months there has been much to record and to applaud, thanks to a host of agencies and initiatives. Conversely, there is yet no cause for celebration nor satisfaction. The harsh truth is that six years after the end of the Cold War we are still prisoner to its psychology of distrust, still enmeshed in the vocabulary of mutual assured destruction, still in the thrall of the nuclear era. Worse, strategists persist in conjuring worlds which spiral towards chaos, and concocting threats which they assert can only be discouraged or ex-punged by the existence or employment of nuclear weapons.

It is well that Secretary Stimson did not survive to witness this folly. I can readily imagine his dismay at witnessing mankind's miraculous reprieve from nuclear disaster only to risk losing the race between self-destructiveness and self-control, or seeing technological prowess and mistrust triumph over morality and the rule of law. For my own part, I find it unconscionable, and for that reason I felt increasingly the moral imperative to reenter the public arena.

That resolve was crystallized by an invitation from the Government of Australia in late 1995 to join the Canberra Commission on the Elimination of Nuclear Weapons. I was deeply moved by Prime Minister Keating's forceful condemnation of the resumption of French nuclear testing, and his courageous effort to bring focus to the ensuing international outcry.

I come away from the Canberra Commission experience with decidedly mixed feeling. On the one hand, I was enormously enriched by this year-long association with men and women of such great stature. I was equally gratified by the unanimity of view and the forceful logic of our report. It captured in measured, balanced, and reasoned terms the essence of my own conclusions about the risks and penalties associated with nuclear weapons. Most importantly, it set forth a practical, realistic blueprint for working toward their elimination.

... I can discern the makings of an emerging global consensus that the risks posed by nuclear weapons far outweigh their presumed benefits.

[I am d]isappointed, thus far, by the quality of the debate, by those pundits who simply sniffed imperiously at the goal of elimination, aired their stock Cold War rhetoric, hurled a personal epithet or two, and settled smugly back into their world of exaggerated threats and bygone enemies. [I am also disappointed] by critics who attacked my views by misrepresenting them, such as suggesting that I am proposing unilateral disarmament or a pace of reduction that would jeopardize the security of the nuclear weapon states.

And finally, [I am] dismayed that even among more serious commentators the lessons of fifty years at the nuclear brink can still be so grievously misread; that the assertions and assumptions underpinning an era of desperate threats and risks prevail unchallenged; that a handful of nations cling to the impossible notion that the power of nuclear weapons is so immense their use can be threatened with impunity, yet their proliferation contained.

Albert Einstein recognized this hazardous but very human tendency many years ago, when he warned that "the unleashed power of the atom has changed everything save our modes of thinking, and thus we drift toward unparalleled catastrophe."

How else to explain the assertion that nuclear weapons will infallibly deter major war, in a world that survived the Cuban Missile Crisis no thanks to deterrence, but only by the grace of God? How else to accept the proposition that any civilized nation would respond to the act of a madman by adopting his methods? How otherwise to fathom a historical view that can witness the collapse of communism but fail to imagine a world rid of nuclear weapons? Or finally, to account for the assumption that because we are condemned to live with the knowledge of how to fabricate nuclear weapons, we are powerless to mount a global framework of verification and sanctions which will greatly reduce the likelihood or adequately deal with the consequences of cheating in a world free of nuclear weapons.

Many well meaning friends have counseled me that by championing elimination I risk setting the bar too high, providing an easy target for the cynical and diverting attention from the more immediately achievable. My response is that elimination is the only defensible goal and that goal matters enormously. First and foremost, all of the declared nuclear weapon states are formally committed to nuclear abolition in the letter and the spirit of the nonproliferation treaty. Every President of the United States since Dwight Eisenhower has publicly endorsed elimination. A clear and unequivocal commitment to elimination, sustained by concrete policy and measurable milestones, is essential to give credibility and substance to this long-standing declaratory position. Such a commitment goes far beyond simply seizing the moral high ground. It focuses analysis on a precise end state; all force postures above zero simply become way points along a path leading toward elimination. It shifts the locus of policy attention from numbers to the security climate essential to permit successive reductions. It conditions government at all levels to create and respond to every opportunity for shrinking arsenals, cutting infrastructure and curtailing modernization. It sets the stage for rigorous enforcement of nonproliferation regimes and unrelenting pressures to reduce nuclear arsenals on a global basis. I say again, the goal matters enormously and the only defensible goal is elimination.

But hear me say clearly, and unreservedly, that no one is more conscious than am I that realistic prospects for elimination will evolve over many years. I was in the public arena for too long ever to make the perfect the enemy of the good. I hasten to add, however, my strong conviction that we are far too timorous in imagining the good, we are still too rigidly conditioned by an arms control mentality deeply rooted in the Cold War. We fall too readily into the intellectual trap of judging the goal of elimination against current political conditions. We forget too quickly how seemingly intractable conflicts can suddenly yield under the weight of reason or with a change of leadership. We have lost sight too soon that in the blink of a historical eye the world we knew for a traumatic half-century has been utterly transformed.

How better then, you may well ask, to proceed. As I noted earlier, my own prescription is carefully detailed in the report of the Canberra Commission. It begins not with a call for greater reductions, but rather to initiate immediate, multilteral negotiations toward ending the most regrettable and risk-laden operational practice of the Cold War era: land and sea-based ballistic missiles standing nuclear alert. Why is it that five years after removing bombers, the most stable element of the nuclear triad, from alert, we keep missiles, with their 30-minute flight time, on effectively hair-trigger postures? What possibly can justify this continuing exposure to the associated operational and logistical risks? What could be more corrosive to building and sustaining security relationships built on trust? What could undercut more overtly the credibility of our leadership in advancing a nonproliferation treaty premised on a solemn obligation to eliminate nuclear arsenals?

There are a host of other measures outlined in the Canberra Commission report which should also be given immediate consideration. But this is not the time nor place to debate alternative agendas, although thoughtful debate is both urgent and essential. What matters more is the much larger and defining question upon which the debate must ultimately turn: above all nations, how should the United States see its responsibility for dealing with the conflicted moral legacy of the Cold War? Russia, with its history of authoritarian rule and a staggering burden of social transformation, is ill-equipped to lead on this issue. It falls unavoidably to us to work painfully back through the tangled moral web of this frightful 50-year gauntlet, born of the hellish confluence of two unprecedented historical currents: the bi-polar collision of ideology, and the unleashing of the power of the atom.

As a democracy, the consequences of these cataclysmic forces confronted us with a tortuous and seemingly inextricable dilemma: how to put at the service of our national survival, a weapon whose sheer destructiveness was antithetical to the very values upon which our society was based. Over time, as arsenals multiplied on both sides and the rhetoric of mutual annihilation grew more heated, we were forced to think about the unthinkable, justify the unjustifiable, rationalize the irrational. Ultimately, we contrived a new and desperate theology to ease our moral anguish, and we called it deterrence.

I spent much of my military career serving the ends of deterrence, as did millions of others. I want very much to believe that in the end that it was the nuclear force that I and others commanded and operated that prevented World War

III and created the conditions leading to the collapse of the Soviet Empire. But, in truth, I do not and I cannot know that. It will be decades before the hideously complex era of the Cold War is adequately understood, with its bewildering interactions of human fears and inhuman technology. Nor would it much matter that informed assessments are still well beyond our intellectual reach, except for the crucial and alarming fact that, forgetting the desperate circumstances which gave it birth, and long after their miraculous resolution, we continue to espouse deterrence as if it were now an infallible panacea. And worse, others are listening, have converted to our theology, are building their arsenals, are poised to rekindle the nuclear arms race, and to rewaken the specter of nuclear war.

What a stunning, perverse turn of events. In the words of my friend, Jonathan Schell, we face the dismal prospect that:

"The Cold War was not the apogee of the age of nuclear weapons, to be succeeded by an age of nuclear disarmament. Instead, it may well prove to have simply been a period of initiation, in which not only Americans and Russians, but Indians and Pakistanis, Israelis and Iraqis, were adapting to the horror of threatening the deaths of millions of people, were learning to think about the unthinkable. If this is so, will history judge that the Cold War proved only a sort of modern day Trojan Horse, whereby nuclear weapons were smuggled into the life of the world, made an acceptable part of the way the world works? Surely not, surely we still comprehend that to threaten the deaths of tens of hundreds of millions of people presages an atrocity beyond anything in the record of mankind? Or have we, in a silent and incomprehensible moral revolution, come to regard such threats as ordinary, as normal and proper policy for any self-respecting nation."

This cannot be the moral legacy of the Cold War. And it is our responsibility to ensure that it will not be. We have won, through Herculean courage and sacrifice, the opportunity to reset mankind's moral compass, to renew belief in a world free from fear and deprivation, to win global affirmation for the sanctity of life, the right of liberty, and the opportunity to pursue a joyous existence.

Winston Churchill once remarked about the nuclear era that, "the stone age may return on the gleaming wings of science."

POSTSCRIPT

Does the World Need to Have Nuclear Weapons at All?

Do arms, nuclear or otherwise, provoke war or provide security? To begin your further consideration, find out more about the current nuclear arsenals at the Web site of the Stockholm International Peace Research Institute at http://www.sipri.se/.

Many analysts argue that weapons are necessary for survival in a predatory world. As political scientist Hans Morgenthau once put it, "Men do not fight because they have arms. They have arms because they . . . fight." This logic suspects that disarmament would actually increase the likelihood of war or domination by tempting aggressors to cheat and spring their weapons on an unsuspecting and defenseless victim.

The power of nuclear weapons makes the relationship between weapons and war particularly important. The contention that nuclear arms are dangerous and that they decrease security is the prevailing view among political leaders, scholars, and others. But it is not a universally accepted view. British prime minister Winston Churchill once suggested that nuclear weapons may have rendered nuclear war and even large-scale conventional war between nuclear powers too dangerous to fight. Some would point to the absence of a U.S.–USSR war during decades of overt confrontation as proof that nuclear arms do provide security. Secretary of State James A. Baker III made this point in 1991, declaring, "I am not prepared to walk away from the concept of nuclear deterrence that has kept the peace for more than 40 years."

It is also well to ponder whether the risks of having or not having nuclear weapons have changed now that the cold war is over. More on the role of these weapons in this new political period can be found in Robert A. Manning, "The Nuclear Age: The Next Chapter," *Foreign Policy* (Winter 1997–1998). Of special note is the impact of the further spread of nuclear weapons to two countries, India and Pakistan, which have a history of enmity and which engaged in a pitched border clash in mid-1999. More on this impact can be found in William Walker, "International Nuclear Relations After the Indian and Pakistani Test Explosions," *International Affairs* (Winter 1998).

The decision whether or not to eliminate all nuclear weapons is a cosmic roll of the dice. If, as Churchill and Baker suggest, nuclear weapons have eliminated war between major powers, then such weapons are a force for peace, however scary they may be. If Churchill and Baker are wrong, and war has not occurred for other reasons, and if nuclear war is possible by inadvertence or conscious decision, then they are gravely mistaken by advocating the retention of the vehicles of Armageddon.

ISSUE 9

Should a Permanent UN Military Force Be Established?

YES: Joseph E. Schwartzberg, from "A New Perspective on Peacekeeping: Lessons from Bosnia and Elsewhere," *Global Governance* (vol. 3, no. 1, 1997)

NO: John F. Hillen III, from "Policing the New World Order: The Operational Utility of a Permanent U.N. Army," *Strategic Review* (Spring 1994)

ISSUE SUMMARY

YES: Joseph E. Schwartzberg, a professor of geography, proposes a standing UN Peace Corps military force of international volunteers to better enable the UN to meet its peacekeeping mission.

NO: John F. Hillen III, a lieutenant in the U.S. Army and a doctoral student in international relations, criticizes the idea of a permanent UN army on several grounds and concludes that such a force is unworkable.

The United Nations seeks to maintain and restore peace through a variety of methods. These include creating norms against violence, providing a forum to debate questions as an alternative to war, making efforts to prevent the proliferation of weapons, diplomatic intervention (such as mediation), and the placing of diplomatic and economic sanctions. Additionally, and at the heart of the issue here, the UN can dispatch troops under its banner or authorize member countries to use their forces to carry out UN mandates.

UN forces involving a substantial number of military or police personnel have been used more than two dozen times in the organization's nearly 50-year history and have involved troops and police from more than 75 countries. There is, therefore, a significant history of UN forces. Nevertheless, recent events and attitude changes have engendered renewed debate over the military role of the UN.

The increased number of UN operations is one factor contributing to the debate. Of all UN operations throughout history, about half are currently active. Furthermore, several of the recent missions, including the UN presence in Bosnia, Somalia, and Rwanda, have included large numbers of troops and, thus, have been very costly. Increased calls for UN peacekeeping operations and the sometimes sizable nature of those operations has increased the UN's annual peacekeeping budget from $235 million in 1987 to approximately $1.3 billion in fiscal year (FY) 1997.

A second factor that has sparked controversy about UN forces are the successes and failures of their missions. Often UN forces have played an important part in the peace process; other times they have been unsuccessful. The limited mandate (role, instructions) and strength (personnel, armaments) of UN forces has frequently left them as helpless bystanders.

A third shift that has raised concerns about UN forces is the change in the international system. With the cold war ended, some people are trying to promote a new world order. This new world order would require countries to live up to the mandate of the UN charter that they only use force unilaterally for immediate self-defense or unless they are authorized to use force by the UN or a regional organization (such as the Organization of American States). This means that collective action under UN auspices is becoming more normal, unilateral action by a country more the exception. The UN-authorized war against Iraq in 1991 is an example of this trend.

Two potential changes in the operation of UN forces apply to the issue here. The first is to increase the scope of the mission of UN forces. To date, UN forces have operated according to two concepts: *collective security* and *peacekeeping*. Collective security is the idea that aggression against anyone is a threat to everyone. Therefore, the collective body should cooperate to prevent and, if necessary, defeat aggression. The second, long-standing UN role of peacekeeping usually involves acting as a buffer between two sides to provide an atmosphere that will allow them to settle their differences, or at least to not fight. Neither collective security nor peacekeeping, however, precisely apply to situations such as domestic civil wars, in which there is no international aggressor and/or clearly identifiable aggressor. Some people consider this a gap in what the UN does to prevent the scourge of war and, therefore, would augment the UN's role to include *peacemaking*. This would involve intervening in either international or civil wars, with or without the consent of any of the participants, to force the warring parties to desist.

The second potential change for UN forces relates to proposals to create, at maximum, a standing UN army or, at least, a ready reserve of troops. These troops would remain with the forces of their home countries but would train for UN operations and be instantly available to the UN.

The immediate background to the issue debated here began with a January 1992 summit meeting of the leaders of the 15 countries with seats on the Security Council. The leaders called on the UN secretary-general Boutros Boutros-Ghali (1991–1996) to report on ways to enhance UN ability "for preventative diplomacy, for peacemaking, and for peacekeeping." In response, the secretary-general issued a report entitled *An Agenda for Peace,* in which he recommended the establishment of a 100,000-soldier UN rapid deployment force and other strategies to enhance UN peacekeeping. In the following selections, Joseph E. Schwartzberg supports the idea of a permanent UN Peace Corps to pave the way to lasting international peace and security. John F. Hillen III argues that the secretary-general's recommendations and other such proposals are mostly ill-conceived and should not be supported.

YES
Joseph E. Schwartzberg

A NEW PERSPECTIVE ON PEACEKEEPING: LESSONS FROM BOSNIA AND ELSEWHERE

The threat to use force is neither credible nor effective if there is no ability or preparedness to actually use it.

—The Commission on Global Governance, 1995

The cited passage, made with specific reference to the Bosnian peacekeeping fiasco, offers a lesson that the international community can ignore only at its peril. A corollary is that the stronger and more credible a peacekeeping force is and the sooner the willingness to apply it is made clear, the less likely will be the necessity of actually employing it in an overt combat role. It follows, then, that the willingness to invest substantially in peacekeeping, though seemingly expensive in the short term, is likely to prove exceedingly economical in the longer term. One is reminded in this context of the admonition "If you think education is expensive, just try ignorance." Similarly, one might observe, "If you think peacekeeping is expensive, try anarchy."

Regrettably, as recent experience has demonstrated, the international community—despite the painful lessons of Bosnia, Somalia, Rwanda, and, I would argue, Iraq—has yet to learn that an ounce of prevention is worth a pound of cure. As surely as the lack of preventive health measures with respect to the human body or the lack of timely preventive maintenance for an automobile engine will exact a future penalty, so too will continued failure to fund and empower effectively UN peacekeeping efforts. In recognition of that simple truth, this essay sets forth a proposal for a cost-effective UN Peace Corps. It discusses the increasing need for such an entity, specifies the functions that such a corps could perform in both peacetime and emergency situations, indicates the means by which the corps may be recruited and trained, outlines the essential elements for its command and control, estimates its likely costs and benefits, and suggests the transitional arrangements that would smooth the way from the present ad hoc mode of peacekeeping to a more efficient and dependable system.

THE GROWING NEED

While falling short of the recommendations set forth in this essay, a number of thoughtful recent calls have been made to establish a standing all-volunteer force of peacekeepers, directly under UN command. Such a force, it is asserted, would be able to provide a needed rapid response in situations of grave threat to the peace and function until such time as nationally recruited standby contingents could be brought to bear to help stabilize the situation and prevent either new outbreaks of hostilities or the expansion of armed conflicts already under way. Had even a small, elite, rapid-reaction force been available in the case of Rwanda, there can be little doubt that it would have averted the slaughter of hundreds of thousands of innocent civilians in the genocidal orgy of 1994. As the commander of UNAMIR (the UN Assistance Mission for Rwanda), Maj. Gen. Roméo Dallaire, observed: "In Rwanda, the international community's inaction... contributed to the Hutu extremists' belief that they could carry out their genocide.... UNAMIR could have saved the lives of hundreds of thousands of people.... A force of 5,000 personnel rapidly deployed could have prevented the massacres... that did not commence in earnest until early May, nearly a month after the start of the war."

Similarly, timely intervention of a small interpositionary force of UN peacekeepers might have dissuaded Saddam Hussein's 1991 invasion of Kuwait. It is also likely, though by no means certain, that had such a peacekeeping force been available early in 1992, the Bosnian cataclysm might somehow have been prevented. But it does seem clear that the presence of a small UN interpositionary force in Macedonia has been among the factors that have prevented the Balkan conflict from spilling southward into that republic and that have averted, thus far, the anticipated Serbian crackdown on Albanian separatists in the neighboring, formerly autonomous, area of Kosovo.

As matters transpired, the forces introduced into Bosnia and other republics of the former Yugoslavia were too few and too late; they lacked funding, logistical support, and a clear mandate to prevent several waves of "ethnic cleansing," other massive violations of human rights, and untold destruction of property. Because of those initial inadequacies, the subsequent infusion into Bosnia of an additional relatively small UN peacekeeping force, no matter how well trained and commanded it might have been, would not have sufficed to restore peace to the region. Moreover, the Bosnian Serbs' successful defiance (for a time) of UN peacekeepers in Bosnia led to the ultimate withdrawal of all UN forces (similar to the case with U.S. forces in the Somali UN operation once the going got rough). These facts point to two important conclusions. The first is that the required scale of future UN peacekeeping missions will often exceed what would have been necessary for the success of comparable missions in the past. The second is the need to put future UN missions under direct and exclusive UN command and to staff them with volunteer soldiers who are not subject to unpredictable recall by the leaders of individual UN member nations responding to domestic political pressures.

Although operations such as the one currently being mounted by NATO in Bosnia may appear to be a feasible alternative to UN peacekeeping in certain contexts, one can hardly expect NATO to take on the role of the world's police force.

The legitimacy of its doing so would surely be called into question, especially when a single power, the United States, occupies so prominent a position within NATO. Moreover, as we shall see, most of the many future conflicts that seem likely to call for UN intervention lie outside the area of NATO's concern.

In the brief period since the dismantling of the Berlin Wall and the ending of the Cold War, several dozen new conflicts have erupted around the planet. Most of these are civil wars pitting repressed ethnic minorities against dominant national groups; but many of the conflicts threaten to involve neighboring nations in which most or a substantial part of the population identifies strongly with one or another party in the struggle. As of 1990, I had enumerated some 321 linguistic minorities in the world—mainly in Africa, Asia, and Eastern Europe—with populations of half a million or more, most of whom had ample reason to be dissatisfied with the system of governance under which they were living. In addition to the potential disputes relating to linguistic minorities are those that involve scores of religious and racial minorities. These figures suggest hundreds of wars waiting to happen. The downfall of repressive regimes in many parts of the world, the easing of restraints formerly imposed by the United States and the Soviet Union on the political behavior of their client states, the spread of the notion of representative democracy and of the idea of national self-determination, and the power of the telecommunications revolution jointly conduce to a greater likelihood of ethnic conflict in the foreseeable future than at any time in the past. While many potential conflicts will undoubtedly be averted—because of continuing repression or, less frequently, through enlightened statesmanship (as in the former Czechoslovakia)—many others will not. And more than a few of the potential conflicts seem likely to become sufficiently serious to call for various forms of international intervention, in some instances by regional organizations such as the OAS, but—given the meager resources of most such organizations—more often by the UN. Ideally, this intervention will be mediatory and not entail the use of armed peacekeepers, but experience suggests that resort to peacekeeping and to the use of interpositionary forces to prevent the eruption or spread of armed conflict will, from time to time, be necessary.

Apart from ethnic and religious struggles, there are in the world scores of other potential conflict situations involving territorial disputes. In addition to traditional disputes over boundaries on land, there are literally hundreds of new maritime boundaries that have yet to be determined because of the coming-into-force of the UN Comprehensive Law of the Sea Treaty; and many of these sea boundaries, especially with regard to the newly established "exclusive economic zones," are even now (as in the South China Sea) being hotly contested. Finally, in a world of burgeoning populations and dwindling resources, the likelihood of strife with respect to such vital needs as arable land, fresh water, and petroleum is certain to increase. Thus, there can be little doubt that the post–Cold War period, far from having ushered in a new era of peace, remains fraught with danger.

For these reasons, a strong case can be made that the world increasingly requires a globally recruited, all-volunteer, elite, highly trained, multipurpose UN Peace Corps (UNPC) larger than any such force proposed to date. Admittedly, the problems to be solved in establishing a

UNPC are dauntingly complex. The cost of such a body would obviously be high, with annual expenditures substantially greater than those allocated for current UN peacekeeping operations. Further, given the present reluctance (especially in the United States) to fund existing UN commitments, it would be unrealistic to anticipate widespread early support for the far-reaching recommendations set forth in this essay. Nevertheless, I make the case that the ultimate benefits would enormously outweigh the costs, not merely with respect to conflicts and destruction averted, but also in the vast reductions in national military expenditures that the proposed new force would permit. I also indicate numerous other realizable benefits of a nonmilitary nature. If the arguments I set forth prove persuasive, the support that now seems unattainable may yet be forthcoming, and a planned sequence of steps toward the establishment of the envisaged UNPC might soon be initiated.

None of the recommendations I propose should be taken to imply that the application of military force is the preferred means of dealing with international or intranational conflict. Much more desirable is the whole range of preventive diplomacy and peacemaking measures spelled out in Boutros Boutros-Ghali's *Agenda for Peace*, and it is obviously potentially more fruitful to refine the tools for effective mediation than to develop measures for dealing with armed strife after preventive diplomacy fails. However, in the foreseeable future, failures will at times occur, and the international community must be ready and able to deal with them.

It is also important to stress at the outset that for military missions to be lastingly effective, decisions by the Security Council to sanction them must be per-ceived as legitimate and not made primarily in the interests of only one or a small coterie of the council's most powerful states. While legitimacy alone provides no guarantee of a mission's success, it seems obvious that compliance with the actions of a legitimately empowered force is more likely than with those of one whose legitimacy is open to question. Hence, the establishment of a more democratic Security Council, better representing the world's people than does the present council, will significantly enhance the probability of success of whatever missions it may order.

FUNCTIONS OF THE UNPC

The more numerous and worthwhile the tasks the proposed UNPC can perform, the greater will be the willingness to provide it with political and financial support. Thus, rather than thinking solely in terms of being able to respond rapidly to pressing military emergencies, one should also consider a multiplicity of additional functions the corps might appropriately perform, many of which could keep units productively occupied during the (one hopes) long periods during which they are not required to play an active, specifically military role.

In the relatively narrow military mode are such functions as patrolling cease-fire lines and monitoring violations, protecting civilian populations in zones of conflict and overseeing the evacuation of refugees from areas of danger, guarding emergency relief supplies to war-affected areas, establishing interpositionary forces to prevent conflicts from spreading to countries under palpable threat of invasion (the first such example of this is the UN force in Macedonia), and—when the Security Council deems it necessary—engaging in peace-enforcing operations under Chapter VII of the UN Charter. Distinctively different functions would be to restore, in concert with civilian specialists, some semblance of normalcy in failed states or in situations in which sovereignty is being transferred from one state to another. (The recent experiences in Cambodia and Somalia provide useful lessons in the former regard and those in West New Guinea/Iran Barat, in 1962–1963, in the latter.) Other vital functions, more likely to be undertaken following the conclusion of conflict than in times of open combat, are clearing minefields, disposing of ordnance, and dismantling selected military installations and/or weapons-making plants (for example, with respect to operations following the Gulf War).

There is no reason why units of the UNPC, when not actively engaged in military activities, should not be employed, in cooperation with other agencies, in a broad range of peace-building projects of a developmental and humanitarian nature. These might include constructing or upgrading roads, airports, and other components of the infrastructure of host countries; establishing projects to improve local drinking-water supplies, sanitation, and other aspects of public health; participating in training activities that would enhance the skills of the local citizenry; responding globally to urgent needs in times of famine, earthquakes, flooding, and other natural catastrophes; providing logistic support to nongovernmental organizations (NGOs) and specialized UN agencies dealing with such catastrophes; and creating and maintaining strategically situated supply depots to facilitate the provision of emergency disaster relief. Finally, election monitoring presents yet another potential task.

Admittedly, all these functions are already being performed on a limited scale by the UN Development Program or, as in the case of election monitoring, through various teams established by the UN on an ad hoc basis; but the scope for enhancing such worthy efforts through the participation of the UNPC would be enormous. Cost-sharing arrangements for such activities would have to be worked out through contracts involving host governments, various agencies within the UN system, NGOs, and others.

The UNPC would provide additional benefits in the training of its internationally recruited male and female volunteers, especially for the many who are likely to come from developing countries. Apart from the valuable technical skills the volunteers would be taught, one must consider the habits of discipline and devotion to duty and the esprit de corps that a well-run, elite military unit would impart. Such intangible benefits have enormous potential to contribute to nation building and social development once the volunteers complete their terms of service and return to their countries of origin. Service in the corps would, as a rule, provide a badge of honor and respect for its veterans and enhance their ability to later function as effective development agents in their home settings. (The experience of veterans of Gurkha units recruited to both the British and the Indian armies is instructive in this regard.) Moreover, the service would bring the elite of different countries into close working contact with one another and thereby help break down negative cultural and gender stereotypes and establish enduring bonds of international amity. The service would also greatly enhance the ability of many volunteers to communicate in one or more new languages, the economic and social benefits of which should be obvious. Apart from the benefits from work-related activities are those that would stem from recreational pastimes, such as organized sporting events (including matches between UNPC and host-country teams), cultural activities within the host country, and foreign travel during periods of paid leave. Finally, the establishment of a corps of men and women inspired with an ethos of global service and common allegiance to humanity, rather than to specific countries, would help forge a new, much-needed planetary consciousness.

RECRUITMENT AND TRAINING

Service in the UNPC would be open equally to qualified men and women from all parts of the world. This presupposes the establishment of offices for the screening, testing, and selection of would-be volunteers. Most of these offices could be permanently attached to those of the already existing network of UN country coordinators, while others would operate perhaps for only one or two months per year, at a sufficiently well distributed set of localities so as to make the option of enlisting a practicable one in areas where the costs of travel are high in relation to average income levels. The physical, mental, and moral requirements for eligibility at all ranks should be sufficiently high to ensure that the corps would be an elite body. Establishing the requisite physical, mental, and behavioral standards and the means to ensure that they were faithfully adhered to would be the task of a specially appointed subcommission of those powers entrusted with drawing up the interim arrangements leading up to the establishment of the UNPC (as will be discussed in the final section of this essay).

All recruits would undergo an initial period of rigorous basic training, the length of which would vary depending on whether preliminary language instruction was necessary.... Terms of service, following the successful completion of basic training, would be four additional years for all noncommissioned ranks, which could be renewed only once; a few exceptions could be made for needed specialists. This stricture would preclude the creation of a large body of career soldiers.... To ensure continuity of command, training, and operational functions, however, the length of permissible service for officers and a small cadre of key noncommissioned officers should be longer than for lower ranks.

On pragmatic grounds, the number of operating languages within the corps would have to be limited. For an initial period, English, French, and Spanish would best serve, given their global distribution and their status as either official or auxiliary languages in a substantial majority of the world's countries. Moreover, while not all recruits would initially be proficient in any of those three tongues, those whose native language was close to one of the UNPC languages would be able to learn the new language well enough to use it effectively within six months or so following recruitment.... Within each command (to be discussed below), a single language would be selected for training and for most operational purposes....

Compensation, in terms of salaries and other benefits, would be generous. In addition to the usual provision of uniforms, food, billeting, other necessities, and paid leave time, all personnel would receive a salary appropriate for the area in which they served and a supplemental amount deposited in a home-country bank account would become available to them on honorable conclusion of their period of service. A system of postservice educational benefits (comparable to the remarkably successful GI Bill of Rights for veterans of the armed forces of the United States) should also be instituted. Service, therefore, would be regarded not merely as a job, but as a hard-won privilege. This would be essential to maintain high morale and to create a healthy esprit de corps. It would also greatly enhance the respect accorded to the UNPC wherever it may be called on to serve.

COMMAND AND CONTROL

Largely following the 1989 recommendations of the Norwegian Commission of Experts, the chain of command for the UNPC would run from the Security Council through the secretary-general and an International Military Staff Committee within the Secretariat to a UN Central Command and thence to three regional commands. Taking into consideration numerous geographical, logistical, and political factors, the following division of responsibilities is suggested: a Western Command for the Americas, the operating language for which would be Spanish; a dual Central Command for Europe, Africa, and the Middle East, one component of which would use French and the other English; and an Eastern Command for the balance of Asia and Oceania, the operating language for which would be English. There could be some units within each command, however, using languages other than the official command language. . . .

The subordination of English within the Western Command structure and the lack of Russian- and Chinese-speaking commands may appear to some to be significant shortcomings. But, as a practical matter, one must recognize that in the foreseeable future the UNPC is unlikely to be called upon to intervene in crises originating in or involving the United States, Russia, or China, or, for that matter, any other veto-wielding permanent member of either the present or an expanded future Security Council. Nor, in all likelihood, would the UNPC be asked to intervene in the areas of a substantial number of other states (e.g., Canada or the Scandinavian countries) whose commitment to peace appears firm. Should any of the world's larger powers become guilty in the near future of armed aggression, that would represent a threat to world peace of such a magnitude that it is not likely that armed intervention, even by the UNPC, would be particularly efficacious. Other ad hoc mechanisms for dealing with the issue would have to be devised. Ultimately, elimination of the veto in the Security Council would go a long way toward remedying this admitted limitation of the present proposal (as well as of all others that call for standing UN peacekeeping forces); but an even more fundamental requisite is an essentially disarmed world. The achievement of that worthy goal, however, will necessitate overcoming a host of political obstacles that cannot be addressed within the scope of this brief essay.

Normally, troops from only one regional command would be used in a specific military mission; and one would hope that the size of the force at its disposal would suffice to carry out effectively whatever task it might be assigned. Nevertheless, one must anticipate instances when obdurate military resistance to a given UNPC intervention would be of such a magnitude that it would become necessary to draw on forces from other commands. Thus, each command would provide, in effect, a strategic reserve for the others. It is further conceivable that an occasion might arise when available units from the combined UNPC commands would be unequal to a specific military assignment. In such a case, the UNPC would still form the nucleus and spearhead of the force assigned by the Security Council to meet the threat; but it would have to be supplemented by additional units provided by individual member states (as originally envisaged in Chapter VII of the UN Charter). In such a case, a resolute mustering of the necessary military would be essential....

The headquarters of each regional command, along with a substantial part of the staff, should be placed on bases leased from reasonably stable countries with relatively democratic regimes within the regions where they are likely to be needed. The countries selected should offer adequate facilities for logistical support by both sea and air from powers capable of providing such support. If the system were currently in place, suitable candidates might be Costa Rica or Ecuador for the Western Command; Morocco or Senegal for the French-speaking component of the Central Command and Egypt or South Africa for the English-speaking component; and the Philippines or Malaysia for the Eastern Command. A limited number of additional bases, including supply depots, could be established at appropriate leased sites in each of the three commands. Preference would be given in all cases to sites in countries with democratic regimes, thereby providing an incentive for maintaining such governments....

In its initial phase, the UNPC would rely on the larger powers for naval and air support, using leased vessels and aircraft in much the same way as in present UN peacekeeping missions. In time, however, there is no reason in principle why the UNPC should not acquire its own ships, aircraft, and personnel.

A final, but crucial, requirement with respect to the UNPC command and control is that the criteria for intervention and the rules of engagement once intervention is sanctioned by the Security Council must be clearly specified.

COSTS AND BENEFITS

As noted, the costs of establishing and maintaining the proposed UNPC would be great. Annual expenditures would undoubtedly be substantially greater than that of the combined ongoing UN peacekeeping operations. Such peacekeeping costs peaked at more than $3.5 billion in 1994; but, because of severe budgetary constraints requiring the termination or curtailment of a number of missions, the figure has since fallen to roughly $1.6 billion in 1996.

At present, the annual cost per man/woman in uniform in the world's major armed forces (including land, sea, and air forces) varies over a remarkably wide range. Sample figures, calculated to the nearest $1,000 [range from] India $4,000... to the United States $173,000. For the countries toward the upper end of this spectrum, however, a very large part of the expenses indicated derives from the high costs of sophisticated equipment, especially for offensive weapons systems for the air force and navy.... However, relatively little in the way of high-tech lethal ordnance would be appropriate for the UNPC. In light of these considerations, it seems reasonable to suggest a cost per soldier in the neighborhood of $40,000 per year.

If, then, we assume a total force of three hundred thousand in all three commands once the UNPC attains full strength, and average annual maintenance costs of $40,000 per soldier, ... that would yield a total of $12 billion when the UNPC is functioning in a nonmilitary mode. Actual military operations would, of course, add significantly to this sum, especially with respect to the leasing of needed ships and aircraft for logistic support. In the initial years of the UNPC, costs would obviously be different from what they would be once the commands were brought to full strength. On the one hand, there would be substantial start-up costs for recruiting and for building and stocking military bases (though significant savings might be realized in this regard by utilizing UNPC cadres themselves for much of the work). On the other hand, the number of personnel initially involved would be substantially less than the full complement, and the costs for postservice benefits would, for some years, be negligible.

While the anticipated expenses of the UNPC may at first appear prohibitively large, they pale in comparison to the world's national military expenditures, which in 1992 totaled $815 billion, or to the Clinton administration's budgeted $1,302 billion for military expenditures over the period 1995–1999 for the United States alone. One should also compare the likely costs of the UNPC with the vastly greater costs of the wars it could avert. For example, while reliable figures for the Gulf War are hard to come by, it is estimated to have cost the victorious allies more than $100 billion, not to mention the incalculable losses to Iraq, Kuwait, and other countries (with respect to lives lost, destruction of property and military equipment, damaged economic infrastructure, and massive environmental degradation) and the subsequent expenses—to both victor and vanquished—of maintaining UN-mandated sanctions against Iraq. On a much more modest scale, we may consider the comparably tragic costs of the UN's recent involvement in Rwanda, where the needed funding and rapid deployment capability was so conspicuously lacking.

> During the slow process of creating UNAMIR, the Security Council made it clear that it wanted the operation conducted at minimal expense. Only a fraction of the US$200 million estimated cost of the operation was ever received by the UN. Only a portion of the troops required to implement UNAMIR's mandate ever arrived in the theatre. The lack of funding and material support for UNAMIR stands in sharp contrast to the money spent by the international community in aid and human resource support once the crisis attracted the attention of the international media. The United States alone provided US$350 million in aid in the first six weeks of the Goma tragedy.

How many more Rwandas will it take for the global community to liberate itself from its self-defeating, penny-wise and pound-foolish mode of response to looming threats of genocide, aggression, and other catastrophic events?

While nobody can accurately foretell the future, it is nevertheless in order to indulge in a bit of plausible economic speculation. Let us suppose that, in some future year X, the costs of the UNPC, including those of actual military operations, total $20 billion (roughly five times the UN expenditures on peacekeeping in 1994). Let us also suppose that the sense of heightened regional and global security generated by the UNPC's capacity to contain conflicts before they get out of control (contrary to what happened, for example, in the former Yugoslavia) will induce the world's nations to reduce annual military expenditures by roughly a fourth, say by $200 billion. If these hypothetical figures are accepted (though there is no compelling reason to suppose that the savings in national military expenditures could not be much greater), they alone would yield a cost-benefit ratio of 10:1, making the UNPC an incredibly good investment. One should also consider the enormous additional savings that would accrue from the many instances in which the very existence of a UNPC will have averted destructive wars —or the imputed value of preventing even a single campaign of genocide on the scale of the one recently witnessed in Rwanda. Finally, one must consider the numerous tangible and intangible benefits that would flow from the UNPC's manifold nonmilitary functions. Though those anticipated benefits are admittedly largely unquantifiable, they alone might more than compensate for the UNPC's cost. Thus, unless the foregoing assumptions are deemed incredibly wide of the mark, by any reasonable economic or political calculus the UNPC would clearly warrant implementation.

Since the anticipated costs of the UNPC substantially exceed the present costs of the entire UN system, one might reasonably consider how such an undertaking could best be financed. Although many creative proposals for enhancing UN revenues have been put forward, the one that appears most appropriate with respect to the UNPC would be a proportional and progressive levy on the defense expenditures and/or on international arms sales of all UN member nations. Apart from their inherent logic, such levies would provide a significant inducement for disarmament. Regrettably, however, while numerous workable ideas have been advanced, they are yet to be accompanied by the requisite will to effect the needed systemic change. What is now necessary is for enough governments to overcome their myopia and distrust with respect to financing and empowering the UN and to recognize the magnitude of the savings and other benefits that would very rapidly accrue from prudent investment in bold peacekeeping initiatives.

TRANSITIONAL ARRANGEMENTS

What has been provided here is a general outline, not a plan capable of being effected in the short term. To get from where we are at present to the proposed UNPC, the UN should first enhance its capability for timely reaction to crises. This will require the establishment of a rapid deployment force of relatively modest size, backed up by standby national contingents capable of responding swiftly and credibly to future threats to the peace up to a level significantly greater than those faced in the former Yugoslavia. Even that reasonable and limited goal, however, will not be reached without a clear determination on the part of the international community, and especially its leading powers, to take effective, timely, and credible military action to prevent future aggression, genocide, and other flagrant abuses of human rights.

As future peacekeeping successes are achieved, and as the recognition spreads that there are indeed reliable international mechanisms for preventing or containing violence, the justification for maintaining large national military establishments will diminish. Then, given popular pressure for reducing tax burdens, nations should be increasingly willing to divert portions of their military budgets away from their individual defense establishments and toward supporting a UNPC. ...

Well-thought-out plans to meet widely sensed and urgent needs are likely to elicit the needed popular and diplomatic support. This would be true even if only the purely military needs for a UNPC were being considered. But as has been indicated, numerous and substantial nonmilitary, developmental, and humanitarian benefits—many of the latter in situations calling for a rapid-response capability—would also result from the establishment of a multipurpose UNPC. Such ongoing benefits, in addition to the narrower military raison d'être for such a force, should go far toward making it internationally acceptable.

NO

John F. Hillen III

POLICING THE NEW WORLD ORDER: THE OPERATIONAL UTILITY OF A PERMANENT U.N. ARMY

Proposals to create a U.N. Army are not new. They are designed to provide a mechanism and structure that will allow the U.N. to exercise its mandate while circumventing the problem that usually hobbles U.N. operations: the lack of a common political will. Political obstacles aside, there are operational reasons for rejecting a standing U.N. Army. The most important reason for this rejection is that such a force is redundant if employed at the lower end of the U.N. military operations spectrum (observation missions and first generation peacekeeping) but incapable of having any real impact at the upper end (second generation peacekeeping and enforcement).

In the three years immediately following the end of the Cold War, there was a heady optimism about the renewed capacity of the United Nations to enforce resolutions concerning international peace and security. Now, due to the apparent impotency of United Nations forces in Bosnia and Somalia, the mood has swung back toward the pessimism characteristic of the Cold War era. This has not stopped debate about mechanisms that the U.N. can use to enforce its resolutions, including an idea that never quite seems to go away for long: a permanent U.N. Army. Proponents say that such a force could rise above the ebb and flow of national interests and provide a genuinely useful security tool for the United Nations. However, what many of these observers fail to realize is that the limited operational capabilities of a permanent U.N. Army would rarely allow it to influence situations like Bosnia and Somalia. In some respects, it is a worthwhile idea, but it is self-defeating in that the force could make little impact on the very problems it was created to alleviate. . . .

A RECURRING THEME

The idea of a permanent force for the U.N. is not envisaged by the U.N. Charter: it is in fact a concept that seeks to rectify a weakness in the Charter.

From John F. Hillen III, "Policing the New World Order: The Operational Utility of a Permanent U.N. Army," *Strategic Review* (Spring 1994). Copyright © 1994 by John F. Hillen III. Reprinted by permission. Notes omitted.

Article 43 of the U.N. Charter was intended to create for the U.N. continued access to the massive forces of the victorious World War II alliance. Even the most modest of proposals for U.N. forces constituted under Article 43 visualized 12 Army divisions, 900 combat aircraft, and almost 50 capital warships. The charter structure for using these forces visualized a fairly consistent process. The Security Council could determine a threat to international peace and security (Article 39), order action to redress such a threat by land, sea, and air forces under U.N. authority (Article 42), and call said forces to its service through the agreements reached according to Article 43. However, this security structure was doomed from the start because the critical agreements of Article 43 never materialized.

Thus, all proposals for a permanent U.N. Army have a common goal: to provide the U.N. with the mechanism and structure necessary to exercise its mandate: to maintain international peace and security....

[C]urrent proposals for a permanent U.N. Army are fueled by the desire for a tool that the U.N. can employ without being buffeted by the tides of a fickle international community. This most recent revival of the call for a permanent U.N. force does not seek to harness international consensus for the United Nations... but to institutionalize a security mechanism for the U.N. that does not rely on that consensus. The contemporary rationale for a permanent U.N. force is that it can circumvent the lack of political resolve in such situations as Bosnia.

THE SPECTRUM OF U.N. MILITARY OPERATIONS

Operations involving military personnel conducted under the auspices of the United Nations or its mandates span a broad operational spectrum. This spectrum ranges from unarmed peace observation missions to the conduct of war against an intransigent state. The operational nature of a U.N. military mission can be determined by many different factors, most of which can be subsumed under two categories: 1) the environment in which the force operates; and 2) the level of military effort or force used.

The environment in which the operation takes place could range from completely benign to very hostile. This important factor in the planning of U.N. military missions largely determines the size, nature, and composition of the U.N. force and its tasks. The level of military effort and the force employed reflects the environment and/or opposing forces as well as the nature of the tasks to be performed. By measuring these factors in all U.N. military operations, one can actually plot the spectrum of operations. While it is a continuous spectrum, there are discernible mission subsets: 1) Observation Missions; 2) First Generation Peacekeeping; 3) Second Generation Peacekeeping; and 4) Enforcement Actions.

The first two sets of U.N. military operations share many of the same operational characteristics. These are largely derived from the "principles of peacekeeping" which were recently articulated by the Under Secretary-General for peacekeeping operations.

1. They are United Nations operations. The forces are formed by the U.N. at the outset, commanded in the field

by a U.N.-appointed general, under the ultimate authority of the U.N. Secretary-General, and financed by member states collectively.

2. Peacekeeping forces are deployed with the consent of all the parties involved and only after a political settlement had been reached between warring factions.

3. The forces are committed to strict impartiality. Military observers and peacekeepers can in no way take sides with or against a party to the conflict.

4. Troops are provided by member states on a voluntary basis. During the Cold War era, the superpowers or even "big five" [the permanent members of the Security Council—China, France, Great Britain, the Soviet Union (now Russia), and the United States] rarely participated in these missions, and the majority of troops were supplied by the so-called "middle nations" to reinforce the concept of neutrality.

5. These units operate under rules of engagement that stress the absolute minimum use of force in accomplishing their objectives. This is usually limited to the use of force in self-defense only, but some missions have used force in "situations in which peacekeepers were being prevented by armed persons from fulfilling their mandate."

These five principles are especially applied in earnest in *observation missions*. There have been fifteen of these missions to date, and they represent the low end of the operational spectrum....

FIRST GENERATION PEACEKEEPING

Another class of U.N. military operations guided by the "principles of peacekeep-

ing" are first generation peacekeeping missions. These operations were all initiated during the Cold War era, as an improvised response to "the failure of collective security and the success of early U.N. peace observation missions." There were seven operations of this kind.... Three are still operational: Cyprus, the Golan Heights, and Lebanon, in their 29th, 19th and 15th years respectively. These operations share the salient feature of observation missions. Because peacekeeping forces are deployed after a political settlement and because they must remain strictly neutral, they rely on the goodwill and cooperation of the belligerents to accomplish their mission.

These forces differ from observation missions in that they are made up of entire military units from U.N. member states. These units are organically equipped, organized, trained, and armed (albeit lightly) for combat. They therefore possess some modicum of offensive capability and a credible defensive capacity. First generation peacekeeping forces have usually been deployed in a "buffer" role, physically occupying and controlling neutral territory between belligerents. These missions have focused primarily on ensuring the continued separation of the previously warring factions.

First generation peacekeeping missions do not generally have ambitious tasks: missions are derived from political objectives. The main objective is to contain the armed conflict in order to provide a stable atmosphere in which the conflict can be politically resolved. First generation peacekeeping missions (with the exception of parts of the U.N. intervention in the Congo) have no mandate or capacity to impose a political solution on the belligerents. After all, if deployed in accordance with the "principles of peacekeeping" there should be no need for forceful action in an atmosphere of cooperation. However, the operational environment has generally been more bellicose than that experienced by observation missions and there have been over 750 U.N. peacekeepers killed in these seven missions. That environment, and the more complicated military tasks involved for these combat units place these operations higher on the operational spectrum.

SECOND GENERATION PEACEKEEPING

Second generation peacekeeping missions share some operational characteristics with their Cold War predecessors but transcend the "principles of peacekeeping." The U.N. has initiated five of these operations since the relaxation of the superpower confrontation in 1987–1989: in Namibia, Cambodia, the former Yugoslavia, Somalia and Mozambique. In the main these operations are far more ambitious in their objectives, which include disarming the warring factions, maintaining law and order, restoring civil government and its associated functions, setting up and supervising elections, and delivering humanitarian aid. What makes these second generation tasks so challenging is that they very often take place in an atmosphere of continued fighting between factions, civil turmoil, and general chaos. The rate of U.N. fatalities in these missions is climbing.

There are considerable differences between these missions and those of the first two classes. While second generation peacekeeping forces are formed and deployed with unprecedented Security Council consensus, the warring parties often do not want them. Unlike first generation peacekeeping, a cease-fire is not a *sine qua non* [essential] for U.N. deployment. The U.N. forces involved in these operations face the prospect of having little or no cooperation from the factions on the ground, since second generation peacekeeping missions often consist of heavily armed combat units possessing considerable offensive capability, frequently contributed by the major powers.

The large and combat-heavy force structure of second generation peacekeeping forces means that they are able not only to protect themselves and other U.N. personnel, but also to attempt to impose an agreement on unwilling belligerents. The risks inherent in this have been most graphically portrayed in Bosnia and Somalia. In each case, military force has been employed against particular parties in the conflict. In Bosnia, it has mainly consisted of an enforced flight ban against the Serbs and the low level use of force to protect the delivery of humanitarian aid and keep supply lines open. In Somalia, the U.N. authorized the capture by force of Mohammed Aideed, again clearly taking sides in the attempt to impose a political solution. The offensive use of military force in these missions has not produced great dividends for the "peacekeepers" as yet.

The operational characteristics of most second generation peacekeeping missions bear little resemblance to the five "principles of peacekeeping." 1) While they are U.N. operations, they sometimes must rely nonetheless on other organizations or member states for complex operational capabilities that the U.N. does not possess. The use of NATO to enforce the Bosnian flight ban and a U.S. military task force to initially intervene in Somalia are two examples of this. 2) There has been no concrete political settlement in some cases and there is hardly an environment of consent for a U.N. presence. 3) As mentioned above, the doctrine of strict neutrality has not been followed. 4) The forces of the permanent members of the Security Council are often heavily involved. 5) The rules of engagement have been enlarged substantially to allow second generation peacekeepers the capacity to impose a solution on the local parties through the use of force.

In most respects, these missions are only one step short of full-scale enforcement operations. The U.N. has recognized that, considering the innocuous forces and methods employed, traditional peacekeeping can only succeed under favorable political conditions. But second generation peacekeeping military forces are caught on the horns of a prickly dilemma. While lesser operations are governed by the principles of peacekeeping and higher operations are governed by the principles of war, second generation peacekeeping operations are quite simply ungoverned by doctrine of any kind.

ENFORCEMENT

Enforcement actions represent the high end of the operational spectrum, taking place in a bellicose and adversarial environment that necessitates the use of large-scale military force. The operational characteristics of these campaigns are those of war. The role of military forces in this enterprise is obviously more clear cut than the somewhat ambiguous parameters of action in peacekeeping missions. There is no cooperation from the enemy and therefore no need for impartiality. The forces can use purely military doctrine to calculate the force needed to impose the dictates of the U.N. resolution on the aggressor. From a military point of view, this is the only type of U.N. operation where the force can actually create the environment it needs to guarantee success. The only two examples of U.N. collective security operations of this type are Korea in 1950–1953 and Kuwait in 1990–1991.

Each of these situations presented a unique set of circumstances for the exercise of collective security under the auspices of the U.N. In each case the command and control of the operation and the majority of forces were provided by the United States, leading many to dismiss these operations as American wars. However, both were multinational operations authorized by the legislative bodies of the U.N. The fact that the U.N. was essentially following the U.S. lead in both cases illustrates an important characteristic of large-scale enforcement actions. They must have the wholesale participation of a great power in order to bring about the huge resources, sacrifices, and political will required to wage modern war against an intransigent state. Only a few states or groups of states can provide the complex infrastructure and large forces necessary to undertake complicated military enterprises like Operation Desert Storm.

THE PERMANENT U.N. ARMY

Having described the types of military operations in which a U.N. force operates, we must now briefly address the different types of permanent U.N. force proposed. This paper will not consider Article 43-type proposals which would create, on paper, a huge force available to the U.N. for any operation up to major enforcement actions. The main reason for this is that there appears to be no chance that an Article 43 agreement will be signed in the foreseeable future. This is the main reason that [U.N. Secretary-General Boutros] Boutros-Ghali's *An Agenda for Peace* calls for the mobilization of a large force separate from Article 43 agreements. It is an effort to bypass the perpetual deadlock surrounding that luckless article.

Boutros-Ghali proposes "units that would be available on call and would consist of troops that have volunteered for such service." This plan would identify units from member states that could be called upon to build a U.N. force "package" when the Security Council authorizes a mission. Communications units, logistics units, transportation units, medical units, and other expensive sophisticated support elements would be earmarked by member states for U.N. service as well as the traditional light infantry units. These units would have to concentrate the majority of their training on U.N. duties and it has been recommended that their deployments be financed through national defense budgets. Needless to say, the response to these proposals from member states has been tepid at best. "Such modeling assumes that there will be major cuts in national armies as a result of diminishing East-West tensions and that this reduction could be matched by a growth in U.N. military capabilities." That assumption has proved to be naive in the extreme.

The proposal addressed here calls for a supra-national force of U.N. volunteers. Much like the civilian bureaucrats and officials employed by the U.N., these soldiers would be international civil (military) servants. They would be volunteers for international service and would not be under military obligation to any member state: only to the United Nations. They would be recruited, trained, equipped, and paid by the United Nations. The force proposed is usually infantry brigade-size, five to six thousand troops, with organic support and transportation capabilities. There are countless practical difficulties associated with forming such a force, but let us for the moment assume that it can be formed, trained, and deployed by the U.N.

THE UTILITY OF A U.N. ARMY

Naturally, even the most enthusiastic proponents of this small U.N. force recognize that its utility is limited by its size and capabilities. The most important advantage of this force is its rapid reaction capability. Since it is not drawn from member states, with all the attendant difficulties of that process, it can be deployed at the discretion of the Secretary-General on very short notice. The key element contributing to its success would be timeliness. "Clearly, a timely intervention by a relatively small but highly trained force, willing and authorized to take combat risks and representing the will of the international community, could make a decisive difference in the early stages of a crisis." This force would be akin to a small kitchen fire extinguisher, whose greatest utility is in the very earliest stages of a possible fire.

But operationally, we must ask where such a force could really enhance the credibility of the U.N. It is not needed for observation missions, as they are composed of experienced individual military observers. In addition, these missions are formed to observe a previously concluded political settlement. An unarmed observation mission would never be undertaken in a situation where dangerous tensions are at the boiling point and the rapid deployment of combat troops is needed.

Would timely and rapid intervention by such a small force make any difference in first generation peacekeeping missions? As these are also only initiated in response to a completed political agreement, would a rapid deployment force greatly increase the efficiency of the peacekeepers on the ground? "Even a full contingent of peacekeeping troops cannot prevent renewal of hostilities by a determined party. Maintenance of the cease-fire ultimately depends on the willingness of the parties to refrain from fighting." On the other hand, rapid deployment can have a favorable impact. In the case of Cyprus, "Canadian troops arrived... within twenty-four hours of UNFICYP's [U.N. force in Cyprus's] approval. A symbolic presence is perhaps all that is needed in the first days of a cease-fire anyway."

Surprisingly, it is in the conduct of second generation peacekeeping missions that U.N. Army enthusiasts foresee the greatest utility for such a permanent force, despite the bellicose environment frequently associated with these missions. To use this force in such a mission would mean that the U.N. would continue its selective abandonment of its "principles of peacekeeping" which it articulated to define success. In fact, the force is targeted for these difficult missions because "few, if any, governments are willing to commit their own troops to a forceful ground role in a situation which does not threaten their own security and which may well prove to be both violent and open ended."

Thus the paradox of using a permanent U.N. force in these operations is exposed. On the one hand it is proposed as a mechanism to circumvent the unwillingness of member states to get involved in difficult missions such as those of the second generation of peacekeeping. It will replace the ground troops which were never committed by reluctant member states. On the other hand, it is acknowledged that this small and symbolic force would be deployed to impose a solution on an armed party which has not accepted a solution through diplomatic channels. It is genuinely hard to imagine how the timely intervention of such a force could have forced a different outcome in Bosnia or Somalia.

In Bosnia, without the conclusion of a political settlement, any U.N. force in limited numbers operating under peacekeeping rather than enforcement rules of engagement is bound to be hostage to its environment. Because the lack of consensus among member states keeps the mandate and size of the force small and innocuous, any U.N. force is powerless to influence the environment in which it operates. Therefore, dozens of U.N. resolutions on the conflict go unenforced. Rapid reaction by a U.N. military force would not have changed this. Neither unarmed observers nor light infantry with soft-skinned armored vehicles can impose or enforce action in a bellicose combat environment. In both cases, the force is merely a tripwire and its operating imperative is almost solely based on its moral strength as a symbol.

In Somalia, the dilemma stems from the fact that "the basic distinction between peacekeeping and enforcement action... has been blurred. The forceful measures taken by U.S. troops to disarm warring factions, while fully within the mandate of UNOSOM II [U.N. force in Somalia], have highlighted the particular risks of attempting to combine the coercive use of force with peacekeeping objectives." Once again, the basic question is how to use the force to effect the political objectives. Any permanent U.N. force would be faced with exactly the same question no matter when it arrived. Only it might get to face that dilemma a bit sooner.

Naturally, a small, permanent U.N. force would have no great utility in enforcement action either. The fact that large-scale enforcement actions are taking place means that diplomacy or previous intervention has failed. The only scenario in which a permanent U.N. force could be involved at this end of the spectrum was if it was deployed, came under heavy attack, or suffered a similar failure to pacify a volatile environment, and withdrew prior to large scale intervention authorized by an Article 42 resolution.

The only outstanding use of such a force would be in preventative deployments, of which Macedonia is the only current example. In this case, the force does not seek to exercise any sort of operational capability other than limited observation and patrolling. It is a human tripwire, a symbol of the will of the international community. Any violent actions directed against this force (or the peace it seeks to keep) will have to be met with a U.N. response that transcends the organic capacity of this very small and lightly armed force. The soldiers involved are in an unenviable position, as they are powerless to influence their own environment. Their fate rests on the goodwill of the belligerents and the credibility of the United Nations in the eyes of the opposing factions. That bluff has been called in the past and the casualty lists are fast approaching 1000.

OPERATIONAL QUESTIONS

In short, preventative deployment by a permanent U.N. force begs a whole series of operational questions:

1. Under what circumstances will the force be deployed? Guidelines for intervention must be clearly defined. After all, "demand for U.N. peacekeeping since early 1992 has begun to outstrip the supply, whether that supply is measured in money or in national political will." Resources ultimately come from the member states, and are limited no matter what form they take. It is easy to imagine the small force being called upon for almost every potential conflict.

2. Will the U.N. force be governed by the "principles of peacekeeping" or will it be expected to enforce or impose solutions on belligerent factions? If the time-consuming negotiations necessary to obtain the consent of all parties are still underway, the rapid deployment capabilities of this force will have little utility.

3. What explicit mechanisms would be needed to determine the composition and missions of follow-on forces to relieve the rapid reaction force? There must be an organized process by which the crisis is evaluated, and intervention is either continued, upgraded, or abandoned. The involvement of a permanent U.N. force in an open-ended commitment would completely negate its utility.

While such guidelines are necessary, in some cases they will be inadequate to address the *sui generis* [unique] conflicts of the post–Cold War era. On the one hand, doctrine governing the use of a U.N. force must be stringent enough to provide real direction. On the other hand, that same doctrine will rule out intervention in many pressing crises. The doctrine guiding the use of U.N. force must cover a bewildering myriad of crises. It must also have a mechanism which forces decisionmakers to evaluate its immediate utility in a timely manner.

The deployment of a permanent U.N. rapid reaction force would catapult issues onto the U.N. agenda which member states are not ready to address. It could quite easily upset a natural control measure in an organization made up of nation-states. "States may well prefer a situation in which the provision of military force for U.N. activities is managed in an *ad hoc* manner, thereby giving them a greater degree of control over events."

There have been situations where the U.N. Security Council has called for troops to staff operations and the member states have simply failed to comply (Somalia 1992, Georgia 1993). It is reasonable to assume that these same member states would not support the deployment of a force controlled by the Secretary-General, which would require them to provide quick reinforcements. The reaction of member states to calls for collective operations are an important barometer of their willingness to act in common with others. A mechanism which forces or circumvents that common ground could backfire.

CONCLUSION

Even when one completely ignores these attendant political difficulties discussed briefly, it is still obvious that the operational utility of a permanent U.N. force is extremely limited. The value of such a force lies in its preventative role. Other

than that role, it does not fit naturally into the spectrum of U.N. military operations conducted since 1948. Even in a preventative role, its small size, limited operational capabilities, and constrained mandate would limit its effectiveness to operations at the low end of the spectrum.

And at this end of the spectrum, there is not only little need for rapid deployments, but little need for forces other than those constituted by traditional means. When acting as a tripwire and in a symbolic role, an *ad hoc* blue-helmet force or an expensive permanent U.N. Army are scarcely different in terms of operational effectiveness or political viability. The past approach to staffing U.N. operations at the low end of the spectrum has always been adequate, has never been seen as responsible for mission failures, and is an important mechanism for involving states in the maintenance of international peace and security. The strategic utility of such a force is marginal when compared with the current system for staffing U.N. operations at the low end of the spectrum.

Many supporters want the U.N. force to solve problems in operations at the upper end of the operational spectrum. This force could never have the complex operational infrastructure and capabilities to make a difference in missions which entail even modest enforcement operations. The whole issue of staffing and directing U.N. operations at the high end of the spectrum needs much greater attention. Second generation peacekeeping and enforcement missions are quite obviously much more reliant on the vigorous political backing of powerful member states. Beyond the politics involved, these missions require the leadership of a major power for two reasons: 1) large-scale enforcement against an intransigent party is an immensely complicated and expensive enterprise; and 2) only a very few member states have the actual military capability to command and control such a campaign. A small force only under the control of the Secretary-General cannot affect these types of situations.

This dilemma stems from the nature of the post–Cold War world and the attendant difficulties of military intervention. It cannot be solved by the implementation of a single mechanism whose operational utility is very limited.

POSTSCRIPT

Should a Permanent UN Military Force Be Established?

The increase in the use of UN peacekeeping forces is partly the result of the changes from the cold war to the post–cold war era, which can be explored in Steven R. Ratner, *The New UN Peacekeeping: Building Peace in Lands of Conflict After the Cold War* (St. Martin's Press, 1996). Within this larger context, the debate over creating a potentially permanent international police force, even army, is being seriously debated in many forums. A good place to begin exploring this topic further is the report issued by Boutros Boutros-Ghali, *An Agenda for Peace: Preventive Diplomacy, Peacemaking, and Peacekeeping* (United Nations, 1992). It is also worthwhile to look into the Web site for UN peacekeeping, which can be found at http://www.un.org/Depts/dpko/.

Events that have occurred throughout the world have done even more to convince those who advocate a standing UN military force that it is important to act to create a force that can respond quickly to crises and that has the military power to intervene effectively when necessary. The events in Kosovo, the grisly border war between Ethiopia and Eritrea, and the clashes that occurred in May 1999 between India and Pakistan, both of which have nuclear weapons, are just a few examples of the continued fighting that some hope a UN force could prevent or stop. Moreover, advocates argue that the fluid, post–cold war international system presents an opportunity that should not be missed to establish such a force. For more on this perspective, see Lionel Rosenblatt and Larry Thompson, "The Door of Opportunity: Creating a Permanent Peacekeeping Force," *World Policy Journal* (vol. 15, 1998), pp. 36–47.

Other analysts are skeptical of the possibility or wisdom of a standing UN force and its possible uses. Some of these concerns are based on such narrow factors as cost. However, the cost of the entire UN peacekeeping operation comes approximately to a mere one-tenth of one percent of what the world's countries collectively spend on their national military establishments. More substantively, there are worries that a more powerful, proactive UN might undermine the sovereignty of the less developed countries (LDCs), with the UN Security Council serving as a tool of the five big powers that control the council through their veto. From this perspective, UN intervention carries the danger of neocolonial control. Other opposition comes from those who believe a UN force will undermine the national sovereignty of even larger countries. For example, could U.S. troops be placed under UN command with the authorization of Congress? Might there even someday be an international draft?

On the Internet . . .

Commission on Global Governance

Insofar as the study of international law is also about the larger subject of creating a more integrated system of world governance, a good place to view the argument for this direction is the Web site of the Commission on Global Governance, an organization that promotes the creation and strengthening of global measures and institutions to (as the commission sees it) make the world a better place.
http://www.cgg.ch

International Law Association (ILA)

The International Law Association (ILA), which is currently headquartered in London, England, was founded in Brussels, Belgium, in 1873. The association's objectives, under its constitution, include the "study, elucidation and advancement of international law, public and private, the study of comparative law, the making of proposals for the solution of conflicts of law and for the unification of law, and the furthering of international understanding and goodwill." *http://www.ila-hq.org*

The United Nations Treaty Series (UNTS)

The United Nations Treaty Series (UNTS) is a collection of 30,000 treaties, addenda, and other items related to treaties and international agreements that have been filed with the UN Secretariat since 1946. The UNTS includes the texts of treaties in their original language(s) and English and French translations.
http://www.un.org/Depts/Treaty/

Public International Law

The faculties of Economics and Commerce, Education, and Law at the University of Western Australia maintain this Web site, which has extensive links to a range of international law topics, including crime and human rights, and to institutions, such as the International Court of Justice.
http://www.law.ecel.uwa.edu.au/intlaw/

PART 4

International Law Issues

One of the underlying themes of current international relations and, therefore, this book is the growing globalization of world politics. Part of that process is the increase in scope and importance of international law. The issues in this section represent some of the controversies involved with the expansion of international law and whether it does or should restrict traditional sovereign powers of countries by extending the purview of international law ever further into such issues as the right to determine how to best defend itself and the prosecution of crimes.

■ Would the Use of Nuclear Weapons Necessarily Violate the International Law of War?

■ Should an International Criminal Court Be Established?

ISSUE 10

Would the Use of Nuclear Weapons Necessarily Violate the International Law of War?

YES: Abdul G. Koroma, from Dissenting Opinion, *Legality of the Threat or Use of Nuclear Weapons*, International Court of Justice (July 8, 1996)

NO: Stephen M. Schwebel, from Dissenting Opinion, *Legality of the Threat or Use of Nuclear Weapons*, International Court of Justice (July 8, 1996)

ISSUE SUMMARY

YES: Abdul G. Koroma, a justice on the International Court of Justice from Sierra Leone, argues that the destructive power of nuclear weapons means that their use would necessarily violate the law of war.

NO: Stephen M. Schwebel, a justice on the International Court of Justice from the United States, maintains that in some circumstances the use of nuclear weapons can be justified under international law.

This debate hinges on two factors. One is the consequences of nuclear attack. The other is the law of war. With respect to the first factor, there are debates about the global impact of general nuclear war, but there is little controversy about the immediate effect of a nuclear attack. A one-megaton warhead detonated a mile above a city would create a huge fireball with temperatures in the range of 20 million degrees Fahrenheit. Within two and a half miles everything and everyone would be set on fire. That inferno would be quickly snuffed out, however, by an atomizing blast. Death and destruction would be total. In a second two-mile ring, flesh would be charred, blast winds would reach 160 mph, and collapsing buildings and flying glass and metal would crush and shred nearly everyone. Yet another two miles out, most homes would be set on fire, half the population would be dead, and the remainder of the population would probably have been lethally exposed to radiation. Still another four miles out, now ten miles from the blast center, a third of the population would be wounded, normal services would be destroyed, and civil chaos would threaten as panic set in and people fought for medicine, food, and water. Those who survived would face uncertain futures of psychological trauma and devastated lifestyles.

The second factor involves the ancient debate of philosophy and international law about the circumstances in which war can be fought justly and, once engaged in war, how it can be waged justly. What is often referred to as "just war" theory has two parts. The first is the cause of war, traditionally denoted by its Latin translation, *jus ad bellum* (just cause of war). The second part of the just war debate relates to *jus in bello* (just conduct of war). This includes the standards of proportionality and discrimination. Proportionality means that the amount of force used must be proportionate to the threat. Discrimination means that force must not make noncombatants intentional targets. It is this second part, the just conduct of war, that is the topic of this debate.

For this debate the most important difficulty with the standards of just war conduct is that they are vague even if you try to abide by them. For example, almost everyone would agree that it would not have been proportional to the danger to have had initially used nuclear weapons on Iraq when it invaded Kuwait in 1990. But what if Iraq had used chemical weapons against coalition forces once the conventional air and ground war broke out in 1991? Would the British, French, and Americans have been justified according to the standard of proportionality if they had retaliated with nuclear weapons?

Then there is the standard of discrimination. Many Iraqi military and command locations were within or near civilian areas. Given the devastating explosive power of nuclear weapons, any attack on these targets would not have discriminated between civilians and the military and would have killed countless civilians.

The twentieth century has seen significant progress in setting down rules of just war. The Hague Conferences near the turn of the century and the Geneva Convention of 1949 set down some rules about *jus in bello* regarding impermissible weapons, the treatment of prisoners, and other matters. Other treaties have banned the possession and use of biological and chemical weapons, and the International Court of Justice (ICJ) ruled that in most circumstances the use of nuclear weapons would be illegal.

Also in the realm of *jus in bello,* individuals are now sometimes held accountable for war crimes. That happened after World War II, and it is occurring once again for the horrendous violations of international law that were committed in Bosnia and Rwanda. Most recently, the president of Yugoslavia, Slobodan Milosevic, and a number of other Serb leaders were indicted in 1999 by the International War Crime Tribunal in The Hague, the Netherlands, for the actions that they directed in Kosovo.

The controversy over the legitimacy of nuclear weapons was carried to the International Court of Justice when the United Nations General Assembly and the World Health Organization each asked the ICJ to give advisory rulings on the matter. The following selections are part of the court's judgment. In the first, Justice Abdul G. Koroma rejects the idea that nuclear weapons can be either proportional to any provocation or can adequately discriminate between legitimate military and illegitimate civilian targets. Justice Stephen M. Schwebel maintains that existing international law does not preclude the legitimate use of nuclear weapons in some circumstances.

YES

Abdul G. Koroma

DISSENTING OPINION OF ABDUL G. KOROMA

It is a matter of profound regret to me that I have been compelled to append this Dissenting Opinion to the Advisory Opinion rendered by the Court, as I fundamentally disagree with its finding—secured by the President's casting vote—that:

> "in view of the current state of international law, and of the elements of fact at its disposal, the Court cannot conclude definitively **whether the threat or use of nuclear weapons would be lawful or unlawful in an extreme circumstance of self-defence, in which the very survival of a State would be at stake**".

This finding, in my considered opinion, is not only unsustainable on the basis of existing international law, but, as I shall demonstrate later, is totally at variance with the weight and abundance of material presented to the Court. The finding is all the more regrettable in view of the fact that the Court had itself reached a conclusion that:

> "the threat or use of nuclear weapons would generally be contrary to the rules of international law applicable in armed conflict, and in particular the principles and rules of humanitarian law".

A finding with which I concur, save for the word "generally". It is my considered opinion based on the existing law and the available evidence that the use of nuclear weapons in any circumstance would be unlawful under international law. That use would at the very least result in the violation of the principles and rules of international humanitarian law, and would therefore be contrary to that law....

In my view, the prevention of war, by the use of nuclear weapons, is a matter for international law and, if the Court is requested to determine such an issue, it falls within its competence to do so. Its decision can contribute to the prevention of war by ensuring respect for the law.... Today a system of war prevention exists in international law, and comprises the prohibition of the use of force, the collective security provisions of the United Nations Charter [the Charter] for the maintenance of international peace, the obligation to

From *Legality of the Threat or Use of Nuclear Weapons*, Advisory Opinion, International Court of Justice (July 8, 1996). References omitted.

resort to peaceful means for the settlement of international disputes and the regulations on weapons prohibition, arms limitation and disarmament. The Court's Advisory Opinion in this case could have strengthened this regime by serving as a shield of humanity....

Furthermore, all States—both the nuclear-weapon and non-nuclear-weapon States—are agreed that the rules of international law applicable in armed conflict, particularly international humanitarian law, apply to the use of nuclear weapons. This law, which has been formulated and codified to restrict the use of various weapons and methods of warfare, is intended to limit the terrible effects of war. Central to it is the principle of humanity which above all aims to mitigate the effects of war on civilians and combatants alike. It is this law which also establishes a regime on the basis of which the methods and means of warfare are to be judged. Accordingly, it would seem apposite and justifiable for the effects of a conflict involving nuclear weapons —regarded as the ultimate weapon of mass destruction—to be judged against the standards of such a regime.

Despite its findings, the Court has itself recognized that the law of armed conflict, and in particular the principles and rules of humanitarian law—would apply to a conflict involving the use of nuclear weapons. It follows that the Court's finding that it cannot conclude definitively whether the threat or use of nuclear weapons would be lawful or unlawful in an extreme circumstance of self-defence, in which the very survival of a State would be at stake, is a contradiction and can at best be described as the identification of two principles, namely, the obligation to comply with the principles and rules of international law applicable in armed conflict and the right of a State to self-defence including when it considers its very survival to be at stake. These principles are not mutually exclusive and are recognized in international law. However, it has been argued that when the Court is faced with two competing principles or rights, it should jurisprudentially assign a priority to one of them and cause it to prevail. In the opinion of Sir Hersch Lauterpacht, even though the margin of preference for giving a priority to one principle over another may be small, yet, however tenuous, that margin must be decisive. He admits that judicial action along this line may in some respects be indistinguishable from judicial legislation. However, he argues, the Court "may have to effect a compromise—which is not a diplomatic but a legitimate judicial compromise— between competing principles of law", and concludes that:

"there is no decisive reason why the Court should avoid at all cost some such outcome. It is in accordance with the true function of the Court that the dispute submitted to it should be determined by its own decision and not by the contingent operation of an attitude of accommodation on the part of the disputants. There is an embarrassing anticlimax, which is not legally irrelevant, in a situation in which the Court, after prolonged written and oral pleadings, is impelled to leave the settlement of the actual issue to... the parties."

The suggestion that it should be left to individual States to determine whether or not it may be lawful to have recourse to nuclear weapons, is not only an option fraught with serious danger, both for the States that may be directly involved in conflict, and for those nations not involved, but may also suggest that such an option is not legally reprehensible. Accordingly, the Court, instead of leaving it to each State to decide whether or not it would be lawful or unlawful to use nuclear weapons in an extreme circumstance of "State survival", should have determined whether or not it is permissible to use nuclear weapons even in a case involving the survival of the state. The question put to the Court is whether it is lawful to use nuclear weapons and is not about the survival of the state, which is what the Court's reply turned on. If the Court had correctly interpreted the question this would not only have had the effect of declaring the law regarding the use of nuclear weapons but could well have deterred the use of such weapons. Regrettably, the Court refrained not only from performing its judicial function, but, by its "non-finding", appears to have made serious inroads into the present legal restraints relating to the use of nuclear weapons, while throwing the regime of self-defence into doubt by creating a new category called the "survival of the State", seen as constituting an exception to Articles 2, paragraph 4, and 51 of the United Nations Charter and to the principles and rules of humanitarian law. In effect, this kind of restraint would seem to be tantamount to judicial legislation at a time when the Court has itself—rightly in my view—recognized that it "cannot legislate", and, that

> "in the circumstances of the present case, *it is not* called upon *to do so*. Rather its task is to engage in its normal judicial function of ascertaining the existence or otherwise of legal principles and rules applicable to the threat or use of nuclear weapons."

However, just after reaffirming this self-denying ordinance, the Court went on to do just that by proclaiming that it cannot conclude definitively whether or not the threat or use of nuclear weapons would be "lawful or unlawful in an extreme circumstance of self-defence, in which the very survival of a State would be at stake", given the current state of international law and the elements of fact at its disposal. This finding, with respect, is not only untenable in law but legally superfluous. The right of self-defence is inherent and fundamental to all States. It exists within and not outside or above the law. To suggest that it exists outside or above the law is to render it probable that force may be used unilaterally by a State when it by itself considers its survival to be at stake. The right of self-defence is not a licence to use force; it is regulated by law and was never intended to threaten the security of other states.

Thus the Court's finding does not only appear tantamount to judicial legislation which undermines the regime of the non-use of force as enshrined in Article 2, paragraph 4, of the Charter, and that of self-defence as embodied in Article 51, but the doctrine of the survival of the State represents a throwback to the law before the adoption of the United Nations Charter and is even redolent of a period long before that. [Hugo] Grotius, writing in the seventeenth century, stated that: "[t]he right of self-defence... has its origin directly, and chiefly, in the fact that nature commits to each his own protection". Thus, the Court's finding would appear to be tantamount to according to each State the exclusive right to decide for itself to use nuclear weapons when its survival is at stake as that State perceives it—a decision subjected neither to the law nor to third party adjudication. . . .

As already stated, the Court's present finding represents a challenge to some of the fundamental precepts of existing international law including the proscription of the use of force in international relations and the exercise of the right of self-defence. That the Court cannot decide definitively whether the use of nuclear weapons would be lawful or unlawful when the survival of the State is at stake is a confirmation of the assertion that the survival of that State is not only not a matter for the law but that a State, in order to ensure its survival, can wipe out the rest of humanity by having recourse to nuclear weapons. In its historical garb "of the fundamental right of self-preservation", such a right was used in the past as a pretext for the violation of the sovereignty of other States. Such acts are now considered unlawful under contemporary international law. The International Military Tribunal at Nuremburg in 1946 rejected the argument that the State involved had acted in self-defence and that every State must be the judge of whether, in a given case, it is entitled to decide whether to exercise the right of self-defence. The Tribunal held that "whether action taken under the claim of self-defence was in fact aggressive or defensive must ultimately be subject to investigation or adjudication if international law is ever to be enforced".

Similarly, this Court, in the [1968] *Nicaragua* case, rejected the assertion that the right of self-defence is not subject to international law. While noting that Article 51 of the United Nations Charter recognizes a "natural" or "inherent" right of self-defence, it stated that "it is hard to see how this can be other than of a customary nature, even if its present content has been confirmed by the Charter". By its present findings, the Court would appear to be departing from its own jurisprudence by saying that it cannot determine conclusively whether or not it would be lawful for a State to use nuclear weapons.

Be that as it may, it is not as if the Court was compelled to reach such a conclusion, for the law is clear. The use of force is firmly and peremptorily prohibited by Article 2, paragraph 4, of the United Nations Charter. The regime of self-defence or the doctrine of "self-survival", as the Court would prefer to have it, is likewise regulated and subjected to that law. The right of self-defence by a State is clearly stipulated in Article 51 of the Charter, as follows:

Nothing in the present Charter shall impair the inherent right of individual or collective self-defence if an armed attack occurs against a Member of the United Nations, until the Security Council has taken measures necessary to maintain international peace and security. Measures taken by Members in the exercise of this right of self-defence shall be immediately reported to the Security Council and shall not in any way affect the authority and responsibility of the Security Council under the present Charter to take at any time such action as it deems necessary in order to maintain or restore international peace and security."

Thus, the Article permits the exercise of that right subject to the conditions stipulated therein. Firstly, in order to exercise the right, a State must have been the victim of an armed attack and, while exercising such a right, it must observe the principle of proportionality. Secondly, the measure or measures taken in exercise of such a right must be reported to the Security Council and are to be discontinued as soon as the Security Council itself has taken measures necessary for the maintenance of international peace. Article 51 therefore envisages the ability of a State *lawfully* to defend itself against armed attack. The Court emphasized this when it stated that the right of self-defence under Article 51 is conditioned by necessity and proportionality and that these conditions would apply whatever the means of force employed. Moreover, self-defence must also meet the requirements of the law applicable in armed conflict, particularly the principles and rules of international humanitarian law.

The question therefore is not whether a State is entitled to exercise its right of self-defence in an extreme circumstance in which the very survival of that State would be at stake, but rather whether the use of nuclear weapons would be lawful or unlawful under any circumstance including an extreme circumstance in which its very survival was at stake—or, in other words, whether it is possible to conceive of consequences of the use of such weapons which do not entail an infringement of international law applicable in armed conflict, particularly international humanitarian law. As stated above, in terms of the law, the right of self-defence is restricted to the repulse of an armed attack and does not permit of retaliatory or punitive action. Nor is it an exception to the *jus in bello* (conduct of hostilities). Since, in the light of the law and the facts, it is inconceivable that the use of nuclear weapons would not entail an infringement of, at the very least, the law applicable in armed conflict, particularly humanitarian law, it follows that the use of such weapons would be unlawful. Nuclear weapons do not constitute an exception to humanitarian law.

Given these considerations, it is not legally sustainable to find, as the Court has done, that, in view of the present state of the law, it cannot conclude definitively whether the threat or use of nuclear weapons would be lawful or unlawful in an extreme circumstance of self-survival, for as it stated in the *Nicaragua case (1968):*

> "the conduct of States should, in general, be consistent with... rules, and that instances of State conduct inconsistent with a given rule should generally have been treated as breaches of that rule."

Judge Mosler, a former member of this Court has in another context, stated

> "that law cannot recognise any act either of one member or of several members in concert, as being legally valid if it is directed against the very foundation of law". (H. Mosler, The International Society as a Legal Community.)

The Court's finding is also untenable, for, and as already mentioned, the *corpus juris* on which it should have reached its conclusion does indeed exist, and in an ample and substantial form. The Court had itself taken cognizance of this when it noted that the "laws and customs of war" applicable to the matter before it had been codified in The Hague Conventions of 1899 and 1907, based upon the 1868 Declaration of St. Petersburg as well as the results of the Brussels Conference of 1874. The Court also recognized that "The Hague Law" and, more particularly, the Regulations Respecting the Laws and Customs of War on Land, do regulate the rights and duties of belligerent States in the conduct of their hostilities and limit the choice of methods and means of injuring the enemy in wartime. It found that the "Geneva Law" (the Conventions of 1864, 1906, 1929 and 1949), which protects the victims of war and aims to provide safeguards for disabled armed forces personnel and persons not taking part in the hostilities, is equally applicable to the issue before it. It noted that these two branches of law today constitute international humanitarian law which was codified in the 1977 Additional Protocols to the Geneva Conventions of 1949.

It observed that, since the turn of the century, certain weapons, such as explosive projectiles under 400 g, dum-dum bullets and asphyxiating gases, have been specifically prohibited, and that chemical and bacteriological weapons were also prohibited by the 1925 Geneva Gas Protocol. More recently, the Court found, the use of weapons producing "non-detectable fragments", of other types of mines, booby traps and other devices, and of incendiary weapons, was either prohibited or limited depending on the case by the Convention of 10 October 1980 on Prohibitions or Restrictions on the Use of Certain Conventional Weapons Which May Be Deemed to Be Excessively Injurious or to Have Indiscriminate Effects. Such prohibition, it stated, was in line with the rule that "the right of belligerents to adopt means of injuring the enemy is not unlimited" as stated in Article 22 of the 1907 Hague Regulations Respecting the Laws and Customs of War on Land. The Court further noted that the St. Petersburg Declaration had already condemned the use of weapons "which uselessly aggravate the suffering of disabled men or make their death inevitable" and that the aforementioned Regulations annexed to the Hague Convention IV of 1907, prohibit the use of "arms, projectiles, or material calculated to cause unnecessary suffering" (Article 23).

The Court also identified the cardinal principles constituting the fabric of international humanitarian law, the first of which is aimed at the protection of the civilian population and civilian objects and establishes the distinction between combatants and non-combatants. According to those principles, States are obliged not to make civilians the object of attack and must consequently not use weapons that are incapable of distinguishing between civilian and military targets. Secondly, it is prohibited to cause unnecessary suffering to combatants and, accordingly, it is prohibited to use weapons causing them needless harm or that uselessly aggravate their suffering. In this regard, the Court noted that States do not have unlimited freedom of choice in the weapons they can use.

The Court also considered applicable to the matter the Martens Clause, first enunciated in the Hague Convention of 1899 with respect to the laws and customs of war on land, a modern version of which has been codified in Article 1, paragraph 2, of Additional Protocol I of 1977, and reads as follows:

> "In cases not covered by this Protocol or by other international agreements, civilians and combatants remain under the protection and authority of the principles of international law derived from established custom, from the principles of humanity and from the dictates of public conscience."

The Court noted that the principles embodied in the Clause are principles and rules of humanitarian law and, together with the principle of neutrality, apply to nuclear weapons.

It was in the light of the foregoing that the Court recognized that humanitarian law does prohibit the use of certain types of weapons either because of their indiscriminate effect on combatants and civilians or because of the unnecessary and superfluous harm caused to combatants. The Court accordingly held that the principles and rules of international humanitarian law are obligatory and binding on all States as they also constitute intransgressible principles of customary international law.

With regard to the applicability of Additional Protocol I of 1977 to nuclear weapons, the Court recalled that even if not all States are parties to the Protocol, they are nevertheless bound by those rules in the Protocol which, when adopted, constituted an expression of the pre-existing customary law, such as, in particular, the Martens Clause, which is enshrined in Article I of the Protocol.

The Court observed that the fact that certain types of weapons were not specifically mentioned in the Convention does not permit the drawing of any legal conclusions relating to the substantive issues raised by the use of such weapons. It took the view that there can be no doubt that the principles and rules of humanitarian law, which are enshrined in the Geneva Conventions of 1949 and the Additional Protocols of 1977, are applicable to nuclear weapons. Even when it observed that the Conferences of 1949 and 1977 did not specifically address the question of nuclear weapons, the Court stated that it cannot be concluded from this that the established principles and rules of humanitarian law applicable in armed conflict do not apply to nuclear weapons, as such a conclusion would be incompatible with the intrinsically humanitarian character of the legal principles in question which permeate the entire law of armed conflict

and apply to all forms of warfare and to all kinds of weapons.

The Court agreed with the submission that:

"In general, international humanitarian law bears on the threat or use of nuclear weapons as it does of other weapons.

International humanitarian law has evolved to meet contemporary circumstances, and is not limited in its application to weaponry of an earlier time. The fundamental principles of this law endure: to mitigate and circumscribe the cruelty of war for humanitarian reasons."

The Court also observed that none of the States advocating the legality of the use of nuclear weapons under certain circumstances, including the "clean" use of smaller, low-yield, tactical nuclear weapons, had indicated that the principles of humanitarian law do not apply to nuclear weapons, noting that, for instance, the Russian Federation had recognized that "restrictions set by the rules applicable to armed conflicts in respect of means and methods of warfare definitely also extend to nuclear weapons"; that for the United States, "the United States has long shared the view that the law of armed conflict governs the use of nuclear weapons—just as it governs the use of conventional weapons"; while for the United Kingdom, "so far as the customary law of war is concerned, the United Kingdom has always accepted that the use of nuclear weapons is subject to the principles of the *jus in bello*".

With regard to the elements of fact advanced in its findings, the Court noted the definitions of nuclear weapons contained in various treaties and instruments, including those according to which nuclear explosions are "capable of causing massive destruction, generalized damage or massive poisoning" (Paris Accords of 1954), or the preamble of the Tlatelolco Treaty of 1967 which described nuclear weapons "whose terrible effects are suffered, indiscriminately and inexorably, by military forces and civilian population alike, [and which] constitute through the persistence of the radioactivity they release, an attack on the integrity of the human species and ultimately may even render the whole earth uninhabitable". It also took note of the fact that nuclear weapons release not only immense quantities of heat and energy, but also powerful and prolonged radiation; that the first two causes of damage are vastly more powerful than such causes of damage in other weapons of mass destruction, and that the phenomenon of radiation is said to be peculiar to nuclear weapons. These characteristics, the Court concluded, render nuclear weapons potentially catastrophic; their destructive power cannot be contained in either space or time, and they have the potential to destroy all civilization and the entire ecosystem of the planet.

With regard to the elements of fact, the Court noted that the radiation released by a nuclear explosion would affect health, agriculture, natural resources and demography over a wide area and that such weapons would be a serious danger to future generations. It further noted that ionizing radiation has the potential to damage the future environment, food and marine ecosystems, and to cause genetic defects and illness in future generations. Also in this regard, the Government of Japan told the Court that the yields of the atomic bombs detonated in Hiroshima on 6 August 1945 and in Nagasaki on 9 August 1945 were the equivalent of 15 kilotons and 22 kilotons of TNT

respectively. The bomb blast produced a big fireball, followed by extremely high temperatures of some several million degrees centigrade, and extremely high pressures of several hundred thousand atmospheres. It also emitted a great deal of radiation. According to the delegation, the fireball, which lasted for about 10 seconds, raised the ground temperature at the hypocentre to somewhere between 3,000°C and 4,000°C, and the heat caused the scorching of wood buildings over a radius of approximately 3 kilometres from the hypocentre. The number of houses damaged by the atomic bombs was 70,147 in Hiroshima and 18,409 in Nagasaki. People who were within 1,000 m of the hypocentre were exposed to the initial radiation of more than 3.93 Grays. It is estimated that 50 per cent of people who were exposed to more than 3 Grays die of marrow disorder within two months. Induced radiation was emitted from the ground and buildings charged with radioactivity. In addition, soot and dust contaminated by induced radiation was dispersed into the air and whirled up into the stratosphere by the force of the explosion, and this caused radioactive fallout back to the ground over several months.

According to the delegation, the exact number of fatalities was not known, since documents were scarce. It was estimated, however, that the number of people who had died by the end of 1945 amounted to approximately 140,000 in Hiroshima and 74,000 in Nagasaki. The population of the cities at that time was estimated at 350,000 in Hiroshima and 240,000 in Nagasaki. The number of people who died of thermal radiation immediately after the bomb blast, on the same day or within a few days, was not clear. However, 90 to 100 per cent of the people who were exposed to thermal radiation without any shield within 1 k of the hypocentre, died within a week. The early mortality rates for the people who were within 1.5 k to 2 k of the hypocentre were 14 per cent for people with a shield and 83 per cent for the people without a shield. In addition to direct injury from the bomb blast, death was caused by several interrelated factors such as being crushed or buried under buildings, injuries caused by splinters of glass, radiation damage, food shortages or a shortage of doctors and medicines.

Over 320,000 people who survived but were affected by radiation still suffer from various malignant tumours caused by radiation, including leukaemia, thyroid cancer, breast cancer, lung cancer, gastric cancer, cataracts and a variety of other after-effects. More than half a century after the disaster, they are still said to be undergoing medical examinations and treatment.

According to the Mayor of Hiroshima who made a statement before the Court, the atomic bomb which was detonated in Hiroshima produced an enormous destructive power and reduced innocent civilian populations to ashes. Women, the elderly and the newborn were said to have been bathed in deadly radiation. The Court was told that the dropping of the bomb unleashed a mushroom cloud and human skin was burned raw while other victims died in desperate agony. The Mayor further told the Court that when the bomb exploded, enormous pillars of flame leaped up towards the sky and a majority of the buildings crumbled, causing a large number of casualties, many of them fatal.

Later in his statement he described the unique characteristic of the atomic bombing as one whose enormous destruction was instantaneous and universal. Old,

young, male, female, soldiers, civilians were all killed *indiscriminately*. The entire city of Hiroshima, he said, had been exposed to thermal rays, shock-wave blast and radiation. The bomb purportedly generated heat that reached several million degrees centigrade. The fireball was about 280 metres in diameter, the thermal rays emanating from it were thought to have instantly charred any human being who was outdoors near the hypocentre. The witness further disclosed that according to documented cases, clothing had burst into flames at a distance of 2 kilometres from the hypocentre of the bomb; many fires were ignited simultaneously throughout the city; the entire city was carbonized and reduced to ashes. Yet another phenomenon was a shock-wave which inflicted even greater damage when it ricocheted off the ground and buildings. The blast wind which resulted had, he said, lifted and carried people through the air. All wooden buildings within a radius of 2 kilometres collapsed, while many well beyond that distance were damaged.

The blast and thermal rays combined to burn to ashes or cause the collapse of approximately 70 per cent of the 76,327 dwellings in Hiroshima at the time. The rest were partially destroyed, half-bombed or damaged. The entire city was said to have been instantly devastated by the dropping of the bomb.

On the day the bomb was dropped, the witness further disclosed that there were approximately 350,000 people in Hiroshima, but it was later estimated that some 140,000 had died by the end of December 1945. Hospitals were said to be in ruins with medical staff dead or injured and with no medicines or equipment, and an incredible number of victims died, unable to receive sufficient treatment. Sur-

vivors developed fever, diarrhoea, haem-
orrhaging, and extreme fatigue, many
died abruptly. Such was said to be the pattern of the acute symptoms of the atomic
bomb disease. Other consequences were
a widespread destruction of cells, loss
of blood-producing tissue, and organ
damage. The immune systems of sur-
vivors were weakened and such symptoms as hair loss were conspicuous. Other
experiences recorded were an increase
in leukaemia, cataracts, thyroid cancer,
breast cancer, lung cancer and other can-
cers. As a result of the bombing, children
exposed to radiation suffered mental and
physical retardation. Nothing could be
done for these children medically and
even unborn babies, the Mayor stated,
had been affected. He concluded by saying that exposure to high levels of radiation continues in Hiroshima to this day.

The Mayor of Nagasaki, in his testimony, described effects on his city that
were similar to those experienced by Hiroshima as a result of the atomic bombing
which had taken place during the war.
According to the witness,

> "The explosion of the atomic bomb
> generated an enormous fireball, 200
> metres in radius, almost as though a
> small sun had appeared in the sky.
> The next instant, a ferocious blast
> and wave of heat assailed the ground
> with a thunderous roar. The surface
> temperature of the fireball was about
> 7,000°C, and the heat rays that reached
> the ground were over 3,000°C. The
> explosion instantly killed or injured
> people within a two-kilometre radius
> of the hypocentre, leaving innumerable
> corpses charred like clumps of charcoal
> and scattered in the ruins near the
> hypocentre. In some cases not even a
> trace of the person's remains could be
> found. The blast wind of over 300 metres
> per second slapped down trees and

demolished most buildings. Even iron
reinforced concrete structures were so
badly damaged that they seemed to have
been smashed by a giant hammer. The
fierce flash of heat meanwhile melted
glass and left metal objects contorted like
strands of taffy, and the subsequent fires
burned the ruins of the city to ashes.
Nagasaki became a city of death where
not even the sounds of insects could
be heard. After a while, countless men,
women and children began to gather for
a drink of water at the banks of nearby
Urakami River, their hair and clothing
scorched and their burnt skin hanging
off in sheets like rags. Begging for help,
they died one after another in the water
or in heaps on the banks. Then radiation
began to take its toll, killing people like a
scourge of death expanding in concentric
circles from the hypocentre. Four months
after the atomic bombing, 74,000 were
dead and 75,000 had suffered injuries,
that is, two-thirds of the city population
had fallen victim to this calamity that
came upon Nagasaki like a preview of
the Apocalypse." (CR 95/27.)

The witness went on to state that
even people who were lucky enough
to survive continued to this day to
suffer from the late effects unique to
nuclear weapons. Nuclear weapons, he
concluded, bring in their wake the
indiscriminate devastation of civilian
populations.

Testimony was also given by the delegation of the Marshall Islands which was
the site of 67 nuclear weapons tests from
30 June to 18 August 1958, during the period of the United Nations Pacific Islands
territories trusteeship. The total yield of
those weapons was said to be equivalent
to more than 7,000 bombs of the size of
that which destroyed Hiroshima. Those
nuclear weapon tests were said to have
caused extensive radiation, induced ill-

nesses, deaths and birth defects. Further on in the testimony, it was disclosed that human suffering and damage to the environment occurred at great distances, both in time and in geography, from the sites of detonations even when an effort was made to avoid or mitigate harm. The delegation went on to inform the Court that the unique characteristics of nuclear weapons are that they cause unnecessary suffering and include not only widespread, extensive, radioactive contamination with cumulative adverse effects, but also locally intense radiation with severe, immediate and long-term adverse effects, far-reaching blasts, heat, and light resulting in acute injuries and chronic ailments. Permanent, as well as temporary, blindness from intense light and reduced immunity from radiation exposures were said to be common and unavoidable consequences of the use of nuclear weapons, but which were uncommon or absent from the use of other destructive devices.

The delegation further disclosed that birth defects and extraordinarily prolonged and painful illnesses caused by the radioactive fallout inevitably and profoundly affected the civilian population long after the nuclear weapons tests had been carried out. Such suffering had affected generations born long after the testing of such weapons. It went on to say that, apart from the immediate damage at and near ground zero (where the detonation took place), the area experienced contamination of animals and plants and the poisoning of soil and water. As a consequence, some of the islands were still abandoned and in those that had recently been resettled, the presence of caesium in plants from the radioactive fallout rendered them inedible. Women on some of the other atolls in the islands who had

been assured that their atolls were not affected by radiation, were said to have given birth to "monster babies". A young girl on one of these atolls was said to have no knees, three toes on each foot and a missing arm; her mother had not been born by 1954 when the tests started but had been raised on a contaminated atoll.

In the light of the foregoing the Court, as well as taking cognizance of the unique characteristics of nuclear weapons when used, reached the following conclusions: that nuclear weapons have a destructive capacity unmatched by any conventional weapon; that a single nuclear weapon has the capacity to kill thousands if not millions of human beings; that such weapons cause unnecessary suffering and superfluous injury to combatants and non-combatants alike; and that they are unable to distinguish between civilians and combatants. When recourse is had to such weapons, it can cause damage to generations unborn and produce widespread and long-term effects on the environment, particularly in respect of resources necessary for human survival. In this connection, it should be noted that the radioactive effects of such weapons are not only similar to the effects produced by the use of poison gas which would be in violation of the 1925 Geneva Gas Protocol, but are considered even more harmful.

The above findings by the Court should have led it inexorably to conclude that any use of nuclear weapons is unlawful under international law, in particular the law applicable in armed conflict including humanitarian law. However, instead of this, the Court found that:

"in view of the current state of international law, and of the elements of fact at its disposal, the Court cannot conclude definitively whether the threat or use of nuclear weapons would be lawful or unlawful in an extreme circumstance of self-defence, in which the very survival of a State would be at stake".

This finding that would appear to suggest that nuclear weapons when used in circumstances of a threat to "State survival"—a concept invented by the Court—would constitute an exception to the corpus of humanitarian law which applies in all armed conflicts and makes no exception for nuclear weapons. In my considered opinion, the unlawfulness of the use of nuclear weapons is not predicated on the circumstances in which the use takes place, but rather on the unique and established characteristics of those weapons which under any circumstance would violate international law by their use. It is therefore most inappropriate for the Court's finding to have turned on the question of State survival when what is in issue is the lawfulness of nuclear weapons. Such a misconception of the question deprives the Court's finding of any legal basis.

On the other hand, if the Court had properly perceived the question and intended to give an appropriate reply, it would have found that an overwhelming justification exists on the basis of the law and the facts, which would have enabled it to reach a finding that the use of nuclear weapons in any circumstance would be unlawful. The Court's failure to reach this inevitable conclusion has compelled me to enter a vigorous dissent to its main finding.

I am likewise constrained to mention various other, more general, misgivings with regard to the Advisory Opinion on the whole. While the purpose of the Court's advisory jurisdiction is to provide an authoritative legal opinion and to enlighten the requesting body on certain legal aspects of an issue with which it has to deal when discharging its functions, the device has also been used to secure authoritative interpretations of the provisions of the Charter or the constitutive instruments of specialized agencies, or to provide guidance to various organs of the United Nations in relation to their functions. Furthermore, although the Advisory Opinions of the Court are not legally binding and impose no legal obligations either upon the requesting body or upon States, such Opinions are nonetheless not devoid of effect as they remain the law "recognized by the United Nations". Accordingly, this Court has, on various occasions, used its advisory jurisdiction as a medium of participation in the work of the United Nations, helping the Organization to achieve its objectives. Advisory opinions have enabled the Court to contribute meaningfully to the development and crystallization of the law. For example, in the *Namibia* Advisory Opinion, the Court referred to the development "of international law in regard to the non-self-governing territories, as enshrined in the Charter of the United Nations", which made the principle of self-determination applicable to such territories.

In its [1975] Advisory Opinion on the Western *Sahara*, the Court, citing the *Namibia* Opinion in relation to the principle of self-determination, stated that when questions are asked with reference to that principle, the Court

"must take into consideration the changes which have occurred in the supervening half-century, and its interpretation cannot remain unaffected by the subsequent development of law, through the Charter of the United Nations and by way of customary law...."

The Court's Opinion in the case accordingly referred to Article 1 of the United Nations Charter and to the Declaration on the Granting of Independence to Colonial Countries and Peoples which, it said, "confirm and emphasize that the application of the right of self-determination requires a free and genuine expression of the will of the peoples concerned". Moreover, the Court insisted that "the validity of the principle of self-determination, defined as the need to pay regard to the freely expressed will of peoples is not affected by the fact that in certain cases the General Assembly has dispensed with the requirement of consulting the inhabitants of a given territory". It can therefore be observed that through the medium of its Advisory Opinions, the Court has rendered normative decisions which have enabled the United Nations to achieve its objectives, in some cases even leading to the peaceful settlement of disputes, and has either contributed to the crystallisation and development of the law or, with its imprimatur, affirmed the emergence of the law.

It is therefore to be regretted that, on this occasion, the Court would seem not only to have retreated from this practice of making its contribution to the development of the law on a matter of such vital importance to the General Assembly and to the international community as a whole but may, albeit unintentionally, have cast doubt on established or emerging rules of international law....

In the case under consideration, the Court would appear to have been all too reluctant to take any position of principle on a question involving what the late Judge Nagendra Singh described as the most important aspect of international law facing humanity today. Instead, the Court resolved the issue about the *jus cogens* * character of some of the principles and rules of humanitarian law by saying that the request transmitted to it "does not raise the question of the character of the humanitarian law which would apply to the use of nuclear weapons". With respect they do. A pronouncement by the Court about the character of such rules while not guaranteeing their observance at all times, would nonetheless as they are related to human values already protected by positive legal principles which, taken together, reveal certain criteria of public policy....

The Court's reluctance to take a legal position on some of the important issues which pertain to the question before it could also be discerned from what may be described as a "judicial odyssey" in search of a specific conventional or customary rule specifically authorizing or prohibiting the use of nuclear weapons, which only led to the discovery that no such specific rule exists. Indeed, if such a specific rule did exist, it is more than unlikely that the question would have been brought before the Court in its present form, if at all. On the other hand, the absence of a specific convention prohibiting the use of nuclear weapons should not have suggested to the Court that the use of such weapons might be lawful, as it is generally recognized by States that customary international law embodies principles which are applicable to the use of such weapons. Hence the futile quest for specific legal prohibition can only be attributable to an extreme form of positivism, which is out of keep-

*[These are principles of international law so fundamental that no nation may ignore them or attempt to contract out of them through treaties.— Ed.]

ing with the international jurisprudence —including that of this Court. The futility of such an enterprise was recognized by the British-American Claims Arbitral Tribunal in the *Eastern Extension, Australia and China Telegraph Company* case, where it was held that even if there were no specific rule of international law applicable to a case, it could not be said that there was no rule of international law to which resort might be had.

> "International law, as well as domestic law, may not contain, and generally does not contain, express rules decisive of particular cases; but the function of jurisprudence is to resolve the conflict of opposing rights and interests by applying, in default of any specific provision of law, the corollaries of general principles, and so to find— exactly as in the mathematical sciences —the solution of the problem. This is the method of jurisprudence; it is the method by which the law has been gradually evolved in every country, resulting in the definition and settlement of legal relations as well between States as between private individuals."

Such then has been the jurisprudential approach to issues before the Court. The Court has applied legal principles and rules to resolve the conflict of opposing rights and interests where no specific provision of the law exists, and has relied on the corollaries of general principles in order to find a solution to the problem. The Court's approach has not been restricted to a search for a specific treaty or rule of customary law specifically regulating or applying to a matter before it and, in the absence of such a specific rule or treaty, it has not declared that it cannot definitively conclude or that it is unable to reach a decision or make a determination on that matter. The Court

has in the past—rightly in my view— not imposed such restrictions upon itself when discharging its judicial function to decide disputes in accordance with international law, but has referred to the principles of international law, to equity and to its own jurisprudence in order to define and settle the legal issues referred to it.

On the other hand, the search for specific rules led the Court to overlook or not fully to apply the principles of the United Nations Charter when considering the question before it. One such principle that does not appear to have been given its due weight in the Judgment of the Court is Article 2, paragraph 1, of the Charter of the United Nations, which provides that "The Organization is based on the principle of sovereign equality of all of its Members". The principle of sovereign equality of States is of general application. It presupposes respect for the sovereignty and territorial integrity of all States. International law recognizes the sovereignty of each State over its territory as well as the physical integrity of the civilian population. By virtue of this principle, a State is prohibited from inflicting injury or harm on another State. The principle is bound to be violated if nuclear weapons are used in a given conflict, because of their established and well-known characteristics. The use of such weapons would not only result in the violation of the territorial integrity of non-belligerent States by radioactive contamination, but would involve the death of thousands, if not millions, of the inhabitants of territories not parties to the conflict. This would be in violation of the principle as enshrined in the Charter, an aspect of the matter that would appear not to have been taken fully into consideration by the Court when making its findings.

I am likewise constrained to express my apprehension over some of the other findings in the Advisory Opinion with regard to respect for human rights and genocide, the protection of the natural environment and the policy of deterrence. With regard to genocide, it is stated that genocide would be considered to have been committed if a recourse to nuclear weapons resulted from an intent to destroy, in whole or in part, a national, ethnical, racial or religious group, as such. This reflects the text of the Genocide Convention. However, one must be mindful of the special characteristics of the Convention, its object and purpose, to which the Court itself referred in the *Reservations* case as being to condemn and punish

> "a crime under international law involving a denial of the right of existence of entire human groups, a denial which shocks the conscience of mankind and results in great losses to humanity and which is contrary to moral law and the spirit and aims of the United Nations";

while further pointing out

> "that the principles underlying the Convention are recognized by civilized nations as binding on States, even without any conventional obligation".

It further emphasized the co-operation required in order "to liberate mankind from such an odious scourge" and, given the humanitarian and civilizing purpose of the Convention, it referred to it as intended "to safeguard the very existence of certain human groups", and, "to confirm and endorse the most elementary principles of morality". The Court cannot therefore view with equanimity the killing of thousands, if not millions, of innocent civilians which the use of nuclear weapons would make inevitable, and conclude that genocide has not been committed because the State using such weapons has not manifested any intent to kill so many thousands or millions of people. Indeed, under the Convention, the quantum of the people killed is comprehended as well. It does not appear to me that judicial detachment requires the Court from expressing itself on the abhorrent shocking consequences that a whole population could be wiped out by the use of nuclear weapons during an armed conflict, and the fact that this could be tantamount to genocide, if the consequences of the act could have been foreseen. Such expression of concern may even have a preventive effect on the weapons being used at all.

As to whether recourse to nuclear weapons would violate human rights, in particular the right to human life, the Court found that it was never envisaged that the lawfulness or otherwise of such weapons would be regulated by the International Covenant on Civil and Political Rights. While this is accepted as a legal position, it does seem to me that too narrow a view has been taken of the matter. It should be recalled that both human rights law and international humanitarian law have as their *raison d'être* the protection of the individual as well as the worth and dignity of the human person, both during peacetime or in an armed conflict. It is for this reason, to my mind, that the United Nations Charter, which was adopted immediately after the end of the Second World War in the course of which serious and grave violations of human rights had occurred, undertook to protect the rights of individual human beings whatever their race, colour or creed, emphasizing that such rights were to be protected and respected even during an armed conflict. It should not be forgotten that the Second World War had witnessed the use of the atomic weapon in Hiroshima and Nagasaki, resulting in the deaths of thousands of human beings. The Second World War therefore came to be regarded as the period epitomizing gross violations of human rights. The possibility that the human rights of citizens, in particular their right to life, would be violated during a nuclear conflagration, is a matter which falls within the purview of the Charter and other relevant international legal instruments. Any activity which involves a terrible violation of the principles of the Charter deserves to be considered in the context of both the Charter and the other applicable rules. It is evidently in this context that the Human Rights Committee under the International Covenant on Civil and Political Rights adopted, in November 1984, a "general comment" on Article 6 of the Covenant (Right to Life), according to which the production, testing, possession, deployment and use of nuclear weapons ought to be prohibited and recognized as crimes against humanity. It is to be recalled that Article 6 of the Charter of the Nuremburg Tribunal defined crimes against humanity as "murder, extermination . . . , and other inhumane acts committed against any civilian population, before or during war . . .". It follows that the Nuremburg principles are likewise pertinent to the matter just considered by the Court.

With regard to the protection and safeguarding of the natural environment, the Court reached the conclusion that existing international law does not prohibit the use of nuclear weapons, but that important environmental factors are to be taken into account in the context of the implementation of the principles and rules of law applicable in armed conflict. The Court also found that relevant treaties in relation to the protection of the natural environment could not have intended to deprive a State of the exercise of its right to self-defence under international law. In my view, what is at issue is not whether a State might be denied its right to self-defence under the relevant treaties intended for the protection of the natural environment, but rather that, given the known qualities of nuclear weapons when exploded as well as their radioactive effects which not only contaminate human beings but the natural environment as well including agriculture, food, drinking water and the marine ecosystem over a wide area, it follows that the use of such weapons would not only cause severe and widespread damage to the natural environment, but would deprive human beings of drinking water and other resources needed for survival. In recognition of this, the First Additional Protocol of 1977 makes provision for the preservation of objects indispensable to the survival of the civilian population, such as foodstuffs, agricultural produce, drinking water installations, etc. The Advisory Opinion should have considered the question posed in relation to the protection of the natural environment from this perspective, rather than giving the impression that the argument advanced was about denying a State its legitimate right of self-defence.

The Advisory Opinion considered that the fact of nuclear weapons not having been used for 50 years cannot be regarded as an expression of an *opinio juris*. The legal basis for such a recognition was not elaborated; it was more in the nature of an assertion. However, the Court was unable to find that the conviction of the overwhelming majority of States that the fact that nuclear weapons have not been used for the last 50 years has established an *opinio juris* in favour of the prohibition of such use, was such as to have a bearing on its Opinion. In this connection, the Court should have given due consideration and weight to the statements of the overwhelming majority of States together with the resolutions adopted by various international organizations on the use of nuclear weapons, as evidence of the emergence of an *opinio juris*.

In my view, it was injudicious for the Court to have appeared to give legal recognition to the doctrine of deterrence as a principle of international law. While it is legitimate for judicial notice should be taken of that policy, the Court should have realised that it has the potential of being declared illegal if implemented, as it would involve a nuclear conflict between belligerents with catastrophic consequences for the civilian population not only of the belligerent parties but those of States not involved in such a conflict, and could result in the violation of international law in general and humanitarian law in particular. It would therefore have been prudent for the Court to have refrained from taking a position on this matter, which is essentially non-legal.

... I am of the view that the parties to the 1968 Treaty on the Non-Proliferation of Nuclear Weapons, realising the danger posed to all States by the proliferation of nuclear weapons, entered into a binding commitment to end the nuclear arms race at an early date and to embark on nuclear disarmament. The dangers that those weapons posed for humanity in 1968 are still current today, as is evident from the decision taken in 1995 by the States parties to the Treaty, to make it permanent. The obligations to eliminate those weapons remain binding on those States so as to remove the threat such weapons pose to violate the Charter or the principles and rules of humanitarian law. There is accordingly a correlation between the obligation of nuclear disarmament assumed by those States Parties to the Non-Proliferation Treaty and the obligations assumed by States under the United Nations Charter and under the law applicable in armed conflict, in particular international humanitarian law.

... [I]t is a matter of profound regret that... the Court... failed to reach the only and inescapable finding, namely, that in view of the established facts of the use of such weapons, it is inconceivable that there is any circumstance in which their use would not violate the principles and rules of international law applicable in armed conflict and, in particular, the principles and rules of humanitarian law. By not answering the question and leaving it to States to decide the matter, the Court declined the challenge to reaffirm the applicability of the rules of law and of humanitarian law in particular to nuclear weapons and to ensure the protection of human beings, of generations unborn and of the natural environment against the use of such weapons whose destructive power we have seen, is unable to discriminate between combatants and non-combatants, cannot spare hospitals or prisoner-of-war camps and can cause suffering out of all proportion to military necessity leaving their victims to die as a result of burns after weeks of agony, or to be afflicted for life with painful infirmities. The request by the General Assembly was for the Court, as the guarantor of legality, to affirm that because of these consequences, the use of nuclear weapons is unlawful under international law.

NO

Stephen M. Schwebel

DISSENTING OPINION OF
STEPHEN M. SCHWEBEL

More than any case in the history of the Court, this proceeding presents a titanic tension between State practice and legal principle. It is accordingly the more important not to confuse the international law we have with the international law we need. In the main, the Court's Opinion meets that test. I am in essential though not entire agreement with much of it, and shall, in this opinion, set out my differences. Since however I profoundly disagree with the Court's principal and ultimate holding, I regret to be obliged to dissent.

The essence of the problem is this. Fifty years of the practice of States does not debar, and to that extent supports, the legality of the threat or use of nuclear weapons in certain circumstances. At the same time, principles of international humanitarian law which antedate that practice govern the use of all weapons including nuclear weapons, and it is extraordinarily difficult to reconcile the use—at any rate, some uses—of nuclear weapons with the application of those principles.

One way of surmounting the antinomy between practice and principle would be to put aside practice. That is what those who maintain that the threat or use of nuclear weapons is unlawful in all circumstances do. Another way is to put aside principle, to maintain that the principles of international humanitarian law do not govern nuclear weapons. That has not been done by States, including the nuclear-weapon States, in these proceedings nor should it be done. These principles—essentially proportionality in the degree of force applied, discrimination in the application of force as between combatants and civilians, and avoidance of unnecessary suffering of combatants—evolved in the pre-nuclear age. They do not easily fit the use of weaponry having the characteristics of nuclear weapons. At the same time, it is the fact that the nuclear Powers and their allies have successfully resisted applying further progressive development of humanitarian law to nuclear weapons; the record of the conferences that concluded the Geneva Conventions of 1949 and its Additional Protocols of 1977 establishes that. Nevertheless to hold that inventions in weaponry that post-date the formation of such fundamental principles are not governed by those principles would vitiate international

From *Legality of the Threat or Use of Nuclear Weapons*, Advisory Opinion, International Court of Justice (July 8, 1996). References omitted.

humanitarian law. Nor is it believable that in fashioning these principles the international community meant to exclude their application to post-invented weaponry. The Martens Clause implies the contrary.

Before considering the extent to which the chasm between practice and principle may be bridged—and is bridged by the Court's Opinion—observations on their content are in order.

STATE PRACTICE

State practice demonstrates that nuclear weapons have been manufactured and deployed by States for some 50 years; that in that deployment inheres a threat of possible use; and that the international community, by treaty and through action of the United Nations Security Council, has, far from proscribing the threat or use of nuclear weapons in all circumstances, recognized in effect or in terms that in certain circumstances nuclear weapons may be used or their use threatened.

Not only have the nuclear Powers avowedly and for decades, with vast effort and expense, manufactured, maintained and deployed nuclear weapons. They have affirmed that they are legally entitled to use nuclear weapons in certain circumstances and to threaten their use. They have threatened their use by the hard facts and inexorable implications of the possession and deployment of nuclear weapons; by a posture of readiness to launch nuclear weapons 365 days a year, 24 hours of every day; by the military plans, strategic and tactical, developed and sometimes publicly revealed by them; and, in a very few international crises, by threatening the use of nuclear weapons. In the very doctrine and practice of deterrence, the threat of the possible use of nuclear weapons inheres.

This nuclear practice is not a practice of a lone and secondary persistent objector. This is not a practice of a pariah Government crying out in the wilderness of otherwise adverse international opinion. This is the practice of five of the world's major Powers, of the permanent Members of the Security Council, significantly supported for almost 50 years by their allies and other States sheltering under their nuclear umbrellas. That is to say, it is the practice of States—and a practice supported by a large and weighty number of other States—that together represent the bulk of the world's military and economic and financial and technological power and a very large proportion of its population. This practice has been recognized, accommodated and in some measure accepted by the international community. That measure of acceptance is ambiguous but not meaningless. It is obvious that the alliance structures that have been predicated upon the deployment of nuclear weapons accept the legality of their use in certain circumstances. But what may be less obvious is the effect of the Non-Proliferation Treaty [NPT] and the structure of negative and positive security assurances extended by the nuclear Powers and accepted by the Security Council in pursuance of that Treaty, as well as of reservations by nuclear Powers adhering to regional treaties that govern the possession, deployment and use of nuclear weapons.

THE NUCLEAR NON-PROLIFERATION TREATY

The Treaty on the Non-Proliferation of Nuclear Weapons, concluded in 1968 and indefinitely extended by 175 States Parties in 1995, is of paramount importance. By the terms of Article I, "Each nuclear-weapon State Party to the Treaty undertakes not to transfer to any recipient whatsoever nuclear weapons... or control over such weapons" nor to assist "any non-nuclear weapon State to manufacture or otherwise acquire nuclear weapons...". By the terms of Article II, each non-nuclear weapon State undertakes not to receive nuclear weapons and not to manufacture them. Article III provides that each non-nuclear-weapon State shall accept safeguards to be negotiated with the International Atomic Energy Agency with a view to preventing diversion of nuclear energy from peaceful uses to nuclear weapons. Article IV preserves the right of all Parties to develop peaceful uses of nuclear energy, and Article V provides that potential benefits from peaceful applications of nuclear explosions will be made available to non-nuclear weapon States Party. Article VI provides:

> "Each of the Parties to the Treaty undertakes to pursue negotiations in good faith on effective measures relating to cessation of the nuclear arms race at an early date and to nuclear disarmament, and on a treaty on general and complete disarmament under strict and effective international control."

Article VII provides:

> "Nothing in this Treaty affects the right of any group of States to conclude regional treaties in order to assure the total absence of nuclear weapons in their respective territories."

Article VIII is an amendment clause. Article IX provides that the Treaty shall be open to all States and that, for the purposes of the Treaty, "a nuclear-weapon State is one which has manufactured and exploded a nuclear weapon or other nuclear explosive device prior to 1 January 1967". Article X is an extraordinary withdrawal clause which also contains provision on the basis of which a conference of the Parties may be called to extend the Treaty.

The NPT is thus concerned with the possession rather than the use of nuclear weapons. It establishes a fundamental distinction between States possessing, and States not possessing, nuclear weapons, and a balance of responsibilities between them. It recognizes the possibility of the presence of nuclear weapons in territories in which their total absence has not been prescribed. Nothing in the Treaty authorizes, or prohibits, the use or threat of use of nuclear weapons. However, the Treaty recognizes the legitimacy of the possession of nuclear weapons by the five nuclear Powers, at any rate until the achievement of nuclear disarmament. In 1968, and in 1995, that possession was notoriously characterized by the development, refinement, maintenance and deployment of many thousands of nuclear weapons. If nuclear weapons were not maintained, they might be more dangerous than not; if they were not deployed, the utility of possession would be profoundly affected. Once a Power possesses, maintains and deploys nuclear weapons and the means of their delivery, it places itself in a posture of deterrence.

What does the practice of such possession of nuclear weapons thus import? Nuclear Powers do not possess nuclear arms to no possible purpose. They develop and maintain them at vast expense; they deploy them in their delivery vehicles; and they made and make known their willingness to use them in certain circumstances. They pursue a policy of deterrence, on which the world was on notice when the NPT was concluded and is on notice today. The policy of deterrence differs from that of the threat to use nuclear weapons by its generality. But if a threat of possible use did not inhere in deterrence, deterrence would not deter. If possession by the five nuclear Powers is lawful until the achievement of nuclear disarmament; if possession is the better part of deterrence; if deterrence is the better part of threat, then it follows that the practice of States—including their treaty practice—does not absolutely debar the threat or use of nuclear weapons.

Thus the regime of the Non-Proliferation Treaty constitutes more than acquiescence by the non-nuclear States in the reality of possession of nuclear weapons by the five nuclear Powers. As the representative of the United Kingdom put it in the oral hearings, "The entire structure of the Non Proliferation Treaty ... presupposes that the parties did not regard the use of nuclear weapons as being proscribed in all circumstances." To be sure, the acquiescence of most non-nuclear weapon States in the fact of possession of nuclear weapons by the five nuclear Powers— and the ineluctable implications of that fact—have been accompanied by vehement protest and reservation of rights, as successive resolutions of the General Assembly show. It would be too much to say that acquiescence in this case gives rise to *opinio juris* establishing the legality of the threat or use of nuclear weapons. What it —and the State practice described—does do is to abort the birth or survival of *opinio juris* to the contrary. Moreover, there is more than the practice so far described and the implications of the Nuclear Non-Proliferation Treaty to weigh.

NEGATIVE AND POSITIVE SECURITY ASSURANCES ENDORSED BY THE SECURITY COUNCIL

In connection with the conclusion of the Treaty in 1968 and its indefinite extension in 1995, three nuclear Powers in 1968 and five in 1995 extended negative and positive security assurances to the non-nuclear States Parties to the NPT. In resolution 984 (1995), co-sponsored by the five nuclear Powers, and adopted by the Security Council on 11 April 1995 by unanimous vote,

"The Security Council,

. . .

Recognizing the legitimate interest of non-nuclear-weapon States Parties to the Treaty on the Non-Proliferation of Nuclear Weapons to receive security assurances,

. . .

Taking into consideration the legitimate concern of non-nuclear weapon States that, in conjunction with their adherence to the Treaty on the Non-Proliferation of Nuclear Weapons, further appropriate measures be undertaken to safeguard their security,

. . .

Considering further that, in accordance with the relevant provisions of the Charter of the United Nations, any aggression with the use of nuclear weapons would endanger international peace and security,

1. *Takes note* with appreciation of the statements made by each of the nuclear-weapon States ..., in which they give security assurances against the use of nuclear weapons to non-nuclear weapon States that are Parties to the Treaty on the Non-Proliferation of Nuclear Weapons;

2. *Recognizes* the legitimate interest of non-nuclear-weapon States Parties to the Treaty on the Non-Proliferation of Nuclear Weapons to receive assurances that the Security Council, and above all its nuclear-weapon State permanent members, will act immediately in accordance with the relevant provisions of the Charter of the United Nations, in the event that such States are the victim of an act of, or object of a threat of, aggression in which nuclear weapons are used;

3. *Recognizes further* that, in case of aggression with nuclear weapons or the threat of such aggression against a non-nuclear-weapon State Party to the Treaty on the Non-Proliferation of Nuclear Weapons, any State may bring the matter immediately to the attention of the Security Council to enable the Council to take urgent action to provide assistance, in accordance with the Charter, to the State victim of an act of, or object of a threat of, such aggression; and *recognizes also* that the nuclear-weapon State permanent members of the Security Council will bring the matter immediately to the attention of the Council and seek Council action to provide, in accordance with the Charter, the necessary assistance to the State victim;

. . .

7. *Welcomes* the intention expressed by certain States that they will provide or support immediate assistance, in accordance with the Charter, to any non-nuclear weapon State Party to the Treaty on the Non-Proliferation of Nuclear Weapons that is a victim of an act of, or an object of a threat of, aggression in which nuclear weapons are used;

. . .

9. *Reaffirms* the inherent right, recognized under Article 51 of the Charter, of individual and collective self-defence if an armed attack occurs against a member of the United Nations, until the Security Council has taken measures necessary to maintain international peace and security;

. . .

It is plain—especially by the inclusion of operative paragraph 9 in its context —that the Security Council, in so taking note "with appreciation" in operative paragraph 1 of the negative security assurances of the nuclear Powers, and in so welcoming in operative paragraph 7 "the intention expressed" by the positive security assurances of the nuclear Powers, accepted the possibility of the threat or use of nuclear weapons, particularly to assist a non-nuclear-weapon State that, in the words of paragraph 7—"is a victim of an act of, or an object of a threat of, aggression in which nuclear weapons are used".

This is the plainer in view of the terms of the unilateral security assurances made by four of the nuclear-weapon States which are, with the exception of those of China, largely concordant. They expressly contemplate the use of nuclear weapons in specified circumstances. They implicitly do not debar the use of nuclear weapons against another nuclear Power (or State not party to the NPT), and explicitly do not debar their use against a nuclear-non-weapon State Party that acts in violation of its obligations under the NPT.

For example, the United States reaffirms that it will not use nuclear weapons against non nuclear weapon States Parties to the NPT

"except in the case of an invasion or other attack on the United States . . . its armed forces, its allies, or on a State towards which it has a security commitment, carried out or sustained by such a non-nuclear-weapon State in association or alliance with a nuclear-weapon State".

The exception clearly contemplates the use of nuclear weapons in the specified exceptional circumstances. The United States assurances add: "parties to the Treaty on the Non-Proliferation of Nuclear Weapons must be in compliance" with "their obligations under the Treaty" in order to be "eligible for any benefits of adherence to the Treaty". The United States further "affirms its intention to provide or support immediate assistance" to any non-nuclear-weapon State "that is a victim of an act of, or an object of a threat of, aggression in which nuclear weapons are used". It reaffirms the inherent right of individual or collective self-defence under Article 51 of the Charter "if an armed attack, including a nuclear attack, occurs against a Member of the United Nations . . .". Such affirmations by it—and their unanimous acceptance by the Security Council—demonstrate that nuclear Powers have asserted the legality and that the Security Council has accepted the possibility of the threat or use of nuclear weapons in certain circumstances.

OTHER NUCLEAR TREATIES

As the Court's Opinion recounts, a number of treaties in addition to the NPT limit the acquisition, manufacture, and possession of nuclear weapons; prohibit their deployment or use in specified areas; and regulate their testing. The negotiation and conclusion of these treaties only makes sense in the light of the fact that the international community has not comprehensively outlawed the possession, threat or use of nuclear weapons in all circumstances, whether by treaty or through customary international law. Why conclude these treaties if their essence is already international law, indeed, as some argue, *jus cogens?*

The fact that there is no comprehensive treaty proscribing the threat or use of nuclear weapons in all circumstances is obvious. Yet it is argued that the totality of this disparate treaty-making activity demonstrates an emergent *opinio juris* in favour of the comprehensive outlawry of the threat or use of nuclear weapons; that, even if nuclear weapons were not outlawed decades ago, they are today, or are on the verge of so becoming, by the cumulation of such treaties as well as resolutions of the United Nations General Assembly.

The looseness of that argument is no less obvious. Can it really be supposed that, in recent months, nuclear Powers have adhered to a protocol to the Treaty of Raratonga establishing a nuclear-free zone in the South Pacific because they believe that the threat or use of nuclear weapons already is outlawed in all circumstances and places, there as elsewhere? Can it really be believed that as recently as 15 December 1995, at Bangkok, States signed a Treaty on the South-East Asia Nuclear Weapon-Free Zone, and on 11 April 1996 the States of Africa took the considerable trouble to conclude at Cairo a treaty for the creation of a nuclear-weapons-free zone in Africa, on the understanding that by dint of emergent *opinio juris* customary international law already requires that all zones of the world be nuclear-free?

On the contrary, the various treaties relating to nuclear weapons confirm what the practice described above imports: the threat or use of nuclear weapons is not—certainly, not yet—prohibited in all circumstances, whether by treaty or customary international law. This is the clearer in the light of the terms of the Treaty of Tlatelolco for the Prohibition of Nuclear Weapons in Latin America of 14 February 1967 and the declarations that accompanied adherence to an Additional Protocol under the Treaty of the five nuclear-weapon States. All of the five nuclear-weapon States in so adhering undertook not to use or threaten to use nuclear weapons against the Contracting Parties to the Treaty. But they subjected their undertakings to the possibility of the use of nuclear weapons in certain circumstances, as recounted above in . . . the Court's Opinion. None of the Contracting Parties to the Tlatelolco Treaty objected to the declarations of the five nuclear-weapon States, which is to say that the Contracting Parties to the Treaty recognized the legality of the use of nuclear weapons in certain circumstances.

RESOLUTIONS OF THE GENERAL ASSEMBLY

In its opinion, the Court concludes that the succession of resolutions of the General Assembly on nuclear weapons "still fall short of establishing the existence of an *opinio juris* on the illegality of the use of such weapons". In my view, they do not begin to do so. The seminal resolution, resolution 1653 (XVI) of 24 November 1961, declares that the use of nuclear weapons is "a direct violation of the Charter of the United Nations" and "is contrary to the rules of international law and to the laws of humanity", and that any State using nuclear weapons is to be considered "as committing a crime against mankind and civilization". It somewhat inconsistently concludes by requesting consultations to ascertain views on the possibility of convening a conference for signing a convention on the prohibition of the use of nuclear weapons for war purposes. Resolution 1653 (XVI) was adopted by a vote of 55 to 20, with 26 abstentions. Four of the five nuclear Powers voted against it. Succeeding resolutions providing, as in resolution 36/92 I, that "the use or threat of use of nuclear weapons should . . . be prohibited . . .", have been adopted by varying majorities, in the teeth of strong, sustained and qualitatively important opposition. Any increase in the majority for such resolutions is unimpressive, deriving in some measure from an increase in the membership of the Organization. The continuing opposition, consisting as it does of States that bring together much of the world's military and economic power and a significant percentage of its population, more than suffices to deprive the resolutions in question of legal authority.

The General Assembly has no authority to enact international law. None of the General Assembly's resolutions on nuclear weapons are declaratory of existing international law. The General Assembly can adopt resolutions declaratory of international law only if those resolutions truly reflect what international law is. If a resolution purports to be declaratory of international law, if it is adopted unanimously (or virtually so, qualitatively as well as quantitively) or by consensus, and if it corresponds to State practice, it may be declaratory of international law. The resolutions of which resolution 1653 is the exemplar conspicuously fail to meet these criteria. While purporting to be declaratory of international law (yet calling for consultations about the possibility of concluding a treaty prohibition of what is so declared), they not only do not reflect State practice, they are in conflict with it, as shown above. Forty-six States voted against or abstained upon the resolution, including the majority of the nuclear Powers. It is wholly unconvincing to argue that a majority of the Members of the General Assembly can "declare" international law in opposition to such a body of State practice and over the opposition of such a body of States. Nor are these resolutions authentic interpretations of principles or provisions of the United Nations Charter. The Charter contains not a word about particular weapons, about nuclear weapons, about *jus in bello*. To declare the use of nuclear weapons a violation of the Charter is an innovative interpretation of it, which cannot be treated as an authentic interpretation of Charter principles or provisions giving rise to obligations binding on States under international law. Finally, the repetition of resolutions of the General Assembly in this vein, far from giving rise, in the words of the Court, to "the nascent *opinio juris*", rather demonstrates what the law is not. When faced with continuing and significant opposition, the repetition of General Assembly resolutions is a mark of ineffectuality in law formation as it is in practical effect.

PRINCIPLES OF INTERNATIONAL HUMANITARIAN LAW

While it is not difficult to conclude that the principles of international humanitarian law—above all, proportionality in the application of force, and discrimination between military and civilian targets —govern the use of nuclear weapons, it does not follow that the application of those principles to the threat or use of nuclear weapons "in any circumstance" is easy. Cases at the extremes are relatively clear; cases closer to the centre of the spectrum of possible uses are less so.

At one extreme is the use of strategic nuclear weapons in quantities against enemy cities and industries. This so-called "countervalue" use (as contrasted with "counterforce" uses directly only against enemy nuclear forces and installations) could cause an enormous number of deaths and injuries, running in some cases into the millions; and, in addition to those immediately affected by the heat and blast of those weapons, vast numbers could be affected, many fatally, by spreading radiation. Large-scale "exchanges" of such nuclear weaponry could destroy not only cities but countries, and render continents, perhaps the whole of the earth, uninhabitable, if not at once then through longer-range effects of nuclear fallout. It cannot be accepted that the use of nuclear weapons on a scale which would—or could—result in the deaths of many millions in indiscriminate inferno and by far-reaching fallout, have profoundly pernicious effects in space and time, and render uninhabitable much or all of the earth, could be lawful.

At the other extreme is the use of tactical nuclear weapons against discrete military or naval targets so situated that substantial civilian casualties would not ensue. For example, the use of a nuclear depth-charge to destroy a nuclear submarine that is about to fire nuclear missiles, or has fired one or more of a number of its nuclear missiles, might well be lawful. By the circumstance of its use, the nuclear depth-charge would not give rise to immediate civilian casualties. It would easily meet the test of proportionality; the damage that the submarine's missiles could inflict on the population and territory of the target State would infinitely outweigh that entailed in the destruction of the submarine and its crew. The submarine's destruction by a nuclear weapon would produce radiation in the sea, but far less than the radiation that firing of its missiles would produce on and over land. Nor is it as certain that the use of a conventional depth-charge would discharge the mission successfully; the far greater force of a nuclear weapon could ensure destruction of the submarine whereas a conventional depth-charge might not.

An intermediate case would be the use of nuclear weapons to destroy an enemy army situated in a desert. In certain circumstances, such a use of nuclear weapons might meet the tests of discrimination and proportionality; in others not. The argument that the use of nuclear weapons is inevitably disproportionate raises troubling questions, which the British Attorney General addressed in the Court's oral proceedings in these terms:

"If one is to speak of 'disproportionality', the question arises: disproportionate to what? The answer must be 'to the threat posed to the victim State'. It is by reference to that threat that proportionality must be measured. So one has to look at all the circumstances, in particular the scale, kind and location of the threat. To assume that any defensive use of nuclear weapons must be disproportionate, no matter how serious the threat to the safety and the very survival of the State resorting to such use, is wholly unfounded. Moreover, it suggests an overbearing assumption by the critics of nuclear weapons that they can determine in advance that no threat, including a nuclear, chemical or biological threat, is ever worth the use of any nuclear weapon. It cannot be right to say that if an aggressor hits hard enough, his victim loses the right to take the only measure by which he can defend himself

and reverse the aggression. That would not be the rule of law. It would be an aggressor's charter."

For its part, the body of the Court's Opinion is cautious in treating problems of the application of the principles of international humanitarian law to concrete cases. It evidences a measure of uncertainty in a case in which the tension between State practice and legal principle is unparalleled. It concludes, in Paragraph 2E of the *dispositif*, that,

"It follows from the above-mentioned requirements that the threat or use of nuclear weapons would generally be contrary to the rules of international law applicable in armed conflict, and in particular the principles and rules of international humanitarian law."

That conclusion, while imprecise, is not unreasonable. The use of nuclear weapons is, for the reasons examined above, exceptionally difficult to reconcile with the rules of international law applicable in armed conflict, particularly the principles and rules of international humanitarian law. But that is by no means to say that the use of nuclear weapons, in any and all circumstances, would necessarily and invariably conflict with those rules of international law. On the contrary, as the *dispositif* in effect acknowledges, while they might "generally" do so, in specific cases they might not. It all depends upon the facts of the case.

EXTREME CIRCUMSTANCES OF SELF-DEFENCE AND STATE SURVIVAL

The just-quoted first paragraph of Paragraph 2E of the holdings is followed by the Court's ultimate, paramount—and sharply controverted—conclusion in the case, narrowly adopted by the President's casting vote:

> "However, in view of the current state of international law, and of the elements of fact at its disposal, the Court cannot conclude definitively whether the threat or use of nuclear weapons would be lawful or unlawful in an extreme circumstance of self-defence, in which the very survival of a State would be at stake."

This is an astounding conclusion to be reached by the International Court of Justice. Despite the fact that its Statute "forms an integral part" of the United Nations Charter, and despite the comprehensive and categorical terms of Article 2, paragraph 4, and Article 51 of that Charter, the Court concludes on the supreme issue of the threat or use of force of our age that it has no opinion. In "an extreme circumstance of self-defence, in which the very survival of a State would be at stake", the Court finds that international law and hence the Court have nothing to say. After many months of agonizing appraisal of the law, the Court discovers that there is none. When it comes to the supreme interests of State, the Court discards the legal progress of the Twentieth Century, puts aside the provisions of the Charter of the United Nations of which it is "the principal judicial organ", and proclaims, in terms redolent of *Realpolitik*, its ambivalence about the most important provisions of modern international law. If this was to be its ultimate holding, the Court would have done better to have drawn on its undoubted discretion not to render an Opinion at all....

Indeed, the drafters of the Statute of the Permanent Court of International Justice crafted the provisions of Article 38 of its Statute—provisions which Article 38 of the Statute of this Court maintains—in order, in the words of the President of the Advisory Committee of Jurists, to avoid "especially the blind alley of *non liquet*". To do so, they adopted [a] proposal to empower the Court to apply not only international conventions and international custom but "the general principles of law recognized by civilized nations".

Moreover, far from justifying the Court's inconclusiveness, contemporary events rather demonstrate the legality of the threat or use of nuclear weapons in extraordinary circumstances.

DESERT STORM

The most recent and effective threat of the use of nuclear weapons took place on the eve of "Desert Storm". The circumstances merit exposition, for they constitute a striking illustration of a circumstance in which the perceived threat of the use of nuclear weapons was not only eminently lawful but intensely desirable.

Iraq, condemned by the Security Council for its invasion and annexation of Kuwait and for its attendant grave breaches of international humanitarian law, had demonstrated that it was prepared to use weapons of mass destruction. It had recently and repeatedly used gas in large quantities against the military formations of Iran, with substantial and perhaps decisive effect. It had even used gas against its own Kurdish citizens. There was no ground for believing that legal or humanitarian scruple would prevent it from using weapons of mass destruction—notably chemical, perhaps bacteriological or nuclear weapons—against the coalition forces arrayed against it. Moreover, it was engaged in extraordinary efforts to construct nuclear weapons in violation of its obligations as a Party to the Non-Proliferation Treaty.

General Norman Schwarzkopf stated on 10 January 1996 over national public television in the United States on *"Frontline"*:

> "My nightmare scenario was that our forces would attack into Iraq and find themselves in such a great concentration that they became targeted by chemical weapons or some sort of rudimentary nuclear device that would cause mass casualties.
>
> That's exactly what the Iraqis did in the Iran-Iraq war. They would take the attacking masses of the Iranians, let them run up against their barrier system, and when there were thousands of people massed against the barrier system, they would drop chemical weapons on them and kill thousands of people."

To exorcise that nightmare, the United States took action as described by then Secretary of State James A. Baker in the following terms, in which he recounts his climactic meeting of 9 January 1990 in Geneva with the then Foreign Minister of Iraq, Tariq Aziz:

> "I then made a point 'on the dark side of the issue' that Colin Powell had specifically asked me to deliver in the plainest possible terms. 'If the conflict involves your use of chemical or biological weapons against our forces,' I warned, 'the American people will demand vengeance. We have the means to exact it. With regard to this part of my presentation, that is not a threat, it is a promise. If there is any use of weapons like that, our objective won't just be the liberation of Kuwait, but the elimination of the current Iraqi regime,

and anyone responsible for using those weapons would be held accountable.'

"The President had decided, at Camp David in December, that the best deterrent of the use of weapons of mass destruction by Iraq would be a threat to go after the Ba'ath regime itself. He had also decided that U.S. forces would not retaliate with chemical or nuclear response if the Iraqis attacked with chemical munitions. There was obviously no reason to inform the Iraqis of this. In hope of persuading them to consider more soberly the folly of war, I purposely left the impression that the use of chemical or biological agents by Iraq could invite tactical nuclear retaliation. (We do not really know whether this was the reason; there appears to have been no confirmed use by Iraq of chemical weapons during the war. My own view is that the calculated ambiguity how we might respond has to be part of the reason.)"

In *"Frontline"*, Mr. Baker adds:

> "The president's letter to Saddam Hussein, which Tariq Aziz read in Geneva, made it very clear that if Iraq used weapons of mass destruction, chemical weapons, against United States forces that the American people would —would demand vengeance and that we had the means to achieve it."

Mr. Aziz is then portrayed on the screen immediately thereafter as saying:

> "I read it very carefully and then when I ended reading it, I told him, 'Look, Mr. Secretary, this is not the kind of correspondence between two heads of state. This is a letter of threat and I cannot receive from you a letter of threat to my president,' and I returned it to him."

At another point in the programme, the following statements were made:

"NARRATOR: The Marines waited for a chemical attack. It never came.

TARIQ AZIZ: We didn't think that it was wise to use them. That's all what I can say. That was not—was not wise to use such kind of weapons in such kind of a war with—with such an enemy."

In *The Washington Post* of 26 August 1995, an article datelined United Nations, 25 August was published as follows:

"Iraq has released to the United Nations new evidence that it was prepared to use deadly toxins and bacteria against U.S. and allied forces during the 1991 Persian Gulf War that liberated Kuwait from its Iraqi occupiers, U.N. Ambassador Rolf Ekeus said today.

"Ekeus, the chief U.N. investigator of Iraq's weapons programs, said Iraqi officials admitted to him in Baghdad last week that in December 1990 they loaded three types of biological agents into roughly 200 missile warheads and aircraft bombs that were then distributed to air bases and a missile site.

"The Iraqis began this process the day after the U.N. Security Council voted to authorize using 'all necessary means' to liberate Kuwait, Ekeus said. He said the action was akin to playing 'Russian roulette' with extraordinarily dangerous weapons on the eve of war.

"U.S. and U.N. officials said the Iraqi weapons contained enough biological agents to have killed hundreds of thousands of people and spread horrible diseases in cities or military bases in Israel, Saudi Arabia or wherever Iraq aimed the medium range missiles or squeaked a bomb-laden aircraft through enemy air defenses.

"Ekeus said Iraqi officials claimed they decided not to use the weapons after receiving a strong but ambiguously worded warning from the Bush administration on Jan. 9, 1991, that any use of unconventional warfare would provoke a devastating response.

"Iraq's leadership assumed this meant Washington would retaliate with nuclear weapons, Ekeus said he was told. U.N. officials said they believe the statement by Iraqi Deputy Prime Minister Tariq Aziz is the first authoritative account for why Iraq did not employ the biological or chemical arms at its disposal.

. . .

"Iraqi officials said the documents were hidden by Hussein Kamel Hassan Majeed, the director of Iraq's weapons of mass destruction program who fled to Jordan on Aug. 7 and whose defection prompted Iraq to summon Ekeus to hear the new disclosures. . . .

"Iraq admitted to filling a total of 150 aircraft bombs with botulinum toxin and bacteria capable of causing anthrax disease, each of which is among the most deadly substances known and can kill in extremely small quantities, Ekeus said. It also claimed to have put the two agents into 25 warheads to be carried by a medium range rocket.

"According to what Aziz told Ekeus on Aug. 4, then-Secretary of State James A. Baker III delivered the U.S. threat of grievous retaliation that caused Iraq to hold back during a tense, four-hour meeting in Geneva about five weeks before the beginning of the U.S.-led Desert Storm military campaign. Baker hinted at a U.S. response that would set Iraq back years by reducing its industry to rubble.

"Ekeus said that Aziz told him Iraq 'translated' the warning into a threat that Washington would respond with nuclear arms. In fact, then-Joint Chiefs of Staff Chairman Colin L. Powell and other U.S. military leaders had decided early on that nuclear weapons were not needed and no such retaliatory plans existed." (*The Washington Post*, 26 August 1995, p. A1. See also the report in *The New York Times*, 26 August 1995, p. 3. For a contrasting contention by Iraq that "authority to launch biological and chemical war-heads was pre-delegated in the event that Baghdad was hit by nuclear weapons during the Gulf war", see the 8th Report to the Security Council by the Executive Chairman of the Special Commission (Ambassador Ekeus), U.N. document S/1995/864 of 11 October 1996, p. 11. That Report continues: "This pre-delegation does not exclude the alternative use of such capability and therefore does not constitute proof of only intentions concerning second use."

Finally, there is the following answer by Ambassador Ekeus to a question in the course of testimony in hearings on global proliferation of weapons of mass destruction of 20 March 1996:

" ... I have had conversation with the Deputy Prime Minister of Iraq, Tariq Aziz, in which he made references to his meeting with Secretary of State James Baker in Geneva just before the outbreak of war. He, Tariq Aziz, says that Baker told him to the effect that if such [chemical or biological] weapons were applied there would be a very strong reaction from the United States.

"Tariq Aziz did not imply that Baker mentioned what type of reaction. But he told me that the Iraqi side took it for granted that it meant the use of maybe nuclear weapons against Baghdad, or something like that. And that threat was decisive for them not to use the weapons.

"But this is the story he, Aziz, tells. I think one should be very careful about buying it. I don't say that he must be wrong, but I believe there are strong reasons that this may be an explanation he offers of why Iraq lost the war in Kuwait. This is the story which they gladly tell everyone who talks to them. So I think one should be cautious at least about buying that story. I think still it is an open question." ...

Thus there is on record remarkable evidence indicating that an aggressor was or may have been deterred from using outlawed weapons of mass destruction against forces and countries arrayed against its aggression at the call of the United Nations by what the aggressor perceived to be a threat to use nuclear weapons against it should it first use weapons of mass destruction against the forces of the coalition. Can it seriously be maintained that Mr. Baker's calculated —and apparently successful—threat was unlawful? Surely the principles of the United Nations Charter were sustained rather than transgressed by the threat. "Desert Storm" and the resolutions of the Security Council that preceded and followed it may represent the greatest achievement of the principles of collective security since the founding of the League of Nations. The defeat of this supreme effort of the United Nations to overcome an act of aggression by the use of weapons of mass destruction against coalition forces and countries would have been catastrophic, not only for coalition forces and populations, but for those principles and for the United Nations. But the United Nations did triumph, and to that triumph what Iraq perceived as a threat to use nuclear weapons against it may have made a critical contribution. Nor is this a case of the end justifying the means. It rather demonstrates that, in some circumstances, the threat of the use of nuclear weapons—as long as they remain weapons unproscribed by international law—may be both lawful and rational.

Furthermore, had Iraq employed chemical or biological weapons—prohibited weapons of mass destruction— against coalition forces, that would have been a wrong in international law giving rise to the right of belligerent reprisal. Even if, *arguendo,* the use of nuclear weapons were to be treated as also prohibited, their proportionate use by way of belligerent reprisal in order to deter further use of chemical or biological weapons would have been lawful. At any rate, this would be so if the terms of a prohibition of the use of nuclear weapons did not debar use in reprisal or obligate States "never under any circumstances" to use nuclear weapons, as they will be debarred by those terms from using chemical weapons under Article I of the Convention on the Prohibition of the Development, Production, Stockpiling and Use of Chemical Weapons and on Their Destruction of 1993, should it come into force. In paragraph 46 of its Opinion, the Court states that, on the question of belligerent reprisals, "any" right of such recourse would, "like self-defence, be governed *inter alia* by the principle of proportionality." The citation of that latter principle among others is correct, but any doubt that the Court's reference may raise about the existence of a right of belligerent reprisal is not. Such a doubt would be unsupported not only by the customary law of war and by military manuals of States issued in pursuance of it, which have long affirmed the principle and practice of belligerent reprisal, but by the terms of the Geneva Conventions and its Additional Protocols, which prohibit reprisals not generally but in specific cases (against prisoners-of-war, the wounded, civilians, certain objects and installations, etc.) The far-reaching additional restrictions on reprisals of Protocol I, which bind only its Parties, not only do not altogether prohibit belligerent reprisals; those restrictions as well as other innovations of Protocol I were understood at the time of their preparation and adoption not to govern nuclear weapons.

There is another lesson in this example, namely, that as long as what are sometimes styled as "rogue States" menace the world (whether they are or are not Parties to the NPT), it would be imprudent to set policy on the basis that the threat or use of nuclear weapons is unlawful "in any circumstance". Indeed, it may not only be rogue States but criminals or fanatics whose threats or acts of terrorism conceivably may require a nuclear deterrent or response.

ARTICLE VI OF THE NPT

Finally, I have my doubts about the Court's last operative conclusion in Paragraph 2F: "There exists an obligation to pursue in good faith and bring to a conclusion negotiations leading to nuclear disarmament in all its aspects under strict and effective international control." If this obligation is that only of "Each of the Parties to the Treaty" as Article VI of the Non-Proliferation Treaty states, this is another anodyne asseveration of the obvious.... If it applies to States not party to the NPT, it would be a dubious holding. It would not be a conclusion that was advanced in any quarter in these proceedings; it would have been subjected to no demonstration of authority, to no test of advocacy; and it would not be a conclusion that could easily be reconciled with the fundamentals of international law. In any event, since Paragraph 2F is not responsive to the question put to the Court by the General Assembly, it is to be treated as *dictum.*

POSTSCRIPT

Would the Use of Nuclear Weapons Necessarily Violate the International Law of War?

Ultimately, the International Court of Justice ruled that "the threat of use of nuclear weapons would generally be contrary to the rules of international law applicable in armed conflict." But it went on to say that it was unable to "conclude definitively whether the threat or use of nuclear weapons would be lawful or unlawful in an extreme circumstance of self-defense, in which the very survival of a state would be at stake." For more on the decision, read Michael J. Matheson, "The Opinions of the International Court of Justice on the Threat or Use of Nuclear Weapons," *American Journal of International Law* (Summer 1997) and John Burroughs, *The Legality of Threat or Use of Nuclear Weapons: A Guide to the Historic Opinion of the International Court of Justice* (Transaction Books, 1998).

People on both sides of the controversy found something to cheer in the court's ruling. For some reactions to the test cases in the ICJ, see the series of related articles in the March 1996 issue of the *Bulletin of the Atomic Scientists*. On one hand, those who believe that the use of nuclear weapons can be legitimate were supported by the court's refusal to totally reject the threat or use of nuclear weapons. On the other hand, antinuclear advocates were cheered by the fact that the court implied that severe restrictions existed on threatening to use and using nuclear weapons. This opinion puts any leader who is considering the use of nuclear weapons (except in extremis) on notice that he or she could wind up the defendant in some future war crimes trial. For more on the International Court of Justice, consult the ICJ Web site at http://www.icj-cij.org/icjwww/icj002.htm. It might also be well to look further into the general subject of international law through such publications as Charlotte Ku and Paul F. Diel, eds., *International Law: Classic and Contemporary Readings* (Lynne Rienner, 1998) and Malcolm N. Shaw, *International Law* (Cambridge University Press, 1997).

It is well to remember that *jus in bello* is not simply a topic that involves nuclear weapons. It certainly extends to chemical, biological, and even conventional weapons. President Slobodan Milosevic is subject to arrest for the conduct of the Serb campaign against the Kosovars. How will future leaders, whatever their intentions, know whether or not they might someday be hauled before the International Criminal Court or some other tribunal for war crimes? Did Harry S. Truman violate the law when he ordered the atomic attacks on Japan?

ISSUE 11

Should an International Criminal Court Be Established?

YES: Beth K. Lamont, from "Establishing an International Criminal Court," *The Humanist* (November/December 1998)

NO: Lee A. Casey and David B. Rivkin, Jr., from "Against an International Criminal Court," *Commentary* (May 1998)

ISSUE SUMMARY

YES: Beth K. Lamont, the American Humanist Association's alternative non-governmental organization representative to the UN, argues that by drafting a treaty to establish a global criminal court, the nations of the world have acknowledged the need to advance the importance of international law as a mandatory standard of the conduct of countries and individuals.

NO: Lee A. Casey and David B. Rivkin, Jr., who have both served in the U.S. Justice Department and who now practice law in Washington, D.C., argue that establishing the International Court of Justice will straitjacket U.S. freedom of international action and harm the very quest for justice that it purports to advance.

Historically, international law has focused primarily on the actions of and relations between states. More recently, the status and actions of individuals has become increasingly subject to international law.

The first significant step in this direction was evident in the Nuremberg and Tokyo war crimes trials after World War II. In these panels, prosecutors and judges from the victorious powers prosecuted and tried German and Japanese military and civilian leaders for waging aggressive war, for war crimes, and for crimes against humanity. Most of the accused were convicted; some were executed. There were no subsequent war crimes tribunals through the 1980s and into the mid-1990s. Then, however, separate international judicial tribunals' processes were established to deal with the Holocaust-like events in Bosnia and the genocidal massacres in Rwanda.

The 11-judge tribunal for the Balkans sits in The Hague, the Netherlands. The 6-judge Rwanda tribunal is located in Arusha, Tanzania. These tribunals have indicted numerous people for war crimes and have convicted and imprisoned a few of them. These actions have been applauded by those who believe that individuals should not escape punishment for crimes against humanity that they commit or order. But advocates of this increased and forceful application of international law also feel that the ad hoc tribunals are not enough.

Such advocates are convinced that the next step is the establishment of a permanent International Criminal Court (ICC) to prosecute and try individuals for war crimes and other crimes against humanity. The move for an ICC was given particular impetus when President Bill Clinton proposed just such a court in 1995. Just a year later, the UN convened a conference to lay out a blueprint for the ICC.

Preliminary work led to the convening of a final conference in June 1998 to settle the details of the ICC. Delegates from most of the world's countries met in Rome, where their deliberations were watched and commented on by representatives of 236 nongovernmental organizations (NGOs.) The negotiations were far from smooth. A block of about 50 countries with Canada as its informal leader, which came to be known as the "like-minded group," favored establishing a court with broad and independent jurisdiction.

Other countries wanted to narrowly define the court's jurisdiction and to allow it to conduct only prosecutions that were referred to it by the UN Security Council (UNSC). The hesitant countries also wanted the court to be able to prosecute individuals only with the permission of the accused's home government, and they wanted the right to file treaty reservations exempting their citizens from prosecution in some circumstances. Somewhat ironically, given the impetus that President Clinton had given to the launching of a conference to create the ICC, the United States was one of the principal countries favoring a highly restricted court. U.S. reluctance to support an expansive definition of the ICC's jurisdiction and independence rested on two concerns. One was the fear that U.S. personnel would be especially likely targets of politically motivated prosecutions. The second factor that gave the Clinton administration pause was the requirement that the Senate ratify the treaty. Senate Foreign Relations Committee chairman Jesse Helms has proclaimed that any treaty that gave the UN "a trapping of sovereignty" would be "dead on arrival" in the Senate.

The restrictive approach met with strong opposition. Canada's foreign minister, Lloyd Axworthy, dismissed U.S. concerns as "specious" and an "exercise in realpolitik." The real danger, he said, would be to "create a court to satisfy our consciences" but to leave the "court without power, teeth, or reach." Voicing a similar concern, an Italian diplomat expressed disbelief "that a major democracy . . . would want to have an image of insisting that its soldiers be given license never to be investigated."

In the following selections, Beth K. Lamont and Lee A. Casey and David B. Rivkin, Jr., present their markedly differing views of the wisdom of founding an ICC. Both sets of authors say that they believe in advancing peace and civilized behavior. Where they differ is on whether an ICC would advance or hinder achievement of that goal.

YES

Beth K. Lamont

ESTABLISHING AN INTERNATIONAL CRIMINAL COURT

Because of its status as a U.N. nongovernmental organization (NGO), the American Humanist Association, publisher of the *Humanist*, was invited to attend the negotiations as an observer and informal participant—as were more than three hundred other NGOs. Also in attendance were Amnesty International, Human Rights Watch, the Lawyers Committee for Human Rights, Global Policy Reform, and the World Federalist Movement, among others. Together they comprise the NGO Coalition for an International Court. While the coalition was formed in 1995, some members have been working to create an international criminal court [ICC] since before the United Nations was founded.

In fact, efforts to create an ICC—as described in the book *The Road to Rome* —began back in the nineteenth century when, in 1872, Gustav Moynier, one of the founders of the International Committee of the Red Cross, proposed a permanent court in response to the crimes of the Franco-Prussian War. After the Nuremberg Judgment in 1946, there was renewed interest that resulted in the establishment of an International Law Commission (ILC), and an attempt was made at that time to create a Code of Crimes. In 1948, the U.N. General Assembly adopted the Convention on the Prevention and Punishment of the Crime of Genocide. Many reports and drafts were prepared during the following years, but the Cold War stymied all efforts.

Then in 1989, Trinidad and Tobago moved to resurrect the proposal for a permanent court. In 1994, the ILC presented a draft statute on an ICC to the U.N. General Assembly. Then followed more years of Preparatory Committee meetings, which were attended by governments, international law experts, and NGOs. In 1996, Italy's offer to host an ICC conference was accepted and a July 1998 date was set.

In March 1998, as the conference neared, U.S. Senate Foreign Relations Committee Chair Jesse Helms sent a letter to Secretary of State Madeleine Albright, declaring that the ICC would be "dead on arrival" in the Senate— unless the United States was given veto control over the court. In an op-ed piece for the May 13 *Washington Post*, Lawyers Committee for Human Rights

Chair Norman Dorsen and Century Foundation/Twentieth Century Fund Senior Vice-President Morton H. Halperin called the United States' position

> the most serious roadblock in the way of the success of the Rome conference.... To ensure beyond all doubt that no American can be tried by the ICC, the Clinton administration is insisting that there be an affirmative vote of the U.N. Security Council—subject to a veto by the five permanent members—before the court's prosecutors can begin an investigation.

How can the United States, which purports to be "a nation of laws," be respectful of the law yet simultaneously above it? What must other nations, which have expressed a willingness to subject themselves to the jurisdiction of the court, think of the United States' refusal to do so? What ever happened to its world leadership? Regardless of the Clinton administration's position, what do U.S. citizens want? Perhaps this lapse in logic can be overcome by the democratic process.

* * *

A number of other questions also had to be forcefully hammered out for inclusion in the draft document: What will be the scope of this new International Criminal Court? What will it do? Where will it be located? Which crimes will it try? What will give it power, and will nations willingly accept its jurisdiction? When will it be in force? Who will have the right to bring charges? Who will its judges be and from which countries will they be selected? How can we trust their judgment? Will a nation willingly surrender to the court one of its citizen to be tried? Will the ICC have jurisdiction

over those nations which choose not to participate? What will constitute jurisdiction: the nation in which a crime is committed, the homeland of the accused, or the homeland of the victim? What penalties will the court impose? Will there be capital punishment?

Among the agreements reached were the following:

- The ICC shall be a permanent institution and shall have the power to exercise its jurisdiction over persons for the most serious crimes of international concern.
- The ICC shall be brought into relationship with the United Nations through an agreement to be approved by an assembly of states parties to this statute and the seat of the court shall be established at The Hague in the Netherlands.
- The ICC has jurisdiction in accordance with this statute with respect to the following crimes: the crime of genocide; crimes against humanity; war crimes; and the crime of aggression.

The definitions of these crimes are spelled out in minute detail. *Genocide* is defined generally as "deliberately inflicting on the group conditions of life calculated to bring about its physical destruction in whole or in part." *Crimes against humanity* are defined as

> "enforced disappearance of persons," meaning arrest, detention or abduction of persons by, or with the authorization of, a State or a political organization, followed by a refusal to acknowledge that deprivation of freedom or to give information on the fate or whereabouts of those persons, with the intention of removing them from the protection of the law for a prolonged period of time.

War crimes are defined as "grave breaches of the Geneva Convention of 12 August 1949, namely, any of the following acts against persons or property protected under the provisions of the relevant Geneva Convention." This is followed by fifty-six definitions of *acts of aggression*.

Terrorism and drug-related crimes were adopted into the document in an annexed resolution, despite opposition from the United States, and will be subject to definition at a review conference in the future. The United States argued that, although bringing terrorism and drug-related charges before an international court would not in itself be a problem, other agencies are better equipped to handle an ongoing investigation. Well, of course—at the present time. But this is a rather circuitous argument, in as much as the necessary investigative powers will be placed in the hands of the ICC prosecutor at some future time.

What will constitute the court's power? Each sovereign nation that signs the document will voluntarily relinquish certain state powers and agree to abide by the decisions of the court. Even heads of state and military leaders will be subject to the jurisdiction of the court, and signatory nations are obliged to surrender their own citizens if charged. Also, the new court cannot bring charges retroactively; it can only try crimes that occur after the jurisdiction of the court has been established.

It was also determined that penalties will not include capital punishment because one cannot condone a crime for which one is trying another person. The maximum penalty will be life imprisonment and, for some, a maximum of thirty years imprisonment. Some nations felt that such minimal prison time will make the court a laughingstock in view of the gravity of the crimes being tried; they insisted that executions were needed for a show of authority. Instead, the court will emphasize the concepts of reparation and compensation of victims. Provision has been made for a trust fund to be established for the benefit of victims of crimes and their families. This trust will be funded by fines and forfeiture of money and property.

One of the most crucial elements decided was who has the right to bring charges. Can individuals—such as mothers of the disappeared—accuse their tormentors, or must such charges be brought by the nation in which the crime has occurred? Must the nation of the accused be a party to the treaty and, if not, must it give voluntary consent to the jurisdiction of the court before the accused can be tried? Must all charges be funneled through and approved by the U.N. Security Council?

The good news is that there will be an independent prosecutor, who has the power to take initiative and investigate an alleged crime. This is called the principle of *proprio motu* and was agreed upon by the majority of nations, again over the objections of the United States, which feared an overwhelmed court. The bad news is that this authority can be curbed by the U.N. Security Council, which will have the right to delay investigation for a renewable twelve-month period. And regrettably, no provision has been made to protect any victims, witnesses, or evidence during these periods. How can it be in the best interest of all nations for such a disproportionate amount of power to be concentrated in the hands of only five nations? In addition to the Office of Independent Prosecutor, the

ICC will consist of the Presidency, the Registry, a Pre-Trial Division, a Trial Division, and an Appeals Division. These offices will be filled by eighteen judges of high moral character, only one of whom may be nominated by each nation and elected by secret ballot at an Assembly of States Parties. These judges must have established competence in criminal law, international humanitarian law, and the law of human rights and have "extensive experience in a professional legal capacity which is of relevance to the judicial work of the court." Generally, these judges will serve for nine years and are to reflect an equitable geographical and gender representation.

* * *

All of the still unanswered questions will be resolved in time and with each new step in the development of the court, but the remarkable accomplishment stands. And although the draft document— now referred to as the Rome Treaty— is and will continue to be available for ratification by the participating nations, the next official step is for it to be reviewed and possibly adopted by the U.N. General Assembly. Or perhaps it will be subjected to further negotiations. It must be ratified by at least sixty participating nations in order to make the new court a reality. However, as of October, no nation had ratified the Rome Treaty and only fifty-three states had formally signed it.

So where does the leading superpower of the free world stand in this effort? Perhaps most telling is the report given by David Scheffer, head of the U.S. delegation to the Rome conference and ambassador-at-large, to the Senate Foreign Relations Committee on July 23. In it, he describes the United States as "the most powerful nation committed to the rule of law" but then proceeds to explain in great detail how certain U.S. objectives were not achieved and why the United States voted against the draft document:

> While we successfully defeated initiatives to empower the court with universal jurisdiction, a form of jurisdiction over nonparty states was adopted by the conference despite our strenuous objections. In particular, the treaty specifies that, as a precondition to the jurisdiction of the court over a crime, either the state or territory where the crime was committed or the state of nationality of the perpetrator of the crime must be a party to the treaty or have granted its voluntary consent to the jurisdiction of the court. We sought an amendment to the text that would have required both of these countries to be party to the treaty or, at a minimum, would have required that only the consent of the state of nationality of the perpetrator be obtained before the court could exercise jurisdiction. We asked for a vote on our proposal, but a motion to take no action was overwhelmingly carried by the vote of participating governments in the conference.
>
> We are left with consequences that do not serve the cause of international justice. Since most atrocities are committed internally and most internal conflicts are between warring parties of the same nationality, the worst offenders of international humanitarian law can choose never to join the treaty and be fully insulated from its reach absent a Security Council referral. Yet multinational peacekeeping forces operating in a country that has joined the treaty can be exposed to the court's jurisdiction even if the country of the individual peacekeeper has not joined the treaty. Thus, the treaty purports to establish an arrangement whereby U.S. armed forces operating overseas could conceivably be prosecuted by the international court even

if the United States has not agreed to be bound by the treaty. Not only is this contrary to the most fundamental principles of treaty law, it could inhibit the ability of the United States to use its military to meet alliance obligations and participate in multinational operations, including humanitarian interventions to save civilian lives. Other contributors to peacekeeping operations will similarly be exposed....

Finally, we were confronted on July 17 [1998] with a provision that no reservations to the treaty would be allowed. We had long argued against such a prohibition, and many countries had joined us in this concern. We believed that at a minimum there were certain provisions of the treaty, particularly in the field of state cooperation with the court, where domestic constitutional requirements and national judicial procedures might require a reasonable opportunity for reservations that did not defeat the intent or purpose of the treaty....

The U.S. delegation also sought to achieve other objectives... that in our view are critical. I regret that certain of these objectives were not achieved and therefore we could not support the draft that emerged on July 17.

Because of some myopia, the founding document for the establishment of a new international criminal court is not what NGOs had wanted; much more was advocated. But it is a new beginning, and the tremendous endeavor was not abandoned in despair—as was feared at many seemingly insurmountable impasses. Many clashing concepts were ultimately compromised in the overriding wish not to fail.

Humanist Manifesto II speaks of the need for the "development of a system of world law and a world order based upon a system of transnational federal government." By drafting a document to establish an international criminal court, 150 nations have acknowledged this same need. We should remain hopeful that this willingness of nations to agree to abide by a law greater than themselves, for the greater good of all, will be the dawning of a more humanistic world. But remember: the Rome Treaty wasn't built in a day.

NO

Lee A. Casey and
David B. Rivkin, Jr.

AGAINST AN INTERNATIONAL
CRIMINAL COURT

Although one would not necessarily know it from the newspapers, a half-century of debate over the question of how to bring perpetrators of genocide and other grave crimes to justice is now coming to a head. In June [1998], a gathering of diplomats in Rome will put the finishing touches on a United Nations-sponsored treaty to establish an International Criminal Court (ICC). This document will then be put forward for signature and ratification by the 185 member states of the world body.

Not a moment too soon, many might say. After all, the prosecution of Nazi war criminals at Nuremberg after World War II was undertaken in part to keep the horrors of mass slaughter and aggressive war from recurring. Yet, in places as disparate as Cambodia, Rwanda, and Iraq, such horrors *have* recurred, and recurred again, and the guilty parties have gone unpunished. The need for a standing International Criminal Court would thus appear self-evident, its absence itself a kind of crime.

In the United States, a variety of influential organizations—ranging from the American Bar Association (ABA) to monitoring groups like Human Rights Watch—is backing the UN initiative. With Secretary of State Madeleine Albright leading the charge, the Clinton administration, too, though quibbling about some aspects of the draft now under discussion, has expressed its approval of the treaty's basic outline, and is expected in due course to submit a version to the U.S. Senate for its advice and consent.

If the ICC were to work as advertised—its professed purpose is to indict warring despots and mass murderers, extradite them, try them, and award them their just deserts—it would be no bad thing. There is, however, a problem, and one with especially severe implications for the United States: it will not, and cannot, work as advertised.

* * *

As it is currently conceived, the ICC will be an independent international body that will combine in one institution the functions of fact-finding, prosecution, judgment, sentencing, appeal, and pardon. The ICC's judges and prosecutors will be nominated by the signatory states, and elected by their majority vote. A complaint brought by any signatory state, or by the UN Security Council, will empower the ICC prosecutors to investigate, indict, and try individuals for such offenses as crimes against humanity and violations of the laws of war. Trials will not be by jury. Punishment, up to a maximum sentence of life imprisonment, will be decided by the court, as will requests for clemency and parole. The sole venue for appeal will be the appellate division of the ICC itself. There will be no recourse from its decisions, and no ability to overturn the law it sets.

To begin at the beginning, it is highly questionable whether the Constitution allows the U.S. government to delegate its judicial authority—to delegate, in other words, the right to put Americans on trial for offenses (like planning an allegedly illegal military action) that they have committed on American soil—to an institution that is not a court of the United States. The defining case here is *Ex parte Milligan*, decided shortly after the Civil War, in which the Supreme Court struck down the conviction of a civilian by a military tribunal. Because the military tribunal had not been established under Article III of the Constitution, ruled the Court, it was not "part of the judicial power of the country." The same reasoning would clearly apply to the ICC and render its judgments against Americans unenforceable in the United States.

Even if a way around this could be found—and it would require, at a minimum, that ICC judges be appointed by the U.S. President, be approved by the U.S. Senate, and serve for life—

the ICC would still be unconstitutional. In particular, though the ICC will be empowered to indict and try American citizens, its procedures will fail to provide American defendants who come before it the basic guarantees they enjoy under the Constitution's Bill of Rights.

Thus, the Constitution's Fourth Amendment protects Americans against unreasonable searches and seizures; the Fifth Amendment requires grand-jury indictments, forbids double jeopardy, and gives an assurance of "due process of law"; the Sixth Amendment ensures that in all criminal prosecutions the accused shall have the right to be tried "by an impartial jury of the state and district wherein the crime shall have been committed"; the Eighth Amendment forbids excessive bail and fines, as well as cruel and unusual punishment. None of these rights is adequately preserved in the ICC agreement, and most are not preserved at all.

The absence of these safeguards is all the more disturbing because the Supreme Court stated plainly in an 1890 case, *De Geofroy v. Riggs*, that the constitutional rights of Americans cannot be abridged by the federal government's power to conclude treaties. That power, stated the Court, does not enable the government to "authorize what the Constitution forbids." The Court reiterated this view in a particularly pertinent case, *In re Yamashita*, heard shortly after the end of World War II and dealing with the same subject matter that will come before the ICC. In any conflict between U.S. law and the laws of war, noted the Supreme Court, U.S. law must prevail: "[W]e do not make the laws of war but we respect them so far as they *do not* conflict with the commands of Congress or the Constitution" (emphasis added).

The fact that the constitutional case against the ICC seems straightforward has not prevented the ICC's supporters, including the American Bar Association [ABA], from blithely dismissing it. An organization ostensibly devoted to the rule of law, the ABA describes constitutional objections to the ICC as a "red herring," asserting that since the ICC will not be a "court of the United States," the Bill of Rights will not apply to its proceedings. This analysis is as simple as it is wrong. The protections offered by the Bill of Rights, as we have seen, extend to every act of the entire federal government, including its agreements with other nations.

*   *   *

But now suppose that the ICC treaty were somehow altered to pass constitutional muster—that is, by scrapping the current draft and starting again. Even so, compelling reasons remain for not setting up a supranational criminal court that will be empowered to stand in judgment not only of the usual despots and mass murderers but also, by definition, of the U.S. and its allies.

The danger of politicization and anti-Americanism, inherent in all international institutions, has been driven home time and again by the behavior of such bodies as the International Labor Organization, UNESCO [United Nations Educational, Scientific and Cultural Organization], and the UN itself. While it is true that the level of anti-Americanism may have waned somewhat now that the cold war has drawn to an end and the Soviet Union has disappeared, the United States and its allies still have enemies, and those enemies, if they accede to the ICC treaty, will have a say in the composition of the court's personnel. Add to the mix the many countries that are not overtly hostile to the U.S. but that wish to check an assertive American foreign policy, and inevitably a tremendous potential for mischief will arise.

Here is an example of how things can go awry. The Clinton administration has asserted that if Saddam Hussein further impedes the work of UN inspectors searching for weapons of mass destruction in Iraq, the U.S. has the legal right to strike Baghdad without further action by the UN Security Council. Yet three of the five permanent members of the Council —Russia, China, and France—disagree. They maintain that a U.S. attack would be a violation of the UN mandate and consequently of international law.

If a court like the ICC were in place, a decision to hit Saddam Hussein would leave the President, and each and every American who participated in the formulation and execution of the military operation, vulnerable to investigation and prosecution. How might the court's proceedings unfold? The prosecution might root its case in the civilian casualties that Iraq would inevitably incur in the course of the U.S. strike. If the ICC determined that sufficient evidence existed to hand up an indictment for violation of the laws of war, the United States would be legally bound to surrender the individuals charged, be they military or civilian, Secretary of State or GS-7 file clerk, President or private. While there would be no enforcement mechanism on U.S. soil to compel acquiescence, the ICC could issue international warrants; those under indictment would then be unable to travel overseas for fear of arrest. The ICC could also opt to begin proceedings against U.S. officials *in absentia*.

Naturally, the President and other responsible officials would have a number of defenses at their disposal. They could claim, for example, that the attacks on Iraq had been authorized by previous Security Council resolutions and that civilians were not deliberately targeted. Ultimately, however, the merits of the case would be for the ICC to determine, and the court's findings, as noted above, could not be appealed except to the ICC itself.

* * *

A scenario like this one may seem unlikely. But whether or not it ever comes to pass, the very existence of a court that can at any time initiate investigations of U.S. actions around the globe will almost certainly impose inhibitions on the conduct of American foreign policy. In fact, even the Clinton administration is troubled by the prospect of the ICC's becoming an uncontrollable rogue institution. "We do have concerns about a prosecutor who would act on his or her own authority," admits David Scheffer, the head of the U.S. delegation to the negotiations.

To keep the ICC within acceptable bounds, the administration has sought to revise the mechanism that will trigger its initiation of a case; these proposed revisions, however, fall far short of the mark. For example, the U.S. wants to require "complementarity," which means that the ICC would become involved in prosecuting individuals only if their own government had failed to bring them to justice. But this particular proposal comes with a qualification: the power to determine whether a good-faith effort at prosecution had been made would be retained by the ICC itself. It is a generous loophole, and potentially a lethal one.

The U.S. also wants to require a referral by the UN Security Council before the ICC can investigate any particular conflict or atrocity. This would allow the United States to exercise its veto when American interests are threatened. But one can easily imagine what would happen in practice: on every occasion in which the U.S. considered casting its veto to prevent the ICC from taking action, it would be accused of hypocrisy and lawlessness, and find itself under intense pressure to acquiesce. And such occasions are likely to abound, given the investigatory latitude the ICC is to enjoy.

To understand what is at stake here, let us return to the example of Iraq, and let us suppose that Kuwait, say, were to attempt to bring Saddam Hussein before the ICC for committing war crimes. An ICC investigation into this matter could easily expand to encompass an inquiry of another sort entirely—namely, into the war crimes that Saddam Hussein himself has alleged were committed by the U.S. *against Iraq*. To avert this possibility, the U.S. might then be forced to exercise its veto—and thus block even friendly states like Kuwait from initiating a referral.

Indeed, to avoid having its current or former leadership brought before an international tribunal to answer for American foreign policy, Washington might find itself compelled to veto *any* referral of *any* conflict where American arms were involved. In the end, all the ICC would then have accomplished would be to tie our foreign policy in knots. In the eyes of some around the world, to be sure, this might well seem a desirable goal; but how it would serve our own interests—or, for that matter, the interests of peace and the rule of law—is a mystery.

* * *

Do the palpable flaws of the ICC treaty mean that the world community is helpless to bring outlaws to justice? Hardly. The UN Security Council already possesses the authority to establish tribunals to investigate and punish war crimes. It has, in fact, recently established two: the international criminal tribunal for the former Yugoslavia, and the international criminal tribunal for Rwanda. Unlike the ICC, however, their territorial jurisdiction and temporal duration are limited. Thus far, the Yugoslav tribunal has issued eighteen indictments against 74 individuals, of whom twenty are in custody. It concluded its first trial, of a Serbian concentration-camp guard, last July, sentencing him to prison for twenty years. A number of other cases are to be heard in the next few months. Some may consider this too little, too late; but with sufficient international backing, such courts can accomplish a great deal.

The ICC also promises to accomplish a great deal—but precisely what those accomplishments will be is another matter. In the name of international law, the treaty will undermine our own system of justice. In the name of bringing aggressors to account, it will diminish our own ability to do exactly that, while augmenting the possibility that we or one of our close allies will sooner or later find ourselves in the dock.

The Clinton administration's penchant for multilateralism is by now an old story. Even so, it is astonishing that it has so fervently embraced a document with such obvious faults. Is this really the straitjacket in which the world's greatest power, and its best hope for peace, wishes to place itself?

POSTSCRIPT

Should an International Criminal Court Be Established?

In the end, the debate in Rome over the ICC yielded compromises with the reservations of the United States and some other countries, but, overall, the conference opted to create a relatively strong court by a vote of 120–7 (countries voting no included China, India, and the United States), with 21 abstentions. Kofi Annan, secretary-general of the United Nations, told the delegates in Rome, "Two millennia ago one of this city's most famous sons, Marcus Tullius Cicero, declared that 'in the midst of arms, law stands mute.' As a result of what we are doing here today, there is real hope that that bleak statement will be less true in the future than it has been in the past." Annan's speech and other material related to the ICC can found on the World Wide Web at http://www.un.org/icc/. Another useful Internet site is http://www.iccnow.org.

Once the ICC treaty was adopted by the conference, it was opened to the world's countries for signature and ratification. The treaty will be open for accession by the world's countries until 2001. Once 60 countries have signed and ratified it, the treaty will go into effect. As of June 1999 representatives of 82 countries had signed the ICC treaty, and 3 states had ratified it. Senegal was the first to ratify, followed by Trinidad, Tobago, and San Marino. Such important countries as France, Germany, and Great Britain had signed the treaty by that date; other important countries, such as China, Japan, and the United States, had not.

The following are some of the basic provisions of the treaty:

1. The court's jurisdiction includes genocide and a range of other crimes committed during international and internal wars. Such crimes must be "widespread and systematic" and committed as part of "state, organization, or group policy," not just as individual acts.
2. Except for genocide and complaints brought by the UNSC, the ICC will not be able to prosecute alleged crimes unless either the state of nationality of the accused or the state where the crimes took place has ratified the treaty.
3. Original signatories will have a one-time ability to "opt out" of the court's jurisdiction for war crimes, but not genocide, for a period of seven years.
4. The UNSC can delay a prosecution for a year. The vote to delay will not be subject to veto.
5. The ICC will only be able to try cases when national courts have failed to work.

For Americans, the next important step will be signature by President Bill Clinton or his successor. If and when that takes place, then the treaty will go to the Senate for ratification.

For further reading from a pro-ICC viewpoint, see Bryan F. MacPherson, "Building an International Criminal Court for the Twenty-First Century," *Connecticut Journal of International Law* (Winter 1998). Taking the anti-ICC position is John R. Bolton in "Courting Danger: What's Wrong With the International Court," *The National Interest* (Winter 1998). For a view of the U.S. position, see Aryeh Neier, "Waiting for Justice: The United States and the International Criminal Court," *World Policy Journal* (Fall 1998).

On the Internet . . .

Amnesty International
Information about the current state of human rights throughout the world is available at this Web site. The 1997 Amnesty International report that documents acts of violence in 151 countries is also available.
http://www.amnesty.org

Welcome to Al-Islam.org
This site is an introduction to Islam (if you are a beginner) and a repository for advancing your knowledge about Islam further (if you are a Muslim).
http://www.al-islam.org

Culturelink
This Web site is Culturelink, the Network of Networks for Research and Cooperation in Cultural Development. The overview network of the many networks related to scholarly research and international cooperation in cultural development was established by UNESCO and the Council of Europe.
http://www.unesco.org/culturelink/unmain.html

United Nations Office for Drug Control and Crime Prevention
For a global perspective of the drug control problem and efforts to halt it, a good place to start is the United Nations office that deals with the issue.
http://www.undcp.org/unlinks.html

United Nations Development Fund for Women
The issue of female genital surgery is part of the larger picture of the conditions, rights, and aspirations of the world's women. The United Nations Development Fund for Women (UNIFEM) deals with a broad range of issues related to women. *http://www.unifem.undp.org*

Global Warming: Understanding the Forecast
This site promotes the global warming exhibit on permanent display at Columbia University's Biosphere 2 Center near Tucson, Arizona. The site offers background information on global warming and a complete online, interactive version of the exhibit.
http://www.edf.org/pubs/Brochures/GlobalWarming/

PART 5

Moral, Social, and Environmental Issues

When all is said and done, policy is, or at least ought to be, about values. That is, how do we want our world to be? There are choices to make about what we want to do. It would be easy if these choices were clearly good versus evil. But things are not usually that simple, and the issues in this part present a series of conundrums related to human rights, social tolerance, and the environment.

■ Should Foreign Policymakers Minimize Human Rights Concerns?

■ Do U.S. Efforts to Stem the Flow of Drugs from Abroad Encourage Human Rights Violations?

■ Would World Affairs Be More Peaceful If Women Dominated Politics?

■ Is Islamic Fundamentalism a Threat to Political Stability?

■ Does Ritual Female Genital Surgery Violate Women's Human Rights?

■ Should the Kyoto Treaty Be Supported?

ISSUE 12

Should Foreign Policymakers Minimize Human Rights Concerns?

YES: Alan Tonelson, from "Jettison the Policy," *Foreign Policy* (Winter 1994/1995)

NO: Michael Posner, from "Rally Round Human Rights," *Foreign Policy* (Winter 1994/1995)

ISSUE SUMMARY

YES: Alan Tonelson, a fellow of the Economic Strategy Institute in Washington, D.C., contends that the United States' human rights policy has collapsed and ought to be jettisoned.

NO: Michael Posner, executive director of the Lawyers Committee for Human Rights, maintains that Tonelson's argument is flawed and that the United States should continue to incorporate human rights concerns into its foreign policy decisions.

This debate on the role of human rights and other moral issues in determining foreign policy is one over which realists and idealists disagree strongly.

Realists are averse to applying moral standards to foreign policy. When Adolf Hitler's Nazi Germany invaded Joseph Stalin's communist Soviet Union, Sir Winston Churchill, the prime minister of democratic Great Britain, offered aid to Stalin. When a critic in Parliament challenged the decision of the prime minister, he replied: "If Hitler had invaded Hell, ... [I would] make favorable reference to the devil." It is not that realists are amoral. Instead, they agree with the view of Secretary of State George Shultz (1982–1989) that "we ... have ... to accept that our passionate commitment to moral principles [cannot] be a substitute for sound foreign policy in a world of hard realities and complex choices." This is true, he argues, because "moral impulse, noble as it might be, [can] lead either to futile and perhaps dangerous global crusades, on the one hand, or to escapism and isolationism, equally dangerous, on the other." Similarly, Hans Morgenthau, one of the founders of the academic realists' school, argued that it is unconscionable as well as risky for a state to abandon realpolitik in favor of moralism. He contended that "while the individual has a moral right to sacrifice himself" in defense of a moral principle, "the state has no right to let its moral disapprobation ... get in the way of successful political action, itself inspired by the moral principle of national survival."

Idealists, in contrast, believe that it is both right and wise to consider human rights when making foreign policy decisions. Richard Falk, a leading idealist scholar, criticizes realists for their "tendency to discount... the normative aspirations of society." Some policymakers agree with this view. President Jimmy Carter declared during a speech marking the 30th anniversary of the Universal Declaration of Human Rights of 1948 that Americans should be "proud that our nation stands for more than military might or political might," that "our pursuit of human rights is part of a broad effort to use our great power and our tremendous influence in the service of creating a better world in which human beings can live," and that "human rights is the soul of our foreign policy." Idealists also reject the realists' contention that a country will be at a disadvantage if it applies moral standards to foreign policy making in a dangerous world. Secretary of State Cyrus Vance (1977–1980) once commented that it is a "dangerous illusion" to believe that "pursuing values such as human rights... is incompatible with pursuing U.S. national interests" because we can "never be secure in a world where freedom was threatened everywhere else."

The end of the cold war has, in many ways, made the issue of human rights more acute. During the cold war the human rights abuses of friendly regimes were often ignored in the interests of solidarity as the West faced the threat from the Soviet-led communists. That threat has ended, of course, and with it has died the easy standard that an anticommunist dictator is better than no anticommunist government at all. Idealists now argue that we act on our principles without the fear that we are empowering an enemy. Realists rejoin that the end of the cold war did not mean the end of power politics.

The debate over whether or not to incorporate human rights standards into foreign policy making is not simply a matter of intellectual speculation. The controversy also involves important policy choices. If democracy truly does promote peace, then perhaps the United States, Canada, and other democracies should pressure, even force if possible, other nondemocratic regimes to change. The United States, backed by the United Nations, did that in Haiti. Should the same standard apply to friendly nondemocratic regimes such as Saudi Arabia, which is ruled by a feudal monarchy? Also, what should a country do when the dictates of realpolitik point in one direction and human rights concerns point in another?

YES

Alan Tonelson

JETTISON THE POLICY

President Bill Clinton's team-up with the Haitian military and his [recent] acknowledgment that trade sanctions would not hasten democracy's development in China are only the latest signs that America's human rights policy has collapsed. The signs of America's failure to achieve the policy's objectives appear everywhere: from the halls of power in defiant Beijing to the streets of Port-au-Prince, from the mountains of Bosnia to the tenant farms of rebellious Chiapas in southern Mexico. At least as important, the policy has antagonized or simply turned off numerous democratic countries, as well as endangered a broad range of U.S. strategic and economic interests in key regions around the world.

No one can fairly blame U.S. policy for the world's continuing—and in many respects worsening—human rights situation. But Washington has been so ineffective in combating human rights violations in so many places for so long, and so many of its efforts at promoting democracy—especially their unilateral elements—have entailed such high costs, that the usual explanations seem inadequate.

Rather than blame Secretary of State Warren Christopher's alleged incompetence and Clinton's allegedly naive campaign promises, or struggle to better "balance" human rights concerns with other major U.S. interests, Americans might instead begin asking a fundamental question: Does any government-centered human rights policy make sense in the post–Cold War era? All the evidence indicates that such policies, however morally compelling, are obsolete—swamped, ironically, by the very forces that only yesterday inspired such bipartisan optimism in a new age of human rights progress. The immense tides of information, technology, goods, and capital that now flow so effortlessly across borders have turned Washington's efforts into Cold War relics, as antiquated as fallout shelters—and, in their own way, as falsely comforting.

Since the Cold War spawned U.S. human rights policy, its post–Cold War collapse should come as no surprise. American leaders have spoken out against oppression abroad throughout U.S. history, and the American people fought two global hot wars as well as a cold war against imperialist adversaries. But a systematic, dedicated policy to promote greater respect worldwide for human rights dates back only to the 1970s. Unfortunately, the policy was never rooted in a rigorous critique of prevailing American approaches to world affairs, or in a careful search for alternatives, but in a politically inspired temper tantrum by foreign policy professionals of the Left and Right.

Of course, as left-of-center human rights advocates argued, Washington's Cold War alliances with anticommunist dictators sometimes backfired. Of course, as right-of-center human rights advocates argued, American leaders episodically kept quiet about communist oppression whenever they pursued détente-like policies. And, of course, there was much heartfelt concern at the grassroots level about the moral tone and impact of American foreign policy. But the high-profile politicians and activists across the political spectrum who created and debated official human rights policies were, at bottom, simply venting frustrations over the compromises with evil that no foreign policy in an imperfect, anarchic world can avoid, and using human rights debates to push broader, more questionable agendas.

Liberals and other left-wing opponents of the Vietnam War used the human rights issue to push the broader view that millennial change was sweeping over world affairs, and that the United States could abandon the use of force and power-politicking altogether. They asserted that America's essential foreign policy objectives could be secured with more morally and aesthetically pleasing tools like foreign aid, diplomacy, and acceding to the (usually legitimate) interests of even hostile powers. The political Right used the human rights issue to at-

tack détente with the Soviet Union and the larger belief that peaceful coexistence with other nuclear superpowers not only was necessary, but also could improve national security by reducing tensions and even produce mutually beneficial agreements.

Not surprisingly, given such political and polemical origins, human rights policy rarely advanced U.S. national interests in the 1970s. Relations with both allies and adversaries worsened (including West European countries that criticized the policy's heavy-handed treatment of the former Soviet Union), dictatorial friends were often weakened without generating better replacements (as in Iran and Nicaragua), and equally dictatorial foes remained securely in power (throughout the communist bloc and much of the developing world).

More surprisingly, prominent human rights advocates rarely sounded troubled when their policies failed to significantly improve human rights practices worldwide. Did U.S. policy simply help replace a friendly autocrat with an equally ruthless and hostile successor, as in Iran and Nicaragua? Did American initiatives lead a target regime to crack down on dissenters or aspiring emigrants, as in the Soviet Union? Was America aiming at countries where it had no influence at all, as in Vietnam or Ethiopia?

When advocates did try to answer such questions, their responses spoke volumes about their real priorities. Symbolism was critical. Consistency was essential—never mind that the objects of human rights policy were countries that differed completely in their level of social and economic development, their significance to the United States, and their political relations with America. The United States had to go on record. Americans had to do "what they could"—implying, of course, that salving American consciences was the main point.

For those reasons, moderate critics of the policies were missing the point entirely when they labored mightily to reconcile human rights positions with American strategic and economic interests. U.S. efforts did score limited successes—securing the release of numerous political prisoners during the 1970s (especially in Latin America) and joining in rare global economic sanctions that did advance the cause of reform in South Africa—although how those successes made the United States appreciably more secure or more prosperous was never explained. But human rights activism was never primarily about enhancing national security and welfare, or even alleviating suffering abroad. It was an exercise in therapy. The bottom line, as Jimmy Carter made clear, was to give Americans a foreign policy they could feel good about.

By the early 1980s, human rights policy became bogged down in sterile debates over the relative merits of left- and right-wing dictators, or the relative importance of the more traditional political rights such as free expression and the vote versus social and economic rights (to a job or education). Advancing the national interest or achieving concrete results receded further into the background. Pushing one's left- or right-wing sympathies and elegantly rationalizing them became higher priorities.

HUMAN RIGHTS IN THE AGE OF CLINTON

The end of the Cold War generated broad optimism that human rights would take center stage, not only in U.S. foreign policy, but in world politics as a whole. Economic and trade issues aside, human rights dominated Clinton's intermittent foreign policy rhetoric during the 1992 campaign, as he and other Democrats repeatedly blasted George Bush's alleged indifference to human rights horrors in Tiananmen Square [China], Iraq, and the former Yugoslavia.

And so far—again, leaving economics aside—human rights issues have dominated Clinton's intermittent foreign policy making as president. His inaugural address promised to use American power if necessary whenever "the will and conscience of the international community is defied." His national security adviser Anthony Lake has made the "enlargement" of the world's roster of democratic countries one of America's top foreign policy priorities. And human rights considerations permeate the U.S. foreign policy agenda from Russia to China to Somalia to Bosnia to Haiti.

Clinton's priorities clearly reflected a rapidly emerging bipartisan conventional wisdom. The reasons for optimism were obvious to conservatives and liberals alike—although they disagreed sharply on what some of them were. Both were thrilled by the prospect of an America no longer forced to back dictators for anti-Soviet reasons. Both expected the collapse of Soviet power and Soviet stooges around the world to bring the blessings of national self-determination to numerous captive peoples. And both assumed that the global revolutions in communications and commerce would inevitably carry democratic political ideas and liberal economic practices into even the most repressive and backward societies.

But conservatives were more taken with the role that America, as the last superpower, could play unilaterally in fostering democracy and capitalism. Some even urged the United States to launch a global crusade to help the process along and create a worldwide Pax Democratica shaped by American political principles and by Reaganomics.

Liberals focused on multilateral approaches, churning out blueprints for creating a U.N. that could oust repressive regimes through sanctions or force of arms. As demonstrated most dramatically in 1991 by the establishment of safe havens for Iraq's Kurds, the international community, they argued, was acquiring the right to intervene in sovereign states' internal affairs when rights violations threatened international security or passed some unspecified threshold of savagery.

Yet none of the countries that the president or the world community has focused on have become significantly freer or more democratic places since Clinton's inauguration or since the Soviet Union's demise. In other areas of American concern, notably Russia and its "Near Abroad," the situation has arguably worsened in recent months. Bleaker still is the human rights outlook in those regions that have so far eluded either the administration's or the media's focus—from sub-Saharan Africa to suddenly shaky Mexico to the Arab world.

Even in Western Europe, democracy is deeply troubled as high unemployment and burgeoning immigrant populations have strengthened xenophobic politicians in many countries. And writers such as Jean-François Revel argue convincingly that the rampant corruption of social democratic systems in Italy and France has undermined the public trust in government that is crucial to the survival of democracy.

However, success stories are by no means unknown. So far, they include Taiwan, South Korea, and Chile, and even economically troubled countries such as Argentina, the Czech Republic, and the Baltic states. Nor can prospects for near-term improvement be written off completely in Russia and Mexico.

Still, one of the most comprehensive annual studies of the global human rights picture—the traditionally optimistic Freedom House's *Comparative Survey of Freedom*—concluded at the end of last year that "freedom around the world is in retreat while violence, repression and state control are on the increase." Of course, recent U.S. policy is not exclusively, largely, or even significantly responsible for that. But it is not apparent that official efforts have achieved many durable gains, either.

Even more disturbing has been the global reaction to U.S. human rights policies, especially their unilateral elements. Not a single major power, for example, emulated Washington's linkage of trade relations with human rights progress in China. Some of America's staunchest regional allies, such as Japan and Australia, openly criticized that strategy from the start. Other allies, principally the West Europeans, quietly worked overtime to cut deals with a booming economy that is already the world's third largest.

Furthermore, many East Asian governments—and many Asian voices outside government—have openly challenged U.S. human rights initiatives as arrogant efforts to impose Western values on proud, ancient societies that are doing quite well economically and socially, thank you. Similar resentments are widely expressed in the Arab world and other Islamic countries.

But the best evidence of failure is the administration's zig-zag record on numerous human rights fronts. Human rights issues are a large part of the president's most embarrassing retreats from campaign promises. Clinton has decided to follow the Bush administration's approach to China, finally agreeing that continued economic engagement is the best way to advance America's human rights and broader agendas with the world's most populous country. Even before his inauguration, the president had to endorse his predecessor's policy of returning Haiti's boat people, and in September 1994 he acquiesced in an agreement negotiated mainly by former president Jimmy Carter for joint U.S. administration of Haiti's democratic transition with the very military leaders he had condemned as murderers and rapists the week before. Moreover, bitter experiences in Somalia and Haiti in 1993 have so far led to a lowering of America's peacekeeping goals.

DECLINE IN PUBLIC SUPPORT

In part, U.S. human rights policies are failing because their consistently shaky strategic foundations have crumbled. During the Cold War, a plausible case could be made for denying an ideologically hostile rival superpower targets of opportunity by fostering democratic practices abroad. But in the absence of such a rival, the state of human rights around the world does not have, and has never had, any demonstrable effect on U.S. national security. America's rise to global prominence occurred primarily in periods when democracies were few and far between, and a combination of geography, power, wealth, and social cohesion will continue to be the country's best guarantees of security in a turbulent world.

In the wake of the Cold War, both liberal and conservative human rights advocates (including the president) have argued that democracies rarely fight each other—hence the more there are, the merrier and safer America will be. Yet the jury is still out: Significant numbers of democracies have existed together only in the last 50 years. Furthermore, U.S. leaders obviously have never bought the argument themselves—otherwise, they would not continue to be terrified by the prospect of democratic Germany and Japan carrying out independent foreign policies or going nuclear.

Moreover, strong domestic support for an active human rights policy has been difficult to detect. Although Americans often endorse vigorous human rights policies when talking with pollsters, they have not recently acted or voted as if they cared much about them. Carter made human rights a top foreign policy priority and was rewarded with early retirement —because he let the economy deteriorate and seemed ineffective in dealing with the Soviets. His 1980 opponent, Ronald Reagan, promised to uphold American values against an evil Soviet empire, but his most politically popular foreign policy position was his stand against the military threat he saw emanating from Moscow. And what happened when the greatest White House communicator since Franklin Roosevelt tried to mobilize public support for his Reagan Doctrine policies of arming "freedom fighters" combating pro-Soviet Third World regimes? He failed everywhere except in Afghanistan, where the Soviet occupation arguably threatened the oil-rich Persian Gulf.

What politicians and pundits do not understand—and may not want to understand—is that unlike their leaders, the American people evidently have learned from past mistakes. Vietnam has happened. The Iran hostage crisis has happened. As the 1992 election and its aftermath showed, when voters care deeply about issues—from the economy to [U.S. attorney general nominee] Zoe Baird's nanny problem—they are not shy about making their feelings known. And just as they never filled the streets or flooded Washington's phone banks protesting oppression around the world during the 1970s and 1980s, they have not been demanding the denial of tariff breaks to China or intervention in basket-case countries in the 1990s. If the American people retain any significant missionary impulse, or much optimism that the world craves American guidance on human rights issues, they are hiding their feelings well.

To a depressing degree, however, U.S. human rights policy grinds on along the same well-worn tracks. Despite the China trade decision, another China-like struggle over linking trade relations with human rights practices may be unfolding with Indonesia, and yet another looms with Vietnam. Both controversies have scary implications for America's economic position in rapidly growing Asia (where establishing long-term relationships and, consequently, a reputation for reliability are keys to business success) and other emerging markets.

And as during the 1970s and 1980s, today's human rights skeptics unwittingly play along, accepting the basic assumptions driving human rights policy but pleading for moderation, perspective, and "balancing" human rights considerations with America's strategic and economic objectives.

In the process, critics have periodically aired stronger objections, calling human rights policy arrogant, naive, inconsistent—a juvenile protest against life's built-in imperfections. They are largely correct. Yet two even greater obstacles to a successful government-led U.S. human rights policy are embedded in the very nature of the post–Cold War world.

The first concerns the phenomenon of failed states that has been exposed by the retreat of Soviet power in Eastern Europe and by the end of Cold War confrontation in much of the Third World—in Bosnia, Georgia, Haiti, Somalia, Rwanda, and elsewhere. The often horrendous general conditions and specific outrages that have resulted from the breakdown of governments in those regions are usually described as "human rights violations," but the phrase trivializes the problem. At worst, they are endemic features of deep-rooted ethnic conflicts. At best, they are symptoms of a monumental struggle over issues not of liberalization or democratization, but of minimal coherence or further fragmentation. Welcome to the dark side of national self-determination, as Colonel E. M. House warned Woodrow Wilson nearly 75 years ago.

Outside Western Europe, North America, and East Asia, most "countries" around the world simply do not deserve that label. They may have the trappings of statehood—postage stamps, U.N. membership—but their populations lack a sense of mutual loyalty and obligation, and their politics lack strong institutions, a commitment to the rule of law, and even a tradition of public service as anything more than an opportunity for theft and vengeance. They are straining to reach minimal viability not even as nation-states but as societies. The conceit behind the idea that even the best designed policies, or a few billion dollars' worth of foreign aid, or "how to" democracy courses can make a real difference is, to put it kindly, immense.

As for U.S. human rights policies toward more advanced repressive countries, they are swamped by a similar problem—by the very global economic and cultural interaction responsible for much of the optimism of human rights advocates. Precisely because ideas and capital and technology—and, to a somewhat lesser extent, people—can cross borders so easily, official rhetoric and even sanctions get lost in the shuffle. Government words and deeds form merely one small breeze in the gales of commerce and culture blowing around the world today. Western and American values will not be the only seeds dropped by those winds. But if we consider their spread and growth to be essential, then we are better advised to lead from strength—to energetically add to America's already vast commercial, cultural, and ideological influence around the world, rather than seek to replace it with legislation or executive orders or official oratory.

Leave aside for the moment the op-ed level arguments that dominated the China most-favored-nation debate—for example, over which country has the most leverage, over whether economic relations with America strengthen the Chinese government's economic base and help pacify the population, over whether other countries will rush in to replace American suppliers and investors. Say Americans were to start from scratch on an imaginary campaign to reform China. What would the most promising tools be? "Sense of the Congress" resolutions? Cutbacks in the numbers of American companies that the Chinese can work for or do business with, and that pay Chinese employees higher wages and provide safer working conditions than do China's state-owned enterprises? Or would America send as many businesspeople to China as quickly as it could? The answer should be obvious even to those who do not believe in business-created utopias.

The China issue, however, along with [the recent] controversy over the North American Free Trade Agreement, does bring up one bona fide human rights issue where more effective U.S. government action is needed: the question of how most of America's workforce can benefit from trade with countries that repress labor rights. American workers are already exposed to strong competition from hundreds of millions of workers in developing countries who are highly educated, highly productive, and organized by the world's leading multinational corporations, but who are paid a fraction of what their U.S. counterparts earn and who are systematically denied the right to form independent unions and bargain collectively for wages that bear some relationship to productivity increases, for decent workplaces, and for nonwage benefits—rights and conditions until recently taken for granted in North America and Western Europe. Many more such workers will soon be coming into the world economy from China's interior (as opposed to its already booming coastal regions), from South and Southeast Asia, and, farther down the road, from Russia and Eastern Europe.

Even if all of them work for politically and socially progressive American companies, which they will not, the capacity of those workers to export will exceed by orders of magnitude their capacity to consume. Lack of labor rights is hardly the only reason, but it can create major competitive advantages. As Labor Secretary Robert Reich noted in an April 1994 speech, the problem is part and parcel of the inherent difficulties of commerce between countries at greatly differing levels of economic and social development in an age of highly mobile capital and technology.

Unlike other human rights issues, moreover, labor rights controversies and their resolutions are already having concrete effects on the lives of millions of Americans. But they are best seen not as human rights issues at all, but as challenges in managing interdependence —in ensuring that the great integrative forces shaping the world economy work for the long-term benefit of the great majority of the American people, not against it.

Nor can labor rights controversies be successfully resolved by acting out the stylized morality plays that make up human rights policy today—by issuing the same threats and voluminous reports, by trotting out the same dissidents in front of the press, by fasting, or by any other attempts to dictate the social and economic priorities of other countries. Instead, labor rights problems require

a raft of new trade, technology, foreign investment, and other policies designed to increase America's economic power.

A vibrant industrial base that creates millions of new high-wage jobs can give America the economic leverage needed to negotiate beneficial economic agreements with the rest of the world. A prosperous America can generate enough markets, capital, and technology to give other countries powerful incentives to conform to U.S. labor, environmental, and other standards voluntarily—not as acknowledgements of American moral superiority or as acts of surrender, but simply as the price of access.

As Americans will discover in many foreign policy fields, crusades to bring about utopian change around the world will rarely achieve their goals. The best bets lie in measures that enable the country to survive, flourish, and bargain successfully in the deeply flawed world that we will remain stuck with for many decades. Americans wishing their government to act in moral ways might consider focusing on their own country —which suffers its share of problems and moral outrages, but is also blessed with the institutions and social cohesion to make serious reform more than a pipe dream.

NO

Michael Posner

RALLY ROUND HUMAN RIGHTS

Alan Tonelson has written a provocative but premature obituary to international human rights. He asserts that the tragedies in Bosnia, Somalia, and Haiti prove that it is no longer useful or productive for the U.S. government to challenge state-sponsored murder and torture in other countries and to emphasize human rights as an element of its foreign policy.

Tonelson's postmortem is flawed in at least four basic assumptions: In a relatively short space, he manages to misrepresent the origins of human rights, its scope and objectives, reasonable measures to judge the effectiveness of U.S. human rights policy, and the view of key U.S. allies with respect to this policy.

According to Tonelson, the emphasis on human rights was a product of the Cold War, designed principally to challenge the Soviet Union. From his perspective, the starting point for the discussion was the 1970s. He is wrong, both about the purpose and the timing. Contrary to Tonelson's narrow world view, attention to international human rights has evolved steadily over the last five decades.

The international community in fact began to focus on human rights immediately after World War II. Shaken by the Holocaust and determined to make amends for their slow and inadequate response to the murder of millions of innocent victims, the United States and its allies sought to take steps to prevent similar future occurrences. The United Nations Charter, adopted in 1945, made human rights a central purpose of that new organization. Governments pledged to take joint and separate actions to encourage a more just, humane world.

A year later, the U.N. created its own Commission on Human Rights, with former first lady Eleanor Roosevelt serving as its first chair. Under her stewardship, the commission moved quickly to draft a body of human rights principles—the Universal Declaration of Human Rights, adopted by the U.N. General Assembly in 1948. Working closely with the U.S. Department of State, Roosevelt helped develop two other key treaties, the International Covenant on Civil and Political Rights and the International Covenant on Economic, Social and Cultural Rights. Many other countries participated in those early

From Michael Posner, "Rally Round Human Rights," *Foreign Policy* (Winter 1994/1995). Copyright © 1994 by The Carnegie Endowment for International Peace. Reprinted by permission.

developments and many more, including virtually all key American allies, now view the treaties as the basis for international consideration of those rights.

Official U.S. attention to those issues increased significantly in the 1970s with congressional efforts like the Jackson-Vanik Amendment, which linked trade with the Soviet Union to its willingness to allow emigration by Soviet Jews. As president, Jimmy Carter greatly expanded U.S. initiatives in the area and gave human rights a much higher profile.

Nongovernmental organizations also came of age at that time. Amnesty International was awarded the 1977 Nobel Peace Prize in recognition of its unique role in human rights advocacy. Several key U.S.-based human rights organizations, including Helsinki Watch (now part of Human Rights Watch) and the Lawyers Committee for Human Rights, were also founded during that period. Thus, over the past 50 years, significant progress has been made in developing human rights law and in setting practical objectives for its implementation.

SCOPE AND OBJECTIVES

Tonelson offers a confusing and sometimes contradictory view of the scope and objectives of U.S. human rights policy. On one hand, he criticizes politicians and activists for using human rights "to push broader, more questionable agendas." On the other hand, he urges that we pursue labor rights, not because it is the right thing to do, but to protect the economic well-being of "millions of Americans."

Tonelson also builds straw men, only to tear them down. He refers repeatedly to "human rights advocates," a term he never defines. Using that broad rubric, he notes that conservatives are using

human rights to foster "democracy and capitalism." He then accuses liberals of using human rights to advocate using U.N. sanctions or military force "to oust repressive regimes." While some have indeed used the language of human rights to pursue these broad political objectives, in doing so they are going beyond the core meaning of human rights, which is to challenge governments when they mistreat their own people.

Human rights advocates such as Amnesty International and hundreds of national rights advocacy groups around the world rely on international human rights standards that set minimum requirements for governments. States that ratify international treaties make a pledge to abide by those core legal principles, which include commitments not to torture their own people, subject them to slavery, or engage in political murder. Tonelson blithely dismisses efforts by human rights groups and others to challenge such violations as "an exercise in therapy." On the contrary, human rights advocacy has evolved into a worldwide movement aimed at exposing and combating official misconduct and alleviating suffering. There is now ample evidence that by exposing violations and challenging the violators, lives are being saved.

The international treaties provide a foundation for such efforts, but set forth only broad basic principles. The civil and political covenant, for example, requires governments to allow for a free press, for the right to hold public meetings, and for the right to speak freely. It also requires popular participation in choosing a government. But it neither spells out how that should be accomplished, nor suggests a specific political structure or system. Those who seek to wrap broader economic and political agendas in the flag of human rights, including some in the Clinton administration, are overloading the system.

The treaties are also silent on the sanctions that may be imposed on governments that systematically violate basic human rights. Although there is nothing to prevent the U.N. Security Council from invoking the language of human rights to help justify military action, there is nothing in the treaties that compels it, or even suggests that it should do so.

Some governments, including that of the United States, have linked their provision of bilateral aid and trade privileges to human rights. In the last 20 years, the United States has occasionally withheld or delayed the provision of bilateral aid—particularly military aid—in situations where a sustained pattern of violations was occurring. The connection to military aid is the most direct, given the possibility that the weapons being provided will be used to commit further violations.

It is much more difficult to impose trade sanctions, in part because there is much less agreement on the usefulness of trade restrictions as an instrument of leverage. The Jackson-Vanik Amendment, which restricted trade to the former Soviet Union, was an exception for two reasons: U.S. economic opportunities in the USSR were limited, and such sanctions had bipartisan support in the broader effort to challenge Soviet influence worldwide.

The recent controversy over the linkage between trade and human rights in China was not surprising, given the economic opportunities at stake. Yet the Clinton administration's decision to de-link the two issues by renewing China's most-favored-nation trading status does not mean that future human rights initiatives should be avoided, or that long-term international pressure on the human rights front will be ineffective.

MEASURES OF EFFECTIVENESS

Tonelson's sole criterion for measuring human rights progress appears to be whether U.S. strategic interests are being advanced. That is the wrong place to start. While governments that respect human rights are likely to be more stable and reliable strategic allies, the protection and promotion of basic rights worldwide is important in itself. Consistent with our values and traditions, the U.S. government should promote international initiatives designed to alleviate suffering and to challenge governments that deny basic freedoms to their own people.

Tonelson argues that since human rights are being violated all around the world, the human rights policy must be failing, and therefore should be abandoned. That is akin to arguing that since thousands of businesses go bankrupt each year, we must abandon the free market system. While progress on human rights cannot be evaluated with the precision of a profit and loss statement, there are several useful measures of effectiveness.

The first measure is public attention to and awareness of human rights issues. Twenty years ago it was rare to see any reference to international human rights in the news media. By contrast, in any newspaper today one is likely to see several articles, often including one or more front-page stories, where human rights issues are featured prominently. While growing awareness does not automatically lead to greater respect for human rights, it is an important step toward that goal. Most governments are surprisingly thin-skinned on these issues and will go out of their way to avoid being stigmatized by a broad public spotlight.

A second measure of progress is the extent to which indigenous human rights activists are raising the issue in their own countries. Apparently Tonelson does not see such activists from his perch in Washington, since he makes no reference to the proliferation of national advocates and organizations. In the 1970s there were perhaps a few dozen human rights organizations around the world. Today, there are hundreds of such organizations operating in countries throughout the world. Every day the groups are busy documenting abuses, filing lawsuits, and challenging their own governments when they violate basic human rights. Most of the groups are underfunded and work in very difficult circumstances. Those who participate in such activism frequently do so at personal risk. But they carry on, often relying on international diplomatic pressure from the U.S. government and influential parties to protect them and help reinforce the legitimacy of their efforts.

Many of the Asian governments, like those of China and Singapore, that are most critical of U.S. human rights policy and seek to characterize it as Western-based and culturally biased are among the declining number of regimes that absolutely prevent any independent human rights groups from operating. Their claims of cultural relativism can only be sustained if they can continue to prevent their own people from raising human rights issues. But they are fighting a losing battle. Recent experience in countries as diverse as Chile, Kuwait, Nigeria, South Africa, and Sri Lanka leave no doubt that where people are allowed to organize and advocate their own human rights, they will do so. The common denominators in this area are much stronger than the cultural divisions.

Finally, look around the world and note that progress continues to be made on human rights issues. Contrast the Latin America today with the one of 15 years ago. Tonelson's own criteria also lead him to assert that none of the countries on which Washington has focused its attention since 1991 have become any freer or more democratic. On that he is simply wrong. A great majority of South Africans, among others, would undoubtedly disagree with him.

Even in the many places where governments do continue to commit serious violations, Tonelson offers no viable alternative to challenging the violators. His suggestion that the United States abandon ship rather than risk the embarrassment of future failure adds little more than a rhetorical flourish to his argument.

The fourth broad mistake in Tonelson's analysis is his assertion that U.S. human rights policy is a failure because it has "antagonized or simply turned off numerous democratic countries." To support his proposition, he notes that not a single "major power" followed the Clinton administration's lead in linking human rights and trade in China. He also notes that some of America's strongest allies in the region, such as Australia and Japan, were openly critical of the policy.

While Tonelson is correct in identifying discomfort and in some cases opposition to the U.S. approach, his analysis is incomplete and therefore misleading. A number of key U.S. allies—Canada, Great Britain, the Netherlands, Sweden, Australia—include human rights as a component in their own foreign policies. But they often prefer to pursue those concerns on a multilateral rather than a bilateral basis. Historically, the U.S. government has disdained multilateral institutions, viewing U.N. debates as an exercise in damage control. In the 1980s, U.S. representatives to the U.N. repeatedly opposed resolutions that called for the appointment of special experts to investigate and report on the situations in Guatemala, Haiti, and El Salvador, among others—preferring to address those situations in a less-confrontational manner.

Tonelson also misses another important point, which is the declining U.S. ability to act unilaterally. During the Cold War, the United States invested billions of dollars in bilateral military and economic aid. Most of the money went to the support of strategic allies in the geopolitical confrontation with the Soviet bloc. A number of governments, such as those in El Salvador, Haiti, Indonesia, Liberia, the Philippines, and Zaire, were committing serious human rights violations. In those situations, the United States had enormous influence and could threaten to cut off aid as a means of ultimate leverage. Following the collapse of the Soviet Union, however, Congress drastically reduced foreign aid—particularly military aid—and, concomitantly, U.S. influence and ability to act unilaterally.

To date, both the Clinton administration and the human rights community have been slow to accept the new reality. The real failure of Clinton's China policy was not that he tried to link trade and human rights, but that he tried to do it alone. American companies quickly mobilized when they realized that not only would they be shut out of a huge market, but that their overseas competitors would jump in to fill the void. So while it remains an open question whether linking trade to human rights is a politically viable option for advancing the cause of human rights, in China or elsewhere, it is clear that whatever America's tactical approach is, it can no longer act alone if it is going to be effective.

Concern for human rights is far from obsolete—either as a set of U.N. principles or as an element of U.S. foreign policy. In looking to the future, these issues are likely to loom more prominently than ever before, particularly in those societies that are in transition, such as China, India, Mexico, Nigeria, and Russia. To be effective, U.S. policymakers and activists need to rethink strategies while working more in concert with others who regard human rights as a vital international concern.

POSTSCRIPT

Should Foreign Policymakers Minimize Human Rights Concerns?

The debate over morality and politics is both ancient and continuing. For recent general works on the topic, consult Frances V. Harbour, *Thinking About International Ethics* (Westview Press, 1999) and Mark R. Amztuts, *International Ethics: Concepts, Theories, and Cases in Global Politics* (Rowman & Littlefield, 1999).

There are times when the promotion of human rights standards and the realpolitik pursuit of national interest can be mutually advanced by the same policy choice. Defeating dangerously militaristic and unconscionably evil Nazi Germany is one clear example. However, it is frequently, perhaps most often, the case that there is doubt and debate about the degree to which imperative human rights and realpolitik point in the same direction.

Humanitarian interventions such as the one that led to war between NATO forces and Yugoslavia in 1999 is one such case. When NATO, with the United States in the lead, launched its air war against the Serbs, President Bill Clinton explained what he saw as the moral imperative. "We are not going to just watch as hundreds of thousands of people are brutalized, forced from their homes, their lives shattered, their history erased," Clinton told Americans. As leaders usually do, the president also made a national interest argument for intervention. "If we do not act," he reasoned, "the war will spread. And if it spreads, we will not be able to act without far greater risk and cost. I believe the real challenge of foreign policy is to deal with problems before they harm our vital interests, and that is what we must do in Kosovo."

But whatever the moral impetus to help the Kosovars, and whatever the likelihood that the conflict could have spread, there were countervailing moral and national interest considerations. The air attacks killed a significant number of civilians, Serb and Kosovar alike. The attacks also devastated a good part of the economic infrastructure of Yugoslavia and will leave many of its citizens in desperation for years. The bombing campaign also cost a great deal and put the lives of American and other NATO military personnel on the line. Recent readings on the dilemmas of humanitarian intervention include Jonathan Moore, ed., *Hard Choices: Moral Dilemma in Humanitarian Intervention* (Rowman & Littlefield, 1999).

To learn more about specific foreign policy issues facing the United States and their moral and national interest implications, visit the Web site of the Foreign Policy Association at http://www.fpa.org or that of the Johns Hopkins Foreign Policy Institute at http://www.sais-jhu.edu/centers/fpi/index.html.

ISSUE 13

Do U.S. Efforts to Stem the Flow of Drugs from Abroad Encourage Human Rights Violations?

YES: Eyal Press, from "Clinton Pushes Military Aid: Human-Rights Abusers Lap It Up," *The Progressive* (February 1997)

NO: Barry McCaffrey, from "Hemispheric Drug Control: Fighting Drug Production and Trafficking," *Vital Speeches of the Day* (May 1, 1997)

ISSUE SUMMARY

YES: Eyal Press, a writer and a journalist, argues that in its effort to control drugs at one of their major sources, Latin America, the Clinton administration is threatening human rights in Latin America and constitutional rights in the United States by speeding arms to the military in Latin America and inserting the U.S. military into domestic police work.

NO: General Barry McCaffrey, director of the Office of National Drug Control Policy, contends that alleviating the threat that drugs pose requires cooperation between the United States and the countries of Latin America and that success promises to ameliorate the corrosive effect in both the United States and Latin America of the production, distribution, and consumption of drugs.

There can be little doubt that the use of drugs is widespread in the United States. According to the Office of National Drug Control Policy (ONDCP), in 1997 there were 13.9 million users of illegal drugs. These drug users constitute about 6.4 percent of the U.S. population and include an estimated 4 million chronic drug users. Of these, 3.6 million are chronic cocaine users (primarily crack cocaine) and 810,000 are chronic heroin users. Somewhat modifying the impact of this data is the fact that it represents a drop from the peak year of drug use, 1979, when 25 million Americans (14.1 percent of the population) were using illegal drugs.

The so-called drug epidemic reached such proportions by 1983 that President Ronald Reagan declared a "war on drugs." There are three basic approaches to waging a war on drugs. The first way is to reduce the consumption and impact of drugs through domestic education, treatment, and law enforcement policies. The range of actions has gone from Nancy Reagan's coining the phrase "Just say no," to the establishment of education and treatment programs, to the institution of mandatory sentences for criminals.

The second approach is drug interdiction. This approach involves creating barriers to prevent drugs from entering the United States. This is a daunting task. More than 68 million people arrive annually in the United States from abroad on 830,000 commercial and private aircraft. An additional 8 million come by sea, and an overwhelming 365 million people cross the U.S. border by land, driving or riding in approximately 115 million vehicles. Some 10 million trucks and cargo containers also cross the U.S. border, and 90,000 merchant and passenger ships annually enter U.S. ports carrying about 400 million metric tons of cargo.

The third campaign being conducted as part of the war on drugs involves attacking drug production and trafficking at their sources in Latin America and elsewhere. These targets include 300 metric tons of cocaine, 13 metric tons of heroin, and huge amounts of marijuana. Much more is sent. A total of 145 metric tons of cocaine, for instance, was seized before it reached the United States. Of the imported narcotics, a significant part comes from Latin America. For example, according to U.S. Drug Enforcement Agency estimates, heroin from South America composes 75 percent of all heroin seized in the United States. The largest sources of imported illegal drugs are Colombia and Mexico.

U.S. efforts in the overseas realm has had many aspects. The Federal Bureau of Investigation, the Drug Enforcement Agency, and other agencies that are normally considered "domestic" police agencies have become involved in other countries. The "war" mentality has also led the United States to send weaponry to Latin American and other countries and also to train their military personnel in antidrug efforts. Moreover, Congress requires that the president annually certify that countries that are involved in the drug trade are making progress toward remedying the problem. If they are not cooperating, a variety of economic sanctions are imposed. Finally, symbolizing the war imagery, Barry McCaffrey, the current head of the ONDCP, is a retired general, and he is often referred to as the "drug czar."

The main thrust of the following debate is that the weapons and U.S.-trained troops that are sent to other countries to fight the drug problem have sometimes been used to support repressive regimes and to fight rebels. In reaction to this, since 1994 Congress has required that U.S. military aid go only to troops that "primarily" carry out antidrug activity. Critics charge not only that the money is still diverted to repression but also that the military aid and the allowance of some countries to buy equipment theoretically meant for the antidrug campaign also violates the general U.S. policy of restraining military growth in Latin America. Still, the funding has risen. For example, the combination of military aid to and military purchases by Colombia rose from $51 million in 1995 to $171 million in 1997.

Eyal Press and McCaffrey debate the wisdom of the war on drugs, especially its overseas manifestations, in the following selections. Press contends that the cure is worse than the disease. McCaffrey disagrees, maintaining that there are effective safeguards and a good collaborative relationship between the United States and its Latin American allies in the war on drugs.

YES

Eyal Press

CLINTON PUSHES MILITARY AID: HUMAN-RIGHTS ABUSERS LAP IT UP

At midnight on December 31, 1999, the United States is due to evacuate Panama, removing thousands of troops and ceding control of the Panama Canal to its rightful owners after nearly a century of occupation. But the Clinton Administration is planning to keep the U.S. military in Panama anyway. The stated reason: to fight the drug war.

This past October [1996], U.S. Defense Secretary William Perry informed Latin-American defense ministers at a meeting in Argentina that the United States is negotiating with Panama's President Ernesto Pérez Balladeres to establish a multinational counter-drug center on Howard Air Base in Panama City. Thousands of U.S. troops will remain on the base to provide training and logistical support.

Heading these negotiations is John Negroponte, who served as U.S. ambassador to Honduras during the height of the contra war. Later in his career, while U.S. ambassador to Mexico, Negroponte pushed for heavy military involvement in the so-called drug war.

Now Negroponte is getting his wish. He and General Barry McCaffrey, the four-star general and Gulf War veteran whom Clinton named director of the Office of National Drug Control Policy in 1996, are committed to drawing the United States ever closer to the brutal militaries in the region. And Clinton is all for it.

Before his appointment as Clinton's drug czar, McCaffrey headed the Panama-based U.S. Southern Command, which for years has been at the forefront of military involvement in drug policy. It was McCaffrey who last summer proposed keeping 5,000 U.S. troops in Panama after 1999, a proposal made just as the Southern Command was launching "Operation Laser Strike," which sent hundreds of U.S. troops into the field to help police and military forces in Colombia, Bolivia, and Peru undertake a major counter-narcotics and crop-eradication operation. Before that, U.S. forces under McCaffrey's command provided the Colombian and Peruvian armies with sophisticated radar and surveillance equipment to track the flow and production of drugs in an operation known as "Green Clover."

Despite Republican charges to the contrary, Clinton has hardly been a dove in the drug war. In 1988, Ronald Reagan devoted $4.8 billion to anti-drug efforts. Clinton's latest budget calls for $15.1 billion, with two-thirds earmarked for repressive interdiction and law-enforcement efforts—the same skewed ratio set by Presidents Reagan and Bush.

Lately, Clinton's policy has gone from bad to worse. Beyond the proposed anti-narcotics base in Panama, Clinton is pressing for a series of measures that will augment the U.S. military's role throughout the hemisphere.

In fiscal year 1997, for example, the Administration requested $213 million for the International Narcotics and Law Enforcement account. These funds, which represent a $98 million increase from the previous year's allotment, will be used primarily to arm and train the military and police forces of Colombia, Peru, Bolivia, and Mexico. With barely a whisper from the media, Washington passed money to these forces by slashing $53 million from overseas-development programs specifically earmarked for children.

This fall, Clinton announced at the United Nations that the United States was sending an additional $112 million in military equipment—including helicopters, surveillance aircraft, patrol boats, troop gear, ammunition, training, and assistance—to the Colombian national police and the Colombian, Peruvian, Venezuelan, and Mexican militaries—forces that the Administration asserts "continue to deserve and need our support" in the battle against drugs. Eleven members of Congress promptly sent a letter to

Secretary of State Warren Christopher complaining that Clinton did not notify the proper Congressional committees before announcing this major transfer of weaponry.

Under the guise of the drug war, the Clinton Administration is bolstering repressive security forces responsible for human-rights abuses throughout much of Latin America. "We're looking at a tripling of U.S. military aid to the Andean region—a dramatic increase," says Colletta Youngers of the Washington Office on Latin America. "Beefing up extremely repressive forces in these countries will do nothing to cut off the flow of drugs, but it will lead to more human-rights abuses."

Youngers points out that drugs surfaced as a pretext just as the Cold War came to a close. "Since 1989, the drug issue has become the prime means for military-to-military relations" between the United States and the hemisphere's other armed forces, she says.

Senator Patrick Leahy, Democrat of Vermont, did manage to attach an amendment to the Foreign Operations bill that forbids U.S. assistance to military units that are known human-rights abusers. But "the amendment applies only to aid given under the International Narcotics Funding," says Robin Kirk of Human Rights Watch, who has documented the flow of aid to Colombian security forces. "It's a step in the right direction, but not broad enough."

In Bolivia, the United States has pressured the government to allow the army to participate in anti-narcotics programs despite reports of widespread abuses in the Chapare region, where most Bolivian coca is grown. Washington has also successfully pressed the Mexican military to involve itself in counter-narcotics, providing infusions of anti-drug training and equipment.

Even prior to this change, Mexico was using U.S. counter-narcotics weapons for repressive purposes. Tucked into a footnote of a recent General Accounting Office report on counter-narcotics is the following stunning admission: "During the 1994 uprising in the Mexican state of Chiapas, several U.S.-provided helicopters were used to transport Mexican military personnel to the conflict."

"Most Mexicans will tell you that the involvement of the military in this aspect of civilian life is very troublesome," says Eric Olsen of the Washington Office on Latin America. "This is happening in the states where the military is involved in counterinsurgency, such as Chiapas."

* * *

Besides fueling repression, the renewed drug war comes at an enormous cost to U.S. taxpayers while doing little to stop the flow of drugs. There is no serious evidence that securing the Pentagon's foothold in Panama and Latin America will reduce drug consumption in America. Since 1981, the United States has poured more than $23 billion into the fight against drug trafficking.

Despite enormous expenditures to stop drugs at the source, virtually the same amount of cocaine and heroin continues to flow into the United States. Last year Barry McCaffrey himself acknowledged as much, conceding that "the street price and availability of cocaine in the United States have not been demonstrably affected by the ... counter-drug effort in Latin America."

In 1994, a Rand study commissioned by the U.S. Army and Office of National Drug Control Policy said that to achieve a 1 percent reduction in U.S. cocaine con-sumption, the United States could spend either $34 million on drug-treatment programs, or $783 million (more than twenty times more) on attempting to eradicate the supply of drugs at the source.

Why, then, has Clinton gone the expensive route? Not surprisingly, the primary motivation has been political: Clinton has found it far easier to win elections as a tough guy than by explaining the complexities of the issue. And for the Pentagon, the drug war yields a more tangible benefit, offering the military something to do now that the Cold War is over.

In an excellent exposé for the *Los Angeles Times*, reporters Mark Fineman and Craig Pyes outlined how much of the Pentagon's high-tech military equipment, designed for the Cold War, is now being deployed to track the flow of drugs. U.S. taxpayers are spending $1,500 per hour to operate the Navy's ROTHR system, a multimillion-dollar radar operation invented to help battleships locate Soviet aircraft cruising at high altitudes. Drug-war boosters point to 219 air interdictions in the Caribbean in the past three years, but meanwhile drug traffickers have shifted to using passenger planes that land, undetected, in Mexico and transfer the goods by truck.

On another front, U.S. Customs is planning to spend $30 million on a series of "Backscatter" X-ray systems that can purportedly detect drug shipments by bombarding trucks with radioactive particles. But the scanner, built to identify Soviet missiles in trucks, is patently incapable of locating the packages of heroin and cocaine routinely hauled over the border.

* * *

The fusion of drug and military policies finds its domestic application on the windswept plains of Fort Bliss, Texas; the remote mountain passes of Nogales, Arizona; the California desert; and the Rio Grande—all places where U.S. Special Forces scan the horizons using infrared radar systems and special map coordinates provided by the Army. Last year, according to an investigative report by Jim McGee of *The Washington Post*, more than 8,000 U.S. military personnel took part in 754 counter-drug missions on U.S. soil.

In Utah, soldiers assist the Drug Enforcement Agency with tapping telephones. In Key West, Florida, the government has erected a $13.5 million command center where military officers and federal drug agents work side by side.

The Pentagon's brazen insertion into domestic law enforcement violates the 1878 Posse Comitatus Act, which prohibits military involvement in searches and seizures. But, as one former official told *The Washington Post*, "it's been institutionalized."

Now that he's safely reelected, will President Clinton shift to a more enlightened policy? Don't count on it. At the start of his first term, Clinton acknowledged that the drug war waged by Presidents Reagan and Bush had failed. But the moment he heard criticism from the right, he adopted the very same strategies.

To reorient drug policy at this point, the President would have to push hard against a Republican Congress that is salivating over the Clinton scandals. He would also have to risk challenging, rather than accepting, the right's terms of debate on drug policy—terms that have emerged in large part because they make it so easy for elected officials of dubious moral stature to couch policy in the righteous language of a moral crusade.

NO

Barry McCaffrey

HEMISPHERIC DRUG CONTROL: FIGHTING DRUG PRODUCTION AND TRAFFICKING

Delivered to the 21st Regular Session of the Inter-American Drug Abuse Control Commission [CICAD], Organization of American States, [OAS], Washington, D.C., April 9, 1997

It is an honor to be here with the delegates from the thirty-one member states, including our own OAS Ambassador, Hattie Babbitt, and CICAD Executive Director David Beall. I'm glad to see many of my hemispheric colleagues, including Dr. Marino Costa Bauer, Peruvian Minister of Health, and President of the Peruvian Commission de Lucha Contra el Consumo de Drogas (CONTRADROGAS), Panamanian Attorney General Jose Antonio Sossa, Costa Rican Minister of Justice Juan Diego Castro Fernandez, and Mr. Danny Gill, Chairman of the National Council on Substance Abuse in Barbados. (Hemispheric relations in context.)

We are all encouraged by the positive direction of hemispheric relations. Civil strife and conflict are firmly in the past in Central America. Regional economic integration is developing an almost unstoppable momentum. All our nations are increasingly able to focus on domestic or regional issues as opposed to extra-hemispheric concerns. Perhaps this optimism has been best captured by the December 1994 Summit of the Americas in Miami and its continuing processes of consultation and cooperation. Now when we think of major cities, we frequently associate them with yet another important step toward integration and problem resolution; Buenos Aires, Belo Horizonte, Santiago—the site of next year's second Summit of the Americas—are examples. Our own U.S. role is guided by President Clinton's uplifting vision of mutually respectful relations that benefit all peoples. As you know, his special envoy to the Americas, Thomas F. McLarty, is playing a key role coordinating our government's engagement with the region.

When I speak to U.S. audiences about hemispheric drug control challenges and counterdrug cooperation with our North American, Central American, Caribbean, and South American neighbors and allies, I feel it is important to underscore that the increasingly important U.S. hemispheric relations do not revolve around any single issue. While drug policy concerns are critical to all of our nations, none of us should lose sight of the other realities that define the ways in which our peoples and governments interact. Indeed, the nations of the Americas are increasingly interlinked by history, culture, geography, and commerce.

More than 830 million people in the Western Hemisphere now live under democratic regimes. Collectively, our economies constitute a $13 trillion market. Indeed, intra-hemisphere commerce is already significant. The United States trades more with Brazil than with China; more with Venezuela than with Russia; more with Costa Rica—a nation of three million people—than with one hundred million Eastern Europeans; more with fourteen million Chileans than with almost a billion Indians. By the turn of the century, Latin America will have a $2 trillion economy, will trade more than $600 billion in goods and services, and our trade with the nations to our south will exceed our trade with Europe. One of President Clinton's priorities for his second term of office is to act on this reality by building on the successes of NAFTA [North American Free Trade Agreement] and the 1994 Miami Summit of the Americas.

DRUGS ARE A PRESSING INTERNATIONAL PROBLEM

Although no single issue dominates our hemispheric agenda, the overall problem of illegal drugs and related crimes represents a direct threat to the health and well-being of the peoples of the hemisphere. All of us here... recognize that we cannot afford to let the demand for, and cultivation, production, distribution, trafficking, and sale of illicit narcotics and psychotropic substances interfere with the aspirations of our peoples. Illegal drugs inflict staggering costs on our societies. They kill and sicken our people, sap productivity, drain economies, threaten the environment, and undermine democratic institutions and international order. Drugs are a direct attack on our children and grandchildren. If we are to make inroads against this growing problem, we shall only do so collectively. We can make progress by formulating a common understanding of the problems posed by drug production, trafficking, and consumption and by developing cooperative approaches and solutions. That is exactly the vision spelled out in the CICAD Hemispheric Anti-Drug Strategy. If we act on this vision, we can prevent illegal drugs from darkening the dawn of a new millennium.

THE CONSEQUENCES OF DRUG ABUSE IN THE UNITED STATES

The consequences of illegal drug use have been devastating within the United States. We estimate that in this decade alone, drug use has cost our society more than 100,000 dead and some $300 billion. Each year, more than 500,000 Americans go to hospital emergency rooms because of drug-induced problems. Our children view drugs as the most important problem they face. Drugs and crime threaten all Americans, not just city residents, the poor, or minorities. Americans from every social and economic background, race, and ethnic group are concerned about the interrelated problems of crime, violence, and drugs. We fear the violence that surrounds drug markets. We abhor the effect it has on our children's lives. Americans are especially concerned about the increased use of drugs by young people. Today, dangerous drugs like cocaine, heroin, and methamphetamines are cheaper and more potent than they were at the height of our domestic drug problem fifteen or twenty years ago. In Arizona, ninety percent of homicides last year were related to methamphetamines. No nation can afford such devastating social, health, and criminal consequences.

DEMAND: THE ROOT CAUSE OF THE DRUG PROBLEM

No one should doubt that the demand for illegal drugs lies at the heart of the global drug problem. We in the United States are cognizant that we are a big part of the demand side of the drug equation. However, the percentage of our citizens that consumes drugs is not the central problem. Currently about six percent of our population, or twelve million Americans, use drugs— a fifty percent reduction from 1979's twenty-five million. Even the number of causal cocaine users is down seventy-five percent over the past decade. There are probably 600,000 heroin addicts in the United States. They represent but a fraction of the world's opium/heroin addicts and consume less than two

percent of the global heroin production capacity. A total of about 3.6 million Americans, or less than two percent of our population, is addicted to illegal drugs. This drug usage causes fourteen thousand deaths and costs $67 billion each year.

The problem is that American drug users have enormous quantities of disposable income. A crack addict in New York can afford a $350 a week habit or steal with relative ease $3,000 or more worth of property to maintain that habit. Indeed, Americans spend about $50 billion a year on illegal drugs. Of the estimated three hundred metric tons of cocaine smuggled into the United States every year, the wholesale value at U.S. points of entry is $10 billion. The retail value of that cocaine on our streets is $30 billion. These enormous sums are the reason criminal organizations dominate international traffic in illegal drugs, threaten our communities, and attack our institutions. All of us should recognize that the traffickers of cocaine, heroin, and the other drugs of abuse are actively seeking to develop new markets. If any country successfully reduces consumption of drugs that remain available, these drugs will find new markets. The new markets, along with the addicts and devastation that accompany them, will increasingly be found in those countries that produce the drugs and those through which they transit.

The U.S. National Drug Control Policy, recognizes this reality and prioritizes our efforts accordingly. Our number one goal is to prevent the sixty-eight million Americans under eighteen years of age from becoming a new generation of addicts. We find it unacceptable that drug use rates have doubled among our youth since 1992; we must and will reverse this trend. While we know that we can't arrest our way out of the drug problem, we will continue to uphold our severe drug laws. A million and-a-half Americans are now behind bars, many for drug law violations.

More than a million additional Americans are arrested for drug offenses every year. Incarceration is entirely appropriate for many drug-related crimes. There must be strong incentives to stay clear of drug trafficking, and prison sentences can motivate people to obey the law. Our challenge is to address the problem of chronic drug use by bringing drug testing, assessment, referral, treatment, and supervision within the oversight of the U.S. criminal justice system. We are doing so by increasing the number of drug courts that oversee treatment and rehabilitation for drug law violators and by validating ONDCP's [Office of National Drug Control Policy's] "Break the Cycle" concept. As a nation, we are optimistic that we can substantially reduce the demand for illegal drugs in the United States. One initiative we believe will help us in this effort is the $175 million-a-year anti-drug media campaign, which will be launched in the coming fiscal year.

DRUGS ARE A SHARED PROBLEM THAT MUST BE ADDRESSED BY ALL NATIONS

We recognize that domestic efforts by themselves cannot address what is fundamentally a global problem fueled by powerful, international criminal organizations. All our countries are affected by the drug problem, but not necessarily in the same ways. For some, the most pressing issue is drug consumption. For others, it may be drug-related violence and corruption. Some countries are affected

by illicit production or trafficking. Other countries are beset by all these problems. No country is immune.

THE RESULTS OF HEMISPHERIC COOPERATION HAVE BEEN NOTABLE

Over the past years, countries in the Western Hemisphere have made strong efforts to curtail production of illicit drugs, their trafficking, and the laundering of drug moneys. Peru's bilateral and multilateral counterdrug cooperation has been notable. President Fujimori is committed to eliminating coca destined for illicit drug production. The joint U.S.-Peruvian air interdiction campaign forced down, seized and/or destroyed twenty-three narcotics aircraft in 1995. As a result, narcotics-related flights decreased by 47 percent compared to 1994. This campaign caused coca-base prices to fall to record low levels last year, providing a critical economic disincentive for campesino growers. We believe this drop was an important contributing factor in the Peruvian government's success in reducing coca cultivation by 18 percent last year. Brazil has drafted key money-laundering legislation and passed comprehensive legislation on regulation of precursor chemicals. The government of Panama has been an important supporting player in an increasingly sophisticated and effective regional effort to disrupt drug-trafficking patterns within South America and launch international anti-money-laundering initiatives. Our interdiction efforts in the so-called "transit zone" have been enhanced by eighteen bilateral cooperative agreements we have with a number of Caribbean states. In Colombia, Attorney General Valdivieso,

Foreign Minister Mejia, Minister of Defense Echeverry, Armed Forces Commander General Bedoya, and National Police Director General Serrano continue to oppose narcoguerrillas who are attacking the very institutions of democracy.

U.S.-MEXICAN COUNTERDRUG COOPERATION

By any measure, the United States and Mexico have made significant progress in our joint efforts to face up to the drug problem. Whether we speak of investigations of drug trafficking organizations, anti-smuggling projects, crop-eradication efforts, demand-reduction programs, or anti-crime legislation, our record of cooperation is substantial.

President Zedillo has made an obvious commitment to political, legal, and institutional reform and is dedicated to fighting drug trafficking—which he has identified as the principal threat to Mexico's national security. Under his leadership, Mexican drug seizures have increased notably, with marijuana seizures up 40 percent over 1994 and opium-related seizures up 41 percent. Cocaine, methamphetamine, and precursor chemical seizures also rose significantly.

No other nation in the world has eradicated as many hectares of illegal drugs as has Mexico. Our extensive counterdrug cooperation occurs under the rubric of the U.S./Mexico High Level Contact Group for Drug Control. This bilateral drug control policy group was established in March 1996 and has enabled us to advance our collective effort to thwart drug trafficking and the demand for drugs in both nations.

Our two great nations share many drug problems. However, we have resolved to address them forthrightly while affirming our commitment to the principles of international law, particularly those of national sovereignty, territorial integrity, and nonintervention in the internal affairs of other countries.

THE POTENTIAL FOR PUBLIC-PRIVATE SECTOR ANTI-DRUG COALITIONS

All of us recognize the vital contributions that national drug commissions can make in each of our nations. We also understand that central governments can't resolve every problem. It is worth recognizing some important programs already underway in different nations that promise to reduce social tolerance for illegal drug use. In Brazil, the recently established Associao Parceria Contra Drogas has launched a national anti-drug publicity campaign with substantial corporate and private-sector assistance. In Venezuela, the Alianza para una Venezuela sin Drogas has already increased public awareness of the drug problem. In Puerto Rico, the Alianza para un Puerto Rico sin Drogas has brought together political, business, community, and educational leaders from around the Island to form yet another effective anti-drug coalition. In May, the mayors of many of our cities will be gathering in Sao Paulo, Brazil, to discuss how municipal governments can build similar public private anti-drug ventures.

All of us should encourage and emulate these diverse initiatives. Drug use goes down when citizens, parents, educators, religious leaders, and local law enforcement come together to oppose illegal drugs.

MORE INTERNATIONAL COOPERATION IS NEEDED

As suggested by President Clinton's March 1997 report to Congress on the status of International Drug Trafficking and Abuse, international cooperation requires further strengthening. Illicit poppy cultivation for opium increased 11 percent globally from 1994 to 1995, doubling in one country since 1992. Ominously for the United States, our Drug Enforcement Agency estimates that Colombia was the source of 60 percent of the heroin seized in the United States last year. Ten years ago, there was no opium growing in Colombia. Many valiant Colombians have since died fighting this terrible drug trade. Many source-country governments face major threats to their democratic institutions from drug violence and corruption. Finally, all of us face a terrible threat from billions of dollars in illegal funds that distort our economic development and assault the integrity of our banking systems.

The time has come for all of us, as responsible governments, to understand that the world community cannot allow international criminal organizations to gain a foothold in any country.

The April 1996 meeting in Vienna of the U.N. Commission on Narcotic Drugs and the ECOSOC [Economic and Social Committee] Conference at the U.N. Headquarters in New York last June underscored the international consensus for cooperation that will: limit money laundering, control precursor chemicals, take action against institutions or companies facilitating the drug trade, develop procedures for boarding vessels suspected of carrying illegal drugs, and reduce demand for these substances.

THE UNITED STATES IS COMMITTED TO SUPPORTING INTERNATIONAL COUNTERDRUG EFFORTS

The United States government is absolutely committed to helping all nations achieve full compliance with the goals and objectives set forth by the United Nations in its 1988 convention. We will support regional and sub-regional efforts to address drug production, trafficking, and consumption. We will share information with our partners. We are prepared to assist in institution-building so that judiciaries, legislatures, and law-enforcement agencies successfully can counter international traffickers. We will support an international effort to stop money laundering. The magnitude of drug profits that filter through international financial institutions makes them conspicuous. Such sums are difficult to conceal from attentive bankers and governments working together. The U.S. government will continue working with our hemispheric partners to develop means of identifying and seizing illegal drug proceeds as they pass through banking systems.

WE MUST ALL REDOUBLE OUR COMMITMENT

The drug problem is a shared agony throughout this hemisphere. It affects us all differently. In the United States, drug abuse has enormous health consequences and also generates violent crime and unsafe streets. In Mexico, the problem is different. Geography and a common two thousand-mile border have drawn international drug trafficking organizations to that country as a route to the United States. In the Caribbean, small island nations with constrained resources have difficulty protecting their extensive coast lines. Cooperative action holds the promise of reducing trafficking through this transit zone. In Colombia and Peru, drug cultivation and production now provide resources to narcoguerrilla organizations. While the drug-abuse menace is a common problem for us all, it takes on different forms. All of us must guard against allowing drug-trafficking organizations from gaining a stranglehold on our economies, our families, or our democratic processes.

We are confident that we can continue making significant progress in the Western Hemisphere against drug production and trafficking. The U.S. 1997 National Drug Control Strategy affirms our commitment to helping reduce the availability of cocaine. We identify as a top international drug-policy priority support for the efforts of Bolivia, Colombia, and Peru in reducing coca cultivation. We are in the process of developing a regional initiative, the goal of which is nothing less than complete elimination within the next decade of coca destined for illicit cocaine production. The success of Peruvian drug-control efforts in reducing coca cultivation by 18 percent in the past year causes us to feel optimistic about our ability to achieve cooperatively this ambitious objective.

It is indeed an honor to address this meeting of the Inter-American Drug Abuse Control Commission of the Organization of American States—the world's oldest regional organization. The hemispheric cooperation that is fostered by the OAS has its roots in the ideals of Simon Bolívar, the liberator of northern South America, who envisioned the creation of an association of states in the Americas. His dream is alive as all Americans—North, South, and Central—come together to build a brighter future for this hemisphere.

POSTSCRIPT

Do U.S. Efforts to Stem the Flow of Drugs from Abroad Encourage Human Rights Violations?

Drugs continue to plague the United States. For fiscal year 1999, President Bill Clinton asked Congress to appropriate $17.8 billion for the war's conduct. As noted in the introduction to this debate, there are signs that drug use has declined. Still, victory can hardly be declared, and there continues to be great debate over the extent of the problem and how to best combat it. With respect to the domestic and foreign policy actions of the United States to win the war on drugs, the debate has two sides. One is whether or not abuses of human rights occur (and to what degree). The other is whether or not, to the extent that abuses do occur, the ends justify the means. For an overall view, see the U.S. Drug Policy Web page of the Close Up Foundation at `http://www.closeup.org/drugs.htm`. For more on policy in Latin America, see Diana Jean Schemo and Tim Golden, "Bogota Aid: To Fight Drugs or Rebels?" *The New York Times* (June 2, 1998), p. A1, and Sewall H. Menze, *Cocaine Quagmire: Implementing the U.S. Anti-Drug Policy in the North Andes-Colombia* (University Press of America, 1997).

Proponents of strong action, including military aid, continue to defend their position. Donnie Marshall, deputy administrator of the Drug Enforcement Administration (DEA), United States Department of Justice, testified in March 1999 before the Subcommittee on the Western Hemisphere of the House Committee on International Relations that it is important to understand that "the threat posed by international drug syndicates is ... ominous." Therefore, "the United States must be able to attack the command and control functions of the international syndicates which are directing the flow of drugs into this country." Two Web sites that present this side of the debate are that of the ONDCP at `http://www.whitehousedrugpolicy.gov/whatsnew.html` and that of the DEA at `http://www.usdoj.gov/dea/`.

Critics continue to charge the United States with maintaining an unconscionable policy that has failed. Critic Peter Zirnite, of the Institute of Policy Studies (IPS), in "Militarization of the U.S. Drug Control Program," writes, "Despite [the] militarization and the massive funding for Washington's drug war, illegal drugs are more readily available now, at a higher purity and lower cost, than they were when the drug war was launched." Zinite's article and more can be found at the IPS Web site at `http://www.foreignpolicy-infocus.org/topics/ifdp.html`.

ISSUE 14

Would World Affairs Be More Peaceful If Women Dominated Politics?

YES: **Francis Fukuyama,** from "Women and the Evolution of World Politics," *Foreign Affairs* (September/October 1998)

NO: **Mary Caprioli,** from "The Myth of Women's Pacifism," An Original Essay Written for This Volume (August 1999)

ISSUE SUMMARY

YES: Francis Fukuyama, Hirst Professor of Public Policy at George Mason University, contends that a truly matriarchal world would be less prone to conflict and more conciliatory and cooperative than the largely male-dominated world that we live in now.

NO: Professor of political science Mary Caprioli contends that Fukuyama's argument is based on a number of unproven assumptions and that when women assume more political power and have a chance to act aggressively, they are as apt to do so as men are.

Political scientists are just beginning to examine whether or not gender makes a difference in political attitudes and the actions of specific policymakers and whether or not any gender differences that may exist as a result have a biological origin or are a product of the divergent ways in which males and females are socialized. The ultimate question is whether or not an equal representation of women among policymakers—or, even more radically, a reversal of tradition that would put women firmly in charge of foreign and defense policy—would make an appreciable difference in global affairs. That is what this debate is about.

Certainly there is good evidence that women in the mass public are less likely to countenance war than men. In the United States, for example, polls going back as far as World War II and extending to the present have found that women are less ready than men to resort to war or to continue war. Examining the difference between males and females in their opinions about the use of force against Iraq during the Persian Gulf crisis yields some fascinating results. Polls of men and women in 11 countries found that in 10 of the countries (Belgium, France, Germany, Great Britain, Israel, Italy, Japan, Mexico, Nigeria, and Russia), men were more likely than women to favor using force against Iraq. Only in Turkey were women more bellicose than men. The pro-war average across the 11 societies was 55 percent for men and 47 percent for women. To these findings we can add the opinions in the United States, where 69 percent of the men thought that the benefits of war would be worth the cost in lives; only 49 percent of women agreed.

Yet the attitudes of women who are in positions of authority may be much different from those of other women. So far only about two dozen women have been elected to lead countries, although that number is slowly growing. Yet the relative scarcity of female international leaders makes comparisons with their male counterparts difficult. There can be no doubt, though, that able, sometimes aggressive leadership has been evident in such modern female heads of government as Israel's Golda Meir and India's Indira Gandhi.

Moreover, it would be grossly inaccurate to say, "Men are apt to favor war, women are not." The reality is that favoring or not favoring war in the 11 countries in the study noted above was much more associated with the country itself. There were some countries in which both men and women strongly favored war. In Israel, which was threatened, then attacked, by Iraq, an overwhelming majority of both men (90 percent) and women (86 percent) favored force. In other countries, a majority of both men and women opposed using force.

In a more extended sense, the following readings are also about equal political opportunity for men and women. There are two reasons to favor equal opportunity. The first is more philosophical and rests on justice. This argument holds that equity demands that women have the same ability as men to achieve political office. In most societies these days there are few people who would disagree, at least publicly, with this view.

The second argument in support of political gender equality is more controversial and at the heart of this debate. This is the disagreement over whether or not women would make a policy difference because they are inherently apt to have a different view of politics than men do. Many scholars, feminist and otherwise, agree that there is a deep-seated difference. Feminist scholar Betty Reardon suggests that "from the masculine perspective, peace for the most part has meant the absence of war and the prevention of armed conflict." She terms this "negative peace." By contrast, Reardon maintains that women think more in terms of "positive peace," which includes "conditions of social justice, economic equity and ecological balance." The implication of this is that in a world run much more by women than is now the case, military budgets would go down and budgets for social, educational, and environmental programs would go up. Even though he is not a feminist scholar, as such, Francis Fukuyama, author of the first of the following selections, would fit in with this school of thought.

There are other scholars, feminist and otherwise, who do not think that women and men have "hard-wired" political differences. For them, a matriarchal society would run generally the same as a patriarchal society, no matter what the issue. Mary Caprioli adheres to this line of thought in the second selection, and so the debate is joined.

YES

Francis Fukuyama

WOMEN AND THE EVOLUTION OF WORLD POLITICS

CHIMPANZEE POLITICS

In the world's largest captive chimp colony at the Burger's Zoo in Arnhem, Netherlands, a struggle worthy of Machiavelli unfolded during the late 1970s. As described by primatologist Frans de Waal, the aging alpha male of the colony, Yeroen, was gradually unseated from his position of power by a younger male, Luit. Luit could not have done this on the basis of his own physical strength, but had to enter into an alliance with Nikkie, a still younger male. No sooner was Luit on top, however, than Nikkie turned on him and formed a coalition with the deposed leader to achieve dominance himself. Luit remained in the background as a threat to his rule, so one day he was murdered by Nikkie and Yeroen, his toes and testicles littering the floor of the cage.

Jane Goodall became famous studying a group of about 30 chimps at the Gombe National Park in Tanzania in the 1960s, a group she found on the whole to be peaceful. In the 1970s, this group broke up into what could only be described as two rival gangs in the northern and southern parts of the range. The biological anthropologist Richard Wrangham with Dale Peterson in their 1996 book *Demonic Males* describes what happened next. Parties of four or five males from the northern group would go out, not simply defending their range, but often penetrating into the rival group's territory to pick off individuals caught alone or unprepared. The murders were often grisly, and they were celebrated by the attackers with hooting and feverish excitement. All the males and several of the females in the southern group were eventually killed, and the remaining females forced to join the northern group. The northern Gombe chimps had done, in effect, what Rome did to Carthage in 146 B.C.: extinguished its rival without a trace.

There are several notable aspects to these stories of chimp behavior. First, the violence. Violence within the same species is rare in the animal kingdom, usually restricted to infanticide by males who want to get rid of a rival's offspring and mate with the mother. Only chimps and humans seem to have

From Francis Fukuyama, "Women and the Evolution of World Politics," *Foreign Affairs*, vol. 77, no. 5 (September/October 1998). Copyright © 1998 by The Council on Foreign Relations, Inc. Reprinted by permission of *Foreign Affairs*.

a proclivity for routinely murdering peers. Second is the importance of coalitions and the politics that goes with coalition-building. Chimps, like humans, are intensely social creatures whose lives are preoccupied with achieving and maintaining dominance in status hierarchies. They threaten, plead, cajole, and bribe their fellow chimps to join with them in alliances, and their dominance lasts only as long as they can maintain these social connections.

Finally and most significantly, the violence and the coalition-building is primarily the work of males. Female chimpanzees can be as violent and cruel as the males at times; females compete with one another in hierarchies and form coalitions to do so. But the most murderous violence is the province of males, and the nature of female alliances is different. According to de Waal, female chimps bond with females to whom they feel some emotional attachment; the males are much more likely to make alliances for purely instrumental, calculating reasons. In other words, female chimps have relationships; male chimps practice realpolitik.

Chimpanzees are man's closest evolutionary relative, having descended from a common chimp-like ancestor less than five million years ago. Not only are they very close on a genetic level, they show many behavioral similarities as well. As Wrangham and Peterson note, of the 4,000 mammal and 10 million or more other species, only chimps and humans live in male-bonded, patrilineal communities in which groups of males routinely engage in aggressive, often murderous raiding of their own species. Nearly 30 years ago, the anthropologist Lionel Tiger suggested that men had special psychological resources for bonding with one another, derived from their need to hunt cooperatively, that explained their dominance in group-oriented activities from politics to warfare. Tiger was roundly denounced by feminists at the time for suggesting that there were biologically based psychological differences between the sexes, but more recent research, including evidence from primatology, has confirmed that male bonding is in fact genetic and predates the human species.

THE NOT-SO-NOBLE SAVAGE

It is all too easy to make facile comparisons between animal and human behavior to prove a polemical point, as did the socialists who pointed to bees and ants to prove that nature endorsed collectivism. Skeptics point out that human beings have language, reason, law, culture, and moral values that make them fundamentally different from even their closest animal relative. In fact, for many years anthropologists endorsed what was in effect a modern version of Rousseau's story of the noble savage: people living in hunter-gatherer societies were pacific in nature. If chimps and modern man had a common proclivity for violence, the cause in the latter case had to be found in civilization and not in human nature.

A number of authors have extended the noble savage idea to argue that violence and patriarchy were late inventions, rooted in either the Western Judeo-Christian tradition or the capitalism to which the former gave birth. Friedrich Engels anticipated the work of later feminists by positing the existence of a primordial matriarchy, which was replaced by a violent and repressive patriarchy only with the transition to agricultural societies. The problem with this theory is, as Lawrence Keeley points out in his book *War Before Civilization,* that the most comprehensive recent studies of violence in hunter-gatherer societies suggest that for them war was actually more frequent, and rates of murder higher, than for modern ones.

Surveys of ethnographic data show that only 10–13 percent of primitive societies never or rarely engaged in war or raiding; the others engaged in conflict either continuously or at less than yearly intervals. Closer examination of the peaceful cases shows that they were frequently refugee populations driven into remote locations by prior warfare or groups protected by a more advanced society. Of the Yanomamö tribesmen studied by Napoleon Chagnon in Venezuela, some 30 percent of the men died by violence; the !Kung San of the Kalahari desert, once characterized as the "harmless people," have a higher murder rate than New York or Detroit. The sad archaeological evidence from sites like Jebel Sahaba in Egypt, Talheim in Germany, or Roaix in France indicates that systematic mass killings of men, women, and children occurred in Neolithic times. The Holocaust, Cambodia, and Bosnia have each been described as a unique, and often as a uniquely modern, form of horror. Exceptional and tragic they are indeed, but with precedents stretching back tens if not hundreds of thousands of years.

It is clear that this violence was largely perpetrated by men. While a small minority of human societies have been matrilineal, evidence of a primordial matriarchy in which women dominated men, or were even relatively equal to men, has been hard to find. There was no age of innocence. The line from chimp to modern man is continuous.

It would seem, then, that there is something to the contention of many feminists that phenomena like aggression, violence, war, and intense competition for dominance in a status hierarchy are more closely associated with men than women. Theories of international relations like realism that see international politics as a remorseless struggle for power are in fact what feminists call a gendered perspective, describing the behavior of states controlled by men rather than states per se. A world run by women would follow different rules, it would appear, and it is toward that sort of world that all postindustrial or Western societies are moving. As women gain power in these countries, the latter should become less aggressive, adventurous, competitive, and violent.

The problem with the feminist view is that it sees these attitudes toward violence, power, and status as wholly the products of a patriarchal culture, whereas in fact it appears they are rooted in biology. This makes these attitudes harder to change in men and consequently in societies. Despite the rise of women, men will continue to play a major, if not dominant, part in the governance of postindustrial countries, not to mention less-developed ones. The realms of war and international politics in particular will remain controlled by men for longer than many feminists would like. Most important, the task of resocializing men to be more like women—that is, less violent—will run into limits. What is bred in the bone cannot be altered easily by changes in culture and ideology.

THE RETURN OF BIOLOGY

We are living through a revolutionary period in the life sciences. Hardly a week goes by without the discovery of a gene linked to a disease, condition, or behavior, from cancer to obesity to depression, with the promise of genetic therapies and even the outright manipulation of the human genome just around the corner. But while developments in molecular biology have been receiving the lion's share of the headlines, much progress has been made at the behavioral level as well. The past generation has seen a revival in Darwinian thinking about human psychology, with profound implications for the social sciences.

For much of this century, the social sciences have been premised on Emile Durkheim's dictum that social facts can be explained only by prior social facts and not by biological causes. Revolutions and wars are caused by social facts such as economic change, class inequalities, and shifting alliances. The standard social science model assumes that the human mind is the terrain of ideas, customs, and norms that are the products of man-made culture. Social reality is, in other words, socially constructed: if young boys like to pretend to shoot each other more than young girls, it is only because they have been socialized at an early age to do so.

The social-constructionist view, long dominant in the social sciences, originated as a reaction to the early misuse of Darwinism. Social Darwinists like Herbert Spencer or outright racists like Madsen Grant in the late nineteenth and early twentieth centuries used biology, specifically the analogy of natural selection, to explain and justify everything from class stratification to the domination of much of the world by white Europeans. Then Franz Boas, a Columbia anthropologist, debunked many of these theories of European racial superiority by, among other things, carefully measuring the head sizes of immigrant children and noting that they tended to converge with those of native Americans when fed an American diet. Boas, as well as his well-known students Margaret Mead and Ruth Benedict, argued that apparent differences between human groups could be laid at the doorstep of culture rather than nature. There were, moreover, no cultural universals by which Europeans or Americans could judge other cultures. So-called primitive peoples were not inferior, just different. Hence was born both the social constructivism and the cultural relativism with which the social sciences have been imbued ever since.

But there has been a revolution in modern evolutionary thinking. It has multiple roots; one was ethology, the comparative study of animal behavior. Ethologists like Konrad Lorenz began to notice similarities in behavior across a wide variety of animal species suggesting common evolutionary origins. Contrary to the cultural relativists, they found that not only was it possible to make important generalizations across virtually all human cultures (for example, females are more selective than males in their choice of sexual partners) but even across broad ranges of animal species. Major breakthroughs were made by William Hamilton and Robert Trivers in the 1960s and 1970s in explaining instances of altruism in the animal world not by some sort of instinct towards species survival but rather in terms of "selfish genes" (to use Richard Dawkins' phrase) that made social behavior in an individual animal's interest. Finally, advances in neurophysiology have shown that the brain is not a Lockean tabula rasa waiting to be filled with cultural content, but rather a highly modular organ whose components have been adapted prior to birth to suit the needs of socially oriented primates. Humans are hard-wired to act in certain predictable ways.

The sociobiology that sprang from these theoretical sources tried to provide a deterministic Darwinian explanation for just about everything, so it was perhaps inevitable that a reaction would set in against it as well. But while the term sociobiology has gone into decline, the neo-Darwinian thinking that spawned it has blossomed under the rubric of evolutionary psychology or anthropology and is today an enormous arena of new research and discovery.

Unlike the pseudo-Darwininsts at the turn of the century, most contemporary biologists do not regard race or ethnicity as biologically significant categories. This stands to reason: the different human races have been around only for the past hundred thousand years or so, barely a blink of the eye in evolutionary time. As countless authors have pointed out, race is largely a socially constructed category: since all races can (and do) interbreed, the boundary lines between them are often quite fuzzy.

The same is not true, however, about sex. While some gender roles are indeed socially constructed, virtually all reputable evolutionary biologists today think there are profound differences between the sexes that are genetically rather than culturally rooted, and that these differences extend beyond the body into the realm of the mind. Again, this stands to reason from a Darwinian point of view: sexual reproduction has been going on not for thousands but hundreds of millions of years. Males and females compete not just against their environment but against one another in a process that Darwin labeled "sexual selection," whereby each sex seeks to maximize its own fitness by choosing certain kinds of mates.

The psychological strategies that result from this never-ending arms race between men and women are different for each sex.

In no area is sex-related difference clearer than with respect to violence and aggression. A generation ago, two psychologists, Eleanor Maccoby and Carol Jacklin, produced an authoritative volume on what was then empirically known about differences between the sexes. They showed that certain stereotypes about gender, such as the assertion that girls were more suggestible or had lower self-esteem, were just that, while others, like the idea that girls were less competitive, could not be proven one way or another. On one issue, however, there was virtually no disagreement in the hundreds of studies on the subject: namely, that boys were more aggressive, both verbally and physically, in their dreams, words, and actions than girls. One comes to a similar conclusion by looking at crime statistics. In every known culture, and from what we know of virtually all historical time periods, the vast majority of crimes, particularly violent crimes, are committed by men. Here there is also apparently a genetically determined age specificity to violent aggression: crimes are overwhelmingly committed by young men between the ages of 15 and 30. Perhaps young men are everywhere socialized to behave violently, but this evidence, from different cultures and times, suggests that there is some deeper level of causation at work.

At this point in the discussion, many people become uncomfortable and charges of "biological determinism" arise. Don't we know countless women who are stronger, larger, more decisive, more violent, or more competitive than their male counterparts? Isn't the proportion of female criminals rising relative to males? Isn't work becoming less physical, making sexual differences unimportant? The answer to all of these questions is yes: again, no reputable evolutionary biologist would deny that culture also shapes behavior in countless critical ways and can often overwhelm genetic predispositions. To say that there is a genetic basis for sex difference is simply to make a statistical assertion that the bell curve describing the distribution of a certain characteristic is shifted over a little for men as compared with women. The two curves will overlap for the most part, and there will be countless individuals in each population who will have more of any given characteristic than those of the other sex. Biology is not destiny, as tough-minded female leaders like Margaret Thatcher, Indira Gandhi, and Golda Meir have proven. (It is worth pointing out, however, that in male-dominated societies, it is these kinds of unusual women who will rise to the top.) But the statistical assertion also suggests that broad populations of men and women, as opposed to exceptional individuals, will act in certain predictable ways. It also suggests that these populations are not infinitely plastic in the way that their behavior can be shaped by society.

FEMINISTS AND POWER POLITICS

There is by now an extensive literature on gender and international politics and a vigorous feminist subdiscipline within the field of international relations theory based on the work of scholars like Ann Tickner, Sara Ruddick, Jean Bethke Elshtain, Judith Shapiro, and others. This literature is too diverse to describe succinctly, but it is safe to say that much of it was initially concerned with understanding how international politics is "gendered," that is, run by men to serve male interests and interpreted by other men, consciously and unconsciously, according to male perspectives. Thus, when a realist theorist like Hans Morganthau or Kenneth Waltz argues that states seek to maximize power, they think that they are describing a universal human characteristic when, as Tickner points out, they are portraying the behavior of states run by men.

Virtually all feminists who study international politics seek the laudable goal of greater female participation in all aspects of foreign relations, from executive mansions and foreign ministries to militaries and universities. They disagree as to whether women should get ahead in politics by demonstrating traditional masculine virtues of toughness, aggression, competitiveness, and the willingness to use force when necessary, or whether they should move the very agenda of politics away from male preoccupations with hierarchy and domination. This ambivalence was demonstrated in the feminist reaction to Margaret Thatcher, who by any account was far tougher and more determined than any of the male politicians she came up against. Needless to say, Thatcher's conservative politics did not endear her to most feminists, who much prefer a Mary Robinson [President of Ireland] or Gro Harlem Brundtland [first female prime minister of Norway] as their model of a female leader, despite —or because of—the fact that Thatcher had beaten men at their own game.

Both men and women participate in perpetuating the stereotypical gender identities that associate men with war and competition and women with peace and cooperation. As sophisticated feminists like Jean Bethke Elshtain have pointed out, the traditional dichotomy between the male "just warrior" marching to war and the female "beautiful soul" marching for peace is frequently transcended in practice by women intoxicated by war and by men repulsed by its cruelties. But like many stereotypes, it rests on a truth, amply confirmed by much of the new research in evolutionary biology. Wives and mothers can enthusiastically send their husbands and sons off to war; like Sioux women, they can question their manliness for failing to go into battle or themselves torture prisoners. But statistically speaking it is primarily men who enjoy the experience of aggression and the camaraderie it brings and who revel in the ritualization of war that is, as the anthropologist Robin Fox puts it, another way of understanding diplomacy.

A truly matriarchal world, then, would be less prone to conflict and more conciliatory and cooperative than the one we inhabit now. Where the new biology parts company with feminism is in the causal explanation it gives for this difference in sex roles. The ongoing revolution in the life sciences has almost totally escaped the notice of much of the social sciences and humanities, particularly the parts of the academy concerned with feminism, postmodernism, cultural studies, and the like. While there are some feminists who believe that sex differences have a natural basis, by far the majority are committed to the idea that men and women are psychologically identical, and that any differences in behavior, with regard to violence or any other characteristic, are the result of some prior social construction passed on by the prevailing culture.

THE DEMOCRATIC AND FEMININE PEACE

Once one views international relations through the lens of sex and biology, it never again looks the same. It is very difficult to watch Muslims and Serbs in Bosnia, Hutus and Tutsis in Rwanda, or militias from Liberia and Sierra Leone to Georgia and Afghanistan divide themselves up into what seem like indistinguishable male-bonded groups in order to systematically slaughter one another, and not think of the chimps at Gombe.

The basic social problem that any society faces is to control the aggressive tendencies of its young men. In hunter-gatherer societies, the vast preponderance of violence is over sex, a situation that continues to characterize domestic violent crime in contemporary postindustrial societies. Older men in the community have generally been responsible for socializing younger ones by ritualizing their aggression, often by directing it toward enemies outside the community. Much of that external violence can also be over women. Modern historians assume that the Greeks and Trojans could not possibly have fought a war for ten years over Helen, but many primitive societies like the Yanomamö do exactly that. With the spread of agriculture 10,000 years ago, however, and the accumulation of wealth and land, war turned toward the acquisition of material goods. Channeling aggression outside the community may not lower societies' overall rate of violence, but it at least offers them the possibility of domestic peace between wars.

The core of the feminist agenda for international politics seems fundamentally correct: the violent and aggressive tendencies of men have to be controlled, not simply by redirecting them to external aggression but by constraining those impulses through a web of norms, laws, agreements, contracts, and the like. In addition, more women need to be brought into the domain of international politics as leaders, officials, soldiers, and voters. Only by participating fully in global politics can women both defend their own interests and shift the underlying male agenda.

The feminization of world politics has, of course, been taking place gradually over the past hundred years, with very positive effects. Women have won the right to vote and participate in politics in all developed countries, as well as in many developing countries, and have exercised that right with increasing energy. In the United States and other rich countries, a pronounced gender gap with regard to foreign policy and national security issues endures. American women have always been less supportive than American men of U.S. involvement in war, including World War II, Korea, Vietnam, and the Persian Gulf War, by an average margin of seven to nine percent. They are also consistently less supportive of defense spending and the use of force abroad. In a 1995 Roper survey conducted for the Chicago Council on Foreign Relations, men favored U.S. intervention in Korea in the event of a North Korean attack by a margin of 49 to 40 percent, while women were opposed by a margin of 30 to 54 percent. Similarly, U.S. military action against Iraq in the event it invaded Saudi Arabia was supported by men by a margin of 62 to 31 percent and opposed by women by 43 to 45 percent. While 54 percent of men felt it important to maintain superior world wide military power, only 45 percent of women agreed.

Women, moreover, are less likely than men to see force as a legitimate tool for resolving conflicts.

It is difficult to know how to account for this gender gap; certainly, one cannot move from biology to voting behavior in a single step. Observers have suggested various reasons why women are less willing to use military force than men, including their role as mothers, the fact that many women are feminists (that is, committed to a left-of-center agenda that is generally hostile to U.S. intervention), and partisan affiliation (more women vote Democratic than men). It is unnecessary to know the reason for the correlation between gender and antimilitarism, however, to predict that increasing female political participation will probably make the United States and other democracies less inclined to use power around the world as freely as they have in the past.

Will this shift toward a less status- and military-power-oriented world be a good thing? For relations between states in the so-called democratic zone of peace, the answer is yes. Consideration of gender adds a great deal to the vigorous and interesting debate over the correlation between democracy and peace that has taken place in the past decade. The "democratic peace" argument, which underlies the foreign policy of the Clinton administration as well as its predecessors, is that democracies tend not to fight one another. While the empirical claim has been contested, the correlation between the degree of consolidation of liberal democratic institutions and interdemocratic peace would seem to be one of the few nontrivial generalizations one can make about world politics. Democratic peace theorists have been less persuasive about the reasons democracies are pacific toward one another. The reasons usually cited—the rule of law, respect for individual rights, the commercial nature of most democracies, and the like—are undoubtedly correct. But there is another factor that has generally not been taken into account: developed democracies also tend to be more feminized than authoritarian states, in terms of expansion of female franchise and participation in political decision-making. It should therefore surprise no one that the historically unprecedented shift in the sexual basis of politics should lead to a change in international relations.

THE REALITY OF AGGRESSIVE FANTASIES

On the other hand, if gender roles are not simply socially constructed but rooted in genetics, there will be limits to how much international politics can change. In anything but a totally feminized world, feminized policies could be a liability.

Some feminists talk as if gender identities can be discarded like an old sweater, perhaps by putting young men through mandatory gender studies courses when they are college freshmen. Male attitudes on a host of issues, from child-rearing and housework to "getting in touch with your feelings," have changed dramatically in the past couple of generations due to social pressure. But socialization can accomplish only so much, and efforts to fully feminize young men will probably be no more successful than the Soviet Union's efforts to persuade its people to work on Saturdays on behalf of the heroic Cuban and Vietnamese people. Male tendencies to band together for competitive purposes, seek to dominate status hierarchies, and act out aggressive fantasies toward one another can be rechanneled but never eliminated.

Even if we can assume peaceful relations between democracies, the broader world scene will still be populated by states led by the occasional [bloody dictator]. Machiavelli's critique of Aristotle was that the latter did not take foreign policy into account in building his model of a just city: in a system of competitive states, the best regimes adopt the practices of the worst in order to survive. So even if the democratic, feminized, postindustrial world has evolved into a zone of peace where struggles are more economic than military, it will still have to deal with those parts of the world run by young, ambitious, unconstrained men. If a future Saddam Hussein is not only sitting on the world's oil supplies but is armed to the hilt with chemical, biological, and nuclear weapons, we might be better off being led by women like Margaret Thatcher than, say, Gro Harlem Brundtland. Masculine policies will still be required, though not necessarily masculine leaders. . . .

LIVING LIKE ANIMALS?

In Wrangham and Peterson's *Demonic Males . . .* , the authors come to the pessimistic conclusion that nothing much has changed since early hominids branched off from the primordial chimp ancestor five million years ago. Group solidarity is still based on aggression against other communities; social cooperation is undertaken to achieve higher levels of organized violence. Robin Fox has argued that military technology has developed much faster than man's ability to ritualize violence and direct it into safer channels. The Gombe chimps could kill only a handful of others; modern man can vaporize tens of millions.

While the history of the first half of the twentieth century does not give us great grounds for faith in the possibility of human progress, the situation is not nearly as bleak as these authors would have us believe. Biology, to repeat, is not destiny. Rates of violent homicide appear to be lower today than during mankind's long hunter-gatherer period, despite gas ovens and nuclear weapons. Contrary to the thrust of postmodernist thought, people cannot free themselves entirely from biological nature. But by accepting the fact that people have natures that are often evil, political, economic, and social systems can be designed to mitigate the effects of man's baser instincts.

... [To that end,] Liberal democracy and market economies work well because, unlike socialism, radical feminism, and other utopian schemes, they do not try to change human nature. Rather, they accept biologically grounded nature as a given and seek to constrain it through institutions, laws, and norms. It does not always work, but it is better than living like animals.

NO
Mary Caprioli

THE MYTH OF WOMEN'S PACIFISM

In a recent article in *Foreign Affairs*, Francis Fukuyama asserts that a more feminized world run by women would be more peaceful. Indeed, he concludes that biology is not destiny and that it is better not to live like animals. Presumably, this means that men can learn to be more peaceful in their behavior, and this new pacifism on the part of men would translate into a more peaceful world. What Fukuyama seems to eliminate from his analysis is that if men change their behavior, then so too would women. If a more egalitarian world would change men's behavior, then it would most likely change women's behavior, too. If men were to become more peaceful, women would potentially become more aggressive.

Fukuyama's argument is based on a number of assumptions. In order to conclude that a future world would be more peaceful if only men acted more like women, one must assume that a gender gap exists in support for the use of force. Furthermore, an acceptance of a gender gap assumes a dichotomy based on gender. Not only must there exist only two genders divided by sex, but there must also be a universality of experience for women and men across cultures. In order to understand Fukuyama's argument, it is necessary to have an understanding of gender and to explore the evidence for proclaiming the existence of a gender gap. Any prediction characterizing a future world must be made only after acquiring such understandings.

GENDER

Gender is crucial to any study supporting and explaining the meaning of gender, in which gender is found to be a cause of state bellicosity. Is gender a function of genital-type, to each person's level of testosterone, or the extent to which each individual had been socialized into accepting standards of feminine and masculine attitudes, which would be a cultural measure of gender?

Gender is the crux of any argument based on the existence of a difference between men and women—the existence of a gender gap. We must, therefore, examine whether or not gender is a useful category of analysis. The literature on gender, especially within anthropology, is prolific yet surprisingly monolithic. All define gender as a culturally construed category. If a definition of gender is based on culture, then gender is not a universal category of analysis.

Indeed, the term "gender" is used to designate socially constructed roles attributed to women and men. These gender roles are learned, change over time, and vary both within and between cultures. Gender issues, therefore, have to do with differences in how women and men are supposed to act. In other words, gender definitions control and restrict behaviors. As Klaus Theweleit highlights in his 1993 piece "The Bomb's Womb and the Genders of War" in the edited volume *Gendering War Talk*, women traditionally have not had the power to act violently, which might explain the identified gender gap in support for war. The culturally proscribed role of women based on gender determines women's alternatives. In this instance, the use of violence is simply not an option for women. Women, therefore, are not necessarily choosing not to act violently but do not have the choice to act violently —a very important distinction.

Indeed, women who have obtained the power to act violently have done so. These leaders include prime ministers Margaret Thatcher (Great Britain), Indira Gandhi (India), Golda Meir (Israel), Khalida Zia (Bangladesh), Maria Liberia-Peters (Netherlands-Antilles), Gro Harlem Brundtland (Norway), and Benazir Bhutto (Pakistan). Using Stuart Bremer's 1996 Militarized Interstate Dispute (MID) data set, which covers the time period from 1816 until 1992, it is possible to examine the level of violence sanctioned by female leaders in comparison to male leaders.

Only twenty-four states have placed a female leader in office since 1900, with the first female leader obtaining power in 1960. In this instance, a female leader is defined as a president, prime minister, or any other decision-maker who is essentially the 'decision-maker of last resort' on decisions to use force and other high-level international decisions. Edith Cresson, who was premier of France in 1991–1992, is therefore not considered a leader in this discussion because that position is one of significantly lesser importance than that of the French president, who was a male.

We can compare the behavior of female and male leaders from 1960 until 1992 using MID. MID includes a variable for the level of hostility used during the crisis. Hostility level is divided into five levels coded as follows: 1) no militarized action, 2) threat to use force, 3) display of force, 4) use of force, and 5) war. Both female and male leaders rely on the fourth category, the use of force, most frequently. Furthermore, both female and male leaders' average use of violence is equal. According to this evidence, female leaders are no more peaceful than their male counterparts.

Of course, critics would argue that female leaders in a male world must act more aggressively in order to prove themselves. According to this argument women are still considered to be by nature more pacific than men are. Because women must operate in a social and political environment that has been defined, structured and dominated by men for centuries, they must recondition themselves to act more violently in order to gain power in a "man's world." On the other hand, women's assent to power and growing equality in relation to men may free women from gender stereotypes re-

Table 1
States With Female Leaders Since 1900–1994

STATE	LEADER	YEARS IN OFFICE
Argentina	Isabel Perón	1974–1976
Bangladesh	Khalida Zia	1991–1996
Bolivia	Lidia Gueiler Tejada	1979–1980
Burundi	Sylvie Kingi	1993–1994
Canada	Kim Campbell	1993
Central African Republic	Elisabeth Domitien	1975–1976
Dominica	Mary Eugenia Charles	1980–1995
Haiti	Ertha Pascal-Trouillot	1990–1991
India	Indira Gandhi	1966–1977
		1980–1984
Israel	Golda Meir	1969–1974
Lithuania	Kazimiera Prunskiene	1990–1991
Malta	Agatha Barbara	1982–1987
Netherlands Antilles	Maria Liberia-Peters	1984–1985
		1988–1994
Nicaragua	Violeta Chamorro	1990–1997
Norway	Gro Harlem Brundtland	1981
		1986–1989
		1990–1996
Pakistan	Benazir Bhutto	1988–1990
		1993–1996
Philippines	Corazon C. Aquino	1986–1992
Poland	Hanna Suchocka	1993
Portugal	Maria de Lourdes Pintasilgo	1979
Rwanda	Agathe Uwilingiyimana	1993–1994
Sri Lanka	Sirimavo Bandaranaike	1960–1965
		1970–1977
Turkey	Tansu Ciller	1993–1996
United Kingdom	Margaret Thatcher	1979–1990
Yugoslavia	Milka Planinc	1982–1986

stricting their behavior. In this more equal world, women become free to exercise different alternatives, including the option of using violence.

The power and role of women varies across cultures because power is based on these culturally dependent gender roles. Because all people are born into, and socialized to a particular culture, the argument for biological determinism becomes impossible to prove. The only way to prove conclusively that women are more peaceful would be to raise a number of baby girls from birth in a cultural vacuum. Such an experiment would be unethical at best. Scholars, therefore, must speculate as to the 'nature' of women. For example, do women in power ignore and overcome inherent gender-based characteristics in order to gain and maintain power? Did Margaret Thatcher have to keep her natural tendency to be peaceful in constant check? Conversely, do people who are attracted to power share basic characteristics regardless of gender? Is Thatcher's biological tendency toward violence no different from a 'normal' tendency of any human's tendency toward violence?

The adoption of gender as a category of analysis implies a universality of experience across cultures and over time. This assumption, especially when espoused by educated and predominantly Western and European women, is as biased as some men's assumption of a universal human experience based on a male perspective. Placing women as the center of analysis is no less biased than focusing on men. Furthermore, the acceptance of this dichotomy between the only two recognized genders implies the acceptance that there do exist biological behavioral differences between the genders—an assumption that remains unproven.

Recognizing the exclusion of the female gender, as culturally defined, in most international relations literature is important to understanding the assumptions within existing research. To assume that including two genders or that taking the female-gender perspective will rectify the problems in current research and society is problematic, for both assume a universality of experience. As Third World feminists have clearly detailed, the experience of women is not universal. As scholars we must, therefore, recognize that the absence of a gendered analysis or conversely, the exclusive reliance on gendered analyses as a bias within research. We must understand that classifying an individual's behavior on the basis of gender is not a valid assumption.

Beyond the scope of this discussion, but important to note, is the argument that there are more than two genders. Arguments identifying a gender gap associate gender with sexuality. Furthermore, gender is assumed to include only two genders: the mythical male and female. If gender is equated with sexuality then children, the aged, especially postmenopausal women, gays, and lesbians would all constitute different genders. And, how would hermaphrodites—those 'sexless' people according to definitions of gender as male/female who are 'assigned' a sex at birth—be categorized?

Following a definition of gender based on sex or at least male and female sex organs, gender/sex differences should be the genesis of power inequality between women and men. These gender differences would necessarily have to be universal both between and within cultures. Yet, research conclusively demonstrates that gender changes over time within cultures and is not consistent among different cultures. Nonetheless, scholars continue to attempt to show a gender gap in the support for the use of force.

Often, this feminine pacifism is linked to women's maternal qualities and more specifically to their ability to have children. This argument is prejudiced in that it discounts men's 'maternal' instincts toward their children. As with the argument for two sexes, there exists a gray area in this argument about women's maternal instincts. For example, how would a single man who adopts a child be classified—or women who are infertile—or women who choose never to have children? Would the single dad not have any 'maternal' characteristics while assuming that women who choose not to have children possess 'maternal' characteristics by virtue of being female?

After examining the numerous gray areas surrounding much of the argument in support for women's pacifism, the argument seems rather thin. Yet, some studies do show that women seem to be less supportive of the use of violence than men. Of course, other groups of people including African Americans are also less supportive of the use of violence than are white men.

GENDER GAP

All evidence in support for the existence of a gender gap comes from public opinion surveys of the Western world and in particular of the United States and the United Kingdom. The women of these countries can hardly be representative of women worldwide. In addition, the size of this identified gender gap varies from study to study. Another shortcoming of public opinion surveys is that women are more likely to indicate no opinion in public opinion surveys or merely fail to voice support for war. Little mention is made of political scientist John Mueller's admonition that not voicing support for a war is not the same as opposing it. In this instance, women might be constrained for voicing support for the use of force by gender stereotypes, so they offer no opinion.

Beyond the problems associated with public opinion surveys lie other challenges to a gender-gap theory for the support of violence. For instance, Nancy E. McGlen and Meredith Reid Sarkees in their 1993 book *Women in Foreign Policy: The Insiders* find varying degrees of a gender gap amongst the masses but none with women working within the State Department or the Defense Department. Some scholars might argue that women in the State and Defense Departments are not representative of women in general, or that these women might be forced to act violently to prove themselves in a predominantly male arena, or that they must adhere to traditional, institutional roles. Such arguments may be countered by the idea that these women are free to act violently—they have the opportunity to act violently and they do.

Not only do scholars challenge the existence of a gender gap but also the reasons for a gender gap. Some scholars suggest that the gender gap is created only by those women who identify with the women's movement. This argument suggests that it is not some inherent quality of women that creates a gender gap in support for the use of force but that women who happen to adhere to a feminist ideology of pacifism are more pacifist much in the same way that Democrats tend to be more pacific than Republicans. In keeping with Fukuyama's argument, it would be prudent, therefore, to encourage people to be Democrats in order to ensure world peace. This task should be less difficult than changing every culture of the world to have men change their behavior to act in the way women supposedly do—by not acting violently—and for women's supposed behavior to remain unchanged —to remain pacific.

A parallel discussion to the argument of women's nature would be asking whether or not people are born Democrat. Are party ideologies an inherent characteristic of some individuals, or are some individuals socialized into accepting the ideology of the Democrats? This is similar to questioning whether pacifism is an inherent quality of women or if women are socialized into being more pacific.

Others argue that any current gender gap associated with support for the commitment of armed forces or for war would be eradicated by the inclusion of more women in active duty within the armed forces. This argument follows the one outlined above in that women are not able to act violently and are traditionally excluded from activities and professions that include violence. Once women are included in active duty within the armed forces, they will not only achieve a certain level of equality but will also be free to act violently and support the use of violence.

Indeed, a group's relative position of power within society may determine its proclivity toward peaceful conflict resolution rather than some inherent quality. For example, John Mueller in his numerous research and public opinion surveys found that African Americans were more pacifistic in that as a group, African Americans were largely against escalation and for withdrawal in their general support for World War II, the Korean War, the Vietnam War, and the Persian Gulf War. According to this logic, one's placement in the hierarchy of power would best predict one's support for war as evidenced by women's and African Americans' more dovish nature.

Mark Tessler and Ina Warriner in an article in the January 1997 issue of *World Politics* argue that there is no evidence to show that women are less militaristic than men are. They do, however, find that individuals who are more supportive of equality between women and men are also less supportive of violence as a means of resolving conflict. This argument suggests that the relationship between more pacifist attitudes and international conflict rests upon the degree of gender equality that characterizes a society. Those who express greater concern for the status and role of women, and particularly for equality between women and men, are more likely than other individuals to believe that the international disputes in which their country is involved should be resolved through diplomacy and compromise. In other words, societies that have values that are less gender-based should be more pacific in their international behavior.

This argument that more gender-neutral societies are less internationally bellicose is similar to the theory outlined above that argues that people are more pacifist based on their position in society. In either situation, a society that is hierarchical in nature because it is based on prejudice against such classifications as gender and race will be more internationally bellicose. Once the social hierarchy is abolished in that all people gain the freedom to act as they choose, then differences among separate classifications of people will be eliminated. For instance, women and African Americans may become more aggressive as they gain more equality, more power. So too, may men become more pacific as they are freed from gender stereotypes that demand men to be aggressive.

Admittedly, I am no expert on chimpanzees. I can, however, speculate that female chimps might be more aggressive if they had the opportunity to act aggressively. Within the animal kingdom, power is often based on size. With humans, the base of power varies from physical size, to the size of one's bank account, to the size of one's intellect. Women, therefore, have an increasingly greater opportunity to act violently, an opportunity that her chimpanzee sisters may not enjoy.

THE FUTURE

The future may not be as rosy as Fukuyama suggests, at least not in terms of a global pacifism brought about by the increasing equality of women. Of course, equality in itself seems to be a positive force if only in freeing individuals to act according to their desires rather than by being restricted by cultural stereotypes related to, and defined by gender. This new freedom to act, however, does not necessarily translate into a global peace.

Fukuyama fleetingly mentions that the number of women incarcerated for violent crimes is increasing in proportion to that of men. The important question remains unanswered: Why are more women committing violent crimes? As American society becomes more egalitarian with regard to the sexes, women are gaining more power. This power may not be directed toward pacifist, nurturing ideals. Lord Acton wrote, "Power tends to corrupt, and absolute power corrupts absolutely." Perhaps he was correct.

POSTSCRIPT

Would World Affairs Be More Peaceful If Women Dominated Politics?

Studies of biopolitics, ethology, gender genetics, and other related approaches are just beginning to probe the connection between biology and politics. Also, the so-called nature-versus-nurture debate continues and presents some fascinating questions. Bear in mind that neither Fukuyama nor Caprioli (nor, for that matter, any other serious scholar) argues that "biology is destiny." Rather, all scholars recognize that human behavior is a mix of socialization and genetic coding. It is the ratio of that mix and its manifestations that are the points of controversy. Fukuyama clearly believes that genetics plays a strong role. Caprioli assigns a much greater role to socialization than Fukuyama does in accounting for the fact that women seem less aggressive than men.

There are a number of good books on the general topic of women and gender as they relate to world politics. These books include Vivienne Jabri and Eleanor O'Gorman, eds., *Women, Culture, and International Relations* (Lynne Rienner, 1998); J. Ann Tickner, *Gender in International Relations: Feminist Perspectives on Achieving Global Security* (Columbia University Press, 1994); Jill Sterns, *Gender and International Relations: An Introduction* (Rutgers University Press, 1998); and V. Spike Peterson, ed., *Gendered States: Feminist (Re)Visions of International Relations Theory* (Lynne Rienner, 1992).

Fukuyama suspects that males tend to act like males and females tend to act like females, largely because of evolutionary biology. For a classic ethological view, read Desmond Morris, *The Naked Ape* (Dell, 1976) and Robert Ardrey, *The Territorial Imperative* (Atheneum, 1966). This line of thinking has many critics, some of whom directly dispute what Fukuyama has argued. In addition to Caprioli, more on this perspective can be found in Barbara Ehrenreich and Katha Pollitt, "Fukuyama's Follies," *Foreign Affairs* (January 1999).

Whatever the reality may be, its implications are important because women are increasingly coming to play leading roles. More on this change can be found in Jane S. Jaquette, "Women in Power: From Tokenism to Critical Mass," *Foreign Policy* (Fall 1997). During the past few decades, women have led such important countries as Great Britain, India, and Israel. Just a few short years ago a first was reached when, in Bangladesh, the choice for a country's prime minister came down to two women. Another breakthrough occurred when Madeleine Albright became the first female secretary of state for the United States. For studies of women in foreign policy leadership positions, read Nancy E. McGlen and Meredith Reid Sarkees's *The Status of Women in Foreign Policy* (Headline Series, 1995) and *Women in Foreign Policy* (Routledge, 1993).

ISSUE 15

Is Islamic Fundamentalism a Threat to Political Stability?

YES: Daniel Pipes, from "Same Difference," *National Review* (November 7, 1994)

NO: Zachary Karabell, from "Fundamental Misconceptions: Islamic Foreign Policy," *Foreign Policy* (Winter 1996/1997)

ISSUE SUMMARY

YES: Daniel Pipes, editor of *Middle East Quarterly*, argues that just as those who considered the Soviet threat a myth were naive, so are those who dismiss the threat from Islamic fundamentalists naive.

NO: Zachary Karabell, a researcher in the Kennedy School of Government at Harvard University, holds that it is wrong to view Islam as a monolith whose adherents pose a threat to the stability of the international system.

Several Islamic political concepts are important to this issue. Some tend to bring Muslims together; others work to divide Muslims.

One of the forces that serve to promote Muslim unity is the idea of the *ummah*, the spiritual, cultural, and political community of Muslims. In part, this means that Muslims are less likely than people from the Western cultural tradition to draw distinct lines between the state, religion, and the individual. Belief in the *ummah* also implies that the adherents to Islam should join spiritually and politically in one great Muslim community.

A sense of common history is another factor that works to bring Muslims together. After a triumphant and powerful beginning, including the spread of Islam and its culture into Europe and elsewhere from its Middle Eastern origins, the political fortunes of the Muslims declined slowly after about the year 1500. Part of this decline was due to losses to predominately Christian European powers. By the 1920s almost all Muslim lands were under the control of colonial powers, which were mostly European and Christian.

There are also strong forces that tend to divide Muslims. One of these is the frequent rivalry between the majority Sunni sect and the minority Shi'ite sect. A second factor that divides Muslims is the degree to which they believe in the strict adherence to the *shari'ah*—the law of the Koran, which is composed of God's (Allah's) teachings—to govern both religious and civil conduct. Muslim traditionalists (fundamentalists, according to common usage) want to frame legal systems based on the *shari'ah* and to establish theocratic rule.

As one Muslim theologian argues, "The notion that a majority should rule and the notion of the political party are all Western notions. Islam calls for obedience to the rule, the unification of the nation and advice by religious scholars to the rules." Other Muslims, who are often called secularists, believe that religious and civil law should be kept relatively separate and that Koranic law is flexible enough to allow changes in tradition, such as permitting greater entry of women into business, politics, and other aspects of civil society. There is considerable strife occurring in Algeria, Egypt, and several other Muslim countries based on the traditionalist-secularist struggle.

Nationalism (primary political loyalty to a national state) is a third factor that divides Muslims. Individual Muslim countries are fiercely nationalistic. Achieving full Muslim political unity would necessarily entail giving up patriotism and other manifestations of nationalism. A fourth factor, and one that further solidifies nationalism, is the major ethnic and sectarian differences within Islam. Iranians, Kazakhs, Pakistanis, and many other Muslim peoples are not ethnic Arabs and do not speak Arabic.

These forces of unity and division among Muslims started to be a matter of global concern with the Muslim world's change of fortune since its nadir after World War I. There are now many more independent Muslim countries. Moreover, Muslim countries are becoming increasingly dependent on, among other things, the wealth that petroleum has brought them. By extension, Muslims everywhere have begun to reclaim their heritage in what might be called a "Muslim pride" movement.

The Muslim revival has many interrelated parts. One involves rejecting direct interference by outside powers. Rejection of outside domination entails reaction against the European–North American West, which Muslims closely identify with the Christians and imperial powers that long beset the house of Islam. There is also an intensifying of the efforts of many Muslims to "get back to their roots." That has strengthened the appeal of traditionalism, and there is a struggle in many Islamic countries between the secularists (usually in power) and the traditionalists for control of the government.

The resurgence of Islam as a political force has ramifications for world politics. First, the secularist-traditionalist struggle within countries will, depending on the outcome, influence their foreign policies. Second, intra-Islamic strife has in part already led to international conflict, such as the Iran-Iraq war. Muslims have also tended to unite, be that in support of Afghans, Palestinians, or others who in the Muslims' view are being oppressed. Some Muslims have also reverted to terrorism.

The issue is whether or not resurgent Islam, especially its traditionalist/fundamentalist aspects, represents a threat to political stability. In the following selections, Daniel Pipes argues that the traditionalists are indeed fundamentally antithetical to stability. Zachary Karabell disagrees, arguing that Islamic fundamentalism in the worst-case scenario is confined to one region and that it poses no threat to other regions or to the global system.

YES

Daniel Pipes

SAME DIFFERENCE

The Western confrontation with fundamentalist Islam has in some ways come to resemble the great ideological battle of the twentieth century, that between Marxism–Leninism and liberal democracy. Not only do Americans frame the discussion about Iran and Algeria much as they did the earlier one about the Soviet Union and China, but they also differ among themselves on the question of fundamentalist Islam roughly along the same lines as they did on the Cold War. Liberals say: Co-opt the radicals. Conservatives say: Confront them. As usual, the conservatives are right.

At first glance, how to deal with fundamentalist Islam appears to be a discussion unrelated to anything that has come before. Islam is a religion, not an ideology, so how can the U.S. Government formulate a policy toward it? A closer look reveals that while Islam is indeed a faith, its fundamentalist variant is a form of political ideology. Fundamentalists may be defined, most simply, as those Muslims who agree with the slogan: "Islam is the solution." When it comes to politics, they say that Islam has all the answers. The Malaysian leader Anwar Ibrahim spoke for fundamentalist Muslims everywhere when he asserted some years ago that "we are not socialist, we are not capitalist, we are Islamic." For the fundamentalists, Islam is primarily an "ism," a belief system about ordering power and wealth.

Much distinguishes fundamentalism from Islam as it was traditionally practiced, including its emphasis on public life (rather than faith and personal piety); its leadership by schoolteachers and engineers (rather than religious scholars); and its Westernized quality (e.g., whereas Muslims traditionally did not consider Friday a Sabbath, fundamentalists have turned it into precisely that, imitating the Jewish Saturday and Christian Sunday). In brief, fundamentalism represents a thoroughly modern effort to come to terms with the challenges of modernization.

The great majority of Muslims disagree with the premises of fundamentalist Islam, and a small number do so vocally. A few... have acquired global reputations, but most toil more obscurely. When a newly elected deputy to the Jordanian parliament last fall called fundamentalist Islam "one of the

From Daniel Pipes, "Same Difference," *National Review* (November 7, 1994). Copyright © 1994 by National Review, Inc., 215 Lexington Avenue, New York, NY 10016. Reprinted by permission.

greatest dangers facing our society" and compared it to "a cancer" that "has to be surgically removed," she spoke for many Muslims.

Americans can in good conscience join them in criticizing fundamentalism. As an ideology, fundamentalist Islam can claim none of the sanctity that Islam the religion enjoys.

BATTLE LINES

In responding to fundamentalist Islam, Americans tend, as I have suggested, to divide along familiar liberal and conservative lines. More striking yet, the same people hold roughly the same positions they held vis-à-vis that other quasi-religious ideology, Marxism–Leninism. A left-wing Democrat like George McGovern advocates a soft line, now as then. A right-wing Republican like Jesse Helms argues for a tough line, now as then. Consider the following parallels:

Causes. The Left, in keeping with its materialist outlook, sees Communist or fundamentalist Islamic ideology as a cover for some other motivation, probably an economic one. The Russian Revolution expressed deep-seated class grievances; fundamentalist violence in Algeria, the State Department tells us, expresses "frustration arising from political exclusion and economic misery." In contrast, the Right sees radical utopian ideology as a powerful force in itself, not just as an expression of socio-economic woes. Ideas and ambitions count at least as much as the price of wheat; visions of a new order go far toward accounting for the revolutions of 1917 and 1979.

Solutions. If misery causes radicalism, as the Left argues, then the antidote lies in economic growth and social equity. The West can help in these areas through aid, trade, and open lines of communication. But if, as the Right believes, ambitious intellectuals are the problem, then they must be battled and defeated. In both cases, liberals look to cooperation, conservatives to confrontation.

The West's responsibility. The Left sees Western hostility as a leading reason why things have gone wrong. According to one journalist, the West "made its own sizable contribution" to the current crisis in Algeria. It's the old "blame America first" attitude: just as Americans were responsible for every Soviet trespass from the Gulag to the arms race, so they are now answerable for the appearance [in Iran] of the Ayatollah Khomeini (due to U.S. support for the Shah) and for the many Arab fundamentalist movements (due to U.S. support for Israel). The Right adamantly denies Western culpability in both cases, for that would absolve tyrants of their crimes. We made mistakes, to be sure, but that's because we find it hard to contend with racial utopian movements. Along these lines, [one analyst] argues that "we are at the beginning of what promises to be a long war in which new moral complexities... will present themselves as once they did in the days of Soviet Communism."

A single source. When the State Department disclaims "monolithic international control being exercised over the various Islamic movements," it uses almost the same words it once used to speak of Marxism–Leninism. For decades, American "progressives" insisted that Communist organizations around the world had indigenous sources and did not owe anything to Moscow (a claim easier to make so long as Moscow's archives remained closed). To which conservatives typically replied: Of course there's no "monolithic international control," but there is an awful lot of funding and influence. Teheran administers a network akin to an Islamic Comintern, making its role today not that different from Moscow's then.

The antis. For many decades, the Left saw those Russians, Chinese, and Cubans whose firsthand experience turned them into anti-Communists as marginal elements. In similar fashion, the Left today looks at anti-fundamentalist Muslims as inauthentic. Churches are among the worst offenders here. For example, in one recent analysis, a German priest presented the extremist element as the Muslim community per se. The Right wholeheartedly celebrates the new antis, like the old, as brave individuals bringing advance word of the terrors that result from efforts radically to remake society.

Do moderates exist? The Left distinguishes between those ideologues willing to work within the system (deemed acceptable) and those who rely on violence and sabotage (deemed unacceptable). The Right acknowledges differences in tactics but perceives no major difference in goals. Accordingly, it tends to lump most Communists or fundamentalists together.

Motives. When the other side strikes out aggressively, the Left often excuses its acts by explaining how they are defensive. Invasions by Napoleon and Hitler explain the Soviet presence in Angola; a legacy of colonial oppression accounts for the depths of fundamentalist rage. The Right concludes from events like the downing of a Korean Airlines flight or the World Trade Center bombing that the other side has offensive intentions, and it listens to no excuses.

Fighting words. The two sides draw contrary conclusions from aggressive speech. Liberals dismiss the barrage of threats against the West (Muslim prisoner in a French court: "We Muslims should kill every last one of you [Westerners]") as mere rhetoric. Conservatives listen carefully and conclude that the West needs to protect itself (French Interior Minister Charles Pasqua: fundamentalist groups "represent a threat to us").

Threat to the West. If they are approached with respect, says the Left, Marxist–Leninists and fundamentalist Muslims will leave us alone. Don't treat them as enemies and they won't hurt us. The Right disagrees, holding that all revolutionaries, no matter what their particular outlook (Communist, Fascist, fundamentalist), are deeply anti-Western and invariably target the West. Their weaponry ranges from ICBMs to truck bombs, but their purpose is the same: to challenge the predominance of modern, Western civilization.

And if truck bombs are less threatening than missiles, it should be noted that fundamentalists challenge the West more profoundly than Communists did and do. The latter disagree with our politics but not with our whole view of the world (how could they, as they pay homage to Dead White Males like Marx and Engels?). In contrast, fundamentalist Muslims despise our whole way of life, including the way we dress, mate, and pray. They admire little more than our military and medical technologies. To appease Communists means changing the political and economic spheres; to appease fundamentalists would mean forcing women to wear the veil, scuttling nearly every form of diversion, and overhauling the judicial system.

Future prospects.   In the 1950s, the Left portrayed Marxism–Leninism as the wave of the future; today, it ascribes the same brilliant prospect to fundamentalist Islam. In other words, these radical ideologies are an unstoppable force; stand in their way, and you'll not only get run over, you might even spur them on. But conservatives see utopianism enjoying only a temporary surge. The effort to remake mankind, they say, cannot work; like Communism, fundamentalism has to end up in the dustbin of history.

CONCILIATION OR CONTAINMENT?

Summing up, the Left is more sanguine than the Right about both Communism and fundamentalist Islam. It's hard to imagine a conservative calling the Ayatollah Khomeini "some kind of saint," as did Jimmy Carter's ambassador to the United Nations, Andrew Young. It's about as uncommon to hear a liberal warning, along with France's Defense Minister François Léotard, that "Islamic nationalism in its terrorist version is as dangerous today as National Socialism was in the past." On the scholarly level, a liberal Democrat like John Esposito publishes a book titled *The Islamic Threat: Myth or Reality?*, in which he concludes that the threat is but a myth. In sharp contrast, Walter McDougall, the Pulitzer Prize–winning historian and sometime assistant to Richard Nixon, sees Russia helping the West in "holding the frontier

of Christendom against its common enemy," the Muslim world.

These contrary analyses lead, naturally, to very different prescriptions for U.S. policy. The Left believes that dialogue with the other side, whether Communists or fundamentalist Muslims, has several advantages: it helps us understand their legitimate concerns, signals that we mean them no harm, and reduces mutual hostility. Beyond dialogue, the West can show good will by reducing or even eliminating our military capabilities. Roughly speaking, this is the Clinton Administration's position. In Algeria, for instance, the Administration hopes to defuse a potential explosion by urging the regime to bring in fundamentalist leaders who reject terrorism, thereby isolating the violent extremists.

The Right has little use for dialogue and unilateral disarmament. Communists and fundamentalists being invariably hostile to us, we should show not empathy but resolve, not good will but will power. And what better way to display these intentions than with armed strength? Now as then, conservatives think in terms of containment and rollback. For conservatives, Algeria's regime fits into the tradition of friendly tyrants —states where the rulers treat their own population badly but help the United States fend off a radical ideology. It makes sense to stand by Algiers (or Cairo), just as it earlier made sense to stick by Ky in Saigon or Pinochet in Chile.

Of course, the schemas presented here do not align perfectly. The Reagan Administration searched for "moderates" in Iran (an effort led by none other than Oliver North), and the Bush Administration enunciated a soft policy toward fundamentalism. The Clinton Administration, in contrast, has pursued a quite resolute policy toward Iran.

Interests sometimes count for more than ideology. Circumstance on occasion compels the U.S. Government to aid one enemy against another; thus, we have recently helped fundamentalist Afghans against Communist ones, and Communist Palestinians against fundamentalist ones. The liberal Clinton Administration speaks out against a crackdown on fundamentalists in Algeria, where the stakes are low for Americans, but accepts tough measures in Egypt, where the United States has substantial interests. The conservative French government bemoans the crackdown in Egypt (not so important for it) but encourages tough measures in Algeria (very important).

Still, the basic pattern is clear. And as the lines of debate sort themselves out, the two sides are likely to stick more consistently to their characteristic positions. This suggests that while Marxism–Leninism and fundamentalist Islam are very different phenomena, Westerners respond in similar ways to ideological challenges.

They do so because of a profound divide in outlook. American liberals believe that mankind is by nature peaceful and cooperative; when confronted with aggression and violence, they tend to assume it is motivated by a just cause, such as socio-economic deprivation or exploitation by foreigners. Anger cannot be false, especially if accompanied by high-minded goals. Less naïvely, conservatives know the evil that lurks in men's hearts. They understand the important roles of fanaticism and hatred. Just because an ideology has utopian aims does not mean that its adherents have lofty motives or generous ambitions.

The Left's soft approach to fundamentalist Islam predominates in Washington, and in the universities, the churches, and the media. Indeed, to recall one of the Left's favorite phrases, it has become the hegemonic discourse in the United States. On the other side stand nothing but a handful of scholars, some commentators and politicians, and the great common sense of the American people. Americans know an opponent when they see him, and they are not fooled by the Left's fancy arguments. That common sense prevailed in the Cold War and no doubt will suffice yet again to overcome the follies of the New Class.

NO

Zachary Karabell

FUNDAMENTAL MISCONCEPTIONS: ISLAMIC FOREIGN POLICY

For all the furor surrounding Islamic fundamentalism, there has been surprisingly little attention given to fundamentalist foreign policy. True, Iranian foreign policy has been analyzed and excoriated, and generalizations have been made on the basis of this one case. It is often assumed that fundamentalists approach foreign affairs with the same set of goals as those that drive domestic policy: namely, rejection of the secular state and the establishment of religious law as the foundation of society. It is further thought that lurking behind Islamic fundamentalist foreign policy is a commitment to holy war (jihad) with the non-Muslim world. And there seems to be a consensus among Western powers that fundamentalism poses a threat to the international system.

The Clinton administration has consistently stated that it opposes violence and extremism, but not Islam. The State Department has spoken out against the repressive measures taken by the Algerian government in its ongoing civil war with fundamentalist insurgents. At the same time, the administration has supported with economic and military aid the pro-Western regimes in Egypt, Saudi Arabia, and Turkey. While the U.S. government has taken great pains to differentiate between its opposition to violence and its respect for Islam, it has nonetheless supported governments like Egypt and Algeria that at times use extreme violence to suppress even nonviolent Muslims who oppose those regimes on religious grounds.

The recently passed Iran-Libya Sanctions Act penalizes foreign companies that do business with those two "rogue" states. Administration officials were careful to say that the target of the legislation is terrorism sponsored by these governments and not Islamic fundamentalism. Yet evidence does exist that associates the Saudi government with fundamentalist insurgents, the Pakistani government with the fundamentalist Taliban guerrillas who seized Kabul [Afghanistan], and the Turkish military with violent, extraterritorial reprisals against the Kurds. No action is taken against these regimes; indeed, these countries are courted by the U.S. government as valuable allies. The discrepancy leads to the speculation that policy toward Algeria, Iran, and the

From Zachary Karabell, "Fundamental Misconceptions: Islamic Foreign Policy," *Foreign Policy,* no. 105 (Winter 1996/1997). Copyright © 1996 by The Carnegie Endowment for International Peace. Reprinted by permission.

Muslim world in general is colored by an antipathy toward Islamic fundamentalism and a strong, if unstated, presumption that fundamentalism is a volatile and dangerous force in international affairs. These assumptions are predicated on a misunderstanding of Islamic fundamentalist foreign policy.

We cannot understand fundamentalist foreign policy simply by inferring from the domestic ideology. Fundamentalist foreign policy is different from the realpolitik or the liberal internationalism of U.S. policymakers. It is different from the raison d'état of France and the communism of the People's Republic of China. Islamic civilization is not destined to clash with the rest of the world, and Islamic fundamentalists in power do not necessarily represent a threat to international security. Instead, outside of the Islamic world, most Islamic fundamentalists have no ambition other than the most anodyne desire for security. While fundamentalism is an expansive force within the Islamic world, it neither seeks jihad with nor domination of the non-Muslim world. In this respect, Islamic fundamentalism ought to matter no more to the non-Muslim world than Québécois nationalism matters to Thailand.

There is considerable disagreement about what precisely constitutes "Islamic fundamentalism." At one time or another the label "fundamentalist" has been attached to groups as diverse as Hamas in Israel/Palestine; Hizbollah in Lebanon; the Refah (Welfare) Party in Turkey; the al-Nahda Party in Tunisia; the Muslim Brotherhood in Egypt, Jordan, and Syria; the Armed Islamic Group (GIA) in Algeria; and the Jamaat-i-Islami in Pakistan. Yet there is no unitary Islamic fundamentalism any more than there is a unitary Christian fundamentalism. In the Middle East, fundamentalism ranges from pietist organizations to revolutionary groups committed to the violent overthrow of what they perceive to be un-Islamic regimes.

While there is no monolithic Islam—and no monolithic fundamentalist movement—there is an ongoing struggle in the Islamic world. On one side are largely secular governments; on the other, there are individuals and groups who believe that politics and religion are one and who reject the secular Western division between the state and religion. As the scholar Nazih Ayubi has observed, for fundamentalists, Islam is understood as *din* (a religion), *dunya* (a way of life), and *dawla* (a state). Fundamentalists call for a return to an earlier, supposedly more pure Islam. They want to replace secular, civil law with the *sharia* (Islamic law), and they view the modern state system in the Islamic world as an illegitimate and immoral division of the *umma* (the community of believers). Fundamentalists share this basic ideology, but different groups adopt varying strategies to realize their vision.

FOREIGN POLICY AND IDEOLOGY

What exactly is an Islamic foreign policy? Many of the ruling Iranian elite say that Iran's foreign policy is Islamic, but what does that mean? Does the foreign policy of the state of Iran depart in significant ways from the foreign policies of states in general? The governments of Saudi Arabia and (non-Arab) Pakistan are avowedly Islamic (as opposed to secular), yet they are rarely considered fundamentalist. Though each of these countries attempts to fashion its laws in accordance with the *sharia*, and though the Saudi monarchy is deeply influenced by a group of Islamic puritans (the Wahhabis), they act in foreign policy matters in a more realist fashion than do leaders in Iran and Sudan, who pursue a distinctly fundamentalist foreign policy.

These questions lead to the further conundrum of whether there is anything that can be characterized as an Islamic foreign policy or as a fundamentalist foreign policy. For example, do the policies that fundamentalist Iran pursues as a self-declared Islamic state differ from the policies of the other, more secular Muslim governments in the Middle East, such as Syria or Jordan? In addition, do the policies of Iran, whose citizens follow Shiite Islam, depart in noticeable ways from the policies of another self-declared Islamic state, Sudan, whose Muslims are Sunni? ...

The default setting for foreign policy is realism. Most policymakers, whether American, European, Asian, or Middle Eastern, perceive international politics to be a competition between states for power, influence, and profit. Over time, diplomats and world leaders have developed what amount to rules of engagement.

One of the strongest of these dictates is that the state is inviolable. Even in war, modern states do not usually attempt to obliterate one another. When they do—as Iraq tried with Kuwait in 1990—they are deemed to have broken the cardinal law of international politics and are punished accordingly.

Some states, however, champion an ideology that challenges the legitimacy of states. Cold War Soviet communist rhetoric, for instance, labeled Western states as bourgeois, capitalist tools of oppression. In due time, workers would recognize their common interests, unite,

and liberate themselves from the capitalist state. That ideology, as well as the policies pursued by the Soviet Union that were designed to carry it out, profoundly disturbed the governments of the West.

Like communism, Islamic fundamentalism is an ideology. Where communism rejected capitalist rules of engagement in international affairs, Islamic fundamentalism rejects the notion that the state is an inviolable unit. But unlike communism, Islamic fundamentalism confines its aspirations to one portion of the world— the Muslim world. Thus, when fundamentalists challenge the state, it is the state within the Muslim world that is the target of their animus. Communism sought, and free market capitalism still seeks, world domination. Islamic fundamentalism does not and never will.

Any successful ideology is malleable, and Islamic fundamentalism is no exception. It does not dictate specific action and can—in the hands of adept leaders or intellectuals—justify almost any behavior. Furthermore, the relationship between ideology and actual policy is notoriously opaque. State leaders are perfectly capable of articulating a governing ideology and then acting in ways that contravene that ideology. Any regime often needs an ideology to legitimize its use of force, both internally and externally. This ideology may mask realist motives, but ideology and realism can also coexist. In the particular case of Islamic fundamentalism, ideology matters a great deal. Fundamentalists conceive of the world as two broad but distinct realms: the community of believers and the non-Islamic world. While there are great variations and divisions within each of those worlds, policy toward one is radically different from policy toward the other.

THE UMMA AND
THE MODERN STATE

In a realist world of states, or in an international system in which the United Nations recognizes and sanctifies the state as the primary and morally approved actor in international relations, foreign policy is anything beyond the borders of the state. Yet, for an Islamic regime, state borders within the Islamic world are artificial constructs, created largely by the former colonial or imperialist powers of Europe. Hence they lack true legitimacy.

The lack of respect that political Islam extends to the state as understood by the West characterizes not just fundamentalists in power (Iran and Sudan) but fundamentalists in opposition (Algeria, Lebanon, and Tunisia). As Hassan al-Turabi, the spiritual leader of Sudan's military regime, has said, "The international dimension of the Islamic movement is conditioned by the universality of the umma ... and the artificial irrelevancy of Sudan's borders." In the tradition of one of the foremost spokesmen of modern fundamentalism, Egypt's Sayyid Qutb, many of today's fundamentalist groups attempt to realign the traditional relationship between Islam and the state from one in which Islam serves to legitimize state authority into one in which Islam delegitimizes the state by branding it un-Islamic. The Ayatollah Ruhollah Khomeini did this frequently in his years of opposition to the shah, and even more moderate opposition leaders like Tunisia's al-Ghannouchi label the attempts of the Tunisian and Algerian governments to suppress fundamentalism as "anti-Islamic."

Not all fundamentalist movements seek to undermine the state. Some movements (such as the Muslim Brotherhood in Jordan) seek accommodation with the state, while others (such as Algeria's GIA) are insurgent. Almost all fundamentalist movements nonetheless seek to infuse Islamic principles into the governments of states within the Muslim world. The attempt to invalidate the state is, on the whole, more pronounced in Middle Eastern and African Islamic fundamentalist movements than in those of Southeast Asia. Indonesian and Malaysian movements call for Islamic law and an Islamic state but they do not as frequently assail the concept of the state itself.

Most fundamentalist movements in the Middle East, however, view states as artificial colonial-era dividers of the umma. Western powers drew the state lines of the Gulf emirates, Iraq, Israel, Jordan, Saudi Arabia, and Syria. At the same time, the boundaries of Algeria, Egypt, Iran, Morocco, and Turkey were not invented by the colonial powers. Fundamentalists in these countries cannot attack the state as a Western invention. Instead, they call the rulers of these countries "un-Islamic" and in so doing brand them as illegitimate.

In theory, the umma is one unit. All Muslims, regardless of sect, constitute the umma; hence, division among the believers is a degenerate state of affairs. In the view of many contemporary political fundamentalists, the entire community of believers makes up the universe of action. States are nothing more than lines on a map. Thus, the policies of the Iranian government toward Central Asia or the policies of Sudan toward North Africa are not really "foreign policy" at all. As al-Turabi remarked in 1995 when discussing his Popular Arab and Islamic Conference, "It represents all Muslim nations. First, because these nations cannot express their views in their countries, and, second, because the whole world is drawing closer together. It behooves the Muslims as a single nation to meet and express their views."

The same view is espoused by the Ayatollah Ali Khamenei, the spiritual leader of the Islamic Republic of Iran. As he stated in a March 1995 sermon,

> The Islamic *ummah* should try to preserve unity, cohesion, and solidarity, as the term *ummah* suggests. Today, this great community has a duty to its esteemed prophet, savior, and teacher, to a person who as God's testimony among the *ummah* is the most popular personality. This duty is to preserve the honor and integrity of the Islamic *ummah* through unity and cohesion. This is the duty of the *ummah* today.

> Today the enemies of Islam and the Islamic community are doing their best to pit the members of this community against each other. This is not peculiar to the present time, as the situation has been the same in the past. However, today, this dastardly mission of the enemies is being implemented through systematic thought and comprehensive planning. The reason is that they feel that the Islamic spirit is growing among Muslims, Islam has awakened hearts, and with our nation's great revolution, arrogance has received a blow from Islam. This is why they want to create enmity in the Islamic community.

> All the Muslims who today in some way or another feel the bite of arrogance's lashes on their bodies and souls—such as the nations of Palestine, Bosnia, Chechnya, Kashmir, and Lebanon, and other Muslim nations in Africa and Asia —are subjected to pain and suffering because of the lack of unity and solidarity in the Islamic community. If the Islamic community had enjoyed solidarity, none of these would have happened.

Fundamentalism significantly expands the strategic universe for fundamentalist states and groups. Prior to the 1979 Iranian revolution and the accession of the government of Umar al-Bashir and al-Turabi in Sudan in 1989, neither Iran nor Sudan would have considered events in Bosnia, Chechnya, Kashmir, or Malaysia to be foreign policy concerns. Foreign policy in these countries now rests on the principle that the *umma* is a cohesive political unit. As a result, the universe has expanded. But at the same time, that universe has a finite scope: It stops where Islam stops and therefore is not expansionist toward the Western world or the East Asian world outside of Malaysia and Indonesia.

Ideologically, then, the policies that Iran or Sudan pursue toward the Muslim world are not foreign but rather are aimed at reconstituting the *umma*. No matter that this *umma* was never politically unified as a self-conscious nation stretching from Morocco to Indonesia, the ideal of fundamentalist policy is that the Muslim community is unitary. That position is shared by many of the more prominent opposition fundamentalist groups, such as the al-Nahda Party in Tunisia, the Jamaati-i-Islami in Pakistan, and the Muslim Brotherhood in Jordan, as well as by the Refah Party in Turkey, which is now in a coalition government. They therefore view the *umma* as a community of interests, and other Islamic countries as potential allies.

Within the Islamic world, the ideology of the *umma* is sometimes trumped by pure realpolitik. Iran might ideologically oppose Syria's Hafez al-Assad, but during the Iran-Iraq war Iran and Syria drew closer against the common enemy of Saddam Hussein's Iraq.

In dealing with the non-Islamic world, however, fundamentalist states and opposition groups adopt a more variegated and pragmatic foreign policy that closely approximates the realist paradigm. While Iran and Sudan support, either rhetorically or with arms and money, fundamentalist revolutionary groups that operate within the *umma*, their policies toward China, Europe, India, and the United States are less subversive. Iran might be antagonistic toward the United States and friendly with India, while Sudan might be friendly with China and less so with Japan. Certainly, there is profound antagonism toward the United States, overall, but it is an antagonism that more closely resembles state competition for power. Within the *umma*, fundamentalism rejects the state and thus sees no constraints on actions that might undermine the states in the region; outside of the *umma*, fundamentalists see an antagonistic world dominated by the United States in allegiance with other states and a system that rarely serves Muslim interests. The aim is not to undermine Western states, or to destroy them, but to try to compete internationally for influence, prestige, and power.

FUNDAMENTALIST GOALS

All fundamentalist movements, whether they accommodate the state or challenge it violently, whether they are pietistic or revolutionary, strive for the unification of the *umma*: Yet they differ greatly over how this goal is to be achieved. In part, the differences among the governments of Iran, Sudan, and the numerous opposition groups, such as Tunisia's al-Nahda Party, may have to do with the life-cycle of ideologies: Iran is entering a postrevolutionary phase, Sudan's Islamic regime is newer to power, and the al-Nahda Party is still an outlaw movement subject to intense repression. The al-Nahda Party is so consumed with local problems that its leader, Rashid al-Ghannouchi, talks hardly at all of exporting ideology. In both word and deed, Iranian leaders were more eager to export fundamentalism a decade ago. With the passing of the early revolutionary fervor, Iran's foreign policy is decidedly less ambitious. Even in its relations with the new Muslim states of Central Asia, its policy is more realist and pragmatic, though it is not necessarily status-quo oriented.

The regime in Sudan emphasizes rhetorically an expansionist, revolutionary foreign policy within the *umma*, and at times al-Turabi even suggests that world Islam is the ultimate goal. Asked by a Spanish newspaper if Sudan is destined to save the world, al-Turabi responded, "We are the spearhead of a movement which must free the world from the moral turpitude and atheism in which it is living." The leaders of Sudan sound much like the leaders of Iran did in the first decade of the revolution. Sudan has been accused by the U.S. government and by Egypt and other Arab states of training guerrilla forces at several camps in its northern region. While Sudan denies the allegations, evidence overwhelmingly indicates that the camps do exist. The primary targets of these guerrilla groups are the secular regimes of Algeria and Egypt. However, these insurgent groups do not appear to be directly controlled by the Sudanese government.

Beyond seeking to unify the *umma*, two additional goals of fundamentalist foreign policies are an opposition to Israel and a rejection of U.S. hegemony in international politics. The two are linked, since the existence of the state of Israel is seen by many as the most naked example of Western imperialism and intrusion on the *umma*. The Iranian republic is especially vehement in its rejection of the U.S.-dominated international system. "The Islamic Republic," said Khamenei, "opposes the hegemony of the United States and its influence and interference in Islamic countries and in all oppressed countries." In this view, the international system is the creation of the West and its current standard-bearer, the United States. The rules of the international system—the rules of realism and state power—work to the disadvantage of Iran and, by extension, Islam. And the most visible local way of rejecting that influence is by negating or refusing to recognize the legitimacy of Israel. This attempt to reject "hegemony" is both a function of Islam and a natural reflection of state interests in acquiring a greater share of the international pie.

POLICY IMPLICATIONS

Fundamentalist foreign policy has several discernible characteristics: an embrace of the unity of the *umma*; a refusal to respect the sovereignty of secular states within the *umma*; a rejection of Western hegemony within the Muslim world; and an animus toward Zionism as the most glaring local manifestation of the Western state system that artificially divides the *umma*.

The intensity with which fundamentalist groups and governments seek to realize the goal of a unified *umma* and a destruction of the Western state system within the *umma* differs depending on a variety of factors. In Iran, an initial expansionist ideology has faded as that nation

enters a postrevolutionary phase, and its behavior may in part be explained by theories of revolution. Sudan's al-Turabi has donned the mantle of Islamic revolution, but Sudanese society is not undergoing revolutionary transformations, and the behavior of Sudanese elites can be explained by the demands of their fundamentalist ideology more than by the pressures of revolution. In Tunisia, where the al-Nahda Party represents a nonviolent variant of fundamentalism, local concerns are dominant.

The policy implications of fundamentalist foreign policies differ depending on the nation in question and its perceived relationship to the *umma*. The implications for Israel are not (or should not be) the same as the implications for the United States or France. For the French, the outcome of the civil war in Algeria has substantial economic and political consequences. The prospect of hundreds of thousands of Algerians fleeing to France, combined with French investments in North Africa and French support for the military government, makes the GIA's violent ideology an immediate security concern. Similarly, the rejection not just of Zionism but of Israel that characterizes Hamas and Hizbollah means that fundamentalism is a security concern for the Israeli state.

Yet the ideology of fundamentalism should not be threatening to France itself. The effects of that ideology on a region in which France has vested interests are problematic, but the fact that fundamentalist ideology so rigorously distinguishes between the *umma* and the non-Islamic world means that the boundaries of ambition of the GIA or of the al-Nahda Party do not cross the Mediterranean.

For the United States, then, Islamic fundamentalist foreign policy can be read in several ways. As an ideology that seeks to disrupt the state system of the Middle East, South Asia, Saharan Africa, and Central Asia, it could create severe chaos. Though there is little hard evidence implicating the Iranian or Sudanese governments in many of the plots they are alleged to have masterminded, it is certainly true that Iran financed the Hizbollah in Lebanon, which kidnapped American citizens in the 1980s and helped to perpetuate the Lebanese civil war. The Palestinian fundamentalist faction, Hamas, seems to have received some financial support from Iran, but it also seems to have received support from the Saudis and the Gulf emirates. Given that U.S. foreign policy is geared toward maintaining the status quo, chaos is threatening. As an ideology that more immediately jeopardizes the health and security of allies such as Israel, Hosni Mubarak's regime in Egypt, and, to a lesser extent, France, fundamentalism does pose a threat. And to the extent that the foreign policy of fundamentalism challenges U.S. "hegemony" in the Muslim world, it is antagonistic to the United States.

None of the above need be interpreted as threats to the United States, however, if the United States interprets its security more narrowly. Islamic fundamentalist ideology does not challenge either the United States or the West on its own turf. Fundamentalism is not a global ideology like communism or capitalism, and hence it should not trigger alarm bells in Western states to anywhere near the degree that it currently does. The more U.S. foreign policy seeks global power and the greater the demand for an international system of liberal democracies, the greater will be the threat posed by an Islamic fundamentalism that adamantly and violently rejects that hegemony and the norms of liberalism. If U.S. goals remain relatively limited and the United States attends to issues such as global prosperity and domestic security, then Islamic fundamentalism should not be considered a threat to the United States.

When asked about fundamentalism in the Middle East, most officials, whether at State, CIA, the White House, or the Pentagon, say that it is a pressing concern and that it has become an even more pressing concern in the past few years. Opinions over why it is a concern differ widely. The major U.S. interests in the region are oil, stability, American power, and the Arab-Israeli peace process. U.S. officials see fundamentalism as a potential threat to each of these.

It is difficult to see how political Islam jeopardizes access to oil. After all, even if every oil-producing country were governed by a radical Islamic regime, they would still wish to sell oil to the West, and there would be a rather low limit to how high they could price that oil. One of the lessons of the 1973 and 1979 oil crises was that once the price of oil exceeds a certain maximum, it becomes cheaper for industrial economies to switch to alternate sources of energy. In the interim, producers outside of the Middle East could increase production to compensate for the decline in supply. Therefore Islamic fundamentalism does not constitute a potential threat to oil.

The other issues are trickier. Regimes such as Iran and Sudan are indeed hostile to the Arab-Israeli peace process, and they wish to see the United States removed as a presence in the Middle East.

It is true, therefore, that a fundamentalist sweep of the Middle East could weaken U.S. influence in the region. It could also so radicalize Arab sentiments that it would prevent a comprehensive Middle East peace and undermine Israeli-Palestinian relations. But judging from the problematic Arab-Israeli peace process so far, the more Israel recognizes Palestinian autonomy, the less antagonistic its Muslim neighbors are.

In addition, the diffuse nature of Islamic fundamentalism and the disunity among such fundamentalists suggests that a Middle East dominated by fundamentalism would be less of a problem for the United States than a secular dictator with illusions of grandeur. As the Persian Gulf war ought to have demonstrated, there is a far greater likelihood that U.S. hegemony will be diminished by secular autocrats than by Islamist puritans. There is a long history of Saddam Husseins. Khomeinis, however, are far more unusual, and Khomeini's Iran never posed the kind of military challenge to the region that Hussein's Iraq has.

As for terrorism, fundamentalist ideology suggests that it is the exception rather than the rule. Indeed, outside of a number of highly publicized incidents in the 1980s, such as the highjacking of TWA flight 847 in 1985 and the World Trade Center bombing in 1993, fundamentalist violence outside of the *umma* has been rare. Where it does occur, the motivation is usually retaliation for perceived infringement of the territorial integrity of the *umma* by the United States or other Western nations. The Iranian government has violated the state sovereignty of several European governments by sending assassination teams to murder Iranian opponents of its regime, but as outrageous as that extraterritorial violence is,

it is not violence directed against the non-Islamic world. Nor is the assistance that Iran and Sudan give to fundamentalist insurgencies directed against the West as much as it is directed against governments that Islamic ideologues perceive to be un-Islamic. Indeed, the ideology of fundamentalism suggests that in foreign policy toward the non-Muslim world, there is no reason for antagonism unless the non-Muslim world cooperates in the continued division of the *umma*.

Furthermore, the policies taken by the United States in response to the perceived threat of fundamentalism may well exacerbate the situation. U.S. officials apparently view authoritarianism in the Middle East as an evil preferable to fundamentalism. The United States ends up supporting the very factor that gives the Islamic opposition its greatest strength: the sense that the secular regimes of the Middle East are illegitimate because they are creations of Western hegemony and not true products of Islam and the *umma*.

Because Islamic fundamentalism is expansive within the *umma* and limited without, U.S. policymakers can set aside notions that fundamentalists will not abide by international norms in foreign affairs. Within the *umma*, they may not, but outside of it, they will. Outside of the *umma*, they have no ideological reason not to abide by international norms, and the demands of the international system exercise the same constraints on them as on traditional nation-states.

Once again, the lack of a compelling ideological reason for violence against the United States has meant that fundamentalist governments do not tend to attack the United States with anything other than words. Attacks and plots against the United States and American citizens have been carried out by "freelance" fundamentalists such as Sheikh Omar Abdel Rahman and his followers. The recent bombing of an American military base in Saudi Arabia was probably carried out by an outlaw group opposed to the Saudi government. Despite efforts to link conclusively the policies of groups such as Hizbollah and Hamas to directives from Tehran, no such evidence appears to have been found. If monetary links make Tehran (or Riyadh) responsible for the actions of these groups, then the U.S. government bears responsibility for the victory of the fundamentalist Taliban in Afghanistan through its covert financing of *mujahedeen* rebels fighting Soviet forces in the 1980s.

The United States must avoid the temptation to treat all fundamentalist governments as rogues. Given the lack of action taken against the Saudis and Pakistanis for behavior that elicits condemnation and embargoes against the Iranians, it seems that at present the United States treats fundamentalist foreign policy as inherently lawless and hence threatening.

The United States should reconsider its stringent policy toward Iran, as well as its excessive support for the repressive regimes in Algeria and Saudi Arabia. Fundamentalist Iran has created far fewer difficulties for the United States than has either secular Iraq or divided Lebanon. While relations between Iran and the United States are not likely to be warm, little is gained by current policy toward Iran.

Finally, the United States can afford to pay less attention to Islamic fundamentalism. If fundamentalist foreign policy is understood to be inherently circumscribed, then fundamentalism in the worst-case scenario is confined to one region. Policymakers have been able to normalize relations with communist China because China is not expansionist. So too could policy be normalized with fundamentalist governments. The United States can afford to accommodate fundamentalism, and it should. The attempt to contain it will almost certainly fail, and there is no better way to guarantee continued tension between political Islam and the West.

POSTSCRIPT

Is Islamic Fundamentalism a Threat to Political Stability?

There are nearly 1 billion Muslims in the world, constituting a majority among the Arabs as well as in several non-Arab countries, including Algeria, Indonesia, Iran, Pakistan, the Sudan, and Turkey. There are other countries, such as Nigeria and the Philippines, in which Muslims constitute an important political force. Indeed, only about one of every four Muslims lives in the Middle East. To learn more about Islamic history, read *The Middle East: A Brief History of the Last 2,000 Years* by Bernard Lewis (Scribner, 1997) and Emory C. Bogle, *Islam: Origin and Belief* (University of Texas Press, 1999).

There can be little doubt that the interplay between Islam and politics remains an important issue in world affairs. Fundamentalism remains strong. The civil wars continue in Afghanistan, Algeria, and elsewhere. A fundamentalist prime minister came to power democratically in Turkey in 1996, only to be forced to step down by the country's military in 1997. Hamas and other radical groups continue to wage terrorist attacks on Israel.

From a Western point of view, the images are mixed and the future ramifications are uncertain. Muslim countries, like most less developed countries, face many difficulties in preserving their traditional values while adopting so-called modern practices, which are mostly those promoted by the dominant European–North American powers. Indeed, the rush of technological advancement associated with modernity, the loss of cultural identity, and other aspects of a rate of change unparalleled in world history are troubling for many people in many countries around the world. It is important to note that the traditionalist movement in Muslim countries is part of a larger effort of people to find belonging and meaning in a rapidly changing world dominated by huge, impersonalized governments, businesses, and other organizations. It is possible to argue that some of the causes of Islamic fundamentalism are the same factors that have strengthened the so-called Christian right in the United States and Hindu fundamentalists in India.

Amid the turmoil, there are many signs that Muslim countries are adjusting to what is arguably a spreading homogenization of global culture. As elsewhere, democracy has taken hold in some Muslim countries and struggles to survive or begin in others. Two worthwhile readings on these matters are John L. Esposito, ed., *Political Islam: Revolution, Radicalism, or Reform?* (Lynne Rienner, 1997) and Michael N. Barnett, *Dialogues in Arab Politics: Negotiations in Regional Order* (Columbia University Press, 1998). To explore the various aspects of Islam on the World Wide Web, see http://www.meij.or.jp/home/Link/islam.htm.

ISSUE 16

Does Ritual Female Genital Surgery Violate Women's Human Rights?

YES: Efua Dorkenoo, from "Combating Female Genital Mutilation: An Agenda for the Next Decade," *World Health Statistics Quarterly* (vol. 49, no. 2, 1996)

NO: Eric Winkel, from "A Muslim Perspective on Female Circumcision," *Women and Health* (vol. 23, no. 1, 1995)

ISSUE SUMMARY

YES: Efua Dorkenoo, a consultant on issues of women's health to the World Health Organization, argues that the practice in some regions of the world of performing clitoridectomies on young women and girls violates their fundamental human rights, and she calls for a global ban on the practice.

NO: Scholar Eric Winkel maintains that if the practice of ritual clitoridectomy is to be changed or discarded, the change should come from within Islam and not through the imposition of external cultural values.

There is a practice in some parts of the world that is almost surely shocking to most of those who will ponder this debate. This practice is a traditional rite of puberty that is widely performed in 26 countries of central and northern Africa. It involves a clitoridectomy (the excision of the clitoris), which deprives a woman of all or most sexual sensation. Sometimes, more drastically, it extends to infibulation, the cutting away of all of a female's external genitalia and labial tissue. Critics of the practice use the term *female genital mutilation (FGM)* to describe it. Proponents of the rite refer to it, among other things, as *female circumcision.* To maintain a posture of neutrality, the term *ritual clitoral excision (RCE)* will be used here to designate the practice.

Whatever term is used, the World Health Organization estimates that between 85 million and 114 million girls and women in the world today have undergone RCE and that each year another 2 million girls are subjected to RCE. Since the procedure is seldom performed by trained surgeons under hospital conditions with anesthesia, it is extremely painful and dangerous.

Aside from the psychic scars, the procedure can be dangerous when carried out, as it usually is, by people who are not medically trained, including village elder women, barbers, and physicians who conduct the practice outside the normal clinical setting. These practitioners most often operate in unsanitary conditions using scalpels, knives, shears, or razor blades. There are no accurate figures on the rate of post-RCE health problems, but infections and other complications are reportedly common, and death can result.

Supporters of RCE defend the practice on two grounds. One is tradition. The second rationale is that it supposedly ensures chaste behavior by girls and women.

The clash over the propriety of RCE is at the intersection of individual human rights (and women's rights, in particular) and the right of varied cultural values to exist without conforming to values imposed from the outside. The basic issue here is whether or not universal standards of what is moral —what constitutes human rights—is possible or even desirable. One aspect of determining what is a "human right" involves the conflicting views of so-called positivists and so-called universalists. Positivists hold that there are many standards of morality based on divergent cultural customs. Therefore, in a multicultural world, no single standard exists. Positivists and others who reject the idea of "one morality fits all" charge that an attempt to impose moral standards on others amounts to cultural imperialism.

Universalists rely on the tenets of ideology, theology, natural law, or some other overarching philosophy to argue that universal law and standards of morality are possible. Representing this view, President Bill Clinton has commented that he is "convinced that certain rights are universal" and that he believes that people "everywhere [have the right] to be treated with dignity, to give voice to their opinions, to choose their own leaders, to associate with who they wish, to worship how, when, and where they want."

Taking a related track, there are some advocates of moral reform who argue that some of what passes for culturally based moral and other practices is, in fact, based on the oppression of some in a culture by others in that culture. Burmese political activist and 1991 Nobel Peace Prize winner Aung San Suu Kyi writes that claims about "the national culture can become a bizarre graft of carefully selected historical incidents and distorted social values intended to justify the policies and actions of those in power." As for the charge of cultural imperialism, Suu Kyi contends that "when democracy and human rights are said to run counter to non-Western culture, such culture is usually defined narrowly and presented as monolithic." To avoid this, she counsels, it is possible to conceive of rights "which place human worth above power and liberation above control." The power and control she wishes to subordinate are not just those of government but those of one ethnic group, race, religion, sex, or other societal faction over another. From this perspective, it might be argued that the "cultural norm" that permits—in some cases, demands— RCE is based on the culture of male dominance over women. It should also be noted, however, that there are women who favor the custom.

In the first selection of this debate, Efua Dorkenoo contends that there needs to be a long-term strategy to end what she calls female genital mutilation. Eric Winkel, in the second selection, does not so much defend what he calls female circumcision as contend that it a manifestation of cultural values.

YES

Efua Dorkenoo

COMBATING FEMALE GENITAL MUTILATION: AN AGENDA FOR THE NEXT DECADE

Hosken (1) and Toubia (2) estimate that there are at present over 120 million girls and women who have undergone some form of female genital mutilation [FGM]—sometimes referred to as "female circumcision"—and that 2 million girls per year are at risk of mutilation. Most of the girls and women who have undergone mutilation are reported to live in 28 African countries where it is practised by many ethnic groups, in northern, eastern and western Africa. Some female genital mutilation is practised in the southern parts of the Arabian peninsula and along the Persian Gulf and increasingly, among some immigrant populations in Europe, Australia, Canada and the United States of America. It has also been reported to be practised by a minority ethno-religious group—the Daudi Bohra Muslims, who live in India—and among Muslim populations in Malaysia and Indonesia (3).

The arguments against this traditional practice are based upon recognized human rights standards including the right to health. It is known that the physical and psychological effects of the practice are very extensive and irreversible, affecting the health of girls and women, in particular sexual, reproductive and mental health and well-being. Furthermore, female genital mutilation reinforces the inequities suffered by women in the communities where it is practised, and must be addressed if the health, social and economic development needs of women are to be met.

Despite recognition of the importance of this sensitive issue, there are still major gaps in knowledge about the extent and nature of the problem and the kinds of interventions that can be successful in eliminating it. To begin the process of developing a sound technical basis for policy and action, WHO [World Health Organization] convened a Technical Working Group Meeting on Female Genital Mutilation in July 1995 (4). The recommendations which emanated from this meeting have drawn international attention to female genital mutilation and its health consequences and have contributed to setting the agenda for the next decade for accelerating the elimination of this practice.

DEFINITION

Female genital mutilation entails the removal of part or all of the external female genitalia and/or injury to the female genital organs for cultural or other non-therapeutic reasons. This definition, adopted by the WHO Technical Working Group Meeting on Female Genital Mutilation, encompasses the physical, psychological and human rights aspects of the practice.

CLASSIFICATION OF THE TYPES OF FEMALE GENITAL MUTILATION

In order to strengthen policy formulation including legislation and to clear the path for research and training, the WHO Technical Working Group recommended for adoption the following classification for the different types of female genital mutilation. In Type I, the prepuce (clitoral hood) is removed, sometimes along with part or all of the clitoris. In Type II, both the prepuce and the clitoris and part or all of the labia minora (inner vaginal lips) are removed. Type III (known as infibulation) involves the complete removal of the clitoris and labia minora, together with the inner surface of the labia majora. The raw edges of the labia majora are then stitched together with thorns or silk or catgut sutures, so that when the skin of the remaining labia majora heals, a bridge of scar tissue forms over the vagina. A small opening is preserved, by the insertion of a foreign body, to allow the passage of urine and menstrual blood. Since a physical barrier has been created for sexual intercourse, the infibulated woman has to undergo gradual dilatation by her husband over a period of days, weeks or months to allow for penetrative intercourse. This painful process does not always result in successful vaginal penetration and the opening may have to be re-cut.

Type IV is a new category that encompasses other surgical procedures including manipulation of the genitalia. These include pricking, piercing or incision of the clitoris and/or labia, stretching of the clitoris and/or labia, cauterization by burning of the clitoris and surrounding tissue, introcision, scraping of the vaginal orifice, cuts into the vagina and introduction of substances into the vagina with the aim of tightening or narrowing the vagina.

The commonest type of female genital mutilation is Type II. This constitutes up to 80% of all female genital mutilation practised. The most extreme form is infibulation. This is thought to constitute 15% of FGM and is widespread in Somalia, northern Sudan and Djibouti. It has been reported in parts of Ethiopia, Eritrea, and northern Kenya and small parts of Mali and northern Nigeria.

PRACTITIONERS

Female genital mutilation is usually performed by a traditional practitioner with crude instruments and without anaesthetics. Although WHO has consistently issued statements opposing medicalization of any form of female genital mutilation, among the more affluent and in urban centres, female genital mutilation is increasingly being performed in health care facilities by qualified medical personnel.

AGE

The age at which female genital mutilation is practised varies from area to area. It is performed at a few days old (for example among the nomads of Sudan), at about 7 years old (as in Egypt and in countries in eastern Africa and the horn of Africa) or in adolescence. In Nigeria, for instance, FGM takes place shortly before marriage among the Ibo, but only before the first child among the Aboh in the midwest (5). Most experts agree, however, that the age of which FGM takes place is falling.

REASONS

It is not known when or where the tradition of female genital mutilation originated and a variety of reasons (sociocultural, religious, psychosexual, hygienic, and aesthetic) are given for maintaining it. Female genital mutilation is practised by followers of a number of different religions including Muslims, Christians (Catholics, Protestants and Copts) and animists, and also by non-believers in the countries concerned. Although female genital mutilation is not mentioned in the Koran, it is frequently carried out in some Muslim communities in the genuine belief that it forms part of Islamic tradition.

THE HEALTH COMPLICATIONS OF FEMALE GENITAL MUTILATION

The health effects of FGM depend on the extent of cutting, the skill of the operator, the cleanliness of the tools and the environment, and the physical and psychological state of the girl or woman concerned.

Immediate Complications
Immediate physical complications include haemorrhage and severe pain which can lead to shock and in some cases death. Acute urinary retention and in-fections are common. Injury to adjacent tissue of the urethra, vagina, perineum and rectum can result from the use of crude instruments. Fractures of the clavicle, femur or humerus or dislocation of the hip joint can occur if heavy pressure is applied to the struggling girl during the operation, as often occurs when several adults hold down the girl during the procedure. Group mutilations, in which the same unclean cutting instruments are used on each girl may give rise to a risk of transmission of HIV and hepatitis B but this has not been confirmed. Medium-term problems include delayed healing and the formation of abscesses due to primary infections resulting from faulty healing.

Long-Term Complications
The long-term complications include keloid scar formation, the formation of dermoid cysts and clitoral neuroma, dyspareunia (painful intercourse), chronic pelvic infections and difficulties in menstruation as a result of partial or total occlusion of the vaginal opening. Problems in pregnancy and childbirth are common, particularly following type III mutilation, because the tough scar tissue that forms causes partial or total occlusion of the vaginal opening and prevents dilatation of the birth canal. Prolonged and obstructed labour can lead to tearing of the perineum, haemorrhage, fistula formation and uterine inertia, rupture or prolapse. These complications can lead to neonatal harm (including stillbirth) and even maternal death.

Psychosexual and Psychological Health
Almost all the types of female genital mutilation involve the removal of or damage to part or the whole of the clitoris, which is the main female sexual organ,

equivalent in its anatomy and physiology to the male organ, the penis. Infibulation removes larger parts of the genitals, and closes off the vagina, leaving areas of tough scar tissue in place of the sensitive genitals, thus creating permanent damage and dysfunction. Sexual dysfunction in both partners may be the result of painful intercourse and reduced sensitivity following clitoridectomy and narrowing of the vaginal wall.

FGM may leave a lasting mark on the life and mind of the woman who has undergone it. The psychological complications may be submerged deeply in the child's subconscious mind, and may trigger the onset of behavioural disturbances. The possible loss of trust and confidence in care-givers has been reported as another serious effect of female genital mutilation. In the longer term, women may suffer anxiety, depression, chronic irritability, frigidity and marital conflicts. Many girls and women, traumatized by their experience of FGM, may have no acceptable means of expressing their fears, and suffer in silence.

HUMAN RIGHTS AGREEMENTS TO GUIDE ACTION

There are various international agreements in place that are legally binding on the parties (states) and which prohibit the practice of female genital mutilation. The *United Nations Convention on the Elimination of All Forms of Discrimination Against Women* promotes the rights of women and specifically addresses discriminatory traditional practices (6). The *Convention on the Rights of the Child* protects the right to gender equality, and Article 24.3 of the Convention explicitly requires States to take all effective and appropriate measures to abolish traditional practices prej-

udicial to the health of children (7). Similarly, there are regional human rights agreements such as the *African Charter on Human and Peoples' Rights* and the *African Charter on the Rights and Welfare of the Child* which protect women and children against harmful traditional practices (8, 9). Article 18 of the African Charter on Human and Peoples' Rights specifically requests states to "ensure the elimination of every discrimination against women and also ensure the protection of the rights of women and the child as stipulated in international declarations and conventions."

Article XXI of the African Charter on the Rights and Welfare of the Child obliges state parties to eliminate harmful social and cultural practices affecting the welfare, dignity, normal growth and development of the child.

The *Programme of Action of the International Conference on Population and Development (ICPD)* held in Cairo in 1994 also included recommendations in regard to female genital mutilation, which commit governments and communities to "urgently take steps to stop the practice of female genital mutilation and to protect women and girls from all such similar unnecessary and dangerous practices." (10)

The *Platform for Action of the World Conference on Women,* also included a special section on the girl child and urged governments, international organizations and nongovernmental groups to develop policies and programmes to eliminate all forms of discrimination against the girl child including female genital mutilation (11).

GAPS IN KNOWLEDGE

There have been no comprehensive global surveys of the prevalence of female genital mutilation. Current information on types of mutilation and their prevalence is derived from inadequate, fragmentary data. On the basis of government reports, anecdotal evidence and limited surveys with samples that are not always representative, the prevalence of female genital mutilation is estimated to range from 5% to 98% in African countries (1, 2). Sudan is the only country to have carried out nationwide surveys (12-14). They were based on a national sample which excluded the three southern provinces, where the practice is unknown (except by adoption through marriage to the dominant northern ethnic groups practising FGM), and indicated an initial prevalence of 89% which subsequently declined by 8%. A study by the Nigerian Association of Nurses and Nurse-Midwives (15) conducted in Nigeria in 1985–1986, using a sample of 400 women and men in each state, showed that 13 out of the 21 states had populations practising some form of female genital mutilation, with prevalence ranging from 35% to 90%. However, the data could not be extrapolated to give a national picture. Similar limited surveys exist for Chad, Ethiopia, Gambia, Ghana and Kenya.

Reliable and accurate data on the prevalence, incidence and recurrence rates of the different forms of female genital mutilation or its health consequences will provide baseline information for subsequent evaluations and to inform policy makers and national decision-making processes. At the local level, a rapid-intervention survey may be the most appropriate step. At the national level, more detailed incidence and prevalence rates can be obtained by incorporating modules on female genital mutilation into existing surveys. Existing government surveys (for example, national Demographic and Health Surveys (DHS), household income and expenditure surveys, and fertility surveys) can, with the addition of some extra questions, be used to provide data on female genital mutilation at a fraction of the cost of a specific survey. As has been noted, questions on female genital mutilation were incorporated in the 1989–90 Demographic and Health Survey (DHSI) in the Sudan. The Central African Republic and Côte d'Ivoire have also incorporated a few questions on FGM into their national Demographic and Health Surveys (1994 and 1994–95). Egypt integrated 34 questions on female genital mutilation into its national Demographic and Health Survey in 1995. A full module on female genital mutilation with 20 questions (DHS III) was field-tested in Mali and Eritrea in 1995. These efforts will help to generate reliable incidence and prevalence data for countries in future years.

Where studies of FGM are to be conducted, the magnitude of the practice should be reported for different socio-demographic groups and for each type of genital mutilation. The magnitude of the problem should be expressed in terms of prevalence, incidence and recurrence rates. Repeat surveys of prevalence, incidence and recurrence rates over time will help to establish trends of genital mutilation in a given community or nation.

Further descriptive research providing quantitative and qualitative information is needed to characterize the different forms of genital mutilation and the socio-demographic characteristics of those who practise FGM versus those who do not. Other sociological variables such as the age of the girl, the location, and the persons involved in performing or assisting in the practice are essential information for planning target interventions and health education programmes aimed at certain locations (for example, schools or homes) or populations (for example, nurses, midwives, doctors and traditional birth attendants) that could help eliminate the practice at the source.

Investigations are also needed to gain a better understanding of the sociocultural factors that influence female genital mutilation, including beliefs, class differences, power structures within society, the social/festive character that has built up around mutilation rituals and the links with marriageability. Some beliefs recur in a number of population groups, but there are notable differences and some themes are exclusive to certain areas. Efforts are needed to analyse these factors within countries so that information and communication materials can be adapted to take account of local conditions. Similarly, an accurate analysis of the existing economic incentives that promote the continuation of the practice will suggest measures to counteract them and indicate appropriate areas for intervention.

With regard to the health complications, the physical complications are well known. What is unclear, however, is the actual prevalence of complications and their long term sequelae in relation to gynaecological and obstetric morbidity and their impact on maternal and childhood mortality. The nature and the degree of psychological and sexual damage in different groups are still largely unexplored. Given the scale of the practice of female genital mutilation in many communities, this information is most important for developing clinical support for girls and women who are suffering from the health complications of female genital mutilation.

LESSONS LEARNED

In the last decade, a wide range of organizations and individuals have attempted community-based activities to eliminate FGM. Women's organizations from communities where the practice persists have been leading the campaign for the last decade. With very little resources, they embarked on awareness-raising campaigns and have managed to break the taboo surrounding FGM in their communities. They have also brought the problem to the attention of political, religious and community leaders. Some governments have made statements condemning female genital mutilation; a few have adopted a policy or passed laws banning the practice; but often they have taken little action on the issue. FGM is an issue that cuts across both health and human rights and a major lesson learned from past community actions is that efforts to stop the practice need to go beyond the medical model of disease eradication. A multidisciplinary approach must be developed.

An Agenda for Action

To achieve real change at the grass-roots will require more planning, and more sustained commitment from governments and international agencies to the elimination of FGM. The gaps in knowledge that need to be addressed have been outlined. While voluntary organizations can play a pivotal role in the elimination of FGM, it is important that governments act to initiate, support and coordinate actions against this practice. The broad actions to be taken at the national level, include the need to:

- adopt a clear national policy for the abolition of FGM. This should focus on prevention and rehabilitation. It should also incorporate clear goals, targets and objectives, and schedules for their attainment. Legislation is important, but legislation alone is insufficient. It should be accompanied by appropriate community-based action. Laws and professional codes of ethics should prohibit the medicalization of all the different forms of FGM;

- establish inter-agency coalitions with members from relevant government ministries, nongovernmental organizations and professionals to follow up action on FGM;
- promote research on FGM, including the incidence, prevalence, and health consequences, particularly the impact of FGM on mental and sexual health as well as on the sociocultural determinants of FGM, in order to develop more effective approaches to its elimination;
- organize strong community outreach and family life education programmes for all sectors of the public including village and religious leaders, men and young people; and
- organize training for health workers—physicians, nurses, midwives and also traditional birth attendants and healers —to enable them to work for the abolition of female genital mutilation and to provide clinical and psychological care and support for girls and women who have undergone FGM.

In order to sustain action for the elimination of FGM, activities on FGM must be integrated into existing health education programmes, reproductive health services and population and development strategies at national, regional and at community level.

Given the United Nations commitment to human rights, with emphasis on ad-

vancing and protecting the health and the lives of women and children, including their mental and sexual health, it is the duty of WHO, UNICEF, UNFPA and other UN agencies, as well as bilateral, multilateral and international development agencies, to support policies and programmes that bring an end to this damaging practice in all its forms. Various approaches will need to be developed such as promotion, providing technical support, and mobilizing resources, so that national and local groups can initiate community-based activities aimed at eliminating all harmful practices that affect the health of women and children, especially FGM. WHO, in particular, has a special responsibility to increase knowledge of FGM and promote technically sound policies and approaches for the elimination of FGM, including developing training guidelines to equip health care workers with the appropriate knowledge, skills and attitudes for preventing and eliminating FGM, providing clinical management of the health complications, and ensuring that FGM is incorporated into broader concerns of women's health, reproductive health and human rights.

CONCLUSIONS

Harmful practices such as female genital mutilation persist today in many communities for a variety of reasons. However, the roots of the practice lie in the patriarchal family and in society at large. Although women who are the victims of FGM are the gatekeepers of the practice in their communities, this should be understood within the context of their general powerlessness in male-dominated societies. Promoting gender equity and women's empowerment will invariably lead to a decrease in the incidence and prevalence of FGM within communities and to its total elimination. It has taken some time for women's and children's rights to be accepted as human rights. It is vital that efforts now be made to give the human rights declarations and conventions on women's and children's rights meaning at the national and local levels. A significant shift in societal attitudes towards women and girls is called for. Young people are the adults of tomorrow. Early introduction of gender-sensitive education in schools will help to foster respect for girls' and women's human rights. Finally, as increased education of women appears to be a major factor in decreasing the practice of FGM, efforts to promote female education would have to be central to the long-term strategy for the elimination of this harmful traditional practice.

SUMMARY

Female genital mutilation (FGM)—sometimes locally referred to as "female circumcision"—is a deeply rooted traditional practice that adversely affects the health of girls and women. At present it is estimated that over 120 million girls and women have undergone some form of genital mutilation and that 2 million girls per year are at risk. Most of the girls and women affected live in 28 African countries where the prevalence of female genital mutilation is estimated to range from 5% to 98%. The elimination of female genital mutilation will not only improve women's and children's health; it will also promote gender equity and women's empowerment in the communities where the practice persists. To achieve change will require more planning, and more sustained programmes for its elimination. The political will of governments is essential in order to eliminate this harmful traditional practice and concerted efforts from all concerned are required.

REFERENCES

1. Hosken, F. P. *Female genital mutilation, estimate: total number of girls and women mutilated in Africa,* Lexington, Women's International Network News, 1995.
2. Toubia, N. *Female genital mutilation, a call for global action,* second edition, New York, RAINBO, 1995, 24–25.
3. Hosken, F. P. *The Hosken report, genital and sexual mutilation of females,* fourth revised edition, Women's International Network News, 1993.
4. *Report of a WHO Technical Working Group Meeting on Female Genital Mutilation, 17–19 July, 1995.* Geneva, WHO (forthcoming).
5. Dorkenoo, E. *Cutting the rose: female genital mutilation, the practice and its prevention,* London, Minority Rights Group, 1994.
6. Convention on the elimination of all forms of discrimination against women, in: Brownlie, I. (ed) *Basic documents on human rights,* 3rd edition, Oxford, Oxford University Press, 1992 (pp. 169–181).
7. Convention on the rights of the child, in: Brownlie, I. (ed) *Basic documents on human rights,* 3rd edition, Oxford, Oxford University Press, 1992 (pp. 182–202).
8. African charter on human and peoples' rights, in: Brownlie, I. (ed) *Basic documents on human rights,* 3rd edition, Oxford, Oxford University Press, 1992 (pp. 555–566).
9. African charter on the rights and welfare of the child. Organization of African Unity, Doc. CAB/LEG/153/Rev. 2 (1960).
10. International Conference on Population and Development (ICPD), *Report of the International Conference on Population and Development,* UN Doc. A/CONF. 171.13 (1994).
11. Platform for Action of the World Conference on Women, in Report of the Fourth World Conference on Women, UN Doc. A/CONF. 177/20.
12. El Dareer, A. *Woman, why do you weep?* London, Zed Books, 1982.
13. *The Sudan fertility survey,* Department of Statistics, Ministry of Economic and National Planning, Khartoum, Sudan, 1979.
14. *Sudan demographic and health survey.* Department of Statistics. Ministry of Economic and National Planning, Khartoum, Sudan, 1989/1990.
15. Adebajo, C. O. Female circumcision and other dangerous practices to women's health. In: Kisekka, M. N. *Women's health issues in Nigeria,* Zaria, Tamaza Publishing Company, 1992, 1–11.

NO

Eric Winkel

A MUSLIM PERSPECTIVE ON FEMALE CIRCUMCISION

ABSTRACT. Western observers are unable to understand why women would want to practice clitoridectomy, just as they are perplexed at the vocal, if mostly inarticulate, rejection by many Muslims of the Cairo conference. The battle lines which get drawn have on one side public health professionals, development organizations, and feminists and on the other side conservative and "fundamentalist" Muslims who, if they are heard at all, sound impossibly antediluvian. Many Muslims, including myself, are uncomfortable with both sides. What is needed is an alternative to this polarization. The alternative I propose is the Islamic legal discourse, which might best be described as the discursive arena in which issues of societal importance get worked out.

That positive change can come about from within—using the Islamic discourse—is possible because Islamic discursive systems are broad and nuanced enough to accommodate a wide variety of medical and public health endeavors. Meaningful social change and improved public health could come about by stimulating and recovering the many Islamic sunnah (exemplary) practices which are so conducive to physical and material well-being. By dealing change through existing, and proven, traditional formats, Muslims would be able to effect valuable and meaningful change in their communities. Muslim communities should not become dependent on and indentured to Western agencies and their own nation-states to solve the problems they face, including the tragic consequences of widely practiced infibulation and clitoridectomy; instead we need to apply our own traditional practices and to support an indigenous Islamic legal discourse.

The practice of clitoridectomy has become for western observers a shibboleth which does not admit the possibility of complexity. It is taken as a sure sign of peculiarly backward behavior, an issue "we" all can get behind. It is such that one would be hard pressed to find a debater to argue "for" female circumcision, at least in English. But western observers are often surprised to find that "in fact, most of the women, regardless of age, social status, or ethnic extraction, favored the continuation of this way of life."[1] Similarly, western observers were perplexed at the vocal, if mostly inarticulate, rejection by many Muslims of the Cairo conference. The fact is that the practice of clitorectomy is often linked to Islam, even though those who so link it often admit that it is not found in the Qur'an. Those who link clitorectomy to Islam, then, imply that *Islam* is something which stands in the way of progress, along with related superstitions. Exemplifying this attitude are statements like this: "The convictions" of some observers "are so strong that until significant educational inroads are made... and superstitions give way to scientific reasoning and objective rationalization," this backward practice will continue.[2]

Female circumcision and other issues arising from the Cairo conference seem to bring out a stark polarization. On the one side are public health professionals, development organizations, and feminists. On the other side are conservative and "fundamentalist" Muslims who, if they are heard at all, sound impossibly antediluvian. The two sides seem to be characterized by observers variously as good and bad, pro-woman and anti-woman, or forward and backward. Perhaps it is more accurate to say that female circumcision and issues of the Cairo conference divide people into two groups, those who believe that the western model of development is universal and universally beneficial and those who do not.

Many Muslims, myself included, are in an awkward position when the battle lines get drawn. We agree with the points of the first side without accepting their agenda; and we agree with the agenda of the second side without accepting their points. For example, the agenda of international and national campaigns to eradicate female circumcision is widely perceived by Muslims as racist and ethnocentric. The entire thrust of "development," after all, includes paternalistic and racist notions of who stands in need of education and development, and why. So whether international or national, a campaign to eradicate female circumcision will carry with it a largely hidden agenda to change people's lives according to a particularly western model of development. One observer writes that "the government in Somalia launched a campaign with the help of the Women's Democratic Organization with Edna Ismail (a Christian by name) as one of the local leaders."[3] In such a situation, Muslims will quickly suspect that "female circumcision" is not what is really at stake: what is at stake is Islam itself, the presence of a Christian as a campaign leader suggesting yet another missionary assault on Islam. The code word "Democratic" might also suggest to Muslims, who are so widely portrayed as terrorists, or at least undemocratic, that they and Islam are under attack.

What is needed is an alternative to the polarization presented above. The alternative I propose is the Islamic legal discourse, which might best be described as the discursive arena in which issues of societal importance get worked out. The legal discourse of Islam may be conceived of as a more or less flexible superstructure erected over the shari'ah, which in turn may be defined as the set of injunctions emanating from the Qur'an and sunnah (exemplary prophetic practice). Those who deal with this superstructure, and help it flex and bend to meet new circumstances, may be loosely defined as the 'ulama', those who have knowledge. This amorphous group of people, women and men, are recognized in their communities by their knowledge. There is no institution or bar which certifies them, and their independence is so vital to their cause that they continually warn themselves against "going to kings." Needless to say, the "official 'ulama" usually do not meet either criterion.

The alternative I propose, the Islamic legal discourse, serves three purposes in this paper. First, it clarifies the issue of female circumcision. Second, it demonstrates, to many people for the first time, that Muslims can have articulate and authentically Islamic responses to issues of concern. Finally, this legal discourse is an important way for Muslim communities to deal with new situations in authentic ways.

Without becoming a nominalist, one may appreciate deeply the clarity that the legal discourse of Islam gives issues through its basis in *names*. The first thing the practitioner of the Islamic legal discourse does is to get the names straight. Let us do that now. We have something called male circumcision where the foreskin covering the head of the penis is trimmed back. The legal position is that Muslim males should be circumcised, although some classical scholars produce evidence which suggests that male converts to Islam need not get circumcised if they are fearful of the procedure. Cutting the actual penis is in the same category as amputation of foot or ear or other bodily part, and there is a complex legal discussion about penalties for inten-

tional and unintentional amputation. Female circumcision is classified as sunnah, which in this context means optional. There is no harm in not doing it, and there is some reward in doing it. But removal of the clitoris, clitorectomy, is in the same category as cutting the actual penis. Clitoridectomy is legally parallel to castration, and that is forbidden as an "alteration of Allah's creation." The phrase in the Qur'an is "Let there be no alteration in Allah's creation" [30:30] and has traditionally been used to explain the unlawfulness of tattoos, disfiguration, and castration. It may be explicitly applied to infibulation.

Infibulation is not unique to Muslim societies; nor do the majority of Muslim communities have this practice. Because it is a harm to women—in Islamic terms—and because it is an "alteration of Allah's creation," Muslims should work to eradicate the practice. The following are ways in which Muslims can articulately frame an approach.

Ibn Qudamah [620 A.H./1223 C.E.] is a major commentator to the work of Ahmad ibn Hanbal, who is himself one of the four sunni imams to whom schools of legal discourse trace their origins. The Hanbalis (followers of Ahmad ibn Hanbal) are generally considered the most "strict." Ibn Qudamah writes that "As for circumcision, it is obligatory on men and admirable [makrumah] for women, but it is not obligatory on them. This is the position of the majority of people of knowledge. Ahmad [ibn Hanbal] said ... the women's circumcision is much less [than the man's]." He cites then as evidence for the lightness of the female circumcision a hadith where the prophet, Allah bless and give him peace, says to the "khafidah" (the word means "one who trims back"), "Do not overdo it, because it [the clitoris] is a good fortune for the spouse and a delight to her."[4] Let us look at this hadith in detail.

In the collection of hadith of Abu Dawud [275/888], we have the following, where *haddathana* means "We were told in the form of a hadith".[5]

haddathana Sulayman ibn 'Abd al-Rahman [of Damascus] and 'Abd al-Wahhab ibn 'Abd al-Rahim al-Ashja'i who both said *haddathana* Marwan *haddathana* Muhammad ibn Hasan that 'Abd al-Wahhab (of Kufah) said, from 'Abd al-Malik ibn 'Amir, from Umm 'Atiyah the Ansar, that a women was circumcising in Madinah and the prophet, Allah bless him and give him peace, said to her, "Do not overdo it, because that [clitoris] is lucky for the woman and dear to the husband." [I,] Abu Dawud, am mentioning that the narration from 'Abid-Allah ibn 'Amr from 'Abd al-Malik is narrated according to its meaning [i.e., not narrated literally; we see above that Ibn Qudamah has a slightly different version]. This hadith is not strong. It is *mursal*.[6] Muhammad ibn Hasan is unknown [to the hadith biographers], so this hadith is *da'if* [weak].[7]

The hadith is not considered revelational proof because the chain is not completely secure in its all links from the prophet, Allah bless and give him peace, to the hadith scholars, and because, according to the vast majority of scholars, a hadith, to be part of the sunnah, must be correctly transmitted word for word. But what is interesting is that despite its weak nature, the hadith is transmitted and becomes part of the Islamic legal discourse. It means that the scholars find it important, even though it does not have the exalted status of a verse from the Qur'an or a strong hadith.

What we have here (and this is supported in many other places as well) is that the traditional scholars have posited that their understanding of Islam (that is, their fiqh) is that female circumcision is not required, and if performed, it should be slight, and that the clitoris contributes to the woman's sexual enjoyment, and that that is an enjoyment which is both hers and her husband's.

I have heard that one reason clitorectomy is performed is to make sex unpleasant as a way of maintaining control over unmarried girls' sexuality. Such reasoning clearly goes against the hadith cited above, because there the woman's sexual pleasure is desired by both the woman and the man; as "sex" and "marriage contract" are synonymous in the legal discourse (the word is *nikah*), sexuality is "controlled" by marrying early and often (for example, a divorced woman should be able to find another husband easily). I have heard other reasons proffered as well. The legal discourse insists that every reason must be put to the test of authenticity, which means in this case that clitorectomy to control sexuality or eliminate female sexual pleasure will be found to be illegitimate. And as with the awkwardly drawn battle lines mentioned above, the entire issue of "control" and "autonomy" needs to be reexamined from an authentic discursive perspective.

It is true that sexuality is controlled internally by individuals themselves (men and women) and by a superstructure which carefully maps relationships of daughters, wives, mothers, sons, husbands, and fathers, but this control gets distorted by a male discourse which seeks to apply violent punishments to "dangerous" women to restore an imagined past. The west struggled for three centuries to dismantle a system of gender control—we have or had "good girls" who got married and "bad girls" who had sex—and yet, for many different reasons, women are still not safe, popular music extols humiliating women, and women are special targets of commodification. Muslims need to find a healthy and authentic alternative to both systems.

In the one system, for example, governments have thinly veiled motives for eliminating female circumcision. One researcher writes that "many African countries, including Somalia, took a hard look at the liabilities female circumcision holds for national development."[8] But the interest of "national development" takes no account of the aspirations, traditions, and beliefs of individuals and communities. The motives for eliminating female circumcision are as important as the motives for practicing female circumcision. They equally must be put to the test of Islamic authenticity, and clearly "national development" is a reason not found in the Islamic legal discourse.

That positive change can come about from within is possible because Islamic discursive systems are broad and nuanced enough to accommodate a wide variety of medical and public health endeavors. Valuable social change comes from within. Some Muslim feminists, for example, have found that their voice is most effective when articulated within an Islamic discourse,[9] noting that "feminism" has historically been tainted with colonialism.[10] And Sachiko Murata explains that "the rigidity 'patriarchal' stress of some contemporary Muslims is to be softened," but "Muslims will be able to do this as Muslims—not as imitation Westerners—only if they look once again

at the spiritual and intellectual dimensions of their own tradition."[11]

Meaningful social change and improved health could come about first by stimulating and recovering the many Islamic sunnah practices which are so conducive to physical and material well-being. By dealing with change through existing, and proven, traditional formats, Muslims would be able to effect valuable and meaningful change in their communities. Muslim communities should not become dependent on and indentured to western agencies and their own nation-states to solve the problems they face, including the tragic consequences of widely practiced infibulation and clitoridectomy; we need to apply our own traditional practices and to support an indigenous Islamic legal discourse.

NOTES

1. Daphne Williams Ntiri [1993] 219.

2. Ntiri [1993] 225.

3. Ntiri [1993] 224.

4. Found in Ibn Qudamah's *al-Mughni Sunan al-Fitrah* pp. 70–71.

5. The practice of merely citing a hadith without citing the complete chain of transmission, or at least its ranking by classical scholarship, contributes to the particularly modern problem of "fundamentalism," which seems to enjoy statements like "Islam says" and "Islam is," based on evidence which is often highly discounted in or quite differently applied by classical sources.

6. *Mursal* means the hadith has a missing link in its transmission.

7. Abu Dawud in *Sunan Abu Dawud Kitab al-Adab,* hadith 5271.

8. Ntiri [1993] 224.

9. One group in Malaysia, called Sisters in Islam, assisted by Dr. Amina Wadud, then a colleague of mine in the International Islamic University, in Kuala Lumpur, formulated their projects for social change related to women's issues in distinctly Islamic modes.

10. Leila Ahmed remarks that "colonialism's use of feminism to promote the culture of the colonizers and undermine native culture has ever since imparted to feminism in non-Western societies the taint of having served as an instrument of colonial domination, rendering it suspect in Arab eyes.... That taint has undoubtedly hindered the feminist struggle within Muslim societies" in Leila Ahmed [1992] *Women and Gender in Islam* (New Haven: Yale University Press) 167.

11. Sachiko Murata [1992] *The Tao of Islam: A Sourcebook on Gender Relationships in Islamic Thought.* Albany: State University of New York Press. p. 323.

POSTSCRIPT

Does Ritual Female Genital Surgery Violate Women's Human Rights?

The debate over "ritual clitoral excision" (RCE) is a real one in world politics. One question is whether or not countries and international organizations should put pressure on countries where RCE is practiced to ban the procedure and to prosecute and punish those who practice it as well as, perhaps, parents who allow RCE to be performed on their daughters. There is a concerted effort to end RCE. Waris Dirie, who was born in Somalia and who underwent RCE as a four-year-old, was named special ambassador on female genital mutilation in 1998 by the United Nations Population Fund (UNFPA). "I am going to do everything I can to stop this [RCE]," Dirie said. Changes in the global moral climate have already led a number of countries where the practice was common, such as Egypt, to ban it.

The issue also has domestic ramifications in the United States and other countries. In the United States an unknown number of girls, perhaps numbering into the hundreds, undergo RCE annually. These girls are mostly the daughters of immigrants from the countries in mid- to northern Africa, where the practice is most common. A second domestic aspect of RCE is that a number of women faced with RCE in their homelands have fled to the United States and elsewhere to seek asylum. Canada has passed a law granting asylum to women fleeing oppression because of their gender, and the United States and other countries have also begun to grant asylum based on gender persecution.

One of the easiest aspects of this issue to deal with is the unsanitary conditions in which the ritual is performed. Certainly, it would be hard to oppose a requirement that if RCE is to happen, it should be done under competent medical supervision. But that would mean that it would have to be legal. Just as proponents of abortion argued that it had to be let out of the back alleys to protect women's lives, so proponents of RCE argue that it cannot be kept in the back alleys.

The second question is whether or not the practice should be banned altogether. It is probable that most of those who read this debate will viscerally respond that RCE should be abolished. In coming to that decision, however, one should keep in mind cultural contexts and perhaps the old adage "What is good for the goose is good for the gander." Much of the world community is appalled by the use of capital punishment in the United States and consider it immoral. Illustrative of that, the United Nations has named a monitor to report on potential human rights violations by the United States. It remains to be seen how the same Americans who object to RCE would react if they themselves were found to be violating global human rights standards.

More on changes in the status of Muslim women can be found in Farida Shaheed, "Constructing Identities: Culture, Women's Agency and the Muslim World," *International Social Science Journal* (March 1999). For a published view of RCE, see *Female Genital Mutilation: A Joint WHO/UNICEF/UNFPA Statement*, published by the World Health Organization (WHO). There are numerous Web sites on the subject, all seemingly from the anti-RCE perspective. These include the Female Genital Mutilation Education and Networking Project's http://www.fgmnetwork.org/index.html and the WHO's http://www.who.int/frh-whd/topics/fgm.htm.

Another interesting parallel is between male and female circumcision. Certainly, male circumcision is much less radical than RCE. But, like RCE, it is based partly on religion. Also like RCE, male circumcision is widely performed in only a few countries; it is performed on nonconsenting children; it is painful; it is sometimes performed by religious figures rather than physicians; and it generally carries no health benefits, according to numerous national medical societies. These include the American Academy of Pediatrics, which in 1999 adopted the statement "Existing evidence does not justify recommending routine circumcision." For more on this view, visit the Circumcision Resource Center's Web site at http://www.circumcision.org. It might be helpful to compare Western-based male circumcision to non-Western-based female circumcision. They certainly are not the same, but considering both will help you to forcefully bring in the matter of cultural perspective.

ISSUE 17

Should the Kyoto Treaty Be Supported?

YES: Bill Clinton, from "Kyoto Conference on Climate Change Reaches Agreement to Limit Emission of Greenhouse Gases," *Foreign Policy Bulletin* (January/February 1998)

NO: J. Kenneth Blackwell, from "The Kyoto Protocol: Using Provisional Science for a World Power Grab," *Vital Speeches of the Day* (November 1, 1998)

ISSUE SUMMARY

YES: Bill Clinton, president of the United States, contends that we have a clear responsibility and a great opportunity to conquer global warming— which he terms "one of the most important challenges of the 21st century— by supporting the Kyoto treaty.

NO: J. Kenneth Blackwell, treasurer of the state of Ohio, argues that the U.S. administration's support of the Kyoto treaty is based on inadequate climatological data and that abiding by the treaty will cause severe economic hardships for Americans.

We live in an era of almost incomprehensible technological boom. In a very short time—less than a long lifetime in many cases—technology has brought some amazing things. If you talked to a 100-year-old person, he or she would remember a time before airplanes, before automobiles were common, before air conditioning, before electric refrigerators, and before medicines that could control polio and a host of other deadly diseases were available.

But these advances have had by-products. A great deal of prosperity has come about through industrialization, electrification, the burgeoning of private and commercial vehicles, and a host of other inventions and improvements that, in order to work, consume massive amounts of fossil fuel (mostly coal, petroleum, and natural gas). The burning of fossil fuels sends carbon dioxide (CO_2) into the atmosphere. The discharge of CO_2 from burning wood, animals exhaling, and some other sources is nearly as old as Earth itself, but the twentieth century's advances have rapidly increased the level of discharge. Since 1950 alone, global CO_2 emissions have increased 278 percent, with more than 26 billion tons of CO_2 now being discharged annually. There are now almost 850 billion tons of CO_2 in the atmosphere.

Many analysts believe that as a result of this buildup of CO_2, we are experiencing a gradual pattern of global warming. The reason, according to these scientists, is the *greenhouse effect*. As CO_2 accumulates in the upper atmosphere, it creates a blanket effect, trapping heat and preventing the nightly cooling of the Earth. Other gases, especially methane and chlorofluorocarbons (CFCs, such as freon), also contribute to the thermal blanket.

Many scientists and others believe that global warming is evident in changing climatological data. It is estimated that in the last century the Earth's average temperature has risen about 1.1 degrees Fahrenheit. In fact, of the 10 warmest years since global record keeping began in 1856, 9 of those years occurred in the 19 years between 1980 and 1998. Many weather experts also see an increase in the number and intensity of hurricanes and other catastrophic weather events, and they attribute these to global warming.

Not everyone believes that global warming caused by a CO_2 buildup is occurring or worries about it. Some scientists do not believe that future temperature increases will be significant, either because they will not occur or because offsetting factors, such as increased cloudiness, will ease the effect. Others believe that recent temperature increases reflect natural trends in the Earth's warming and cooling process.

Whatever the reality may be, the 1990s has seen efforts to constrain and cut back CO_2 emissions. The Earth Summit held in Rio de Janeiro in 1992 was the first of these efforts. At Rio, most of the economically developed countries (EDCs) signed the Global Warming Convention and agreed to a voluntarily stabilize emissions at their 1990 levels by the year 2000. They also resolved to reconvene in 1997 to review progress under the agreement. However, five years later many of the EDCs, including the United States, had made no progress toward meeting the goals set in 1992.

The 1997 meeting was held in Kyoto, Japan. The negotiations were too complex to detail here. The more important point for this debate is the treaty's provisions. They are:

1. The EDCs must reduce CO_2 and other greenhouse gas emissions by 6 to 8 percent below their respective 1990 levels by 2012. The U.S. cut will be 7 percent; Europe's will be 8 percent; Japan's 6 percent.
2. EDCs can trade emissions quotas among themselves.
3. No sanctions for failure to meet standards were set. The parties to the treaty will meet in the future to establish sanctions.
4. The less developed countries (LDCs), including China and India, are exempt from binding standards but may opt to adopt voluntary goals.
5. The treaty will go into effect when ratified by at least 55 countries representing at least 55 percent of the world's emissions of greenhouse gases.

Bill Clinton and J. Kenneth Blackwell debate the wisdom of the Kyoto treaty in the following selections. Clinton argues that the threat of global warming requires action, and he predicts that energy savings and other economic advantages will offset any negative economic consequences. Blackwell argues that it is not clear that a carbon dioxide–driven crisis is upon us, and he contends that the Kyoto treaty will damage the U.S. economy.

YES

Bill Clinton

KYOTO CONFERENCE ON CLIMATE CHANGE REACHES AGREEMENT TO LIMIT EMISSION OF GREENHOUSE GASES

REMARKS BY THE PRESIDENT, OCTOBER 22, 1997

President [Bill] Clinton delivered his remarks at the National Geographic Society, Washington, DC.

... [W]hat sustains any civilization, and now what will sustain all of our civilizations, is the constant effort at renewal, the ability to avoid denial and to proceed into the future in a way that is realistic and humane, but resolute.... [N]ot long after I started running for President, I went back to my *alma mater* at Georgetown and began a series of three speeches outlining my vision for America in the 21st century—how we could keep the American Dream alive for all of our people, how we could maintain America's leadership for peace and freedom and prosperity, and how we could come together across the lines that divide us as one America.

And together, we've made a lot of progress... now that the Vice President and I have been privileged to work at this task. At the threshold of a new century, our economy is thriving, our social fabric is mending, we've helped to lead the world toward greater peace and cooperation.

I think this has happened, in no small measure, in part because we had a different philosophy about the role of government. Today, it is smaller and more focused and more oriented toward giving people the tools and the conditions they need to solve their own problems and toward working in partnership with our citizens. More important, I believe it's happened because we made tough choices but not false choices.

On the economy, we made the choice to balance the budget and to invest in our people and our future. On crime, we made the choice to be tough and smart about prevention and changing the conditions in which crime occurs. On welfare, we made the choice to require work, but also to support the children of people who have been on welfare. On families, we made the choice to help parents find more and better jobs and to have the necessary time and resources for their children. And on the environment, we made the choice to clean our air, water, and land, to improve our food supply, and to grow the economy.

This kind of commonsense approach, rooted in our most basic values and our enduring optimism about the capacity of free people to meet the challenges of every age must be brought to bear on the work that remains to pave the way for our people and for the world toward a new century and a new millennium.

Today we have a clear responsibility and a golden opportunity to conquer one of the most important challenges of the 21st century—the challenge of climate change—with an environmentally sound and economically strong strategy, to achieve meaningful reductions in greenhouse gases in the United States and throughout the industrialized and the developing world. It is a strategy that, if properly implemented, will create a wealth of new opportunities for entrepreneurs at home, uphold our leadership abroad, and harness the power of free markets to free our planet from an unacceptable risk; a strategy as consistent with our commitment to reject false choices.

America can stand up for our national interest and stand up for the common interest of the international community. America can build on prosperity today and ensure a healthy planet for our children tomorrow.

In so many ways the problem of climate change reflects the new realities of the new century. Many previous threats could be met within our own borders, but global warming requires an international

solution. Many previous threats came from single enemies, but global warming derives from millions of sources. Many previous threats posed clear and present danger; global warming is far more subtle, warning us not with roaring tanks or burning rivers but with invisible gases, slow changes in our surroundings, increasingly severe climatic disruptions that, thank God, have not yet hit home for most Americans. But make no mistake, the problem is real. And if we do not change our course now, the consequences sooner or later will be destructive for America and for the world.

The vast majority of the world's climate scientists have concluded that if the countries of the world do not work together to cut the emission of greenhouse gases, then temperatures will rise and will disrupt the climate. In fact, most scientists say the process has already begun. Disruptive weather events are increasing. Disease-bearing insects are moving to areas that used to be too cold for them. Average temperatures are rising. Glacial formations are receding.

Scientists don't yet know what the precise consequences will be. But we do know enough now to know that the Industrial Age has dramatically increased greenhouse gases in the atmosphere, where they take a century or more to dissipate; and that the process must be slowed, then stopped, then reduced if we want to continue our economic progress and preserve the quality of life in the United States and throughout our planet. We know what we have to do.

Greenhouse gas emissions are caused mostly by the inefficient burning of coal or oil for energy. Roughly a third of these emissions come from industry, a third from transportation, a third from residential and commercial buildings. In each case, the conversion of fuel to energy use is extremely inefficient and could be made much cleaner with existing technologies or those already on the horizon, in ways that will not weaken the economy but in fact will add to our strength in new businesses and new jobs. If we do this properly, we will not jeopardize our prosperity—we will increase it.

With that principle in mind, I'm announcing the instruction I'm giving to our negotiators as they pursue a realistic and effective international climate change treaty. And I'm announcing a far-reaching proposal that provides flexible market-based and cost-effective ways to achieve meaningful reductions here in America. I want to emphasize that we cannot wait until the treaty is negotiated and ratified to act. The United States has less than 5 percent of the world's people, enjoys 22 percent of the world's wealth, but emits more than 25 percent of the world's greenhouse gases. We must begin now to take out our insurance policy on the future.

In the international climate negotiations, the United States will pursue a comprehensive framework that includes three elements, which, taken together, will enable us to build a strong and robust global agreement. **First,** the United States proposes at Kyoto that we commit to the binding and realistic target of returning to emissions of 1990 levels between 2008 and 2012. And we should not stop there. We should commit to reduce emissions below 1990 levels in the five-year period thereafter, and we must work toward further reductions in the years ahead.

The industrialized nations tried to reduce emissions to 1990 levels once before with a voluntary approach, but regrettably, most of us—including especially the United States—fell short. We must find new resolve to achieve these reductions, and to do that we simply must commit to binding limits.

Second, we will embrace flexible mechanisms for meeting these limits. We propose an innovative, joint implementation system that allows a firm in one country to invest in a project that reduces emissions in another country and receive credit for those reductions at home. And we propose an international system of emissions trading. These innovations will cut worldwide pollution, keep costs low, and help developing countries protect their environment, too, without sacrificing their economic growth.

Third, both industrialized and developing countries must participate in meeting the challenge of climate change. The industrialized world must lead, but developing countries also must be engaged. The United States will not assume binding obligations unless key developing nations meaningfully participate in this effort.

As President Carlos Menem [of Argentina] stated forcefully last week when I visited him in Argentina, a global problem such as climate change requires a global answer. If the entire industrialized world reduces emissions over the next several decades, but emissions from the developing world continue to grow at their current pace, concentrations of greenhouse gasses in the atmosphere will continue to climb. Developing countries have an opportunity to chart a different energy future consistent with their growth potential and their legitimate economic aspirations.

What Argentina, with dramatic projected economic growth, recognizes is true for other countries as well: We can and we must work together on this problem in a way that benefits us all. Here at home, we must move forward by unleashing the full power of free markets and technological innovations to meet the challenge of climate change. I propose a sweeping plan to provide incentives and lift road blocks to help our companies and our citizens find new and creative ways of reducing greenhouse gas emissions.

First, we must enact tax cuts and make research and development investments worth up to $5 billion over the next five years—targeted incentives to encourage energy efficiency and the use of cleaner energy sources.

Second, we must urge companies to take early actions to reduce emissions by ensuring that they receive appropriate credit for showing the way.

Third, we must create a market system for reducing emissions wherever they can be achieved most inexpensively, here or abroad; a system that will draw on our successful experience with acid rain permit trading.

Fourth, we must reinvent how the federal government, the nation's largest energy consumer, buys and uses energy. Through new technology, renewable energy resources, innovative partnerships with private firms and assessments of greenhouse gas emissions from major federal projects, the federal government will play an important role in helping our nation to meet its goal. Today, as a down payment on our million solar roof initiative, I commit the federal government to have 20,000 systems on federal buildings by 2010.

Fifth, we must unleash competition in the electricity industry, to remove outdated regulations and save Americans billions of dollars. We must do it in a way that leads to even greater progress in cleaning our air and delivers a signif-

icant down payment in reducing greenhouse gas emissions. Today, two-thirds of the energy used to provide electricity is squandered in waste heat. We can do much, much better.

Sixth, we must continue to encourage key industry sectors to prepare their own greenhouse gas reduction plans. And we must, along with state and local government, remove the barriers to the most energy efficient usage possible. There are ways the federal government can help industry to achieve meaningful reductions voluntarily, and we will redouble our efforts to do so.

This plan is sensible and sound. Since it's a long-term problem requiring a long-term solution, it will be phased in over time. But we want to get moving now. We will start with our package of strong market incentives, tax cuts, and cooperative efforts with industry. We want to stimulate early action and encourage leadership. And as we reduce our emissions over the next decade with these efforts, we will perform regular reviews to see what works best for the environment, the economy, and our national security.

After we have accumulated a decade of experience, a decade of data, a decade of technological innovation, we will launch a broad emissions trading initiative to ensure that we hit our binding targets. At that time, if there are dislocations caused by the changing patterns of energy use in America, we have a moral obligation to respond to those to help the workers and the enterprises affected—no less than we do today by any change in our economy which affects people through no fault of their own.

This plan plays to our strengths—innovation, creativity, entrepreneurship. Our companies already are showing the way by developing tremendous environmental technologies and implementing commonsense conservation solutions.

Just yesterday, Secretary [Frederico] Pena announced a dramatic breakthrough in fuel cell technology, funded by the Department of Energy [DOE] research—a breakthrough that will clear the way toward developing cars that are twice as efficient as today's models and reduce pollution by 90 percent. The breakthrough was made possible by our path-breaking partnership with the auto industry to create a new generation of vehicles. A different design, producing similar results, has been developed by a project funded by the Defense Advanced Research Products Agency and the Commerce Department's National Institute of Science and Technology.

The Energy Department discovery is amazing in what it does. Today, gasoline is used very inefficiently in internal combustion engines—about 80 percent of its energy capacity is lost. The DOE project announced yesterday by A.D. Little and Company uses 84 percent of the gasoline directly going into the fuel cell. That's increased efficiency of more than four times traditional engine usage.

And I might add, from the point of view of all the people that are involved in the present system, continuing to use gasoline means that you don't have to change any of the distribution systems that are out there. It's a very important, but by no means the only, discovery that's been made that points the way toward the future we have to embrace.

I also want to emphasize, however, that most of the technologies available for meeting this goal through market mechanisms are already out there—we simply have to take advantage of them. For example, in the town of West Branch,

Iowa, a science teacher named Hector Ibarra challenged his 6th graders to apply their classroom experiments to making their school more energy efficient. The class got a $14,000 loan from a local bank and put in place easily available solutions. The students cut the energy use in their school by 70 percent. Their savings were so impressive that the bank decided to upgrade its own energy efficiency.

Following the lead of these 6th graders, other major companies in America have shown similar results. You have only to look at the proven results achieved by companies like Southwire, Dow Chemical, Dupont, Kraft, Interface Carpetmakers, and any number of others in every sector of our economy to see what can be done.

Our industries have produced a large group of efficient new refrigerators, computers, washer/dryers, and other appliances that use far less energy, save money, and cut pollution. The revolution in lighting alone is truly amazing. One compact fluorescent lamp, used by one person over its lifetime, can save nearly a ton of carbon dioxide emissions from the atmosphere, and save the consumer money.

If over the next 15 years everyone were to buy only those energy-efficient products marked in stores with EPA's [Environmental Protection Agency's] distinctive "Energy Star" label, we could shrink our energy bills by a total of about $100 billion over the next 15 years and dramatically cut greenhouse gas emissions.

Despite these win-win innovations and commitments that are emerging literally every day, I know full well that some will criticize our targets and timetables as too ambitious. And, of course, others will say we haven't gone far enough.

But before the debate begins in earnest, let's remember that over the past generation, we've produced tremendous environmental progress, including in the area of energy efficiency, at far less expense than anyone could have imagined. And in the process, whole new industries have been built.

In the past three decades, while our economy has grown, we have raised, not lowered, the standards for the water our children drink. While our factories have been expanding, we have required them to clean up their toxic waste. While we've had record numbers of new homes, our refrigerators save more energy and more money for our consumers.

In 1970, when smog was choking our cities, the federal government proposed new standards for tailpipe emissions. Many environmental leaders claim[ed] the standards would do little to head off catastrophe. Industry experts predicted the cost of compliance would devastate the industry. It turned out both sides were wrong. Both underestimated the ingenuity of the American people. Auto makers comply with today's much stricter emissions standards for far less than half the cost predicted, and new cars emit on average only 5 percent of the pollutants of the cars built in 1970.

We've seen this pattern over and over and over again. We saw it when we joined together in the '70s to restrict the use of the carcinogen, vinyl chloride. Some in the plastics industry predicted massive bankruptcies, but chemists discovered more cost-effective substitutes and the industries thrived. We saw this when we phased out lead and gasoline. And we see it in our acid rain trading program —now 40 percent ahead of schedule—at costs less than 50 percent of even the most optimistic cost projections. We see it as

the chlorofluorocarbons are being taken out of the atmosphere at virtually no cost in ways that apparently are beginning finally to show some thickening of the ozone layer again.

The lesson here is simple: Environmental initiatives, if sensibly designed, flexibly implemented, cost less than expected and provide unforeseen economic opportunities. So while we recognize that the challenge we take on today is larger than any environmental mission we have accepted in the past, climate change can bring us together around what America does best—we innovate, we compete, we find solutions to problems, and we do it in a way that promotes entrepreneurship and strengthens the American economy.

If we do it right, protecting the climate will yield not costs, but profits; not burdens, but benefits; not sacrifice, but a higher standard of living. There is a huge body of business evidence now showing that energy savings give better service at lower cost with higher profit. We have to tear down barriers to successful markets and we have to create incentives to enter them. I call on American business to lead the way, but I call upon government at every level—federal, state, and local—to give business the tools they need to get the job done, and also to set an example in all our operations.

And let us remember that the challenge we face today is not simply about targets and timetables. It's about our most fundamental values and our deepest obligations.

Later . . . I'm going to have the honor of meeting with Ecumenical Patriarch Bartholomew I, the spiritual leader of three hundred million Orthodox Christians—a man who has always stressed the deep obligations inherent in God's gift to the natural world. He reminds us that the first part of the word "ecology" derives from the Greek word for house. In his words, in order to change the behavior toward the house we all share, we must rediscover spiritual linkages that may have been lost and reassert human values. Of course, he is right. It is our solemn obligation to move forward with courage and foresight to pass our home on to our children and future generations.

I hope you believe with me that this is just another challenge in America's long history, one that we can meet in the way we have met all past challenges. I hope that you believe with me that the evidence is clear that we can do it in a way that grows the economy, not with denial, but with a firm and glad embrace of yet another challenge of renewal. We should be glad that we are alive today to embrace this challenge, and we should do it secure in the knowledge that our children and grandchildren will thank us for the endeavor.

NO

J. Kenneth Blackwell

THE KYOTO PROTOCOL

Delivered to the American Legislative Exchange Council Annual Meeting, Panel on Global Climate Change, Chicago, Illinois, August 21, 1998

I am delighted ... to discuss the implications of what has become over the past decade a very hot domestic and international public policy issue, an issue which is likely to stay hot for at least the next decade. The subject is global warming, and what makes it hot is not just the content of the questions, but the nature of the actions being proposed to deal with it. I have to make one more play on the temperature idea by promising that, in contrast to some of the advocates of immediate and drastic remedial action, I shall try to bring more light than heat to the subject.

An appropriate way to begin our discussion is to recall a remark attributed to J. Pierpont Morgan. A woman is said to have approached him at a social gathering roughly a hundred years ago and asked, "Mr. Morgan, what is the stock market going to do?"

The financier reportedly hesitated a moment before giving the woman the full benefit of his years of money-accumulating experience. "Madam," he said, "the stock market will fluctuate."

If J. Pierpont Morgan had been born a hundred years later and specialized in climate instead of money, and if he were asked now what the world climate is going to do, the same answer would be right on the money.

"Madam, the climate will fluctuate."

I do not mean to suggest by this that we can ignore the possibility that this time Henny Penny may be right. The sky may be warming. The seas may rise. And it would be irresponsible to sit idly by doing nothing if there is a real chance that all the world's coastal cities will go under water in the next fifty or one hundred years.

Neither, however, do I believe it responsible to rush to the binding international agreement the Administration is proposing to replace the voluntary approach we agreed to in Rio de Janeiro in 1992 [at the UN-sponsored conference on the environment].

From J. Kenneth Blackwell, "The Kyoto Protocol: Using Provisional Science for a World Power Grab," *Vital Speeches of the Day* (August 21, 1998). Copyright © 1998 by J. Kenneth Blackwell. Reprinted by permission of *Vital Speeches of the Day*.

The Administration's proposal is a fast answer to incompletely formulated questions based on inadequate data. Fast answers all too often are half-baked. In this case, the kindest thing we can say about the fast answer is that it is not fast at all. At best, it is half fast.

Just for starters, we do not know whether global warming is taking place now. It is true that surface temperature readings have gone up by about one degree Fahrenheit over the past century. Over the past decade, however, satellite temperature data, which is the most accurate measurement we have, shows that modest global cooling has occurred. At this point, we simply do not know whether global temperatures are rising, falling or staying about the same. What we do know is that the Kyoto Protocol will not answer this question. Only time and serious scientific study will produce an answer.

The action proposed in the Kyoto Protocol is setting limits in developed countries on the release into the atmosphere of CO_2, one of the greenhouse gases so named because they help trap heat in the atmosphere.

I will parenthetically add here that if there were no greenhouse gases, the earth's temperature would be about 30 degrees colder than it is, a level which would not sustain life as we know it. The question is not whether greenhouse gases are good or bad—they are inarguably good and necessary—but whether human activity, more specifically, industrial activity, is producing too much of them.

Back to the point, if global warming is taking place, we do not know the extent to which man-made greenhouse gases may be responsible. We do know that the biggest influence on global temperatures is the eleven-year cycle of solar activity. Sunspots waxing and waning produce more than half of the temperature changes experienced on earth. And we have a long way to go in understanding this subject. For years, climatologists believed that the sun's energy output was constant, but some now believe the solar constant may not be constant at all. Variation in solar activity may well account for the one degree rise in surface temperature recorded over the past hundred years. This one degree change may thus be an entirely natural progression following the Little Ice Age which ended about the time Mr. Morgan was sharing his wisdom on the stock market, and it may well prove to be cyclical.

Even if in the face of all the scientific uncertainties, we could properly conclude that a worldwide cap on man-made CO_2 emissions would end whatever potential threat global warming may represent, there is little reason to believe that the Kyoto Protocol will accomplish that objective. Even its supporters concede that emissions from China and India alone are likely to overwhelm the proposed reductions by the U.S. and Western Europe before the target date for the reductions is reached.

Although the proposed Climate Treaty is not an answer to either the objective of understanding global warming or capping CO_2 emissions, we can be certain that it will accomplish other objectives. I think it will be helpful to consider some of them.

First, and from a public policy standpoint, more important even than the kind of possible consequences of global warming the alarmists predict, is the impact such a treaty will have on domestic and international governance. If we want to hasten the day when the United Nations will be transformed from an association of sovereign states into a one-world governing body, the Climate Treaty will be a huge step in that direction.

Some international entity will have to be formed and empowered to measure and enforce emission mandates. Many Americans bridled at the 55 mile per hour national speed limit. Imagine that fast answer expanded to cover all matters involving energy consumption, and imagine it administered out of, say, Geneva instead of Washington, D.C. That's the path we are on if we accept binding international mandates.

It is true that the United States has entered other binding international environment agreements which have not seriously eroded our sovereignty. Examples include limitations on Fluorocarbons—CFC's—and on international hazardous waste disposal. But these agreements have not had the sweeping economic implications of limitations on CO_2 emissions, and they have not required setting up a world body with the power to make and enforce decisions directly affecting the economies of both participating and non-participating countries. Unlike CFC's and waste, CO_2 emissions are directly tied to the economic activity which produces income and wealth for nations, corporations, institutions and individuals.

With today's energy producing and consuming technology—indeed, with the technology foreseeable in the lifetimes of every person in this room—the zero sum game inherent in the Kyoto Protocol's transfer of CO_2 emissions, and therefore production and consumption of energy-intensive products and processes, will carry with it a corresponding transfer of wealth.

Let's say we and other developed nations are willing to make this sacrifice to produce temperatures two to six degrees cooler and sea levels six inches to three feet lower, reductions consistent with the upward changes the alarmists predict will take place with no action. Once the sovereignty transfer is accomplished, what kind of sanctions will be given the new supergovernment to enforce its mandates? Some form of coercion will surely be required to make the agreement binding.

Otherwise we might just as well stay with the voluntary approach which is in place now as the outcome of the 1992 Rio de Janeiro agreement.

Should the super-government have troops to enforce its dictates? Nobody is suggesting that, at least not yet in public.

If not armed force, what would work? The approach most mentioned so far is trade restrictions. A country that failed to meet its mandated reductions would find an upcharge on its exports as they crossed the borders of other participating countries. But who would collect this duty? Who would keep or distribute it? The advocates of a binding treaty have a lot of thinking to do on this point, and then a lot of persuading before the citizens of participating countries buy into it.

A consideration secondary only to the sovereignty issue is the economic impact on participating countries.

Many people complain about the fact that in the U.S., combined federal, state and local taxes take more of an average household's income than food, clothing and shelter. The Climate Treaty will address that complaint in several ways.

Before Vice President [Al] Gore went to Japan and pulled off what the Administration has spun as a diplomatic coup, the U.S. CO_2 emission cap most discussed was a return to 1990 levels by the year 2010. Gore's coup was to get Japan's mandated reduction to six percent below 1990 in exchange to our accepting a seven percent reduction.

Given the carbon tax required to meet only the reduction to 1990 levels, and using mainstream economic assumptions, personal incomes will go down substantially. In my home state of Ohio, real income per capita will drop almost 10%. The impact in Illinois will be about the same. This should make anti-tax people happy, because with no change in our income tax rates, taxpayers will pay less.

The good news does not stop with the reduction in income, and therefore income taxes. Housing and food prices will go up about 10%, and the cost of clothing will go up along with all other manufactured goods. Some skeptics will argue that the increased cost of the necessities should be accounted for as taxes, but we will at least have the appearance of a change in the relationship of taxes versus basics.

Third, we should see some public health benefits from this proposal. Service jobs are usually less hazardous than manufacturing jobs, so those among the 34,000 Ohioans and 28,000 Illinoisans who lose their manufacturing jobs but exchange them for service jobs may thereby find work where they are less likely to suffer on-the-job injuries. This may not compute, because total employment is projected to fall by more than 58,000 jobs in Ohio and 180,000 in Illinois, but even so the workers who do not out-migrate in search of jobs are surely safer sitting at home than going into the perilous workplace. And these fortunate citizens will be encouraged to improve their health in other ways. Many will almost certainly choose to exercise more, at least during the winter, because their household energy bills will be several hundred dollars higher, so they will have to keep moving to stay warm. With food costs up nearly ten percent, meat consumption should go down, still another heart-healthy benefit.

Fourth, increasing the cost of gasoline by fifty cents a gallon will surely reduce exposure to highway accidents. If people cannot afford to drive, they are less likely to be hurt as long as they do not walk on the road.

I would like to wrap up my remarks with a grossly partisan political comment. With the benefit of 20-20 hindsight, it is clear that President George Bush made at least two mistakes in his presidency, both having to do with the timing of major events.

First, he should not have won the Gulf War so long before he had to run for reelection—the 1992 outcome would quite likely have been different if he had still had the approval ratings in the 90's he enjoyed immediately after the war. Second, he should not have signed on to the Democratic Party's tax increase so close to the election. President Clinton certainly learned from that mistake.

But on the global warming subject, President Bush was right in 1992 when he agreed to voluntary, not mandatory, CO_2 caps, and to continued scientific scrutiny of the warming phenomenon to see what future action would be indicated, what action would work, and what action would be worth what it cost.

With the 1992 agreement as a foundation, we should view the next decade as an asset, and we should use it to take advantage of three windows of opportunity.

First is the scientific work. We need to know whether global warming is in fact taking place, and if it is, how much is taking place, what is really causing it, and what will arrest it.

Second, if capping CO_2 emissions is necessary, we need an approach which will cap them globally instead of simple-mindedly transferring caps from one part of the globe to another with no meaningful overall reduction.

Third, we need to work with China, India, Brazil, Mexico and other developing nations to help them meet their growing energy needs by transferring technology, not American sovereignty and jobs.

POSTSCRIPT

Should the Kyoto Treaty Be Supported?

The debate over whether or not to take the strong measures required by the Kyoto treaty involves momentous decisions. One indication is that the Clinton administration signed the treaty but has not yet asked the Senate to ratify it.

Like most environmental problems, the negative impacts of global warming will be slow to build up and, therefore, are somewhat hard to see. Average temperatures will rise most years in fractions of degrees. Patterns of storms, rain, and other weather factors that strongly govern the climate of any region will also change slowly. Although some coastal cities may disappear and some now-fertile areas may become deserts, that is many years in the future. Besides, other regions may benefit. Marginal agricultural areas in northern regions may someday flourish. To make matters more confusing, the Earth warms and cools in long cycles, and some scientists believe that to the degree there is a general warming, it is all or mostly the result of this natural phenomenon. If that is true, cutting back on greenhouse gases will have little or no effect.

However, if we ignore global warming, there will only be an escalating buildup of greenhouse gases; EDCs will continue to emit them, and emissions from LDCs will rise as part of their modernization efforts. If those who are alarmed about global warming are correct, and we ignore it, there will be many devastating effects that will affect large portions of the globe.

Then there is the matter of the effects of programs to ease global warming. Those who recommend caution in responding to demands that global warming be halted also point out that significantly reducing CO_2 emissions will not be easy. It might well require substantial lifestyle changes in the industrialized countries. For example, cars might have to be much smaller, gasoline prices higher, and electricity production and consumption curtailed. Costs would also be enormous. The Union of Concerned Scientists (UCS) has concluded that a program to cut CO_2 emissions by 70 percent over a 40-year period would cost the U.S. economy $2.7 trillion.

But there will also be benefits. The UCS also projects a $5 trillion savings in fuel costs. Others have pointed to the economic stimulus that would be provided by creating alternative energy technologies. Losses from storm damages would also drop. A stabilization of the climate would stabilize the lifestyles of people in coastal and other areas that would be most strongly affected by global warming.

In the end, the question is this: Should the United States and other countries bet trillions in economic costs that emissions-driven global warming is occurring, or bet the atmosphere that it is not occurring? Given the fact that CO_2 stays in the atmosphere for centuries and that, if it is having a climatic effect, it will take several lifetimes to begin to reverse significantly, then there is little room to defer the decision. Place your bets, ladies and gentlemen!

An interactive Web site on global warming is available at `http://www.edf.org/pubs/brochures/globalwarming/`. For a more extended view that global warming is a crisis, see Albert K. Bates and Albert Gore, Jr., *Climate in Crisis: The Greenhouse Effect and What We Can Do* (Book Pub, 1990). For the opposite view, consult Gale Moore, *Climate of Fear: Why We Shouldn't Worry About Global Warming* (Cato Institute, 1998). In addition to the general matter of whether or not to adopt the Kyoto treaty, there are a number of objections to specific parts of the treaty. Two such expositions are Richard N. Cooper, "Toward a Real Global Warming Treaty," *Foreign Affairs* (March/April 1998) and Henry D. Jacoby, Ronald G. Prinn, and Richard Schmalensee, "Kyoto's Unfinished Business," *Foreign Affairs* (July/August 1998).

CONTRIBUTORS
TO THIS VOLUME

EDITOR

JOHN T. ROURKE, Ph.D., is a professor of political science at the University of Connecticut for campuses in Storrs and Hartford, Connecticut. He has written numerous articles and papers, and he is the author of *Congress and the Presidency in U.S. Foreign Policymaking* (Westview Press, 1985); *The United States, the Soviet Union, and China: Comparative Foreign Policymaking and Implementation* (Brooks/Cole, 1989); and *International Politics on the World Stage,* 7th ed. (Dushkin/McGraw-Hill, 1999). He is also coauthor, with Ralph G. Carter and Mark A. Boyer, of *Making American Foreign Policy,* 2d ed. (Brown & Benchmark, 1996). Professor Rourke enjoys teaching introductory political science classes—which he does each semester—and he plays an active role in the university's internship program as well as advises one of its political clubs. In addition, he has served as a staff member of Connecticut's legislature and has been involved in political campaigns at the local, state, and national levels.

STAFF

Theodore Knight   List Manager
David Brackley   Senior Developmental Editor
Juliana Poggio   Developmental Editor
Rose Gleich   Administrative Assistant
Brenda S. Filley   Production Manager
Juliana Arbo   Typesetting Supervisor
Diane Barker   Proofreader
Lara Johnson   Design/Advertising Coordinator
Richard Tietjen   Publishing Systems Manager
Larry Killian   Copier Coordinator

AUTHORS

GREGORY ALBO teaches in the Department of Political Science at York University in Toronto, Canada.

TOM BETHELL is a *National Review* contributing editor and a visiting media fellow at the Hoover Institution.

J. KENNETH BLACKWELL is the treasurer of the state of Ohio.

GEORGE LEE BUTLER was commander in chief of the U.S. Strategic Air Command from 1991 to 1992 and the U.S. Strategic Command from 1992 to 1994, with responsibility for all U.S. Air Force and Navy deterrent forces. He was closely involved in the development of U.S. nuclear doctrine. General Butler has also served as deputy to General Colin Powell.

MARY CAPRIOLI is an assistant professor of political science at the University of Massachusetts–Dartmouth.

LEE A. CASEY has served in the U.S. Department of Justice and now practices law in Washington, D.C.

BILL CLINTON became the 42d president of the United States in 1993. He taught at the University of Arkansas in the early 1970s, became Arkansas state attorney general in 1976, and was elected governor of Arkansas in 1978. He is the author of *My Plans for a Second Term* (Carol Publishing Group, 1995) and coauthor, with Al Gore, of *Putting People First: How We Can All Change* (Times Books, 1992).

CARL CONETTA is codirector of the Project on Defense Alternatives at the Commonwealth Institute in Cambridge, Massachusetts. He is coauthor, with Charles Knight, of *Defense Sufficiency and Cooperation: A U.S. Military Posture for the Post–Cold War Era* (Commonwealth Institute, 1998).

EFUA DORKENOO is a consultant in women, health and development in the World Health Organization's Division of Family Planning and Reproductive Health in Geneva, Switzerland. She is the author of *Cutting the Rose: Female Genital Mutilation: The Practice and Its Prevention* (Minority Rights Publications, 1995).

EDITORS OF *THE ECONOMIST* publish articles dealing with national as well as international affairs. Topics range from world politics and current affairs to business, finance, and science. *The Economist* is published weekly by The Economist Newspaper.

DOUGLAS J. FEITH, an attorney in Washington, D.C., served as deputy assistant secretary of defense and as a Middle East specialist on the White House National Security Council staff during the Reagan administration. He is the author of *Israel's Legitimacy in Law and History* (Center for Near East Policy Research, 1994).

FRANCIS FUKUYAMA, a former deputy director of the U.S. State Department's policy planning staff, is a senior researcher at the RAND Corporation in Santa Monica, California. He is also a fellow of the Johns Hopkins University School for Advanced International Studies' Foreign Policy Institute and director of its telecommunications project. He is the author of *The Great Disruption* (Simon & Schuster, 1999).

JAMES P. GRANT is executive director of the United Nations Children's Fund.

JOHN F. HILLEN III is a defense analyst at the Heritage Foundation and author of

Blue Helmets in War and Peace: The Strategy of UN Military Operations (Brassey's, 1997).

ZACHARY KARABELL is a researcher in Harvard University's Kennedy School of Government.

HERBERT C. KELMAN is the Richard Clarke Cabot Professor of Social Ethics at Harvard University. He is also director of the Program on International Conflict Analysis and Resolution at the Weatherhead Center for International Affairs and cochair of Harvard's Middle East Seminar. He is the author of *Crimes of Obedience: Toward a Social Psychology of Authority and Responsibility* (Yale University Press, 1990).

CHARLES KNIGHT is codirector of the Project on Defense Alternatives at the Commonwealth Institute in Cambridge, Massachusetts. He is coauthor, with Carl Conetta, of *Vital Force: A Proposal for the Overhaul of the U.N. Peace Operating System and for the Creation of a U.N. Legion* (Commonwealth Institute, 1995).

ABDUL G. KOROMA is a judge, from Sierra Leone, on the International Court of Justice. His term expires in 2003.

BETH K. LAMONT is the American Humanist Association's (AHA) alternate nongovernmental organization representative to the United Nations and program director for the Humanist Society of Metropolitan New York: The Corliss Lamont Chapter. She is also an initiator of the Division of Humanist Advocacy and a former chair of the AHA Chapter Assembly. She has been involved in numerous humanistic endeavors throughout her life.

GREG MASTEL is vice president for policy planning and administration at the Economic Strategy Institute in Washington, D.C., an organization devoted to changing American attitudes on issues of trade, competitiveness, and economic policy issues that affect America's overall economic performance, the creation of good jobs, and the welfare of individual industries.

BARRY McCAFFREY is director of the Office of National Drug Control Policy (ONDCP) at the White House. He serves as the senior drug policy official in the executive branch and as the president's chief drug policy spokesman, and he is also a member of the National Security Council.

DANIEL PIPES is editor of the *Middle East Quarterly* and the author of three books on Islam and politics.

MICHAEL POSNER is executive director of the Lawyers Committee for Human Rights.

EYAL PRESS is a writer and a frequent contributor to the *Progressive.*

PETER REDDAWAY is a professor of political science and international affairs in the Elliott School of International Affairs and Department of Political Science at George Washington University in Washington, D.C., where he is also a member of the Institute for European, Russian and Eurasian Studies. His many publications include *Russia's Political Hospitals: The Abuse of Psychiatry in the Soviet Union* (Gollancz, 1977), which won the 1978 Guttmacher Award of the American Psychiatric Association, and *Soviet Psychiatric Abuse: The Shadow Over World Psychiatry* (Gollancz, 1984), both of which were coauthored with S. Bloch.

DAVID B. RIVKIN, JR., has served in the U.S. Department of Justice and now practices law in Washington, D.C.

ROBERT S. ROSS teaches political science at Boston College and is a research associate at the John King Fairbank Center for East Asian Research at Harvard University. He is the author of *Negotiating Cooperation: The United States and China, 1969–1989* (Stanford University Press, 1995).

JOSEPH E. SCHWARTZBERG, primarily a South Asian specialist, has taught political geography at the Universities of Pennsylvania and Minnesota since 1960. He is a national board member of the World Federalist Association (WFA) and president of the WFA's Minnesota chapter.

STEPHEN M. SCHWEBEL is president of the International Court of Justice starting the year 2000. His term ends in 2006.

STEPHEN SESTANOVICH is ambassador-at-large for the United States and special adviser to the secretary of state for the New Independent States.

DOMINIC A. TARANTINO was chairman of Price Waterhouse World Firm, Ltd., until his retirement in June 1998.

ALAN TONELSON is research director of the Economic Strategy Institute in Washington, D.C., which is a research organization that studies U.S. economics, technology, and national security policy. His essays on American politics and foreign policy have appeared in numerous publications, including the *New York Times, Foreign Policy,* and the *Harvard Business Review.* He is coeditor, with Clyde V. Prestowitz, Jr., and Ronald A.

Morse, of *Powernomics: Economics and Strategy After the Cold War* (Madison Books, 1991).

MANUEL VELASQUEZ is the Charles Dirksen Professor of Business Ethics at Santa Clara University, where he teaches courses in the legal, political, and social environment of the firm; business strategy; and business ethics. He has published numerous articles in such journals as *Academy of Management Review, Business Ethics Quarterly, Social Justice Research,* and the *Business and Professional Ethics Journal,* and he is the author of *Business Ethics: Concepts and Cases,* 4th ed. (Prentice Hall, 1998). He received his B.A. from Gonzaga University and his Ph.D. from the University of California at Berkeley.

MURRAY WEIDENBAUM is the Mallinckrodt Distinguished University Professor in and director of the Center for the Study of American Business at Washington University in St. Louis, Missouri. His publications include *Public Policy Toward Corporate Takeovers* (Transaction, 1987), coedited with Kenneth Chilton.

ERIC WINKEL is a Fulbright Scholar in the Center for Area Studies at Quaid-i-Azam University in Islamabad, Pakistan. He is the author of *Mysteries of Purity: Ibn al-'Arabi's Asrar al-Taharah* (Cross Cultural Publications, 1995).

R. JAMES WOOLSEY is former director of the Central Intelligence Agency. He is coauthor, with David M. Abshire and Richard R. Burt, of *The Atlantic Alliance Transformed* (Westview Press, 1992).

INDEX